COMPUTER SYSTEMS ARCHITECTURE

CHAPMAN & HALL/CRC
TEXTBOOKS IN COMPUTING

Series Editors

John Impagliazzo
Professor Emeritus, Hofstra University

Andrew McGettrick
Department of Computer
and Information Sciences
University of Strathclyde

Aims and Scope

This series covers traditional areas of computing, as well as related technical areas, such as software engineering, artificial intelligence, computer engineering, information systems, and information technology. The series will accommodate textbooks for undergraduate and graduate students, generally adhering to worldwide curriculum standards from professional societies. The editors wish to encourage new and imaginative ideas and proposals, and are keen to help and encourage new authors. The editors welcome proposals that: provide groundbreaking and imaginative perspectives on aspects of computing; present topics in a new and exciting context; open up opportunities for emerging areas, such as multi-media, security, and mobile systems; capture new developments and applications in emerging fields of computing; and address topics that provide support for computing, such as mathematics, statistics, life and physical sciences, and business.

Published Titles

CHAPMAN & HALL/CRC
TEXTBOOKS IN COMPUTING

COMPUTER SYSTEMS ARCHITECTURE

Aharon Yadin

Yezreel Valley College (YVC)

Israel

CRC Press
Taylor & Francis Group
Boca Raton London New York

CRC Press is an imprint of the
Taylor & Francis Group, an informa business

A CHAPMAN & HALL BOOK

CRC Press
Taylor & Francis Group
6000 Broken Sound Parkway NW, Suite 300
Boca Raton, FL 33487-2742

© 2016 by Taylor & Francis Group, LLC
CRC Press is an imprint of Taylor & Francis Group, an Informa business

Printed on acid-free paper
Version Date: 20160120

International Standard Book Number-13: 978-1-4822-3105-2 (Hardback)

Library of Congress Cataloging-in-Publication Data

Names: Yadin, Aharon, author.
Title: Computer systems architecture / Aharon Yadin.
Description: Boca Raton : Taylor & Francis Group, CRC Press, 2016. | Series:
Chapman & Hall/CRC textbooks in computing | Includes bibliographical
references and index.
Identifiers: LCCN 2015048879 | ISBN 9781482231052
Subjects: LCSH: Computer architecture.
Classification: LCC QA76.9.A73 Y335 2016 | DDC 004.2/2--dc23
LC record available at http://lccn.loc.gov/2015048879

Visit the Taylor & Francis Web site at
http://www.taylorandfrancis.com

and the CRC Press Web site at
http://www.crcpress.com

Printed and bound in the United States of America by Publishers Graphics, LLC on sustainably sourced paper.

Contents

Preface

THE PURPOSE OF THIS BOOK is to provide the necessary understanding of and background of hardware for IT (information technology) people. The term IT refers to a variety of disciples related to computer-based systems such as software engineering, information systems, computer science, and so on. Each one of these disciplines has its own focus and emphasis. In most cases, the hardware platform is viewed as an existing infrastructure, and it is sometimes insufficiently addressed or understood. Furthermore, technological developments in hardware in recent decades were aimed mainly at defining the hardware as a separated platform. As such, IT personnel, and especially software designers and developers, may regard it as a required layer of a computing solution, but a layer that they do not have to understand. In a sense, it is like using a car; the driver drives it but does not care about the internal mechanics. On the other hand, recent architectural developments, such as cloud computing,* virtualization,† and the abstractions required for implementing modern computing systems, emphasize the importance of an understanding of hardware. For example, desktop virtualization provides the capability to access any application, using any device. The user may use a desktop computer, a laptop, a tablet, a smartphone, and even appliances that have not yet been invented, and the application will work properly.

For that reason, this book is not about computer organization, but rather concerns ongoing issues related to computer hardware and the solutions provided by the industry for these issues.

Figure 0.1 defines most of the layers in a computer system, going top-down from the application (or program), which is usually developed using a high-level programming language, such as C#, C++, Java, and so on. In some cases, the compiler‡ translates the

---

* Cloud computing is a relatively new computing infrastructure that has the potential to revolutionize the whole industry. Cloud computing became feasible due to several technological developments that have now matured and are capable of providing a coherent computing infrastructure. Cloud computing is based on the success of some of the most well known web-based applications, such Google's search engine and Amazon's virtual store. These and other applications paved the way for Internet-based applications that provide services to a large and extremely dynamic customer population. Based on the experience gathered, cloud computing is based on flexible and on-demand provision of computing servers that reside somewhere in the network. As such, it has the potential to significantly change the whole computing industry and especially information technology (IT) departments within organizations by providing a better service at a fraction of the cost.

† Virtualization is the possibility of executing an application regardless of the physical infrastructure.

‡ A compiler is the software tool that is responsible for translating the high-level programming language instructions into machine instructions, which are the only instructions understood by the hardware. For each programming language, there is a different compiler. Furthermore, usually a compiler will produce the running program that is suitable for a specific hardware. Similarly, the tool that translates assembly-language instructions into machine language is called an assembler.

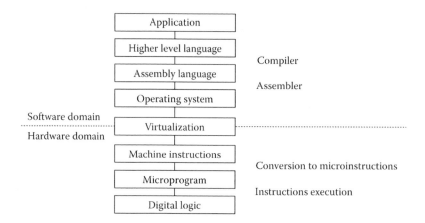

FIGURE 0.1   System layers.

high-level programming languages' instructions into assembly language, which represents the mnemonics of the instructions the machine understands. In other cases, the high-level programming languages are compiled directly into the machine language. The translated program (executable) will be able to run using services provided by the operating system, which is an additional software component, usually considered part of the infrastructure. The next level, which is a mixed software–hardware layer, is virtualization, which provides the possibility of defining virtual machines (this will be elaborated on in Chapter 10, "Additional Architectures"). The next level is the machine instructions. These binary values represent the instructions to be executed and are the only instructions the machine recognizes. In most modern computers, the binary instructions are designed using predefined building blocks, sometimes called microinstructions (this will be elaborated on in Chapter 4, "Central Processing Unit"). These building blocks are defined in the next layer of Figure 0.1. The last level is the digital circuits that understand and execute these building blocks and the instructions they produce. For quite some time, the separation between hardware and software was somewhat clear, as outlined by the dotted line in Figure 0.1.

Although the separation between software and hardware was clearly defined in the early days of computing, developers had to understand some hardware principles to produce reliable and fast working software. Even the recent technological developments related to cloud computing, which draw an even clearer line between the hardware and software layers of the solution, did not manage to establish a distinct separation. Furthermore, as more and more hardware components are implemented using programmable chips, software engineering methods are being used as part of the hardware development process. For example, the modular approach of defining new instructions using building blocks is a concept borrowed from systems engineering, wherein a system is usually defined using subsystems. Each subsystem is further divided into smaller and smaller parts, right up to the single function or method. This means that even the second stage of Figure 0.1, which consists of defining the common hardware blocks, is actually software based, so the once-clear separation becomes very blurred. Cloud computing, which emerged in the last decade, is intended to provide a computing infrastructure while reducing costs and allowing customers to concentrate on their core business rather than on computing-related issues. One of the main developments that led to cloud computing is virtualization (explained in Chapter 10, "Additional Architectures"). Virtualization is a software layer that creates scalable "virtual machines." These machines hide the underlying physical hardware. In many cases, the operating system enters the gap between the hardware and software by providing a layer of interface. On one hand, it provides tools and application programming interfaces (APIs) for software development, to ease access to the hardware. On the other hand, it accesses the hardware using specially developed functions that assure a higher degree of flexibility and efficiency. Due to the complex nature of software, in many cases there is a need for an additional layer above the operating system, which provides additional common functionality such as .net by Microsoft or J2EE by Oracle Corporation. These environments ease the process of software development by relieving the developer of system functions such as memory management, data encryptions, and so on. Using these virtual environments' frameworks, the developer can concentrate purely on the application's logic instead of spending time "reinventing the wheel" and developing libraries of common services.

Although all these new developments undermine the importance of hardware for software development, a basic understanding of hardware components and their effect on execution is still very important. Software can be developed with a minimal understanding of hardware; however, for developing good software that is both reliable and efficient, some understanding of hardware is of paramount importance. As part of the first stages of the software engineering process, in which the system's functionality is defined, this hardware understanding becomes vital. After the requirements are defined, the system analysis stage defines the functionality of the new system. For a simple program, the levels of abstraction provided by cloud computing and the operating system as well as additional development frameworks (such as .net a J2EE), may be sufficient. However, for a larger or even an organizational software system, some hardware understanding is needed, for example as part of the feasibility study* and calculations regarding return on investment (ROI†). After the "what" has been defined (what the system will do) as part of the design stage, the "how" is defined (how the system will be implemented). At this stage, an understanding of hardware becomes even more important. Several design decisions may have severe implications, and understanding the hardware components and their interaction with the planned software helps to produce a better design. For example, most modern computers utilize multiple cores (this will be elaborated on in the subsequent chapters). This means that such a system can execute several tasks in parallel. In a sense, it is like a dual-line telephone system that supports two calls in parallel. The telephone provides the functionality; however, a single person cannot use it. The person can switch between the lines but cannot talk simultaneously with two other people (unless it is a conference

---

* A feasibility study is done as part of the system engineering stage in order to assess the feasibility of the required system, which relates to the efforts required, the resources, and the possible implications for the working procedures and infrastructure.

† One of the criteria for deciding about new projects' development is the return on investment (ROI). For each such project, the anticipated benefits are compared to the planned and required resources' costs. The systems with the higher ROI will usually be implemented first.

call). However, when using a multiple-core system, the application can be developed using multithreading* which will better utilize the hardware platform and provide a superior user experience when using the newly developed system. A very simple but clear system engineering example may relate to a web-based application. The old traditional application supported one user, accepted the user's input, performed the required function, produced the result, and then asked for the next input, and so on. A web-based application that has to support a varying number of concurrent users should be designed differently. There will be a small task that collects the users' input requests. This task will not handle the requests, just store them. There will be some (or even many) other tasks that are responsible for fetching the requests that were entered and executing each one of them. This software architecture can be implemented on a single-core processor, but it will be much more efficient using multiple cores, and in extreme cases, it will require virtualization (in which several physical systems will act as a single virtual machine). Another example that demonstrates the importance of hardware understanding is related to large dimensional arrays. If a program performs some calculations on an array with two (or more) dimensions, the order of indexing the array may have significant performance implications, especially when very large arrays are involved. Understanding the way the memory works and building the program accordingly may substantially speed up its execution, even on a cloud platform. It should be noted, however, that some of the compilers are able to modify the code so it will benefit from the specific hardware it is running on.

There are many hardware books that were intended for hardware engineers and, as such, provide a very detailed explanation of the various aspects of hardware. This book, however, was written especially for IT people, for whom various aspects of hardware engineering are less important. The aim of the book is to provide a brief historic description of the trends in computing solutions that led to the current available infrastructures. The historic perspective is important, since some of the stages repeat themselves when new computerized appliances emerge. For example, when the mobile-telephone revolution started, the hardware attributes of mobile devices followed some of the developments in computer systems, for example, regarding memory and its utilizations. Furthermore, many of the less sophisticated appliances use hardware components and technologies that were used in various stages during the history of computers. For example, a simple alarm system uses an embedded computer, but since its functionality is limited, it usually mimics the architecture of computer systems 20 or 30 years old. Nevertheless, the components resemble the components of modern systems (processor, memory, and input and output devices).

The historic perspective and the various development stages are important due to the emerging trend of being connected "always and everywhere." The Internet of Things, which aims to connect billions of embedded computing devices and create a global interconnected network, provides an additional aspect to the necessity of understanding hardware and its historic evolution.

---

* Multithreading is a capability that exists in most programming languages and provides the means to define several threads of execution within the same process. These threads share some of the processes' resources but execute independently, thus better utilizing hardware resources (cores).

THE HUMAN COMPUTER

When trying to relate to computer components and architectures, an amazing resemblance to the human body's functionality is discovered. The human body, as well as that of any other living creature, is composed of different components, each one with a clearly defined purpose. This modular approach (which, at least at present, is for humans very limited, since only a small fraction of organs can be replaced), is well known in the engineered solutions and machines that surround us. Modern computers provide, of course, the same modularity; however, the first computers were different.

For better understanding the various computer hardware components, we will refer to human processing mechanisms. When considering human thinking, there are several organs involved. The brain, which processes information, is similar to the computer's processor. The brain controls all activities as well as behavior and feelings. This process is based on previous experiences, whether learned or acquired. Similarly, the processor acts on the data it receives based on the program that was loaded. In this sense, the program loaded into the system provides the rules for processing, similar to the way in which experience provides the human brain with a blueprint for behavior. In this sense, the program developed by software engineers may be considered as instructing or teaching the computer how to react to various events. This is similar to teaching students how to act in a given situation, for example, when engineering a computerized solution.

The human memory is even more interesting in its relation to the computer memory. Many researchers regard the human memory as a hierarchy of three levels of memory:

- A temporary (or sensory) memory, which is used as a buffer that stores data received from the various senses. Every sense has its own buffer, which contains all the data received. This data undergoes some initial processing, during which most of it is classified as irrelevant and is discarded. The information that may be relevant is copied to the working memory for additional processing. An example is the vast amounts of data we as human beings are exposed to. For example, while driving a car, we constantly see the surroundings. These images and sounds are transferred to the visual sensory memory, where most of it is classified as irrelevant, and it disappears. This is done in order to reduce the data overload, and, as a matter of fact, we even do not remember many of the scenes we have seen or sounds we heard. The sensory memory is the mechanism that allows humans (like other living creatures) to be part of the environment and constantly react to important situations. For most creatures, these situations may involve threats or opportunities (e.g., acquiring or hunting for food).

- Short-term memory (or the working memory), which is the memory used for processing data. It receives only the information that was classified as important or relevant. Here, it is analyzed to determine the proper required action. The short-term memory has a relatively fast access time (tens of milliseconds); however, it has a limited capacity. The data in the short-term memory is kept for a short time; the length of this time depends on the flow of additional "important" data that is being received, the person's situation, and their age. Due to its limited capacity, this memory is affected by environmental disturbances, which may cause the data to disappear; then, a special search process will be required (to remember the last thing we were thinking or talking about). Talking on the phone or text messaging while driving is a good example of a disturbance in short-term memory processing, as is a disturbing noise during an exam.

- Long-term memory, which is used for storing information for a long and even unlimited duration. This memory has a very large capacity and can hold large amounts of data items. The access time to that data is long, and it becomes even slower with age. The retrieval mechanisms are unreliable. Sometimes we may try to remember some fact but cannot. This is not because the specific data item was removed, but because the retrieval process is not adequate. Sometime later, we may recall the missing data, which implies that it was stored in memory and was not lost, simply that the pointer that links the data was not clear. For information to be stored in the long-term memory, it has to be very important, or a constant rehearsal is required.

Relating back to computers, all three types of the human memory are present. Unfortunately, as will be elaborated on in this book, although modern computers use a similar memory hierarchy, it took time before it was designed and developed. The long-term memory in computers refers to the various storage devices, such as disks (hard drives). These devices are used for storing the information for a long duration. Among the storage devices we may find magnetic tapes, which were used in the past but were, almost totally, replaced by better, more reliable technologies and disks (magnetic, optical, and electronic, such as solid-state disks). The short-term memory is the memory (or random access memory [RAM]) and it is the working area. For the processor to run a program, it has to be loaded into memory as well as the data it requires. This is usually a limited capacity memory, although in a modern system it may consist of billions of bytes (or characters); it is significantly smaller, nevertheless, than the storage, which may be several orders of magnitude larger. The third level of the sensory memory is implemented in computers by registers as well as the cache memory. Registers are a small working area inside the processor that is intended for the data currently being used and processed. Cache memory is a fast but limited memory used for the recently used instructions and data. Furthermore, due to its contribution to the system's performance, cache memory is implemented using several levels. The closer the cache is to the processor, the faster and smaller it is.

The last and most trivial components are the various senses that act as our input devices (sensors in embedded and real-time systems) and sense the environment; and the muscles that control movement and speech, which represent output devices (actuators in real time systems).

Regarding behavior, in addition to the behavioral blueprints that regulate our behavior in various situations, sometimes the brain tries to correct errors it thinks were introduced by our inherent limitations. One such famous example is the Kanizsa* triangle.

---

* Kanizsa Gaetano was an Italian psychologist who published an article about illusory contours, which discussed various visual illusions.

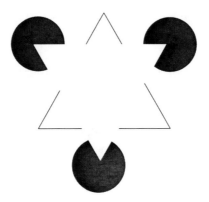

FIGURE 0.2   The Kanizsa triangle.

Most humans will interpret the picture as a white triangle placed on top of three circles. This is an example of a visual illusion, since there is no white triangle but only three circles, each of which has a missing part (similar to the "creature" from the famous Pac-Man game). The erroneous interpretation is due to the brain's attempt to overcome a known limitation. We live in a three-dimensional world; however, drawings, such as Figure 0.2, that are printed on paper cannot convey the three-dimensional experience and are limited in providing just two dimensions. The brain, which is aware of this fact, tries to correct the problem by interpreting the figure as a three-dimensional object. This "recovery" is done automatically without active conscious involvement. Another example of a process that is done automatically among all creatures is the instinctive reflexes, such as moving the hand after we touch a hot surface, or an animal that attacks or runs away when a threat is perceived. These reflexes are managed without the brain's involvement, mainly in order to save time in dealing with a potential dangerous situation. Computers have adopted similar "behavior" using a different approach. One such example is during communications, in which error correction codes (ECC) are used to assess the correctness of the messages sent and received. It is an automatic process in which the system tries to correct mistakes and provide the right interpretation before it gets to the user program (just like the Kanizsa illusions). In cases of error, the controller issues a resend request without even involving the processor. Roughly, this can be viewed as the controller reflex to the erroneous message received. The idea behind this behavior is to relieve the software engineering process of the need to check the integrity of the data received from another component or by communication.

CHAPTER ORGANIZATION

The book was designed to enhance students' understanding regarding the hardware infrastructure used in various software engineering projects. As such, it covers the main hardware components and, in some cases, the logic that the components' development followed. The historic perspective is important because sometimes when new computerized appliances are invented, the old design considerations may surface again. One such example is the memory management used by old mobile telephones before they emerged into fully operational computer systems, as is the case with smart phones. For a better and a gradual understanding, the text in the book is divided into 11 different chapters:

- Chapter 1, "Introduction and Historic Perspective," provides an introduction and a historic perspective, from the initial need for computers, followed by the first developments and additional technological directions, up to modern cloud computing. The historic perspective relates to computers and systems in general. Historic aspects that relate to various components of the system will be elaborated on as part of the appropriate chapter.

- Chapter 2, "Data Representation," describes the computers' data representation. It starts with various numeric systems, followed by the way computers represent and store numbers, and it includes a brief section on computer arithmetic.

- Chapter 3, "Hardware Architecture," provides a brief explanation regarding computer architecture and how this term and its underlying meaning changed over the years.

- Chapter 4, "Central Processing Unit," provides an explanation about the processor (or central processing unit [CPU]). Once again, it includes a brief historic development, since some of the previous implementations are still available and are used by simple appliances, such as calculators. The chapter includes a large section on performance enhancements, which, although performed by the hardware, resemble the algorithms used by software engineers.

- Chapter 5, "Memory," describes computer memory and discusses its organization, hierarchy, and performance considerations as applied by the operating system, which are important for software engineers.

- Chapter 6, "Cache Memory," describes cache memory, which is an important level in the memory hierarchy responsible for significant performance increase. The chapter concludes with various possible architectures that are the cornerstone of modern and future systems.

- Chapter 7, "Bus," describes the bus system, which is responsible for the movement of data between the various computers' hardware components. Due to the changing definition of buses in modern architectures, various algorithms for ensuring data integrity are discussed as part of the chapter.

- Chapter 8, "Input and Output," provides a brief description of input and output (I/O) components and discusses various methods for performing I/O. Various aspects relevant to software engineering, such as buffers and buffer flushing, are explained.

- Chapter 9, "Storage," describes the various nonvolatile storage devices (the bottom part of the memory hierarchy). For obvious reasons, most of the chapter is dedicated to hard drives and technologies for enhancing performance and reliability. As with previous cases, the methods used are related to hardware (the disk controller), but the algorithms used are implemented using software and are relevant for software engineers.

- Chapter 10, "Additional Architectures," describes additional system architectures, with a special emphasis on virtualization and cloud computing.

- Chapter 11, "Software Architectures," briefly describes the emergence of software-based systems, from the prearchitectural era through some of the architectures that were developed to cope with various market requirements. It concludes with current and future trends.

Author

Aharon Yadin has over 40 years of IT experience spanning a variety of fields and disciplines, gained while working and consulting in the high-tech industry. These activities include systems analysis and design, systems architecture design and configuration, the analysis of current and emerging trends in software and hardware technologies, IT project management, benchmarking and system performance and evaluation, research and the commercialization of research results. For the last 15 years, Aharon has been engaged in academia. As a senior lecturer, he teaches, lectures, and conducts research projects. In parallel to these academic activities, Aharon consults numerous local and international organizations regarding innovative solutions, security issues, and the use of new technologies. Aharon is the author of nine instructional and text books covering various areas of computing and has published dozens of papers.

CHAPTER 1

Introduction and Historic Perspective

INTRODUCTION AND HISTORIC PERSPECTIVE

The need for computers or computing devices, which were originally intended just for counting, is as old as humankind. This need for a counting mechanism was developed as part of the verbal communication between humans in ancient times. Such a mechanism was needed in order to express ideas related to quantities such as the number of sheep in the herd, the time that had passed since a specific event, or the distance from some place. Only at a later stage did the counting mechanism develop into a system that started using symbols for representing quantities. These symbols led to another significant development, which supported simple arithmetic operations.

An interesting insight into the representation of quantities in ancient times can be found in Latin. It can be safely assumed that in the beginning, people used their fingers to represent quantities, since the origin of the word "digit," the cornerstone to our numbering system, is the Latin word *digitus*, which means "finger." Similarly, and based on the same logic, one can assume that the first calculations were performed using pebbles, since *calculus* in Latin means "pebble." One of the oldest machines used for calculations was the abacus, invented in the ancient civilization of Mesopotamia about 5000 years ago. It was later spread to other civilizations, such as the Egyptian, Persian, Chinese, Greek, and so on. Some abacus variations are still being used in various remote locations around the globe. The device was intended to represent numbers (quantities) and to help in simple arithmetic such as additions and subtractions. Nevertheless, it is difficult to use it for more complex calculations. During the centuries that followed, many other various calculating devices were invented. One of these devices is the Napier Bones, a small and sophisticated device intended for complex calculations such as multiplications and divisions. It was invented in the early seventeenth century by John Napier, a Scottish mathematician who also discovered logarithms, among other things. The device was made of 10 ivory rods on which the multiplication table was engraved (Figure 1.1).

1	1	2	3	4	5	6	7	8	9
2	0 / 2	0 / 4	0 / 6	0 / 8	1 / 0	1 / 2	1 / 4	1 / 6	1 / 8
3	0 / 3	0 / 6	0 / 9	1 / 2	1 / 5	1 / 8	2 / 1	2 / 4	2 / 7
4	0 / 4	0 / 8	1 / 2	1 / 6	2 / 0	2 / 2	2 / 8	3 / 2	3 / 6
5	0 / 5	1 / 0	1 / 5	2 / 0	2 / 5	3 / 0	3 / 5	4 / 0	4 / 5
6	0 / 6	1 / 2	1 / 8	2 / 4	3 / 0	3 / 6	4 / 2	4 / 8	5 / 4
7	0 / 7	1 / 4	2 / 1	2 / 8	3 / 5	4 / 2	4 / 9	5 / 6	6 / 3
8	0 / 8	1 / 6	2 / 4	3 / 2	4 / 0	4 / 8	5 / 6	6 / 4	7 / 2
9	0 / 9	1 / 8	2 / 7	3 / 6	4 / 5	5 / 4	6 / 3	7 / 2	8 / 1

FIGURE 1.1 The Napier Bones scheme.

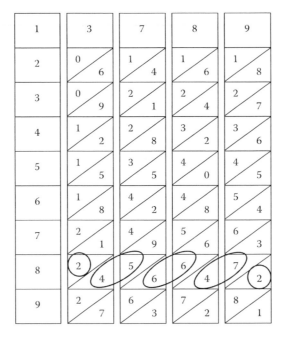

FIGURE 1.2 The Napier Bones example.

For performing a specific multiplication, only the relevant rods were used. The multiplication itself resembles the common multiplication process taught today in elementary schools, which starts from the least significant digit and continues to all higher-order digits. Let us assume we want to use the Napier Bones to multiply 3789 by 8. The rods to be selected and used will be 3, 7, 8, and 9 (Figure 1.2). We start the process of multiplication from right to left by writing down the numbers in row 8. The least significant digit (units) will be 2; the second (tens) will be 1 (4 + 7 = 11, which is larger than 9 so it produces a carryover and we write down only the units digit). The third digit (hundreds) will be 3 (adding the two diagonal digits and carry over 6 + 6 + 1 = 13, producing an additional carryover). The fourth digit (thousands) will be 0 (5 + 4 + 1 = 10) and the last digit (ten thousands) will be 3 (2 plus the carryover). The result obtained is 30312 (3789 * 8 = 30312).

The discovery of logarithms significantly contributed to lowering the complexity of calculations since it replaced multiplications and divisions by additions and subtractions. The slide rule, which was invented in the seventeenth century, was based on logarithms behavior. Described as a mechanical analog computer, the slide rule was used by scientists and engineers for over 300 years until it was gradually replaced by the electronic calculator. In its simplest form, the rule was based on two sliding logarithmic scales that could be aligned to produce the result of the multiplication or division.

There are several logarithms' rules used for simplifying expressions. For example

$$\log(xy) = \log(x) + \log(y)$$

$$\text{and } \log\left(\frac{x}{y}\right) = \log(x) - \log(y)$$

Multiplication is actually aligning the two slides, one after the other, by moving the upper scale to the right up to position x on the lower scale. The result is the number on the lower scale that scales with the y on the upper scale. For example, let us assume we have to multiply 2 by 4. We align the upper scale so that 1 is aligned with 2 on the lower scale, and then 4 on the upper scale is aligned with the result (Figure 1.3).

The race to invent a device for simplifying mathematical calculations continued with a device invented by Blaise Pascal, a French mathematician. This device was a mechanical calculator that used a set of interconnected wheels, a concept similar to the mechanisms in mechanical clocks.

However, many view Charles Babbage as the real "father of the computer." He was an English mathematician who invented a device considered to be the first mechanical computer. Although it did not materialize, it paved the way for other newer ideas. Since additions and subtractions can be relatively easily implemented using a mechanical wheel, Babbage, like his predecessors, was looking for ways to replace complex mathematical computations such as polynomial functions by a set of simple operations using only additions and subtractions. The device was called the difference engine, since it overcame the need for multiplications and divisions by a method of finite differences.

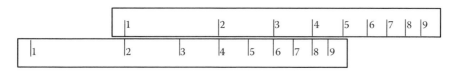

FIGURE 1.3 The slide rule example.

TABLE 1.1   Differences Table

X	The Function Value $9x^2 + 3x + 12$	First Difference	Second Difference
0	12		
1	24	12	
2	54	30	18
3	102	48	18
4	168	66	18
5	252	84	18
6	354	102	18
7	474	120	18

The main idea behind the method is to create a series of differences that replace the more complex calculations. The first set is calculated by the difference of each two consecutive values of the polynomial. The second set is calculated by the difference between any two consecutive values of the first set, and so on. The last set will consist of constants. The polynomial degree defines the number of sets to be calculated. For a polynomial degree of n, there will be $n + 1$ sets, where the first set is the polynomial values and the last set consists of a constant. The number of differences sets for such a polynomial is n.

For example, let us assume we want to calculate the differences for the function $9x^2 + 3x + 12$ (as described by Table 1.1).

From a mathematics point of view, it is quite simple to prove that for a second-degree polynomial, the second level of differences is constant.

The first level is calculated by

$$\text{Diff1}_n = 9x^2 + 3x + 12 - \left(9^* (x-1)^2 + 3^* (x-1) + 12\right)$$

$$= 9x^2 + 3x + 12 - 9x^2 + 15x + 18$$

$$= 18x - 6$$

The second level is calculated by

$$\text{Diff2}_n = 18x - 6 - \left(18^* (x-1) - 6\right)$$

$$= 18$$

After the initial values were calculated, the process can be reversed, which provides an easy way to calculate the values of the polynomial without the need for multiplications. To calculate the value of the polynomial for $x = 8$, we have to start with the last set of constants:

$$\text{Set } 3 = 18,18,18,18,18,18,18,18,18\ldots$$

Then we build the second set by starting with the first difference ($f(2)$–$f(1)$) and adding the constant to every object in the set:

$$\text{Set } 2 = 12, 30, 48, 66, 84, 102, 120, 138\ldots$$

The last stage is building the first set, since this is a second-degree polynomial. This is done by starting with the value of $f(0)$ and then adding this value to all objects:

$$\text{Set } 1 = 12, 24, 54, 102, 168, 252, 354, 474, 612\ldots$$

The required value ($f(8)$) is given at the ninth location (since the set starts with object 0).

Although Babbage planned the differences engine, he never built it. His son Henry continued the work and built a device using parts found in his father's laboratory. However, it took an additional 150 years to fully complete the device by using better production technologies and better building materials. Several devices were built, all based on Babbage's original drawings.

Babbage himself realized that the "real" solution for a computing device cannot be implemented using the differences engine, so he abandoned this idea and started working on an analytical engine.

Although the analytical engine idea did not proceed beyond the drawing board, the principles expressed (a processing unit, a control unit, memory, input and output devices) are the cornerstones of modern computers. The analytical engine as designed by Babbage had a 1000-cell memory, each cell capable of storing up to 50 digits. To allow better memory utilization, the analytical engine included a mechanism for writing out some of the cells for creating additional space for new numbers. This idea is widely used by most of the general-purpose computers utilizing virtual memory and various storage devices. However, the most important aspect of the analytical engine was the understanding that the machine should be able to execute various programs and not just the one it was designed for. This understanding, which later led to the development of programming languages, is one of the unique characteristics of computers.

By separating the software or the executed programs from the hardware, computers and computer-based devices can be made to assume various different roles. Unlike all other machines or appliances that are designed to perform a specific task, computers can be made to change their behavior by loading different applications. After the computer (desktop, laptop, tablet, etc.) is started, it waits for the user's instructions. When a word-processing application is launched, the computer "transforms" into a word-processing machine. If the user starts a browser, the computer "transforms" into a device that provides the means to surf the web. On the other hand, if the user prefers to launch a game, then the computer becomes a gaming console. It should be noted, however, that the computer hardware does not change, just the software loaded and executed. Computers' many identity changes are possible due to the separation between software and hardware, which was initially designed by Babbage in his analytical engine.

Due to the vast spread of computers and their usage in various other devices, the multifunctionality or identity changes are not confined to computers only. Modern cellular phones, for example, utilize several processors and provide much more than the basic and original purpose of making phone calls. These small devices have emerged as mobile personal information centers providing web connectivity, a local database for various types of information (contact lists, photos, text, videos, music, etc.), and an entertainment center for playing music, video, and games; by loading other applications, the phone's identity is transformed even further.

The First Computers

Herman Hollerith, who in the late nineteenth century invented a tabulation machine based on punched cards, is considered by many as the "father" of modern computers. This is mainly due to his practical contribution to advancing the subject. As has been the case many times in the past and present, technical developments were triggered by a need to solve a concrete problem.

During the second half of the nineteenth century, large waves of immigrants came to the United States hoping for better lives. These hundreds of thousands of new inhabitants required a population census, especially considering that the U.S. constitution requires a census every ten years. The technology available at that time was based on manual registration. Due to the size of the United States and the number of citizens involved, completing such a census using the available technology would have required a very long time. Since the census was used not just for counting the population but also for gathering important information expressed by questions, the solution required additional tabulations. The 1880 census took almost 10 years to complete, and it was tabulated by hand. In addition to the very long time involved, the main problem in using the manual technology was that by the time it was complete, the results obtained were incorrect and sometimes even irrelevant. It was clear that for the 1890 census, another way had to be used. It of course had to be more reliable and especially faster. The census office issued a Request for Proposals (RFP) for a solution to the problem. In modern times, we refer to a new technology; in the nineteenth century, however, the census office was looking for a new way of conducting the census. The winning proposal by Herman Hollerith was based on a machine that could read data stored on punched cards. The data obtained in the census was recorded on the cards by punching holes in them. The machines could "read" the data by using a metal brush. The brush sensed the holes in the card by passing through the holes and closing an electrical circuit.

Hollerith, who was a statistician, did not intend to develop a new technology but a tool capable of dealing with huge amounts of data and especially of helping to organize and tabulate these data. The newly invented technology of the punched card was used by computers for several decades afterward. During the first half of the twentieth century, punched cards were widely used for storing and entering data into computers, and they served as one of the first input/output media. Only during the 1980s were punched cards replaced by other more modern devices.

The 1890 census was completed in about 6 months and used $5 million (U.S.) less that the budget allocated. The most important issue, however, is not the technology or the time and money it saved, but the first occurrence of a machine that replaced humans in managing large amounts of data, which recorded Hollerith as one of the founders of modern computing. The technology was used in other countries as well, and as a result, Hollerith founded the Tabulating Machines Company, which won the 1900 RFP for the census. In 1911, by merging two other companies, it grew and became CTR (Computing Tabulating Recording Company), which in 1924 changed its name to IBM (International Business Machines).

The Hollerith punched cards that were used until the 1980s had 12 rows and 80 columns (Figure 1.4). Each card could hold up to 80 characters (digits, letters, and special symbols), one per column. Ten rows were marked by numbers (0–9), and two rows representing 11–12 were left blank. Digits were encoded by a hole in rows 0–9 that represents the digit, while other characters were encoded by a combination of holes (0–9 and 11–12).

The Hollerith punched cards advanced the technological state of the art but were used mainly for storing information and tabulating it, and they later became the primary source of input and output media.

The modern era of computing started with the Mark I, an electromechanical computer developed by Howard H. Aiken, which was funded and built by IBM and shipped to Harvard University in 1944. The computer was physically very large (over 50 feet long), and since it used mechanical relays, it was very noisy. The idea behind the architecture was based on the analytical engine designed by Babbage but was implemented using an electrical motor. While modern computers use binary arithmetic, the Mark I used decimal numbers, and the execution times were slow even when compared to the human brain:

- Three additions/subtractions per second

- Four to six seconds for multiplications

- Fifteen seconds for divisions

The execution instructions were read one at a time from punched paper tape, and the data was entered using manual switches representing numbers.

FIGURE 1.4 Punched card.

Based on the experience gathered from the Mark I, both Harvard and IBM developed new and more advanced computer models. However, another important landmark in computer history was the Electronic Numerical Integrator and Computer (ENIAC).

The ENIAC was the first electronic computer without mechanical parts. Due to its ability to run various programs, it is considered the first general-purpose computer. The main purpose behind its design was to ease the tedious work involved in calculating and preparing artillery-firing tables. Design and construction of the machine was carried out at the University of Pennsylvania and was led by John Mauchly and Presper Eckert. The project started in 1943 and the computer became operational in 1946. It was too late to contribute to the war efforts, but since it was operational until 1955, it was used for many other heavy computational projects such as the hydrogen bomb.

The ENIAC, like all other computers at that time, was very large, and it spread over 1800 square feet. It used over 17,000 vacuum tubes, which at that time were not too reliable. As a result, the computer was nonoperational for a large period and it was up only half of the time. However, when it was working, it was the fastest available computer, capable of performing 5000 additions/subtractions, 357 multiplications, and 38 divisions per second.

The most important feature, and the one that advanced computing technology, is the understanding that a computer should be a general-purpose machine that can execute many different programs. This principle is currently one of the main cornerstones of computer architectures. It led to the development of many programming languages and directly contributed to the wide usage of computers as standalone systems as well as being embedded in many machines, devices, and appliances.

Attributes of the First Computers

Computing technology did not appear suddenly but was developed gradually over time. The first computers were different from the computers that followed and significantly different from the current modern ones. Because most civilizations used the decimal system, the first computers were designed to work in the same way. Only at later stages was it understood that for electrical devices such as computers, a binary system is more suitable and much more efficient.

A second significant difference relates to size. The rapid technological advancements in electronics and minimization did not exist in the early days of computing, and for that reason the computers were very large, consumed huge amounts of electricity, and were limited in the scope of solutions they could provide. A significant step forward was achieved with the invention of the transistor (1947). The transistor is a semiconductor device that can amplify and switch signals. The transistors replaced the vacuum tubes and the electromechanical switches, which were significantly larger, consumed large amounts of electricity, and were insufficiently reliable. The transistor invention, which changed the electronics market forever, provided a substantial step in the advancement of the modern technologies. The transistor supports electronic circuits' minimization as well as the integration of millions—and in recent years even billions—of transistors on a single chip. These attributes revolutionized the computer industry as well as the whole electronics market.

In the first computers, the "programming" was performed using manual switches or by reading a punched paper tape. The computer read one instruction, executed it, and then proceeded to the next one. The idea of loading a program into memory or the "stored programs model" appeared only at later stages.

Another important change was the introduction of registers. Registers are fast buffers in the processing unit for holding temporary data. If compared to the human body (see the preface), registers are an equivalent hardware component to sensory data. Although registers are not used for storing all sensory data and ignoring the irrelevant parts (as in humans), they are an important part of the instruction's execution. The first computers did not have any registers and saved temporary variables in memory or in the stack. Only later was the one-register (called "accumulator") computer designed. This accumulator was used for intermediary results used in more complex calculations. It worked in a similar way to the display in the common simple calculator. Later on, the importance of registers was realized, and current computers partly enhance the execution speed by including hundreds of registers.

Von Neumann Architecture

John von Neumann, who worked on the hydrogen bomb project, was partially involved with the ENIAC project as well, mainly due to its potential in solving complex computations needed for the bomb. Through his involvement, von Neumann designed a computer architecture that is used even now in the design of modern computers. In fact, the principle of modularity was later applied to system engineering as well. The von Neumann architecture consists of a shared memory (equivalent to the short-term memory in humans) that is used for storing both instructions and data. The model defines several different but interconnected components comprising the computer architecture. The model is referred to as the stored program model, since it allows different programs to be loaded into the computer's memory, contrary to the single program that was available in the early models. An important principle that stemmed from the von Neumann architecture and advanced the usage of computers while lowering their prices is modularity. The model defines several functional units with a distinct separation between them (Figure 1.5). For example,

- Separating the processing unit from the memory. The processing unit (or the processor) is responsible for executing the instructions and is not related in any way to the location of the instructions or the data. The processor is the computerized equivalent

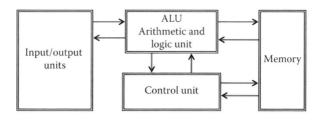

FIGURE 1.5　The von Neumann model.

of the brain in human body. A special component within the control unit inside the processor is responsible for fetching the instructions and the operands required for its execution. A similar component is responsible for collecting the result of the executed instruction and storing it in the designated location.

- Defining a unique mechanism for storing data in and retrieving data from memory. The underlying meaning is that the computer system can regard the programs as data and load the program into its memory for execution. This mechanism is the basis for the stored program model. The separation of memory from the processor, and the understanding that data and programs are variables that can change, paved the way for modern computers. Such computers are capable of running many programs in parallel. These programs change the functionality of the system as defined by each program. Furthermore, the ability to run several programs/applications in parallel allows the computer to provide different functionalities to different users as well as different functionalities to the same user in different windows.

- Separating the execution unit from the control unit. Originally, the two units were combined into the execution unit, which is responsible for executing the programs' instructions. After the separation, the control unit is responsible for scheduling the execution as well as for providing everything necessary for execution (instructions, operands), while the execution unit only executes the instructions.

- Separating the input and output units from other components of the system as well as separating each unit from the other units. The result, for example, is the high degree of modularity we all enjoy with the personal computer. Due to this separation, one may buy a computer from some manufacturer, while the mouse and keyboard can be acquired separately and connected to the computer, along with any other input and output devices. This high degree of modularity is rarely found in other electronic devices, unless these devices use embedded computers. In electronic devices, one may replace electronic components, but usually using other original or compatible components. These replaced components have to be fully compatible and provide identical functionality. The computer, through its standard interfaces, allows the user to replace a component, for example a hard drive, with another totally different device. Instead of a rotating hard drive, one may install a new solid-state drive that performs much faster or, alternatively, another rotating hard drive with a significantly larger capacity.

Figure 1.5 depicts the main components of the model:

- The ALU (arithmetic and logic unit) is responsible for executing the instruction on the basis of data received form the control unit.

- The CU (control unit) is responsible for scheduling the instructions for execution, fetching the instructions, and decoding and fetching the operands, if they exist.

- The input and output units provide the mechanism to connect to the outside world (users, other systems, various devices and appliances).

- The memory is for storing the instructions and data.

The first implementation of the von Neumann architecture was at the Institute of Advanced Technology (IAS) (at Princeton University). The IAS computer had the ability to load programs, in contrast to the previously manual switches settings. The computer was designed especially for complex mathematical computations, used binary numbers, and had several registers.

Computers' Evolution

The rapid technological development and progress that has taken place over the last few decades is even far beyond experts' expectations. Computers' influence on our lives as well as their contribution to our society was significantly underestimated by many who tried to assess future computing trends. The following are some of the better-known predictions:

- In 1948, an article published by *Popular Mechanics* predicted that future computers may weigh no more than 1.5 tons. This was mentioned as significant progress, and the article could not foresee that the weight of computers would continue to decline three or four orders of magnitude.

- In 1977, Ken Olson, one of the cofounders of Digital Equipment Corporation, expressed his opinion about computers and said that there was no reason why anyone would want a computer in their home.

The invention of the transistor was one of the driving forces behind the rapid developments, and it influenced the whole electronics market, not just computers. The large-scale miniaturization and integration of billions of transistors on a single chip paved the way for continuous waves of new generations of computers, each one faster than the one before, with advanced capabilities and lower power consumption.

Table 1.2 describes the exponential growth of transistors within a single chip as applied in the Intel line of processors. Other companies may have different but very close numbers.

It should be noted, however, that the increase in the number of transistors is not related only to the processor but also to the additional capabilities that were added in order to increase its functionality and performance. One important component is cache memory (explained later in this book—see Chapter 6, "Cache Memory"), which is a significant factor in enhancing the machine's execution speed. Furthermore, recent new developments emphasize increasing the number of cores inside the processor, which produces additional performance gains.

The number of transistors per chip continues to grow; however, due to global changes, such as the energy crisis as well as the huge demand for mobile and electricity-efficient processors, other courses of action are being explored. Instead of increasing the processor

TABLE 1.2   Number of Transistors

Chip[a]	Clock speed	Year of introduction	Transistors
4004	108 kHz	1971	2,300
8008	200 kHz	1972	3,500
8080	2 MHz	1974	6,000
8086	4.77 MHz	1978	29,000
Intel286™	6 MHz	1982	134,000
Intel386™ DX processor	16 MHz	1985	275,000
Intel486™ DX processor	25 MHz	1989	1,200,000
Intel® Pentium® processor	60 MHz	1993	3,100,000
Intel® Pentium® II processor	233 MHz	1997	7,500,000
Intel® Pentium® III processor	600 MHz	1999	28,000,000
Intel® Pentium® 4 processor	1.4 GHz	2000	42,000,000
Intel® Itanium® 2 processor	900 MHz	2002	220,000,000
Dual Core Intel® Itanium® 2 processor	1.4 GHz	2006	1,720,000,000
Intel® Core i7® Sandy Bridge	3.3 GHz	2011	2,270,000,000
18-core Xeon Haswell-E5		2014	5,560,000,000

[a] Intel, Microprocessor quick reference guide. 2008, http://www.intel.com/pressroom/kits/quickreffam.htm#XeonIII.

speed, a lot of effort is being put into reducing the required power consumption and heat dispersion.

For example, in an article published in the *New York Times*[1] on September 9, 2011, Mr. Urs Hoelzle, Google's senior vice president for technical infrastructure, revealed some data about Google's electricity consumption. The Google data centers responsible for searches, YouTube videos, Gmail, and so on, constantly consume 260 megawatts. Furthermore, in another article[2] published in September 2013, Google announced it will buy all the electricity generated by a 240-megawatt wind farm built in Texas. These two examples demonstrate the reasoning behind the new research directions. In addition to the efforts being spent in finding new ways for mainly increasing processing speed, significant research is being conducted into the design of new lighter and faster chips that use less energy.

In 2008, as part of its analysis of the state of the personal computer (PC) industry, Gartner, a leading information technology research and advisory company, estimated that the number of PCs in use worldwide surpassed 1 billion units[3]. Gartner's analysts estimate the worldwide installed base will surpass 2 billion by 2014. In a recent report by Gartner[4], more detailed shipments data was revealed. According to that report, shipments of traditional PCs will decline over the coming years, while mobile-phone shipments will continue to grow.

These new trends, which are fueled by new consumers' demands for constantly connection to the network, have affected the race to include more transistors in a chip. Mobility, light weight, and low power consumption have become a prominent factor in purchase decisions and have to be considered in hardware design processes as well.

Moore's Law

In a paper published in *Electronics* on April 19, 1965, Gordon Moore, then Fairchild Semiconductor's director of research and development (R&D) wrote an interesting projection about the number of components in an integrated circuit. The projection that the number of components per circuit would double every year was based on extrapolating the number of components used at that time. Moore, who later was to be one of the founders of Intel, changed his projection to a doubling of the number of components every 24 months. Moore's law[5] is thus not actually a physical law but an observation that shaped the semiconductor industry and all electronics devices that use these circuits. The importance of Moore's law is not merely in the number of components per integrated circuit but also in the fact that the performance of these devices is closely linked to the number of components. Contrary to the common belief that Moore suggested that the number of components will double every 18 months, this was in fact a modification made by David House, an Intel executive at that time, who spoke about the computers' performance and not specifically about the number of components in the circuit. Moore's law, which is basically applicable to hardware, influences software and system engineering processes as well. Even problems that seem unsolvable due to lack of computer power will be solved in a couple of years due to the rapid advancements in computing technologies as predicted by the law.

Classification of Computers

There are many ways to classify computers, however over the years, the dominant classification has been according to the systems' use. Generally speaking, there are three main groups of computers and computer-based systems:

- Microcomputers, which are usually small, low cost, and intended for one user or one device. Almost every office and house has a personal computer; these usually include a display, keyboard, and mouse and are used for a large variety of applications, from network access to business, educational, and entertainment applications and even games. The wide spread of PCs and the fact that over 300 million have been sold annually in recent years has reduced their prices, and currently these PCs are the dominant platform for application development and solutions in many fields. Such PCs use a large variety of hardware and software components and are used for many purposes. Although a large proportion of the current PCs are laptops, for very specific tasks a subcategory of microcomputers has been developed. This subcategory manifested itself in tablets and PDAs (personal digital assistants), which utilize a different input device such as a touch screen, which in most cases is an integral part of the device. This is contrary to the design of ordinary PCs, which is based on modularity and supports intermixing input and output devices. These new mobile devices, along with the modern mobile telephones, are the main focus of current engineering efforts, mainly due to their vast potential (as was demonstrated by the worldwide device shipment—Table 1.3). Furthermore, the integration of the mobile networks and the Internet has provided mobile phones with all the functionality that was previously available only to desktop and laptop computers. The fact that in many organizations

TABLE 1.3   Worldwide Device Shipments (Thousands of Units)

Device Type	2014	2015	2016	2017
PC (desk based and notebook)	277,118	252,881	243,628	236,341
Ultra mobile	36,699	53,452	74,134	90,945
Tablet	227,080	236,778	257,985	276,026
Mobile phone	1,878,968	1,943,952	2,017,861	2,055,954
Total	2,419,864	2,487,062	2,593,608	2,659,265

most of the workforce is on the move (travelling sales people, service and repair technicians, appraisers, etc.) requires the integration of these mobile devices into the operational computing network. This integration is important for better management control as well as more intelligent and fact-oriented decision making. A very clear example is the various shipment companies such as FedEx, UPS, and others that have equipped all their dispatchers with handheld devices. Every operation, such as picking up a parcel, loading it onto an airplane, bringing it to a delivery center, and so on, is recorded and sent in real time to the control center. The information system at the control center is integrated into the website, which provides the capability for each customer to track almost in real time the location of his or her parcel. Another very large market segment that is using many microcomputers is that for various embedded devices. As most of the devices and appliances that surround us become more complex and highly sophisticated, the need for integrating a computer arises. In the twenty-first century, most home appliances utilize some computerized system. This is also the case with vehicles, industrial machinery, medical equipment, and so on. All these devices are based on microcomputers.

- Minicomputers, which are generally used in a multiuser environment. Historically, these computers were developed to provide a solution for a specific department rather than for entire organizations. Prior to the advancements in network technologies, these minicomputers could support a geographically remote department. With the rapid advancements in PC performance, as predicted by Moore's law, in recent years minicomputers have transformed into small servers, sometimes utilizing a standard PC. These servers act as a platform for a specific application, such as a print server that manages all printers and handles all print tasks or a mail server that manages all the organization's mail.

- Mainframes, which are large organizational computer systems that act as the main computational infrastructure. These systems host an organization's databases and provide applications to support all business processes. Mainframes are usually very powerful and support many concurrent users. Originally, the mainframes were proprietary systems with a proprietary operating system. At the beginning of the twenty-first century, many of the mainframes were replaced by large servers, which provide the same functionality. Some of these servers are built using many off-the-shelf microprocessors working in parallel. To provide the required power and functionality, new server farms were built to host many servers working and sharing the same facility. These farms provide an additional level of parallelism and a potential for unlimited computing power. Furthermore, new developments in computing technologies provide tools for defining virtual machines, which are usually made up of many physical systems working together as one virtual system. Other modern trends use this virtualization combined with high-speed communications for providing cloud computing. The cloud-computing technology allows an organization to acquire computing services from a third-party provider (this will be elaborated on in Chapter 10, "Additional Architectures").

Historic Perspective

The first computers developed in the mid-twentieth century were physically very large and expensive. These systems used proprietary operating systems and required a special cooling facility, mainly due to the vacuum tubes, which produced heat. These computers could run only one program (or process) at a specific time and supported only batch processing. Unlike the modern interactive mode of operation, in batch processing the computing program runs off-line without any user involvement or interaction. The data required for the program is provided in advance. The batch programs were loaded into the system and the operating system was responsible for running these programs one after the other. The fact that the system executed only one program at a given time meant that the program had to run to completion before the next program in the queue could start running. This mode of operation was extremely inefficient. Even in the early days of computing, the input and output (I/O) devices were significantly slower than the processor. However, since only one program was executed, the processor had to wait for the I/O operations. The bottom line was that not only was the system very expensive, but also that this mode of operation prevented it from working efficiently. This was especially noticed when the program had to perform lots of inputs and outputs.

These limitations were among the triggers for efforts to advance computing technology, mainly by providing mechanisms to run several programs in parallel. Initially these were batch jobs and only later included interactive sessions as well. When one program was waiting for an event, such as the users entering some input, the processor could be utilized to execute another program. To enable the execution of multiple programs in parallel, special hardware modifications were required—for example, to provide the necessary separation between the running programs. The operating systems had to be modified as well in order to protect each program and its working space from unauthorized access as well as to assure that each program was accessing only its working space.

Working interactively provided a significant benefit for users, since they could get the required reply instantaneously. This fueled the shift from batch systems to more interactive systems. The large difference between the processor speed and the I/O devices speed produced a new idea of time-sharing systems, which is currently used by most computer systems. Since the processor was fast enough to support many interactive clients, the operating systems were modified to support many concurrent users who share the computer system. Each user feels as if he or she is the only user served by the system, but actually, the system is fast enough to support all of them. This of course required additional modifications and enhancements to the operating system in terms of scheduling the algorithms that are responsible for providing a balanced share of the system to all working clients. However, the ability to provide service for many concurrent users was among the enablers for the wide adoption of computer systems in spite of their very high price.

The first stage in implementing time-sharing computing used "dumb terminals." These were simple devices used for communicating with the computer system. Such terminals had a keyboard as the input device and a printing mechanism for displaying the computer's replies. Only at a later stage was the output device replaced by a screen as used by most modern systems. These terminals were purely mechanical, and each character type on the keyboard was transmitted to the computer. The computer sent the command to the printing mechanism to print the typed character. In the early implementations, each such terminal was connected to the computer by a separate communication line (Figure 1.6). Furthermore, each of the vendors had specific and proprietary terminals designed for its computer, which were quite expensive.

Figure 1.6 depicts a computer that supports numerous terminals, each connected using a separate communication line.

The high costs associated with computers led computing departments to try and load the processor to its maximum capacity in order to justify these costs. On the other hand, a fully loaded system works more slowly, which became unbearable for many users who originally experienced fast turnaround times. Rapid technological development, as predicted by Moore's law, produced new generations of computers that were physically smaller, were usually slower, and did not require special cooling systems. For computer manufacturers, it provided a new market segment. As the price of a computer system decreased from

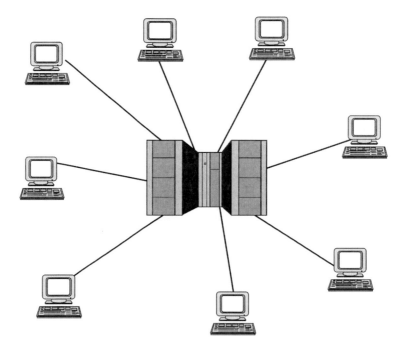

FIGURE 1.6   Terminal connectivity.

millions of dollars to hundreds of thousands and later to tens of thousands, computers were offered to departments. Instead of a large computer center managed by the computing department, many smaller departmental computers started to appear. The main advantage of the departmental computer was that it provided a better response time since the department's users did not have to compete for the computer resources with all the other users in the organization. In most cases, these departmental computers used a proprietary operating system and utilized special proprietary terminals.

In parallel to the appearance of the departmental computers, another significant technological development started to emerge—communications. The original means of connecting a terminal to the computer was to use a dedicated line for each terminal. However, sometimes the users' offices were located in a far and distant area. In many cases, in such a distant office, there were several terminals that had to be connected. Using a separate line for each terminal was very expensive and unjustified, especially in cases where the utilization of these lines was very low. The solution that was suggested was a concentrator, which is a small communication device that can use one communication line to transfer the data produced by several sources working in parallel (Figure 1.7). Like the time sharing used by the computer's processor, the concentrator assumes that the communication line is faster that the users' interaction, so sharing the communication line among several users produces a significant cost saving with minimal negative impact. By using such concentrators, the organization could increase the number of terminals at remote locations without deploying a new communication lines and by using the existing infrastructure. In many cases, adding a terminal at a remote location was cheaper compared to adding a terminal at the local site.

The upper part (on the left side of Figure 1.7) depicts a remote site with four terminals. Prior to using concentrators, there was a need to deploy a separate communication line for

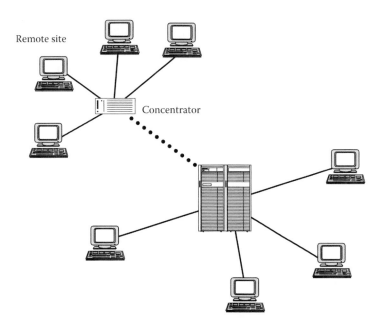

FIGURE 1.7   A concentrator example.

each one of the terminals. The concentrator uses one line for all four terminals, reducing costs by 75%. In addition to the one-time costs associated with such a deployment, there are additional reoccurring maintenance costs. Usually, an organization cannot deploy communication lines outside its campus, so an external communication provider has to be involved. Such a provider usually charges a maintenance fee for its services. A concentrator that supports several logical data streams on one physical line reduces these communication costs as well. There is a pair of concentrators on each line that transparently handle the data stream. The computer on one side and each one of the terminals on the other side do not even know they do not share a dedicated line.

Personal Computers

Microcomputers, which are characterized by a single-chip processor, emerged in the early 1970s. One of the first microcomputers was the Intel 4004, which was introduced in 1971 and used 4 bits. In the 1970s, various companies explored the microprocessor capabilities for various applications. During the first half of that decade, the software systems developed were very specific, for example a dedicated engineering device. However, during the second half of that decade, more "off-the-shelf" applications started to appear, such as spreadsheets and games. Some of the 1970s microcomputers, and especially those used for games, connected to a television screen in order to lower costs.

In the early 1980s, IBM worked secretly on evaluating the potential of the "new" microcomputers. There were even rumors of IBM's intention to buy Atari, a highly experienced arcade company. Atari entered the consumer market consciousness in the early 1970s with a microcomputer-based device dedicated to graphic games. Atari's most famous gaming device, the Atari 800, had an integrated basic programming language, providing a simple and affordable personal computing device. The microcomputer market experienced a steady growth, although a large portion of this was dedicated to arcade games. Realizing the vast market potential, IBM decided to enter the market by developing its own hardware platform. In 1981, the first IBM microcomputer was introduced. It was based on an 8088 microprocessor, had 16 KB (kilobytes) of memory (expandable to 256 KB) and a floppy drive for storing data. Its name was the Personal Computer, a name that is being used even currently. Furthermore, IBM's entrance into the market provided the required legitimacy, and slowly the technology emerged as a platform for commercial applications as well.

The personal computer was a significant landmark in IBM's history as it was the first time a whole computer was based on off-the-shelf components without any special IBM developments. Furthermore, even marketing efforts for the new computer were innovative, as the systems were sold in ordinary commercial store chains. The operating system for the new computers was developed by a small company headed by Bill Gates, who successfully persuaded IBM to let him sell the product to other companies as well.

Several months after the introduction of the personal computer, it was selected as the Machine of the Year by *Time* magazine. This was a tribute to the PC's contribution and especially its future contribution to human welfare. In fact, the PC started a revolution in the computing industry, which still affects modern architectures. In many cases, these computing architectures do not use just the Personal Computer, but also some of its mobile, lightweight derivatives.

The first PCs were very simple and quite primitive. As was the case with the first large computers, the PC was originally intended for one user and could run only one application at any given time. However, technological developments for large computers were adopted for PCs as well, which gradually enhanced their capabilities. The first PCs were used for standalone problem solving, such as spreadsheets used by managers as part of the management process or simple applications for task management and tracking. However, the PC, like any other computer, could run other applications as well. One of the first applications that was developed and was very successful was an emulation of proprietary terminals.

The organizational computers at that time used only proprietary terminals that were designed and manufactured by the hardware manufacturer. This meant that the prices of these terminals were defined solely by the vendor. Without any competition, the customers had to pay the required price, even if it was high and unreasonable. The PCs that could run an application that emulated these proprietary terminals provided compatible devices but at a significantly cheaper price. In a very short time, the prices of the proprietary terminals plunged. However, due to the large numbers of PCs manufactured and sold and the fact many companies entered the market and offered their version of the computers, PCs' prices decreased as well. In retrospect, the trend of using a PC with an emulation application for replacing the proprietary terminals was the main reason that the number of proprietary terminals is currently close to none.

The immediate result of introducing the PC-based terminals into organizations was systems with some proprietary terminals as well as some PCs. Furthermore, such a PC can act not only as a terminal but can be used for other tasks as well. Some of the PCs were used as standalone systems and were not connected to the main computer (Figure 1.8).

Slowly but surely, the PC established its role in organizations. The reasonable price and the variety of available applications and games increased its prevalence. On the other hand, the increase in the number of systems sold decreased their market price. PCs started to appear in each and every office and in most houses. At one point in time, the price stabilized at approximately $1000 per PC. This price remained constant for several decades and, as predicted by Moore's law, delaying the purchase provided a faster system for the same amount of money. Only in the first and second decades of the twenty-first century did the price of PCs decline further, and this was caused by a new generation of personal devices such as smart phones, tablets, and so on.

The technology that was implemented in PCs was largely copied from the technology developed for large computers, but without spending funds on research and development. This fact, combined with the large quantities of PCs being manufactured, (hundreds of millions per year), was the main reason for the sharp decline in PC prices. Several years after its introduction, the PC successfully competed with large systems that were several years older and several orders of magnitude more expensive. However, it should be noted that the systems' speed is just one parameter for measuring the systems' performance. To lower the price, and since PCs were initially intended for the single user, their ability to support vast amounts of information transfers was compromised. So even though a PC can

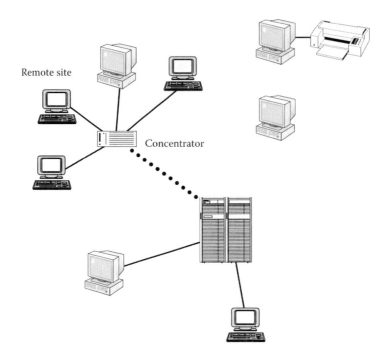

FIGURE 1.8   PCs as a replacement for terminals.

run a specific program like a large system does, when it comes to handling large amounts of traffic or massive input and output requirements, PCs fall short compared to these large computers or modern servers.

Computer Networks

As time passed, the PC continued to be developed and its capabilities increased too. It became faster and supported larger memories, and the functionality it provided increased as well. Slowly, the PC became the standard infrastructure for small business applications, connecting several users working concurrently. As a result, PCs were required to support larger files. To better address this need, computer networks started to evolve. These networks were designed to provide the connectivity of several PCs working in a common workgroup and sharing hardware resources. The reasons that contributed to the development of networks were

- The need to access common files: Every organization maintains common files that contain or manage organizational constants, for example VAT or dates of holidays, and so on. Usually the responsible person will update the value in a specific table or file, and all users and applications access this file. Without a network that allows all computing devices to access the specific file, it will be necessary to create replications of the file. In such a case, it is just a matter of time until one copy will be forgotten, which will create inconsistent and unreliable results. The best and easiest way to prevent this situation is by providing a mechanism that allows all computing devices to access a common file.

- Sharing files: After the PC became a common working platform, the need to share the work done by various users arose. In modern society, many projects are developed by teams, and in such cases, the exchange of ideas and pieces of unfinished work is required. Originally, this was achieved by a common file that was shared by the group members. However, even for this solution, a network has to be deployed. In the second stage, there was a need for collaborative work among team members as well as among members of different teams sharing the same project. Furthermore, the teams are sometimes located at dispersed locations, and a data communication network is the only feasible solution.

- Central backup: The first PCs sometimes had various reliability problems. The users, who in most cases did not have the proper computing knowledge, did not have good backup procedures. After many events in which the users lost their data, which usually translated into many lost hours of work, it was evident that a reliable mechanism of backups (and restoration) should be implemented. Since an organization's computer department had the required knowledge and the proper tools, procedures, and hardware devices, it could provide the best solution. Although it is possible to implement backup procedures for each PC, transferring the responsibility to the computer department is safer, cheaper, and more efficient. In addition, the various backup devices were usually connected to large computers and were not largely available for the PCs. As the use of PCs increased in many organizations, information—and sometimes even critical information—was stored on PCs. No organization will accept the situation that historic and critical information can be lost due to users not being computer experts. This reason by itself is a significant enabler for implementing networks.

- Sharing unique and expensive peripherals: When organizations were using mainly central computers, it was possible to purchase a unique or expensive device to be shared by all users. Currently a laser printer, for example, is affordable for many private users; however, in the early 1980s, such devices were extremely expensive. The PC revolution required the necessary adaptations, and currently most peripheral devices can be connected to the PC. However, to access the device from other PCs, a network is required. Furthermore, it does not make sense to equip all PCs with even ordinary and relatively cheap I/O devices such as scanners and printers, let alone expensive devices. Most organizations provide these peripheral devices per a group of PCs, and for accessing these devices, a network is required.

- Working in a network: The issue that significantly contributed to the development of networks was the need to work in a connected environment. The development of e-mail systems, chat facilities, message boards, forums, and so on could not have been achieved without an underlying network. Currently, online communication is an integral part of modern life and it is very difficult to imagine the world without it. All these capabilities materialized only after networks were developed. Initially, they were developed to connect PCs within the organizations and later to connect them to other PCs at external organizations and in remote locations.

- Remote work: By utilizing the network, one user can access and actually work on a different computer, even if the remote computer is geographically far away. Although in the first stages of the network development it was not possible to work on a remote system, this capability was developed in order to provide a solution to a real problem. Remote work differs from collaborative work (previously described) in that it means working on special-purpose computers or systems that have a special software installed, such as parallel systems that contain a large number of computers and are used for running extremely large applications in a reasonable time. For example, for an accurate weather prediction, a very large model has to be analyzed. In order to provide the prediction in time, a large and usually massive parallel system is used. However, not all weather centers can afford such a system, so they use a common system that is sometimes funded through mutual agreements (e.g., ECMWF—the European Center for Medium-Range Weather Forecasts, which is located in the United Kingdom and is partially supported by the European member states).

- The Internet: The Internet, which became widely known during the late 1980s, started originally as a military research and development project by the Defense Advanced Research Projects Agency (DARPA). The capabilities of the new network and its potential use triggered the development of many software and hardware tools. These tools enabled PCs to be part of the network and to assume an active role in many of the services provided. Currently, many applications utilize the Internet, unless it is prohibited for security reasons.

It should be noted that the first stages in networking consisted mainly of connecting one computer to another or connecting several computers to a server (Figure 1.9). Only at a later stage was the wide-area network (WAN) developed, providing Internet connectivity as well as connecting systems all over the world. In addition, the Internet, which is being used as a global connectivity infrastructure, is used not only by computers but also by

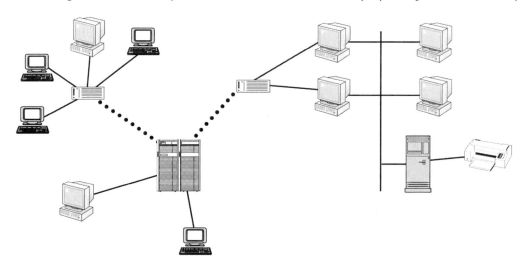

FIGURE 1.9 Appearance of organizational networks.

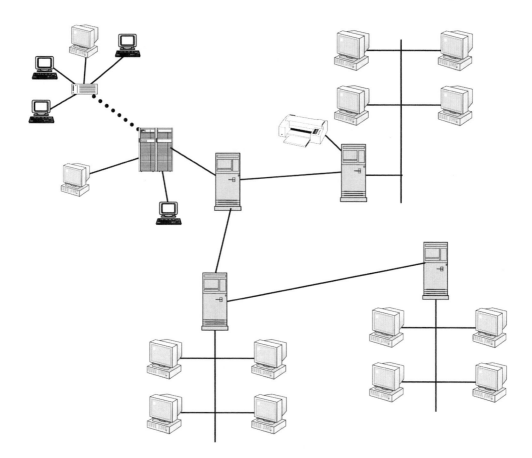

FIGURE 1.10   Multiple networks.

many types of appliances, such as web cameras, vending machines, elevators, GPS devices, and so on.

Computer networks continued to evolve, and after several years, while organizations still used a central system, the number of networks increased very fast. Originally, there was one server that connected several PCs, and later this model replicated itself. Additional servers were installed; each one supports another group of PCs, while the organizational network connects all of them (Figure 1.10).

1970s Computers: The First Mainframes

The main computers during the 1970s were responsible for all organizational computations, including scientific computations, data processing, data entry, word processing, and so on. Using such an expensive computer (sometimes the price was millions of dollars) was very wasteful; however, this was the only solution, since the personal computer appeared only a decade later. In spite of their high cost, such computers were not very efficient at performing all these types of computations. However, several companies started a process of differentiation and aimed at designing computers that were suitable for some types of computations, such as scientific, data processing, and so on.

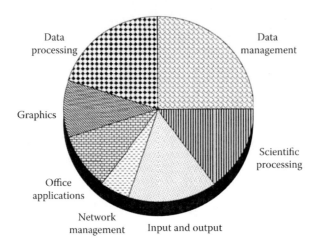

FIGURE 1.11 Types of computations.

Nevertheless, the price of such a computer was still very high, and so most organizations, even the large ones, could not afford more than one computer. The existing computer had to handle all types of computations. When more computers started to offer interactive capabilities, their inefficiency increased dramatically. The first computer terminals* were "dumb" terminals, which did not have any computational capabilities. Each character entered was submitted to the main computer. The computer had to temporarily stop the program that was running,† start a small system utility to check the entered character, and, if it was valid, send a command to the terminal to display or print it. If the character was not valid, an error message had to be displayed. The computer had to interrupt the running program since a longer delay, for example of 200–300 milliseconds, would have been noticed by the user. Only after the system utility finished processing the character would the original program that was running at the time the character was received continue its execution.

Among the types of computations performed by the 1970s computer one may find (Figure 1.11)

- Scientific computing that served the R&D departments. These were unique and custom-made software programs developed especially for the organization's needs, or various off-the-shelf packages.

- Data processing such as inventory management, procurements, human resources management, and so on.

- Handling all input and output.

---

* A terminal is a device that is used by interactive users in order to communicate with a computer. It usually consists of a keyboard for entering data and a printer for displaying the data. In modern terminals, the printing device was replaced by a screen that displays the data as well as graphics.

† The process of entering a signal to stop the computer and let it handle some external situation is called *interrupt*. The running program is stopped temporarily or interrupted for another more critical event.

- Graphics as part of special applications that were used for creating and drawing various graphs, such as the visual representation of a specific program. The graphics produced were plotted using special output devices called plotters.

- Office applications such as word processing or spreadsheets.

- Network management.

- Storage management and so on.

1980s Computers: The Last Mainframes

The rapid development in computing technology and the "birth" of personal computers, as well as their constantly increasing capabilities, changed the way organizations perceived their computing environment. The new emerging platforms, which were significantly cheaper than the large organization computers, provided some superior functionality. For some types of computing, a simple price/performance calculation was sufficient to change the running platform. For example, a simple word-processing program executed on a central computer is not only inefficient but is also cumbersome and expensive. Instead of the mainframe's lengthy process of interrupting the running program for each character typed, using a dedicated PC is much faster and significantly cheaper.

As a result of the trend for finding the best platform for each type of computation, the mainframes continued to concentrate only on some types, while other types were migrated to dedicated and task-oriented machines (Figure 1.12).

The right side of Figure 1.12 refers to the standard mainframes and the types of computations that remain. The left side refers to the types that were migrated to other more efficient and cheaper platforms. The large difference in the platforms' prices was due to their different capabilities as well as the fact that most of the mainframes were proprietary platforms while most of the PCs and later servers were off-the-shelf solutions. These off-the-shelf solutions were usually manufactured in very large quantities by various manufacturers and were significantly cheaper.

It should be added that for supporting these distributed architectures, wherein some types of computations are performed on a variety of platforms, new

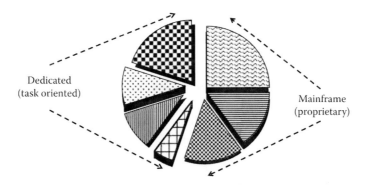

FIGURE 1.12   Changes in computing environments.

developments in the networking technologies were required. In addition to the developments already described, additional functionality was required, such as automatic transfer of jobs according to their type. Such transfers cannot be performed manually by the users since, due to the dynamic nature of computing platforms, a specific machine may be replaced by another. These replacements should be fully transparent to the users.

All these new functionalities added to the networks, which transferred jobs to the appropriate system and rerouted the results back to the user or printed them on the closest printer, paved the way for new and more distributed architectures.

"The Network Is the Computer"

During the 1980s, Scott McNealy—one of Sun Microsystems' founders and later its CEO until the company was acquired by the Oracle Corporation in January 2010—was advocating for a new computing system based on a networked environment. At that time, many criticized the idea, claiming it represented Sun Microsystems' efforts to overcome its limitations. As a new computer manufacturer, Sun Microsystems concentrated on small and medium computers and especially cheap ones. The environment used for operating these computers was a normal air-conditioned room, in contrast to the special and very expensive cooling systems used by the mainframes of that time. It is not clear if McNealy was trying to offer a high-end solution based on Sun's platforms or if he really believed in the new trend, but he managed to accurately forecast the future and probably helped move toward it. The main idea represented by the networked environment is the understanding that computing becomes an integrative environment in which computers and resources are connected seamlessly. The computer user does not know and does not care about the specific system that provides the application that he or she is running. The service is provided by a networked environment in which many heterogeneous systems collaborate to provide the required solution. To support this idea, Sun developed the Java programming language, which defines a universal architecture capable of running common code on a variety of platforms. These platforms include various appliances not usually considered as computers (e.g., TV sets). According to a very conservative estimate, there are many billions of appliances capable of running Java.

The idea represented by Sun Microsystems is another stage in the development of a networked environment, which paved the way for the modern interconnected world as we all know it. Today's simple browsing represents Sun's idea in a very clear way. During our browsing session, we receive various computing services from various systems that are spread all over the world. In most cases, we do not even know where the system is located, which system it is, what operating system it is using, and so on. Even if there is a way to find out about the server that provides the service, no one really cares about it. A basic network component is responsible for all the needed migration, so that the solution we receive is clear and readable. A simple analogy for the required migration is the use of the cellular telephone network. Everyone possesses a cellular device that is capable of communicating with all other devices on the network, not just the ones that are similar or the ones that are using the same network protocols. In this example, the network is responsible for all the migrations needed for connecting all these devices.

As can be seen in Figure 1.13, a user is receiving organizational computing services from a network of computers. Sometimes these services are performed on the local system (the one used by the user), and sometimes it is performed on a nearby server. At other times, it may be executed on a remote organizational server, and it may even be that it is executed on an external system that is not related to the organization at all (e.g., search services). In most cases, the user does not know where the service originated.

The fast penetration of the Internet network and the various services it provides create a cycle that continues to grow and at an increasing pace (Figure 1.14). According to a survey conducted by the "World Internet Stats"[6] in 2006 the total number of users surpassed one billion. This meant that 15% of the world's population was using the Internet. According to the latest statistics (from December 2014), an estimated 3.08 billion users are using the Internet, and this represents a 42.4% penetration.

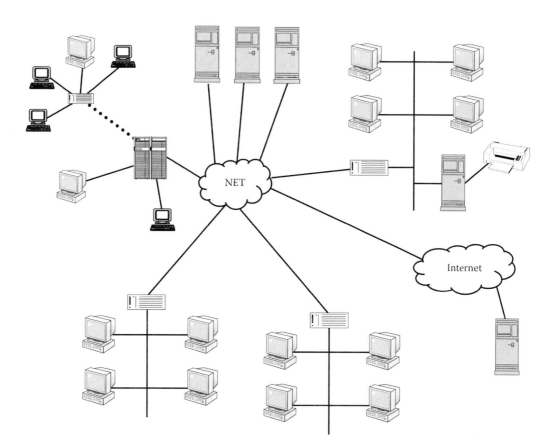

FIGURE 1.13   Changing computing environment.

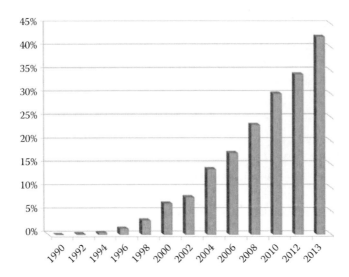

FIGURE 1.14   Internet penetration percentage.

It should be noted that this penetration is not confined only to computers, but also involves many types of equipment such as cellular phones, Internet cameras, GPS devices, and many other appliances.

Network Computers

During the 1990s, in parallel to the rapid entrance of the PC into the computing world, a small number of companies dominated the market and enjoyed economic prosperity and a solid increase in their business. The two dominant players were Microsoft, which was responsible for selling most of the software for the PCs; and Intel, which was the major supplier for hardware components. To understand the behavior of the market, one has to follow market trends. Every couple of years, Microsoft upgrades its operating system as well as its widely used Office suite. Sometimes this involves major changes that even require a rewrite of portions of the code. Due to the fact that the world is interconnected and that in most cases the products are not upwardly compatible, there is a need to upgrade the software. For marketing purposes, Microsoft does not charge maintenance fees and does not upgrade old products, except when security issues are involved. Unfortunately, this means that Microsoft does not offer an upgrade to the new product, and users have to purchase the new upgraded product. For example, let us assume a user receives an Office file (Word, Excel, PowerPoint) as an attachment to a mail message. If this new file was created by a new version, there is a chance that the receiving user will not be able to open it, especially if he or she is using an older version. This means that sometimes upgrading the software on the PC is driven by external events. Furthermore, due to rapid and significant developments in PC technology during the 1980s, many software upgrades required a hardware upgrade as well or, as seldom was the case, the purchase of a new PC. This mode of operation required large sums of money in order to maintain computing capabilities in the home or in an organization. It should be noted that many other niche companies managed to take part in the growing market and enjoyed these ways of renewing purchases. However, there were other companies that did not participate in this activity, and they were looking for a way to increase their market share in parallel or instead of the leading companies.

In May 1996, five computing companies (Apple, Oracle, IBM, Netscape, and Sun) formed a new alliance and defined a new computing concept: The network computer.* This idea, revolutionary at that time, stemmed from several assumptions:

- Computers are connected: Most personal computers are connected to some network or even to several networks. Sometimes it is an organizational network or a home network, and in many cases, it is a wide-area network like the Internet.

- The network is not a bottleneck anymore: The recent new developments related to networking technologies enabled fast data transfers. Even though, at the time of the announcement of the new concept, the transfer rates were still moderate, it was safe to assume that it would drastically change. In retrospect, this was a very true and logical assumption. The ADSL† technology that allowed home computers to be connected to the networks by using a telephone line was cheap and significantly faster compared to previous technologies.

- The interconnectivity of computers manifests itself in a cost increase, as demonstrated by the Microsoft model. Some new releases of Office, for example, changed the format of the files, as was the case with the introduction of Office XML formats. This meant that for accessing these files, an upgrade was required. However, in most cases, an upgrade was not available and the user had to purchase a new license. This cycle of continuous expenditure just to remain operational was unique to the PC industry, which originally was dominated by the Microsoft infrastructure. During the 1980s, Gartner, a world leader in IT consultancy, introduced the term TCO (total cost of ownership) as a measure of the total costs associated with computing that span all its life cycle: purchase, operation, upgrade, and decommission. In research that was published back then, it was written that although the PC itself costs about $1,000, the real cost (including management, support, maintenance, backups, upgrades, infrastructure, etc.) may reach $10,000 a year.

Computing Attributes

To better understand the factors contributing to these high costs, we need to identify the computer attributes that utilize most of the budget. In a very simple and schematic way, one may describe the system as an integration of six components: the processor, memory,

---

* A network computer is a term that originated in the 1990s and defined a new computing architecture. It should be noted, however, that it is not directly related to networked computers, which usually refer to computers linked together. A network computer has to be connected to the network but has very distinct attributes that are different from those of networked computers.

† Asymmetric digital subscriber line (ADSL) is a fast data communication technology that enables high transfer rates.

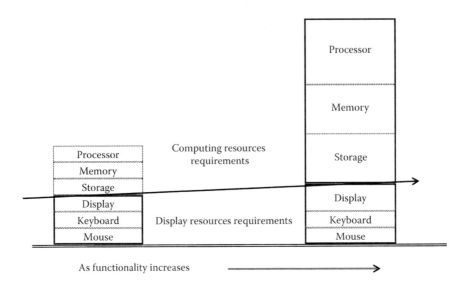

FIGURE 1.15   Computing attributes.

storage, display, keyboard, and mouse. From analyzing the upgrades done in PCs, we may conclude that most upgrades are related to computing components (processor, memory, and storage), while display resources have remained almost unchanged over the years. It should be noted that the displays' technology improved from a monochrome to a large color screen with increased resolution, but this improvement is minimal compared to the improvements in the processing components. The current mice are more advanced than the mice 30 years ago and instead of mechanical mice, we use ergonometric, optical, and wireless mice with improved resolution; however, the functionality has remained identical—a device that is used to point at and select data on the screen. Even the keyboard has remained almost unchanged. The new keyboards may have additional buttons for controlling the system or some applications, but the basic functionality is unchanged. These devices that are used by humans did not have to be faster due to our limitations in using them. Computing resources, on the other hand, have enjoyed a significant increase in performance. PC processing power increased by over four orders of magnitude between the years 1982 and 2010 (from a 4.77 MHz 8080 processor to the new 3.0 GHz multiple core chips). The PC's internal memory capacity increased as well by over five orders of magnitude (from 640 KB to the modern 4 and 8 GB*). The external storage, however, increased by over seven orders of magnitude, from floppy disks containing 360 KB to modern disks with over 2 TB.

Figure 1.15 depicts the changes in computing resources as the functionality of the applications increases. Usually the significant increase occurs in the computing resources, while the display resources seldom change. The cost associated with replacing keyboards and mice is not high, and for that reason, when buying a new desktop PC, users usually replace their keyboards and mice. The five computing companies' alliance drew a parallel

---

* G, which represents giga (bytes), is 10^9.

line between computing behavior and the telephone or the TV sets. In these two cases, on the user's side there is a simple device (like the display resources), and for that reason, there is no frequent need for upgrades. The center (telephone exchange or the TV broadcasting station) has heavy duty and very powerful machines that are capable of handling the tasks. There is a clear line that differentiates the two, and upgrading one side has no effect on the other. It should be noted, however, that the twenty-first century is somewhat different. The current generation replaces or upgrades cellular devices not because they have stopped working but due to aggressive and very successful marketing campaigns.

The clear differentiation between the client side and the central service provider was the trigger for the network computer idea. The network computer was intended to be a "thin" computer system that functions by utilizing the network. For that reason, such a system does not need a storage device, since all the information is stored on a networked server somewhere. If and when this information is needed, it will be loaded through the network. Furthermore, even booting up* the system can be done by loading the necessary pieces of software from the network. Each such network computer has the display resources required (screen, keyboard, and mouse) but very limited computing resources. Contrary to the dumb terminals (see the section "Historic Perspective" in this chapter), the network computer performs some of the applications locally using its own memory and processing power. Nevertheless, the computing resources are significantly limited compared to standard (nonnetwork) computers. The fact that the network computers provide similar functionality but without the frequent need for upgrades means a lowered TCO. Furthermore, because originally such computers did not have storage resources, they provided a better and more secure computing environment that could not be attacked by viruses and other malicious attempts. The original network computer model addressed the high costs associated with maintenance as well. Every change introduced is performed on the central copy of the application, and when the application is needed by the network computers, the newer version will be loaded. It should be noted that currently there are several ways to load or upgrade applications on a remote PC without the need to physically access it. However, when this model was suggested, the remote access capabilities were limited and the information technology (IT) people had to get to each system and install the new version. An additional cost factor that contributed to the high TCO for standard PCs was user involvement. In many cases, the users were trying to correct various computing technical problems, which led to a waste of production hours. This was due both to their inexperience in dealing with the problem and the fact that they were not doing the tasks they were hired for. With network computers, the possibilities for users to solve problems are limited, and everything is done from the center.

In the first years after the idea was published, many were overwhelmed and many articles and surveys were published with estimates that network computing would decrease the TCO by at least 30%. By the end of the 1990s, the advisory firm International Data

---

* Booting or booting up is the initial operation the computer performs after it has been powered up. Usually, it starts with a preliminary hardware test, and then it loads a small piece of software that will load the entire operating system. Initially, the term was attributed to the famous story about Baron Munchausen's adventures by Rudolf Erich Raspe, in which the Baron pulls himself out of the swamp by pulling his hair.

Corporation (IDC) predicted that by 2005 half of computer shipments will be network computers. In retrospect, this did not happen.

For a successful implementation of the network computer model, a new infrastructure of renting software had to be put on place. Since network computers did not have any storage resources, no application of data files could be saved locally. The intention was that a new service-providers market would emerge in which companies would provide software for rent. Unlike the normal model in which the user purchases a software package, with network computers the idea was that such a user would rent the software for a specific period of time. This idea was borrowed from other utilities such as telephone or electricity. The user subscribes to the service but pays according to the actual usage. It should be noted that similar markets such as ISP (internet service providers) existed already; however, with Microsoft's domination of the PC software industry, such a software rental model could not be implemented without Microsoft's active participation. Microsoft, which understood the potential negative impact such a model might have on its business, did not participate. At that time, the business model Microsoft used was based on repeated sales. Most users then were using Windows 98, and it was anticipated that they would upgrade to Windows 2000 and in a couple of years upgrade once again to Windows XP. Although this was referred to as an upgrade, the users actually bought a new license (sometimes with a price reduction). Network computers, if implemented, could lower the number of licenses bought, which could affect Microsoft's revenues.

Although network computers did not evolve as expected by various analysts, some follow-on initiatives for lowering the costs associated with personal computing emerged. One direction developed and matured into the open-source development model, in which free-to-use software alternatives are offered to the wider public. In addition, some companies such as Citrix were developed that offered various terminal-based solutions, partially implementing the idea of network computers. It may even be that the modern trend of cloud computing (which will be discussed later) partially originated in the idea of network computers.

Terminal Services

In parallel with its attempts to stop the network computer idea, Microsoft started working on a concept that was similar but would assure the future revenue stream. The Terminal Services was Microsoft's partial answer to network computers. These are a set of software tools that allow terminals (Windows-based PCs) to access applications and data stored on a central server. The various developments supporting the Terminal Services technology were intended to save money and time. The fact that the applications were installed, managed, and maintained on a single server saved time and money. For larger organizations, the time saved was even more significant. Installing an application on thousands of PCs not only requires a lot of time but is also a complex logistic operation that is sometimes even impossible, especially if the systems are geographically remote and differences between the versions require simultaneous installations.

Supporting and maintaining the applications from a central location is cheaper and more efficient, which provides additional organizational saving at the IT department, decreasing downtime and increasing the users' work effectively. An additional difference between the two architectures is due to the execution environment. In the standard PC, the application runs on the PC, and this is one of the main triggers for the continuous requirements for upgrade; in the network computer, however, some part may be executed remotely on the server. This means that the requirements for computing resources on the client side are minimal, which translates into a longer period between hardware upgrades. Even old and relatively slow PCs can be used as network computers since most of the resources are on the server side.

The Microsoft implementation provided an additional layer of functionality to the original idea of network computers. The system included various components that could be installed on any Windows-based system and not only on network computers. Furthermore, with the Terminal Services in place, Microsoft stopped opposing the idea of network computers. This happened only after Microsoft had changed its licensing mechanism, ensuring that even for network computer configurations, users would have to purchase a license for each connected PC. This, of course, undermined the main idea of network computers, which stemmed from trying to lower the costs associated with computing. The new licensing mechanism prevented new players from entering the software rental business, and only after this threat disappeared did Microsoft start offering a solution similar to the one expressed by the network computers. It should be noted, however, that Microsoft realized the market trends and started to offer various price discounts, for example on site licenses or volume discounts.

Microsoft's implementation of the network computers concept provided the means for achieving an additional strategic target. For quite some time, Microsoft was trying to establish itself as the dominant solution for desktop computing in organizations. A survey published in May 2007[7] by Awio Web Services revealed that Microsoft operating systems (Windows XP, Windows 2000, Windows Vista, Windows 98, Windows 2003, and Windows ME) were found on 94.2% of the systems sampled. This means that, back then, Microsoft dominated the desktop market, while Apple was in second place with 4.4%. Unfortunately, the same survey in September 2014[8] revealed a different picture. Microsoft is still the main and dominant player; however, its operating systems were found on only 61.4% of desktop computers, which represents a significant decline.

Client/Server

A relevant technology related to the network computers as well as to the Terminal Services is client/server technology. Like other computing technologies, client/server technology evolved over time and went through numerous configurations. In the first stages, it was mainly a natural development of the mainframe and the appearance of organizational networks (see the section "Computer Networks" in this chapter). The technology was developed in order to better utilize the PC's potential capabilities and to lighten the burden of highly expensive organizational computing resources. In essence, the idea behind client/server technology is to provide various mechanisms for sharing the work between the client side (the desktop PC) and the server side (the organizational mainframe).

File Server

Originally, PCs' networks were intended mainly for file sharing. The architecture was simple and consisted of several personal computers sharing a network with a server that was used as the central point for file storage (Figure 1.16).

The application was executed on the client (the local personal computer), and each time data was needed, the whole file was transferred from the server. This mode of operation was efficient only if the number of connected computers was small and the amount of files transferred and their sizes were not too large. An additional problem associated with this type of implementation is the need for a locking mechanism to assure that while a file is being processed by one personal computer no other computers can access or modify it. The operating system had to be amended so it would be able to keep track of the files and their usage and even provide mechanisms to overcome problematic situations. For example, consider a case in which a user is working on a file but forgot to release it and went home. All other users that need to access the file are put on hold until the file becomes available, but this may take a while. This means that although the file server technology was a good idea for providing sharing mechanisms, it has its limitations. It is useful when the number of connected personal computers is relatively small and the amount of files transferred is not large, and even than some error situation may occur.

The original implementations of the file server architecture were intended to overcome another limitation of PCs. The first PCs had limited storage, while the server was equipped with robust and high-volume storage resources. In this way, an organization was able to maintain one copy of organizational data that is always up to date. It was also easier to develop backup procedures for data protection.

Due to the inherent limitations of the file servers' original implementation, mainly the need to transfer the whole file each time a piece of information was required (Figure 1.17), a more flexible architecture was developed. The files on the server could be "mounted" on the local personal computer and all the files would appear as a new "virtual" drive. This meant that the file was actually managed by the local operating system (with some

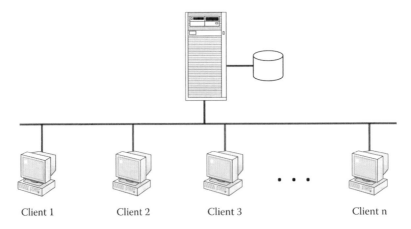

Client 1   Client 2   Client 3   Client n

FIGURE 1.16   Client/server architecture.

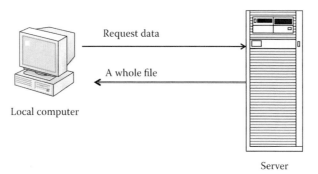

FIGURE 1.17   Information transfer in a file server architecture.

required modifications) and the application could read just the information needed instead of moving the whole file through the network.

A similar architecture is implemented in database* applications. The database (the data) is located on the server, and each local personal computer runs a copy of the database management system[†] (DBMS) software. The processing is performed locally, but the data is stored remotely (on the server). Each time the application needs to access or modify the data, the whole file is transferred as described in Figure 1.17.

Client/Server

The inherent limitations of the file server architecture triggered the development of the more advanced client/server architecture. In this implementation, the database server replaced the file server. When working with a relational database[‡], the application communicates with the DBMS, sends the query and gets the results. The DBMS in this case accesses the database and retrieves just the needed data and sends it back to the client. This mode of operation dramatically reduces the amount of data transferred. Instead of the whole file, only the specific record (or records) is being sent back.

Contrary to the file server architecture, in which most of the processing is performed on the local personal computer, in a client/server architecture the processing is split between the client and the server. It should be noted that the architecture originated in the local

---

* A database is an organized collection of information that that provides an easy and efficient way to store and retrieve that information. Usually, the data stored in the database and the information extracted represent an image of the reality in which the organization functions.

[†] DBMS is the software system that manages the database. It is responsible for accepting data, storing it in the proper location (cataloging it), and retrieving it when needed. The DBMS can be seen as a software layer between the actual tables and the applications (and users) accessing the data. On one hand, it interacts with the data consumers (users and applications), and on the other hand, it handles the data (defines, manipulates, retrieves, and manages).

[‡] A relational database is an advanced form of database. The original databases were used flat files in which all data was stored in a long text file and each record was separated by a special character. The relational database, on the other hand, is based on tables, each one representing some type of information (customers, products, employees, etc.). Each column in a table represents an attribute (or field in a record, such as customer name, telephone number, address, etc.), and each row represents a different entity. It is called a relational database due to the relations that are maintained. Some columns in a table can be used as keys, but other tables provide the means to create new tables from the existing ones. These relationships increase the flexibility and efficiency of the database without the need to duplicate the data.

area network* (LAN); however, it can be implemented in a wide area network† (WAN) as well. The server provides a set of services that are known by all the clients. This means that the client knows the server but the server does not have to know who the clients are.

Like any other technology, client/server architecture provides benefits but also has some drawbacks. The main benefits are

- Ease of use: It is easy and convenient to develop distributed applications (including distributed data). The data can reside on remote servers even at different locations. There is no difference in the local system behavior even when services are migrated from one server to another due to the consolidation of servers or the addition of new ones.

- Efficient use of resources: The network is not overloaded with transferring files that are not needed. The application execution is divided between the local system (the client) and the remote (the server). This mechanism may prevent unnecessary and costly hardware upgrades. When the need for upgrades arises, it can be done by migrating services to new hardware in a seamless way that does not interrupt the user's work.

The drawbacks associated with client/server architecture stem from its capabilities (a distributed system in which the data is sometimes not stored in one central location).

- When the organizational data is dispersed among several (or maybe many) locations, it is difficult to create one single model of the whole organizational data. This may lead to unnecessary duplicates and even integrity issues.

- There might be cases in which additional work will be needed in management of the data resources.

- It is possible that not all services are known to the clients. In such cases, an additional service is required. The new service will be responsible for service discovery.

It should be noted, however, that the abovementioned drawbacks are not directly related to client/server architecture but to a bad implementation of the architecture. One of the important issues in implementing an information system is to provide the various executing levels with the relevant information for better decision making. Sometimes this means that managers have to be able to access all the organizational resources, including the organizational data. In such cases, a bad implementation of the client/server architecture is one that allows some of the data to be kept on local PCs. This data is usually known only to the particular user and hidden from other users or managers, and this issue manifests itself in the quality of the decision-making process.

---

* A local area network (LAN) is a network (hardware and software components that provide networking capabilities) for a group of systems in a close proximity, such as a home, a working group, a department, one building, and so on.
† A wide area network (WAN) is a network that spans a large geographic area. It often may contain several LANs and provides the means to communicate over a broad-area telecommunications network.

There are several alternatives in implementing a client/server architecture, but in all of these, the local PC is performing some part of the computations. This architecture stems from the idea that a PC is a computer by itself and can be used not just as a replacement for dumb terminals (see the section "Personal Computers" in this chapter) but as a computing resource that can be used to offload the central computer. In addition, there are functions that are better performed by the local PC due to its proximity to the user, such as handing input and output.

In implementing a client/server architecture, there are two main alternatives for configuring the desktop computer (the client):

- Thin client, which is only marginally involved in the process. Most of the processing and storage management are done by the server while the client is responsible only for the data entry and display. This was the preferred model for customers who used mainframes for many years and who were used to the central computer being the dominant part of the system. In these cases, most of the work is still done on the server (which replaces the mainframe) and the clients assume a marginal supporting role. This implementation requires a powerful server to ensure it is capable of handling the required workload and it does not become a bottleneck. The thin clients are similar to the old dumb terminals with some more capabilities.

- Thick client is a more powerful computer that handles a significant part of the processing. The server manages the database (it acts as the organizational storage resource), but all other processing as well as display is done locally. This alternative was more difficult to manage since most software is stored locally and upgrades are more complex and more time consuming. This of course was just in the beginning since, as with many other cases, several tools were developed to address this limitation, and currently remote installations have become the preferred way of managing these sometimes far-from-the-center systems.

In implementing client/server architecture, there are several possibilities:

- Two-tier architecture: This involves two computers, the local client and the remote server. As with all client/server architectures, the processing is split between the two based on the type of client (thin or thick) or the way the application was developed. Usually, the DMBS will reside on the server as well as procedures that can be executed remotely and simplify the applications' development, such as stored procedures. The two-tier (or two layers) architecture provides a good solution when the number of users working with the server is limited. If there are many users, the response time may deteriorate significantly. This is due to the fact that the server maintains an open communications link with every client, even if there is no work to be performed. In addition, in cases where it is anticipated that the number of clients will increase, it is advisable not to use this architecture due to the complexity in splitting services or increasing the number of servers.

- Three-tier architecture: This was developed in order to overcome the limitations of the two-tier architecture. In this architecture, a new layer (tier) was added between the client and the server. Of course there are many ways of implementing this new layer, for example by adding a messages server, application servers, transactions' monitoring, and so on. The central layer can provide queuing services; when the client sends a request, the queuing server enters it into the queue and will ensure it is executed when the time arrives. This means that the burden of making sure it runs was removed from the client. This architecture is useful when dealing with many clients, and it is very flexible and can accommodate changes and the introduction of new servers. On the other hand, the efforts for developing the application in this case are heavier. The flexible and modular approach of three-tier architecture enables the integration of old servers that contain large quantities of valued information into a modern solution. Sometimes, especially as part of software development, the three tiers (or layers) are called by different names, although the meaning remains identical. The first layer is the presentation layer, which is responsible for the communication with the user (input from the user and display of the results). This layer is implemented by the local PC. The second layer is the application (or the logic to be performed as part of the application). This layer is sometimes implemented on the server, as is the case with thin clients, and sometimes it is implemented on the client, especially when it is a thick client. This layer may even be split between the two systems (client and server). The third layer is the data layer, and it is implemented on the server side.

The rapid technological advancements changed and are still changing the definitions and their implementations. The establishment of two- and three-tier architectures paved the way for more tiers if needed, for example, four-tier architecture, which includes an additional layer or even a different division of functionality into layers. The J2EE* architecture that was developed by Sun Microsystems (currently part of Oracle Corporation) is a multitier architecture that implements the client tier and the functionality it provides: the Web tier provides the tools necessary for the web-based operations; the Business tier provides the solution for the specific business segment; and the EIS (Enterprise Information System) tier provides the database. These logical tiers can be implemented using several physical machines based on the specific infrastructure used.

The additional layer can be used for providing additional services as part of this layer or by adding new layers. A very simple and highly required service is the TP monitor (transaction processing monitor), which manages transactions' queues, schedules the work, and provides a mechanism for setting the priority of the various transactions. TP monitor technology had already emerged several decades ago due to the need to synchronize many users (clients) who are working on one system. With the wide spread of

---

* Java 2 Platform Enterprise Edition (J2EE) is a platform for the development and implementation of Java-based organizational applications. The platform is an enhancement of the previous standard edition (SE), which provides additional layers for increased reliability and sustainability.

web-based systems, in which the number of concurrent users is unknown but the system has to be able to handle all these requests, a TP monitor becomes a must. The software components that provide the distributed processing functionality are sometimes called middleware since they bridge between the clients' requests for the various services available and the systems that provide these services. In addition to managing the work, this technology can

- Manipulate several databases as part of a single transaction
- Connect to a variety of data sources (including flat files), nonrelational databases, and data that resides on nonstandard platforms such as proprietary systems
- Provide mechanisms for transactions priority setting
- Provide for better and elaborated security infrastructure

The following four figures are used to visualize the possible architectures while addressing the four basic applications components previously defined: the presentation layer, the business-logic layer, the DBMS layer, and the data layer (Figure 1.18).

The figure depicts a schematic view of the mainframe architecture. The dumb terminal did not have any computing capabilities, and all processing, including the presentation layer, was performed on the server side. It should be noted, however, that this model was used during the 1970s and early 1980s before the division of the applications into layers was developed. Nevertheless, Figure 1.18 represents the situation in which all the execution parts were performed by the mainframe and the client provided just simple data entry and output services—originally printing the result and later displaying it.

Figure 1.19 depicts the thin client architecture. This is exactly the network computer model envisioned by the original five computing companies (see the section "Network Computers" in this chapter). The local computer is intended just for the presentation layer, handling input and output; thus, it does not need a fast processing unit and since it cannot save file locally, it does not need large storage capabilities. All business logic, the applications, and the data storage are kept on the server side.

Figure 1.20 depicts a distributed process. The application, in this case, is split between the client and the server in which some parts are performed locally and others remotely.

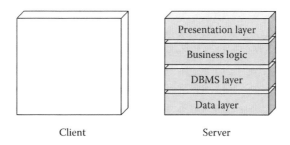

Client   Server

FIGURE 1.18   Mainframe-type architecture.

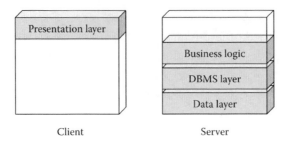

FIGURE 1.19   Thin client architecture.

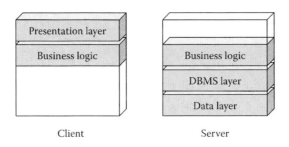

FIGURE 1.20   Distributed processing architecture.

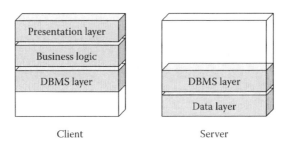

FIGURE 1.21   Thick client architecture.

The DBMS as well as the data is on the server. For supporting this architecture, one can no longer use a thin client since the client is responsible for running part of the application, so it has to have the required infrastructure to support it. The client may need some storage capabilities to save the temporary data it processes. As part of the system analysis and design, the specific architecture will be designed, and this will affect the architecture and implementation. After the architecture has been defined and the application developed, changes involving moving some functionality from the server to the client may be quite difficult to implement. It should be noted that the network computer model suggested supports this type of configuration as well.

Figure 1.21 is about a thick client with an expanded configuration that enables it to execute the entire business-logic layer as well as some of the DMBS layer (Figure 1.22).

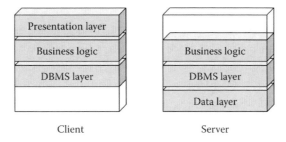

FIGURE 1.22   A thick client expanded architecture.

Since the time the network computer idea was first brought up, many devices that partially implemented the idea have been introduced. During these years, and after using various types of thin clients, some general insight was developed:

- The configuration needed for a thin client is significantly smaller than the average PC. However, a more interesting point is the fact that the gap between network terminals and ordinary PCs is constantly widening. This is mainly due to the increase in hardware requirements for PCs that follows new releases of Windows.

- There is no difference between working on a standard PC and on a network terminal. In many cases, the user is unaware of the specific configuration he or she is using.

- The functionality is very similar to the Windows-based operating system, with a similar windows mechanism.

- The amount of physical memory required by the network terminal is minimal, although with the memory pricing trends, the modern thin clients utilize standard amounts of memory (2–4 GB).

- The total cost of ownership is lower (sometimes significantly lower) compared to standard PCs. Not only is the original configuration simpler, it is more easily maintained.

- The thin client that adopted a new mode of operation in which the processing is done remotely provides new capabilities adopted from other operating systems such as UNIX. The user can initiate a long process, disconnect from the server, and let the process continue its operation off-line. When the user connects to the system once again, the system will remember that the process is still running (or waiting) and will offer to reconnect the user to that process.

- Thin clients provide better security against malware since there is no local storage. It should be noted, however, that the server can still be attacked by viruses, for example, but usually the servers are managed by professionals in the IT department with better security procedures.

- Thin clients allow for longer usage of the personal computer (as was the main idea represented in the network terminal). As a result, the need for upgrades is decreased, and this lowers the costs associated with computing.

The accumulated experience gathered leads to the conclusion that the network terminal represented a good idea, which unfortunately at the time was premature.

Additional "Computers"

In addition to the "standard" computers that have been described in this chapter, over the years additional development of special-purpose computing devices took place. These are other devices sometimes with a specific functionality for some special needs. Even so some of these devices are augmented in the organizational network due to the added value they provide. A very famous and clear example is the handheld device, including smart phones. Although in many cases the original intention was different, some of these devices provide tremendous benefits to the organization. For example, they provide online and sometimes real-time updates even if the updating person is not in the office. The fact that most appliances and devices utilize computers provides limitless opportunities for new and advanced developments, such as elevators or cars that are capable of reporting problems long before the user has even noticed or been affected. All the embedded processors used in a variety of appliances and equipment that surround us are actually computers that can be used in a variety of novel ways.

The idea represented in the development of the Java programming language (see the section "The Network is the Computer" in this chapter) was based on the understanding that the world will become a large system of interconnected devices. In the first decade of the twenty-first century, it is referred to as the "Network of Things" or the "Internet of Things." In both cases, it is a huge system of integrated "things" that collaborate. These "things" can be all the physical things in our lives (clothes, glasses, home appliances, etc.). Each of these things will be programmable, acting as an entity in the network. The technology will provide capabilities to "program" or change the functionality of some of the "things." This may sound like science fiction; however, one should take into account that if the capabilities of current mobile phones were ideas mentioned two decades ago, the response may have been similar. However, currently software developers can use SDK (software development kits) provided by manufacturers and develop special features that can be loaded onto their phone, augmenting its functionality.

As a matter of fact, in the twenty-first century, humans are surrounded by many systems, and sometimes we are unaware of the degree of their penetration into our lives. Many of these systems are computer based and as such provide all the functionality made available by a computer. Electronic games, watches, air conditioning, music players, cameras, traffic lights and control, and medical equipment represent just a fraction of these. In many cases, these "things" have to communicate with a central point or a larger server that controls and manages their operation.

In recent years, the server concept that has existed for decades has changed significantly. Being aware of the large costs associated with computing, some large companies started to offer a different computing model that is based on service. This model, which will be elaborated upon in Chapter 10, "Additional Architectures", is referred to as cloud computing and is basically a variation of a client/server architecture in which the servers are maintained by many large companies and reside in some remote location. The connectivity is performed through the Internet. One of the major benefits is economical. As with all other types of service, the client pays just for usage, in contrast to the "standard" computing model in which the organization has to purchase all the equipment necessary for handing peak requirements. For Internet-based online systems, such peaks can be very high, requiring a large and complex configuration that is seldom used. In the cloud computing model, the supplier has a very large configuration that can accommodate even the largest peaks, and this configuration is available for the customers whenever they require it. The cloud-computing model provides additional outsourcing capabilities such as reducing space and IT staff, which are translated into additional cost savings.

Key Takeaway

- *The difference engine*: A "computer" invented by Charles Babbage that was intended for complex calculations and used only additions, since it was used on finite differences.

- *The punched card*: A card made of stiff paper that was originally used by Herman Hollerith for storing data.

- *ENIAC*: The first electronic computer without any mechanical parts.

- *Von Neumann architecture*: A computer architecture that was designed in the late 1940s and has been used since. It defines a modular approach and consists of the main computers' components (processor, memory, I/O devices, communication links).

- *Registers*: Fast buffers inside the processing unit used for holding temporary data. The first generation of computers did not have any registers; then, computers with one register (called "accumulator") emerged, and only later did the number of registers increase up to hundreds in modern systems.

- *ALU (arithmetic and logic unit)*: A part of the processor that is responsible just for executing the instructions.

- *CU (control unit)*: A part of the processor that is responsible for all other aspects except execution, such as bringing the instruction from memory, decoding it, bringing the operands and transferring all the required data to the ALU for execution.

- *Moore's Law*: An observation made by Gordon Moore regarding the technical development of the electronics market. According to the observation, every 18 months the number of components in the single chip doubles and the expected performance is roughly proportional to the number of components.

- *Classification of computers*: Categorizing computers by their size or functionality (minicomputers, microcomputers, mainframes, servers, supercomputers).

- *A time-sharing computer*: A computer system that is intended for running several users/tasks in parallel. Most of the current modern computers and even some appliances, such as smart phones, support time sharing.

- *Computer networks*: Computer networks evolved as a logical enhancement of personal computers. Features like sharing resources, accessing common data, central support, backup service, and so on are among the motivations behind the development of networks.

- *The personal computer*: Introduced in the early 1980s, this is based on a microprocessor and originally was intended for a single user running a single task. Since then, the computer has advanced and it has become the dominant platform for most computing systems of various sizes.

- *"The network is the computer"*: A slogan coined during the 1980s by Sun Microsystems that clearly predicted future computing trends. The idea, which has since materialized, was that the services provided by computers will be by many distributed systems, even if geographically dispersed. The user that works on its computer does not know and does not care which specific computer is providing the service.

- *Network computers*: An idea that emerged during the second half of the 1990s that defined a new computing concept (similar to the dumb terminals of the first computers). Instead of personal computers that constantly have to be upgraded, a small computing device is used for accessing the network, and most computing resources will be in the network. This idea, although it took some time to materialize, paved the way for most modern computing environments.

- *Client/server*: A computing architecture in which the application is divided between components that are being executed on the local computer (client) and components that are executed on the server. This architecture has been implemented, with some modifications, in many Internet-based applications and services.

- *The server concept*: As part of the division of work between the local computer and computers on the network, many services are being provided by dedicated computers. Some relevant examples may be file server, print server, database server, and so on.

- *File server*: A concept for overcoming some of the PC's limitations. The server is connected to the network and provides access to its files. The concept was later enhanced to support many other types of servers, such as print servers, e-mail servers, compute intensive servers, and so on.

- *Thin client*: This is mainly involved with the presentation layer, while all or most of the business-logic computation is done on the server.

- *Thick client*: This is a powerful computer used for the presentation layer as well as some or all of the business logic.

- *Tier architecture*: A general term used for defining a client/server architecture. In its minimal configuration (two tier), there are two components or layers. A more complex architecture will consist of three tiers: presentation, business logic, and data. Additional tiers have evolved over time with additional responsibilities such as access, security, and so on.

- *J2EE*: Java 2 Platform Enterprise Edition is a platform for the development and implementation of Java-based organizational applications. The platform is an enhancement of the previous SE (Standard Edition) and provides additional layers for increased reliability and sustainability.

REFERENCES

1. Glanz, J. (2007). Google details, and defends, its use of electricity. *New York Times*, September 8. http://www.nytimes.com/2011/09/09/technology/google-details-and-defends-its-use-of-electricity.html?_r=1&.
2. Woody, T. (2013). Google is on the way to quietly becoming an electric utility. *Quartz*, September 18. http://qz.com/125407/google-is-on-the-way-to-quietly-becoming-an-electric-utility/.
3. van der Meulen, R. and Pettey, C. (2008). Gartner says more than 1 billion PCs in use worldwide and headed to 2 billion units by 2014. *Gartner Newsroom*, June 23. http://www.gartner.com/newsroom/id/703807.
4. van der Meulen, R. and Rivera, J. (2015). Gartner says global devices shipments to grow 2.8 Percent in 2015. *Gartner Newsroom*, March 19. http://www.gartner.com/newsroom/id/3010017.
5. Moore, G. E. (1965). Cramming more components onto integrated circuits. *Electronics*, 38, 114–117. (Reprinted in *Proc. IEEE*, 86, 82–85, 1998.)
6. Internet World Stats. (2015). Internet users in the world by regions: November 2015. *Miniwatts Marketing Group*. http://www.internetworldstats.com/stats.htm.
7. W3 Counter. (2015). May 2007 market share. *Awio Web Services*. http://www.w3counter.com/globalstats.php?year=2007&month=5.
8. W3 Counter. (2015). September 2014 market share. *Awio Web Services*. http://www.w3counter.com/globalstats.php?year=2014&month=9.

CHAPTER 2

Data Representation

DATA REPRESENTATION

The widespread availability of computers and computer-based systems requires a precise definition of data representation. Although human communication with computers is at a high level and most users do not care about the internal representation, it is needed to assure proper functioning of the system. This definition is not different from the "protocols" that were defined in order to provide communications between humans themselves, such as the natural languages. Writing was developed in order to provide a mechanism for representing language in a more visual form. This is done by a set of symbols (letters and numbers) that represent sounds defined in the language. Only after the language was defined could the writing symbols (letters, numbers) be developed, and this paved the way for written communication between humans, that is, books and newspapers as well as information displayed and printed by computers. The agreed-upon convention for representing a natural language was developed in the early stages of human development, and it provided the mechanism for written communication that is not confined to face-to-face discussions. Very well-known examples are ancient Egyptian hieroglyphs and the Cuneiform scripts, which were used over 5000 years ago. Rapid technological advancements and the development of analog and later digital communication links provide the means to communicate with people even if they are far away. For establishing such communications, the various systems (i.e., telephone, telegraph, facsimile, etc.) had to use a predefined encoding system. Such a system that has already been mentioned was the Hollerith punched card, which used the holes in the card to represent data.

The fast development of the Internet and the fact it is a global system required special attention to data representation standards. These standards provide the basic platform for data transfers between all connected devices. Furthermore, since all modern computers use the binary system, the standards have to define the binary representation of data as well. This data may include numbers (integers, real and complex numbers), text, and special symbols. An important aspect of the representation system applicable to numbers is its ability to support computations (as will be explained in the section "Computer's Arithmetic" in this chapter).

Numerical Systems

From the dawn of history, humans needed a mechanism that would allow the measurement of quantities. As such, basic verbal communication was developed to include a system to quantify size. Over the years, various civilizations have developed numerous such numerical systems, used originally for counting and later for computations as well. Such numerical systems are a prerequisite for data representation, since first the system has to be put in place and only later is its representation defined.

Every numerical system has to use symbols (numerals) for representing quantities. A delicate balance regarding the number of the symbols used as the numeric system has to be maintained. On one hand, the number of symbols should be relatively small, so it will be easier for humans to remember and use the system. On the other hand, it should not be too small, as this would require long representation (or many numerals, as will be elaborated on and explained in the section "Binary System" in this chapter). The system, of course, should be able to cover the whole spectrum of numbers (i.e., be infinite).

There are numerous archeological evidences of such number systems developed in ancient times. Originally, these systems were intended for measuring and counting, for example, the size of a herd, an amount of people, and so on. The ancient Egyptians extended the hieroglyphics system to include numbers as well. The system was based on several symbols, each one representing a value. The system was based on decimal (base 10) numerals, and each number was defined by its components. Each power of 10 had a different symbol. The basic numerals' (symbols) values were 1, 10, 100, 1000, 10,000, 100,000, 1,000,000 (Table 2.1).

For calculating the value of the number, one had to follow the simple rules of addition. For example the "number" $\text{I}\!\!\text{I}\cap|||||$ represents 2015 and is calculated as the sum of the numerals (1000 + 1000 + 10 + 1 + 1 + 1 + 1 + 1).

TABLE 2.1   Ancient Egyptian Numerals

Numeral	Value
|	1
∩	10
ℓ	100
↑	1,000
ℓ	10,000
🦅	100,000
𓁨	1,000,000

TABLE 2.2   Roman Numerals

Numeral	Value
I	1
V	5
X	10
L	50
C	100
D	500
M	1000

The Roman numerical system, which is still sometimes used, was a bit more complicated. It used numerals (Table 2.2), but calculating the number represented required additions and simple subtractions.

In general, the value is calculated by summing all numerals; however, to simplify the calculation and minimize the repetitions of numerals, some values are figured out by subtractions. For example, while the Egyptians represented the value of four by four lines (repeating the value one four times), the Romans define four as five minus one. The logic implemented is that all numerals are written in consecutive order, from the large to the small. However, if the left numeral is smaller than the consecutive one, it has to be subtracted. For example, the Roman number MMXIV represents the value of 2014:

$$M + M + X + (V - I) = 1000 + 1000 + 10 + (5 - 1) = 2014$$

Similarly, MCMXLIV represents the value of 1944:

$$M + (M - C) + (L - X) + (V - I) \;=\; 1000 + (1000 - 100) + (50 - 10) + (5 - 1)$$
$$= 1000 + 900 + 40 + 4 = 1944$$

Decimal Numbering System

The currently most widely used numbering system is the decimal (derived from the Greek word *deca*, which means 10) system, which is based on 10 numerals (digits), each one representing a specific value. A number is written as a list of digits wherein each location corresponds to the specific power of 10 multiplied by the digit in that location.

For example, the number 1987 is calculated as $7 * 10^0 + 8 * 10^1 + 9 * 10^2 + 1 * 10^3$

The general migration formula is

$$Number = \sum_{i=0}^{p-1} d_i {}^* b^i$$

where:

p   defines the location of the digit. The least significant digit is in location 0 and the number increases as we move to the left.

b   is the base of the system, and in this specific case it is the decimal system, so b = 10. There are other systems that use other bases (as will be explained later in this chapter).

d   is the specific digit in that location. Since in this case the base is 10, the possible digits are the ones available in this list: d = {0, 1, 2, 3, 4, 5, 6, 7, 8, 9}. It should be noted that the system's base defines the number of numerals (digits) that exist in the specific system. For each base n, the number of numerals is n. The first numeral will always be zero and the last numeral will be n − 1. So in general for each base n the available digits are [0:n − 1]. For that reason when using the decimal base, the available digits are [0:9].

Other Numbering Systems

The decimal system, although widely used, is just one specific example. There might be many other systems that can be used, and the previously defined formula is applicable to all such systems. When the base is clearly defined, it is sufficient to write the number; however, if it is not clear which base is to be used, the base is added as a subscript digit to the number. For example, 573_8 represents the value of the number 573 written in base 8. Base 8 or octal (derived from the Greek word *octo*, which means 8) is an important base related to computers since it is one of the bases that are powers of 2. The value of 573_8 is calculated in a similar way:

$$573_8 = 3*8^0 + 7*8^1 + 5*8^2 = 3 + 56 + 320 = 379_{10}$$

As with the previous example, the digits that are available in the octal system are [0:7]. Mathematical calculations can be performed in any base; however, since we are familiar with decimal numbers, calculating the value of numbers represented in other bases means translating the number to decimal, that is, converting the number from its base to a decimal number.

Numbers can be defined in any base, but figuring out their value remains the same. For example, the value of 4321_5 is 586_{10}:

$$43215 = 1*5^0 + 2*5^1 + 3*5^2 + 4*5^3 = 1 + 10 + 75 + 500 = 586_{10}$$

Binary System

A very important base, especially when addressing computers, is 2, which represents the binary system. Although the first computers were based on decimal numbers (see "Attributes of the First Computers" in Chapter 1), this changed quickly due to the understanding that computers, like any other electrical circuit, recognize two basic conditions: on and off. This understanding led to the current modern architecture implementations in which computers are based on the binary system. Although there are only two numerals in the binary system, there are no other changes, and calculating the value of a specific number is identical to other bases. The numerals (digits) in the binary system are called bits (binary digit).

For example, $110101_2 = 53_{10}$

$$110101_2 = 1*2^0 + 0*2^1 + 1*2^2 + 0*2^3 + 1*2^4 + 1*2^5 = 1 + 4 + 16 + 32 = 53_{10}$$

The binary system is efficient and convenient for computers; however, for humans, it represents a significant hurdle. As previously stated (see the section "Numerical Systems" in this chapter), a numerical system should have a relatively small number of digits, so it will be easily remembered by humans. On the other hand, this number (of digits) should not be too small, as it would then require many digits to represent a number. With only two digits, the binary system requires many digits to represent large numbers.

For example

$$255_{10} = 11111111_2$$

This means that to represent the number that includes three decimal digits, we need eight bits (or eight binary digits). If the number is significantly larger, the number of bits increases rapidly, and it becomes difficult and sometimes impossible for humans to follow.

For example, a number such as

$$3,212,580_{10} = 1100010000010100100100_2$$

is very difficult to understand due to its length and the fact there are only two digits that repeat themselves. One way to deal with such long binary numbers is to divide the number into groups using some delimiter, as is sometimes done with large decimal numbers by adding the thousands separators. However, even after the delimiter (usually the space character) is added to the number, it is still very difficult to comprehend:

$$3,212,580_{10} = 11\ 0001\ 0000\ 0101\ 0010\ 0100_2$$

The real solution to the problem is to use other numbering systems in which the base is a power of two (i.e., 4, 8 or 16). The octal numbering system, which uses eight digits, is easily converted to and from binary. Each three bits represent an octal digit, and thus octal numbers are shorter compared to the binary numbers. The translation of the three bits into an octal digit is done using the appropriate line in Table 2.3.

For example

$$3,212,580_{10} = 1\ 100\ 010\ 000\ 010\ 100\ 100\ 100_2 = 14202444_8$$

A more interesting and useful base is 16 (or hexadecimal), which uses 16 digits. It is based on the 10 decimal digits with the addition of A, B, C, D, E, and F. It should be noted that while the letters A–F are text characters, when used as part of the hexadecimal system they represent numerals. A is the equivalent of 10, B is 11, C is 12, and so on up to F, which is the equivalent of 15.

TABLE 2.3   Migration Table

Binary (2)	Decimal (10)	Base 4 (4)	Octal (8)	Hexadecimal (16)
0	0	0	0	0
1	1	1	1	1
10	2	2	2	2
11	3	3	3	3
100	4	10	4	4
101	5	11	5	5
110	6	12	6	6
111	7	13	7	7
1000	8	20	10	8
1001	9	21	11	9
1010	10	22	12	A
1011	11	23	13	B
1100	12	30	14	C
1101	13	31	15	D
1110	14	32	16	E
1111	15	33	17	F

The migration of binary numbers to hexadecimal numbers is done by splitting the binary number into groups of four bits and using Table 2.3 for the appropriate value.

For example:

$$3,212,580_{10} = 11\ 0001\ 0000\ 0101\ 0010\ 0100_2 = 310524_{16}$$

Both bases (8 and 16) are powers of two, and this provides a simple and straightforward migration to and from binary numbers. Since $8 = 2^3$, then every three bits represents one octal digit, and since $16 = 2^4$, every 4 bits represents one hexadecimal digit.

For example, the number

$$0101_2 = 5\ \left(\text{in octal, decimal and hexadecimal}\right)$$

This can be easily figured out using the migration formulas described above.

On the other hand, the number

$$1011_2 = 11_{10} = B_{16}$$

The underlining meaning of these migrations is that any binary number can be replaced by an octal or hexadecimal number without any complex calculations, just by grouping the bits and figuring out the value of each such group.

As with the delimiters that separate different groups of thousands in the decimal system, the split used in binary numbers always starts from the right side. For a simple migration, one may use the migration table (Table 2.3).

Using the numbers in the table, it is easy to represent the binary numbers in other bases that are powers of two. For example, we saw already that $255_{10} = 11111111_2$; this now can be easily extended to other bases that are powers of two:

$$255_{10} = 11111111_2 = 3333_4 = 377_8 = FF_{16}$$

or

$$3,212,580_{10} = 1100010000010100100100_2 = 14,202,444_8 = 310,524_{16}$$

The table can also be used for the opposite migration from octal or hexadecimal numbers to their binary equivalence. This is done by replacing each such (octal or hexadecimal) digit by the binary value in the table and concatenating these values.

For example

$$ABCD_{16} = 1010\ 1011\ 1100\ 1101_2$$

or

$$6754_8 = 110\ 111\ 101\ 100_2$$

The first value was obtained by copying the equivalences of the hexadecimal digits. The binary equivalence of A is 1010, the equivalence of B is 1011, and so on.

It should be noted that the values in the migration table were calculated using the migration formula, so there is no need to memorize the table. For example, the value (or the decimal equivalence) of the binary number 1110_2 can be calculated thus:

$$1110_2 = 0*2^0 + 1*2^1 + 1*2^2 + 1*2^3 = 0 + 2 + 4 + 8 = 14_{10}$$

or

$$16_8 = 6*8^0 + 1*8^1 = 6 + 8 = 14_{10}$$

and

$$32_4 = 2*4^0 + 3*4^1 = 2 + 12 = 14_{10}$$

Since E_{16} is the hexadecimal digit that represents 14 then

$$14_{10} = E_{16} = 16_8 = 32_4 = 1110_2$$

Representing Real Numbers

The previous chapters discussed the representation of natural (integers) numbers; however, these numbers are just a subset of a larger group, the real numbers. The logic and description of this group is very similar, since the fractions can be defined as digits multiplied by negative powers of the base. The migration formula that was described earlier with a minor change is relevant to real numbers as well.

$$\text{Number} = \sum_{i=-n}^{p-1} d_i {}^* b^i$$

The only change is related to the index. While in the previous formula for natural numbers, the index (i) starts from zero and goes up to p–1, in the new formula, the index starts from minus n. In this case, n is the number of digits right to the fraction point.

For example, assuming one has to calculate the value of 675.43_8:

$$675.43_8 = 3 * 8^{-2} + 4 * 8^{-1} + 5 * 8^0 + 7 * 8^1 + 6 * 8^2 = 445.546875_{10}$$

or

$$1111.1111_2 = 1 * 2^{-4} + 1 * 2^{-3} + 1 * 2^{-2} + 1 * 2^{-1} + 1 * 2^0 + 1 * 2^1 + 1 * 2^2 + 1 * 2^3$$

$$= 0.0625 + 0.125 + 0.25 + 0.5 + 1 + 2 + 4 + 8 = 15.9375_{10}$$

Converting Natural Numbers

There are several ways to convert numbers between various numeric systems.

- Converting numbers from any base to decimal numbers. This is probably the simpler way, already discussed. Since we are used to the decimal system, such conversions actually calculate the value of the number. This is done by using the migration formula discussed earlier.

  For example,

$$1234_5 = 4 * 5^0 + 3 * 5^1 + 2 * 5^2 + 1 * 5^3 = 4 + 15 + 50 + 125 = 194_{10}$$

- Converting numbers between the binary system to other systems with bases that are a power of two. In these cases, grouping several bits together and calculating the value of the group provides the result. The number of bits in the group depends on the migrating base and is driven from the specific power of two. For base 4, since 4 equals 2^2, then the group consists of 2 bits. For hexadecimal numbers, since 16 equals 2^4 then the group consists of 4 bits.

For example,

$$10110111_2 = 10\ 11\ 01\ 11 = 2313_4$$

or

$$10110111_2 = 1011\ 0111 = B7_{16}$$

- Converting numbers from a system that is a power of 2 to binary numbers. Each digit is broken into its binary equivalence, and the number of bits in the group is determined by the rule described in the opposite conversion.

  For example, the octal number 765 is converted to a binary number one digit at a time, and each digit represents 3 bits:

$$765_8 = 111\ 110\ 101_2$$

or

$$1A2F_{16} = 0001\ 1010\ 0010\ 1111_2$$

- Converting decimal numbers into numbers in a different base. This type of conversion is performed in an iterative way. Each iteration consists of three stages:

  - Divide the number by the new base

  - Collect the remainder and replace the original number by the result (integer)

  - If the result is not zero, go back to the first stage

  For example, let us assume one has to convert the decimal number 37 into a binary number.

$37/2 = 18$	Remainder $= 1$
$18/2 = 9$	Remainder $= 0$
$9/2 = 4$	Remainder $= 1$
$4/2 = 2$	Remainder $= 0$
$2/2 = 1$	Remainder $= 0$
$1/2 = 0$	Remainder $= 0$

Since the result is zero, the conversion ends. The result is the list of the remainder, where the first remainder is the rightmost digit. The conversion result in this case is

$$37_{10} = 100101_2$$

This of course can be easily checked by performing the opposite conversion.

$$100101_2 = 1*2^0 + 0*2^1 + 1*2^2 + 0*2^3 + 0*2^4 + 1*2^5 = 1+4+32 = 37_{10}$$

The method described is relevant for converting any decimal number to any other base. The only difference is that when converting to another based the base is the divisor.

For example, converting 122_{10} to base 7:

$$122/7 = 17 \text{ remainder} = 3$$

$$17/7 = 2 \text{ remainder} = 3$$

$$2/7 = 0 \text{ remainder} = 2$$

So

$$122_{10} = 233_7$$

Once again, it can be easily checked:

$$233_7 = 3*7^0 + 3*7^1 + 2*7^2 = 3+21+98 = 122_{10}$$

- Converting numbers from a base n to a number in base m, where both n and m are not cases described earlier in this chapter. This conversion is performed in two different steps. In the first step, the number is converted to decimal, and in the second step, the decimal number is converted to base m.

For example, migrating 2131_7 to base 5.

Step 1

$$2131_7 = 1*7^0 + 3*7^1 + 1*7^2 + 2*7^3 = 1+21+49+686 = 757_{10}$$

Step 2

$$757/5 = 151 \text{ remainder} = 2$$

$$151/5 = 30 \text{ remainder} = 1$$

$$30/5 = 6 \text{ remainder} = 0$$

$$6/5 = 1 \text{ remainder} = 1$$

$$1/5 = 0 \text{ remainder} = 1$$

So

$$757_{10} = 11012_5 \text{ and the result is:}$$

$$2131_7 = 11012_5$$

Converting Fractions

Converting fractions from any base to decimal is done using the migration formula (see the section "Representing Real Numbers" in this chapter) by multiplying the specific digit by the relevant power. For example,

$$0.321_4 = 1*4^{-3} + 2*4^{-2} + 3*4^{-1} = 0.890625_{10}$$

Conversions of decimal fractions to any other base's fraction is done by multiplying the fraction by the base, collecting the integer part of the result, and continuing the multiplication in an iterative way until the result obtained is 1.0. The result is the integers collected during the process.

For example, converting the decimal number 0.375 to binary:

$$0.375*2 = 0.75$$

$$0.75*2 = 1.5$$

$$0.5*2 = 1.0$$

The result is $0.375_{10} = 0.011_2$
Just for verification, we may recheck:

$$0.011_2 = 1*2^{-3} + 1*2^{-2} + 0*2^{-1} = 0.125 + 0.25 = 0.375_{10}$$

Explanation

The original decimal number is multiplied by the base (in this case, it is two). The binary number that is the result consists of the integer parts of the multiplications. Thus after the first multiplication the result is 0.75, so the integer is zero. This is the first binary digit to be written right to the fraction point. The result of the first multiplication (without the integer) is multiplied once again. The result is 1.5 and the relevant digit is once again the integer, which is written to the right of the previous binary digit. The result without the integer part is multiplied once again. This time the result is 1.0, which means that this was the last cycle of the conversion. The integer part is written to the right of the previous digit to form the result 0.011_2.

It should be noted that there are cases in which a decimal fraction cannot be converted to a binary fraction. In such cases, the multiplication will never produce the value of 1.0.

For example, converting the decimal fraction 0.3 to a binary number:

$$0.3 * 2 = 0.6$$

$$0.6 * 2 = 1.2$$

$$0.2 * 2 = 0.4$$

$$0.4 * 2 = 0.8$$

$$0.8 * 2 = 1.6$$

$$0.6 * 2 = 1.2$$

$$0.2 * 2 = 0.4$$

and so on. So

$$0.3_{10} = 0.010011001100110011...._2$$

Negative Numbers Representation

All the numbers discussed so far have been positive or unsigned numbers; however, as part of representing quantities, there is a need for negative (or signed) numbers as well. For defining negative numbers, we have to allocate a "sign" so the computer will be able to determine that it is a negative number. Such signs are in use in the standard communication between humans, where the minus and plus signs are used. This method is sometimes called "sign and magnitude" since the number consists of two parts. One is the value (magnitude) and the other is the sign. Furthermore, in human communication there is also a convention that a number without a sign is considered positive. When trying to implement the same method with computers, all that is needed is a standard that will define the sign character. It can of course be any symbol, provided everybody knows it and acts accordingly. For example, if we define that numbers starting with the digit 9 are considered negative and numbers starting with 0 are considered positive, then a positive 123 number will be written as 0123 and a negative 123 will be written as 9123. Using this convention, the first digits (0 or 9) are not part of the number and are only used for defining if it is positive or negative.

There are other methods for defining and representing negative numbers. One such method is called radix complement, which is basically complemented to the base. If N is a number with M digits represented in base B, then the radix complement of N is given by

$$C = \left(B^M - N \right)_{Bc}$$

Let us assume we have a decimal number 235. Using the radix complement, its negative value will be calculated by

$$-\left(235 \right)_{10} = 10^3 - 235 = 1000 - 235 = 765_{10Bc}$$

This method is not limited only to decimal numbers and can be applied to any other base. For example, it can be used to calculate the negative value of the binary number 101101:

$$-(101101)_2 = 2^6 - 101101_2 = 1000000_2 - 101101_2 = 010011_{2Bc}$$

Similarly, radix complement can be applied to other bases, for example, octal:

$$-(327)_8 = 8^3 - 327_8 = 1000_8 - 327_8 = 451_{8Bc}$$

A slightly different method is the diminished radix complement, in which the negative number is calculated somewhat differently. Assuming N is a number with M digits represented in Base B, then the diminished radix complement is defined by

$$C = (B^M - 1 - N)_{B-1c}$$

The difference between the two methods is that the radix complement complements to a power of the base, while the diminished radix complement complements to the power of the base minus one. As such, the difference between two negative representations of the same positive number using these two methods is one.

The two methods can be applied to numbers in different bases; however, their main use is related to binary numbers. The convention for binary numbers is that signed numbers with a leading "1" are considered negative, while signed numbers with a leading "0" are considered positive. As such, the format of a binary negative is 1xxxxxx (where x represents any bit), while the format of a binary signed positive number is 0xxxxxx.

The applicable methods for binary signed numbers' representations are

- *Sign and magnitude*: The value of the number is determined by the digits (except the leftmost) and the sign is determined by the leftmost digit. For example, four bits for the value (or magnitude) and one bit for the sign (see also Table 2.3)

$$10_{10} = 01010_2$$

$$-10_{10} = 11010_2$$

$$7_{10} = 00111_2$$

$$-7_{10} = 10111_2$$

The disadvantage of the method is that it defines two values for zero, a positive zero (00000) and a negative zero (10000)

- *One's complement*: This is the special case of the diminished radix complement implemented for binary numbers. Positive numbers are represented in the standard way, including zero as the leftmost bit. The negative number is calculated by complementing each bit (zero becomes one and one becomes zero). Since the positive number was defined using a leading zero, by complementing the number the leftmost bit becomes a one, so the whole number is negative.

For example:

$$10_{10} = 01010_2$$

$$-10_{10} = 10101_2$$

$$7_{10} = 00111_2$$

$$-7_{10} = 11000_2$$

As with the sign and magnitude method, the one's complement method has two values for zero: the positive zero (00000) and the negative zero (11111).

- *Two's complement*: This is the special case of the radix complement implemented for binary numbers. Positive numbers are represented in the standard way, including zero as the leftmost bit. The negative number is calculated by complementing each bit (zero becomes one and one becomes zero) and adding 1 to the result. As with the one's complement method, since the positive number was defined using a leading zero, by complementing the number the leftmost bit becomes a one, so the whole number is negative.

For example:

$$10_{10} = 01010_2$$

$$-10_{10} = 10110_2$$

$$7_{10} = 00111_2$$

$$-7_{10} = 11001_2$$

Contrary to the previous two methods, the two's complement has only one zero (00000).

When obtaining a negative binary number that was encoded in one of the complement methods, it is difficult to immediately calculate its value, and we have to complement it first; only then can we evaluate it. The sign and magnitude method, on the other hand, provides all the necessary information, and the number can be immediately calculated.

Due to the single-zero representation of the two's complement method, this is the method most often used for representing negative binary numbers. The other two methods require special circuits in the computer hardware for assessing, evaluating, and performing calculations using the two representations of zero.

Range of Numbers

There is one large difference between computers and humans in terms of their usage of numbers. Every numerical system has to be able to represent an indefinite number of numbers. This means that such a system is not limited, and any number, large as it is, still has to be represented. Computers, however work in a different way. All data (numbers, text, and symbols) is represented using bits (binary digits), and since the amount of bits reserved for such representations are limited, there is a limit to the largest (and smallest) number that can be represented.

In general, the number of binary unsigned integers that can be represented by n bits is 2^n, which defines all possibilities available within n bits. In modern computers, a byte is defined as 8 bits. As such, a byte can represent 256 (2^8) binary unsigned integers [0:255]. If such a byte is used for representing signed numbers, then the 256 possible values will be divided between positive and negative numbers. Since most computers utilize the two's complement method, then the values X represented by n bits can be defined by

$$-2^{n-1} < X < 2^{n-1} - 1$$

where:

    X   represents the possible values
    n   is the number of bits

As such, for a byte (8 bits) the largest possible positive number is 127_{10} (01111111_2) and the smallest possible negative number is -128_{10} (10000000_2).

Figure 2.1 is a graphical representation of the difference between the standard number line and the way numbers are represented in computers.

The standard definition of numbers is described as a line of numbers that extends endlessly to the right to represent positive numbers and similarly extends endlessly to the

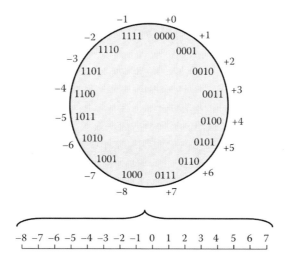

FIGURE 2.1　Range of numbers.

left to represent negative numbers. The computer representation is different since it is like a circle. This means that sometimes an overflow will cause a change of sign and definitely a wrong result. This can be easily understood when performing simple arithmetic (this will be elaborated on in the next section).

For example, the maximum positive value for a signed 8-bit number is 01111111_2 (127_{10}). If we add one to it, the result obtained is 10000000_2 (-128_{10}). This is an overflow, and the result is wrong. The computer hardware is, of course, capable of detecting such an event, which usually happens in two cases:

1. A negative result occurs after two positive numbers are added.

2. A positive result occurs after two negative numbers are added.

The computer hardware will raise a special flag signaling that such an event has happened, and it is the responsibility of the software to check for it.

After understanding the overflow mechanism in the computing numbering system, we can get back to the two's complement. As stated, if N is a number with M digits represented in base B, then the radix complement of N is given by

$$C = \left(B^M - N \right)_{Bc}$$

With binary numbers, which are a special case of any base, the formula becomes

$$C = \left(2^M - N \right)_{2c}$$

We can prove that C is the complement by computing the value C + N:

$$C + N = \left(B^M - N \right) + N = B^M$$

However, B^M will represent an overflow, so the value will be zero.
For example

$$N = 0101$$

$$M = 4 \left(\text{number of digits in N} \right)$$

$$B = 2 \left(\text{for the example, however can be any other base} \right)$$

Then

$$C = \left(2^4 - 0101 \right)_{Bc} = 10000 - 0101 = 1011$$

But

$$C + N = 1011 + 0101 = 10000$$

However, since there are only 4 digits in the number (4 bits in this example), the leading one disappears and the value calculated is zero.

Computer's Arithmetic

Arithmetic operations, for example, additions on numbers in any base, are similar to ordinary decimal arithmetic. In performing a simple addition, we start from the right side of the two numbers, adding two digits in each cycle. The result, if it consists of one digit, is written down, and if consists of two digits, the right digit is written while the left one serves as the carry. In the next cycle, the next two digits are added, including the carry digit, and so on until all digits have been added.

Additions in other bases are performed in a similar way.

For example, consider a standard decimal addition:

Carry	1 0 1
1st number	6 4 7
2nd number	5 3 7
Result	1 1 8 4

- We start by adding the rightmost digit (7 + 7). Since the result is larger than one single digit, the right digit (4) is written and the left digit becomes the carry.

- In the next cycle, the next pair of digits is added (4 + 3) and to the result the carry is added as well. In this case, the result is just one digit, which is written down, and the carry is zero.

- In the third cycle, the process repeats itself, adding the leftmost digits including the carry, which in this specific case is zero. The result is once again larger than one digit, so the right digit is written and the left is the carry for the next cycle.

- In the last cycle, there are no digits, but only the carry that is being copied to the result.

The same process is applied when adding numbers in any other base. For example, consider a case of adding binary numbers:

Carry	1 0 0 1 1
1st number	1 1 0 1 1
2nd number	1 0 0 1 1
Result	1 0 1 1 1 0

- Once again, we start from the rightmost digits and add the two bits. Since the binary system consists of only two digits (0 and 1), the result of the first addition requires more than one digit (two in binary is represented by 10_2). The right digit (0) is the result and the left digit (1) becomes the carry.

- In the next cycle, the second pair of binary digits is added (1 + 1) and on top of the result the carry is added as well. The result (3) once again requires more than one digit (3 in binary is represented by 11_2). Therefore, the right digit is written down as the result and the left digit becomes the carry.

- In the next cycle, the following pair of binary digits is added (0 + 0) and the carry is added to the result. In this case, the result (1) is just one binary digit, which is written as the next digit of the result, and the carry for the next addition is set to zero.

- The process repeats itself until all digits have been added.

We can verify that the addition is correct by converting the two binary numbers to decimal, adding the decimal numbers, and comparing this to the binary result obtained. For example

$$11011_2 = 27_{10}$$

$$10011_2 = 19_{10}$$

$$27_{10} + 19_{10} = 46_{10}$$

and

$$101110_2 = 46_{10}$$

As already noted, the addition method works for any numerical system and not just decimal or binary numbers.

For example, consider a case of adding two hexadecimal numbers:

Carry	1 1 1 0
1st number	9 5 3 A 7
2nd number	A F D C 8
Result	1 4 5 1 6 F

It should be noted that a very common mistake when adding two hexadecimal numbers is related to overflow. Many forget that when adding two hexadecimal numbers, such as 1 + 9, the result is A and not 10.

As with addition, multiplication is performed in a similar way regardless of the numerical system base. However, since we are used to decimal calculations, sometimes it is easier to convert the numbers to decimal numbers, multiply, and convert the result back to the required base.

For example

$$7_8 * 5_8 = 7*_{10} * 5*_{10} = 35_{10} = 43_8$$

or

$$12_7 * 21_7 = 9_{10} * 15_{10} = 135_{10} = 252_7$$

And a hexadecimal example:

$$A1_{16} * 25_{16} = 176_{10} * 37_{10} = 6512_{10} = 1970_{16}$$

Binary long multiplication is similar to other multiplications; however, it is simpler, since there is no need to multiply. The two possible digits are zero and one, so either the number is all zeroes or it is copied. For example, consider multiplying 011011_2 by 1011_2 (these are unsigned numbers):

$$
\begin{array}{r}
0\,1\,1\,0\,1\,1 \\
1\,0\,1\,1 \\
\hline
0\,1\,1\,0\,1\,1 \\
0\,1\,1\,0\,1\,1 \\
0\,0\,0\,0\,0\,0 \\
0\,1\,1\,0\,1\,1 \\
\hline
1\,0\,0\,1\,0\,1\,0\,0\,1
\end{array}
$$

As usual, we can verify the result by converting the numbers to decimal and multiplying using decimal numbers.

$$011011_2 = 27_{10}$$

$$1011_2 = 11_{10}$$

$$27_{10} * 11_{10} = 297_{10}$$

$$100101001_2 = 297_{10}$$

Additions and Subtractions

In order to reduce the costs associated with hardware design, engineers were constantly looking for more efficient ways to implement the machine. This issue will be elaborated on in the following chapters especially regarding the computer's processing unit. However, one aspect of this efficiency is related to the elimination of redundancy functions. Since most computers implement the method of two's complement for representing negative numbers, it implies that the system must have a hardware unit that is capable of converting a positive number into a negative one and vice versa. The direct implication was that there is no need for a subtract unit. Instead of calculating a–b, the computer hardware calculates a + (−b). Figure 2.2 provides a visual explanation of the process involved in addition and/or subtraction. The two operands are the inputs for the calculation. As part of the execution, the second operand is converted by changing its sign (two's complement). A switch in the hardware is used in order to decide if the second operand or the inverted one is to be used in the original value. The switch is triggered based on the instruction in the program. If it is an ADD instruction, the switch will signal to use the original value. On the other hand, if the instruction is SUBTRACT, the switch will impose using the inverted value.

The following example involves subtracting two numbers while using 4-bit binary numbers:

$$3_{10} - 7_{10} = 0011_2 - 0111_2 = 0011_2 + (-0111_2) = 0011_2 + 1001_2 = 1100_2 = (-0100_2) = -4_{10}$$

The decimal numbers are converted to binary numbers. Then the second number (7 or 0111_2) is converted to a negative number, which will be added to the first number. The negative number using two's complement is 1001_2, and this is added using the standard

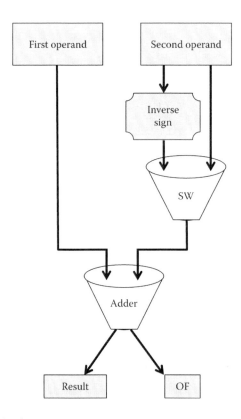

FIGURE 2.2 Addition and subtraction.

adding mechanism. The result obtained (1100_2) is negative, so using two's complement will reveal its true value (-4).

Because the sum of a number and its negative value (calculated using two's complement) is the relevant power of 2, there is another way to calculate the two's complement values.

For example, let us assume a binary number of 8 bits with a value of 97, so the decimal number X is 97 ($x = 97$).

Then

$$X + (-X) = 97_{10} + (-97_{10}) = 0110\ 0001_2 + 1001\ 1111_2 = 1\ 0000\ 0000_2$$

The spaces between the groups of binary numbers were added just for clarity.

This means that we can calculate the negative values (represented in two's complement) by subtracting the original number from 2^N, as can be seen from the formula

$$-X = 2^N - X = \left[\left(2^N - 1 \right) - X \right] + 1$$

However, $2^N - 1 = 1111...1_2$.

This means that converting a binary number using two's complement can be done by scanning the positive number from its right side, copying all the zero bits until the first one bit. This one bit is copied as well, and all other bits to the left of the number are inverted.

For example, the decimal number 68 has to be converted to binary in both positive and negative forms.

$$68_{10} = 0100\ 0100_2$$

Converting to a negative number in the "standard" way:

Original number : 0100 0100

One's complement : 1011 1011

Two's complement : 1011 1100

Direct conversion:

Original number : 0100 0100

Two's complement : 1011 1100

Floating Point

The real numbers (and fractions) described in previous chapters used a format called fixed point. This is due to the decimal or binary point being at a fixed location. The digits to the left of the point represent integers (or the whole part), while the digits to the right of the point represent the fraction part. Such numbers have a fixed number of digits to the right of the point.

For example, the decimal number 12.345 has three digits in its fraction part. Its value will not change if the format is changed and the fraction part increases. If the number is changed to XXXX.YYYY (where X represents integers and Y represents the fraction digits), the number will change, but its value remains the same: 12.345 = 0012.3450.

These rules are relevant to any numbering system and not only to decimal numbers. The decimal number 12.25 when converted to a binary number is 1100.01_2. In this case, changing the fixed-point format will have no effect on the value, assuming of course the format provides the necessary space for all digits.

As such, the equation below is correct:

$$12.25_{10} = 1100.01_2 = 0000\ 1100.0100_2$$

However, using fixed-point numbers has some inherent limitations, especially considering the limited nature of the numbers in computers due to the fixed number of bits. An explicit limitation becomes evident when there is a need to express very large or very small (close to zero) values. For that reason, there is another format for representing numbers that is based on the concept of floating point. Most computers use floating point as the dominant mechanism for representing real numbers, while integers are represented using the standard binary numbering system. To understand the concept of floating point and how it is used in computers, we will start with a brief discussion of scientific notation.

Scientific Notation

When we need to define very large numbers (or alternatively very small numbers), there are some techniques for eliminating or reducing human error. These errors are caused mainly when the numbers include many digits and especially if these are repeating digits. One useful technique is to use thousands separators, so the human eye can easily synchronize even if there are many identical digits. These separators do not change the value and are intended only for clarity. Another example, which has been used already in this book, is to add spaces between groups of binary numbers. It should be noted that when using very large binary numbers, this is a major problem due to the length of the numbers and the fact there are only two digits that repeat.

For example, the decimal number 498000000000, which includes many similar digits that repeat, becomes more readable and clear if it is written as 498,000,000,000. However, it is even more readable if it is written as $4.98 * 10^{11}$.

This type of writing is referred to as scientific notation and is relevant to very small number as well, such as $1.2 * 10^{-27}$ or $3.45 * 10^{-39}$.

The scientific notation format consists of five components:

1. The number's sign

2. The number magnitude (sometimes referred to as significand or mantissa), which represents the significant digits of the number. Usually, the significand has to be normalized, which means that there is one and only one significant digit to the left of the fraction point.

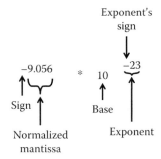

FIGURE 2.3   Scientific notation's components.

3. The base of the number

4. The exponent's sign

5. The value (magnitude) of the exponent

Figure 2.3 is a visual representation of the scientific notation, including its components. The number used in this figure is $-9.056 * 10^{-23}$.

When the value of the mantissa consists of one and only one digit to the left of the fraction point, the number is considered to be normalized. Every number has only one normalized format but may have infinite number of nonnormalized versions.

For example, if we want to represent the fraction 1/1,000,000,000, then

the normalized form will be $1.0 * 10^{-9}$

Nonnormalized numbers are $0.1 * 10^{-8}$, $10.0 * 10^{-10}$, $100.0 * 10^{-11}$, and many others.

It is easy to change nonnormalized numbers into normalized ones, and this is done by changing the location of the fraction point followed by changing the exponent accordingly. Due to the fact that the point's location is not fixed, this format is called floating point. It should be noted, however, that the value of the number does not change due to the point's location movement:

$$10 * 10^{-9} = 0.1 * 10^{-8} = 10.0 * 10^{-10}$$

Scientific notation does not have to be decimal, and it can be implemented using other bases as well. Specifically, it can be used for binary numbers as is demonstrated in Figure 2.4.

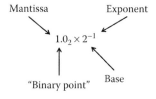

FIGURE 2.4   Binary scientific notation.

Binary scientific notation must, of course, obey the binary rules, and the digits represented in the mantissa have to be binary digits (zero and one).

During the first decades of computer history, several formats for binary floating point were developed. Different formats and implementations provided a higher degree of accuracy (if the mantissa had more bits) or the possibility of supporting a larger range of numbers (if the exponent was larger). However, the variety of floating-point formats that may have provided some marketing advantages to a specific vendor became a major deficiency. Since the days of standalone computers are gone and in the last three decades most computers have become part of a network, connectivity has become important. Computers have to be able to easily integrate with other systems, and different formats of floating-point representations hamper this connected environment. As a result, the understanding that a common standard for floating point is needed was born. After several years of discussions, in 1985 the ANSII/IEEE Standard 754 was established, and since then it has been adopted by most hardware manufacturers. The standard defined the format for 32 bits and 64 bits and also had additional formats for different numbers of bits (16, 128).

THE 754 STANDARD

The ANSI/IEEE standard 754 defines a common format for representing floating-point numbers across many hardware platforms. The standard defines the number of bits allocated for each one of the scientific notation components as well as the definition of these components. For example, for a 32-bit word, the standard defines it thus:

1. The number's sign is the leftmost bit and, when it is on, it means that this is a negative number.

2. The number (value or mantissa) is expressed using the rightmost 23 bits of the binary number. These bits represent the fraction of the normalized binary number. Since a normalized number contains only one significant digit left of the fraction point, then when dealing with binary numbers, the only significant digit is one. For that reason, the format used by the 754 standard does not relate to the significant digit and does not include it as part of the number. One may say that the standard designers did not want to waste a bit for information, that is obvious. For that reason, the 23 bits represent only the fraction (mantissa) and not the whole number. The processor that received the floating-point number "knows" the standard and automatically adds the missing significant digit before the required calculations. After the calculations are over and the result is normalized, the processor will strip the significant digit so the number will follow the standard.

3. Base is another scientific notation component that is not represented in the standard. As with the significant digit that is omitted, since all numbers are binary numbers, the standard's designers did not want to waste bits on an obvious piece of information. Although base is one of the scientific notation components, it does not exist in the 754 format.

4. The exponent's sign is another component that exists in scientific notation; however, the standard did not assign bits for it, and it is part of the exponent value. As with previous cases, the standard tries to be as efficient as possible and not to waste bits on known or duplicate information. The idea is to use these bits for increasing the accuracy of the numbers represented by allocating more bits for the mantissa.

5. The exponent is defined by 8 bits, which are in the middle between the sign bit (on the left) and the mantissa 23 bits (on the right). This 8-bit number is a binary unsigned value, but the real exponent is biased by 127; that is, the value 127 is added to the real number of the exponent, and this is what is stored in the standard.

   For example, if the real exponent is 3, then the number that will be used as part of the 754 standard will be $127 + 3 = 130_{10} = 82_{16} = 1000\ 0010_2$.

   Similarly, if the exponent is (-4), then the 754 exponent will be $0111\ 1011_2$; this was obtained by $-4 + 127 = 123_{10} = 7B_{16} = 0111\ 1011_2$.

This means that although scientific notation is based on 5 components (see "Scientific Notation" above) the implementation of the 754 standard is based on only three of these components as is shown by Figure 2.5.

Figure 2.6 provides a further explanation of the standard and how the various fields are implemented.

The standard was not defined for 32 bits only, and it can be applied for other word sizes as well. For example, in the 64-bits-per-word format, the mantissa is using 52 bits, and for

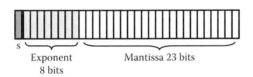

FIGURE 2.5   The 754 standard.

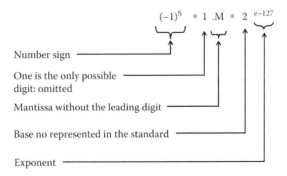

FIGURE 2.6   The 754 standard formula.

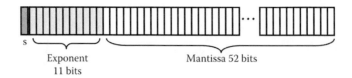

s

Exponent
11 bits

Mantissa 52 bits

FIGURE 2.7   The 754 standard for 64-bit words.

the exponents 11 bits were allocated (see Figure 2.7). This means that the 64-bit numbers are more accurate since there are much more digits to represent the number, and in addition, increasing the size of the exponent provides an increased range of numbers.

Due to the larger number of bits allocated for the exponent, the biased number was also changed. In the 64-bits-per-word standard, the bias is 1023 (instead of the 127 that is used with 32-bit words).

For relevancy for other word sizes, this bias was defined in a general form as well:

$$(-1)^s * 1.M * 2^{e-b}$$

where:

$$b = 2^{n-1} - 1$$

Range of Floating-Point Numbers

Unlike the circular nature of the integers (or natural numbers) represented in a computer (see the section "Range of Numbers" in this chapter), the range of the floating-point numbers is significantly different. Of the seven possible segments of numbers available in the range, floating-point numbers can access only three. For a better explanation of the ranges and the segments, we will use a virtual number system and a virtual floating-point format.

Assuming we have a six-digit decimal number, the applicable format will be as follows:

1. One digit represents the number's sign (0 means positive and 1 means negative, while all other values are invalid).

2. One digit is the significant part of the normalized number.

3. Two digits are allocated for the mantissa.

4. Two digits are allocated for the exponent with a bias of 49.

This means that the format of this system is

$$(-1)^s * D.MM * 10^{e-49}$$

where:

S   is the sign

D.MM   is the normalized number (one significant digit and two digits for the mantissa)

e   is the exponent

Using this imaginary system, a number like 125 will be written as 012551. The steps that are required to build this format are

1. Normalize the original number: $125 = 1.25 * 10^2$

2. Then build the format's exponent by adding the bias (49) to the real exponent: $2 + 49 = 51$

3. Setting the sign a positive $(S = 0)$

The number -0.000571 will be written as 157145.

1. Normalize the original number: $0.000571 = 5.71 * 10^{-4}$

2. Build the format's exponent by adding the bias (49) to the real exponent: $-4 + 49 = 45$

3. Setting the sign a negative $(S = 1)$

Due to the inherent limitations of computer systems and the fact that the words have a definite number of bits, the floating-point representation is limited and cannot address all the indefinite numbers in a specific range.

For a better explanation, we will use an imaginary system that uses decimal numbers. The exponent is based on two decimal digits, and the normalized significant part consists of three digits. Figure 2.8 provides a visual explanation of the floating-point representation's limitations.

From the seven segments shown in the numbers line, only three are accessible by the floating-point representations. The two overflow segments represent numbers that are beyond the possible representations. For example, since the maximum number that can be represented is $9.99*10^{49}$, then it means that 10^{52} is bigger than the maximum possible representation and thus cannot be expressed by this imaginary system. Using 10^{52} will cause a positive overflow. Similarly since the largest negative number is $-9.98*10^{49}$, then -10^{52}

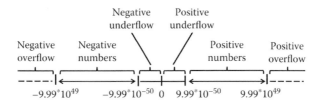

FIGURE 2.8   Definition range example.

cannot be represented either and it will cause a negative overflow. There are two additional ranges (or segments) that are inaccessible. The underflow numbers that are very small numbers (close to the zero) that are too small to be represented. For example, the numbers with an absolute value smaller than 10^{-52}.

The only three accessible segments shown in the figure are

- Positive numbers in the range $9.99 * 10^{-50} \leq X \leq 9.99 * 10^{49}$

- Negative numbers in the range $-9.9 * 10^{49} \leq X \leq -9.99 * 10^{-50}$

- Zero

It should be noted that when the exponent has only two digits, the total number that can be represented is 100 (10^2). One number is reserved for zero, which implies that the two sides, negative and positive, have different magnitudes. Usually the standard will define how the exponent is calculated, but in this specific example, the assumption was that the negative side has one additional value. This is the reason it gets to 10^{-50} while the positive side gets only to 10^{49}. The 754 standard, like the imaginary model described previously, provides access to only three of the segments of the number line. The limits of these segments are different from the limits of the model that was previously described and are based on the specific word size. The 32-bit standard defines 8 bits for the exponent. This means that the maximum magnitude of the exponent is 256 (2^8); however, only 254 of these values are used to represent floating-point numbers, while two values (zero and 255) are reserved for special cases.

Special Numbers

Due to the limitations inherent in the floating-point mechanism, the used values for the exponent in a 32-bit representation are 1–254. Due to the bias used in the formula, the possible exponents are between minus 126 to 127 ($-126 \leq e \leq 127$). When the exponent field is all zeroes or all ones, this denotes some special numbers:

1. A number with a zero exponent and a zero mantissa represents zero. This is a special number that does not follow the 754 format.

2. A number with a zero exponent and a nonzero mantissa is a denormal (a number that is not a normal one). This type is used for representing numbers that are in the underflow segment (or very close to zero). The sign bit (the leftmost bit) defines it as a positive or negative underflow.

3. A number with an exponent where all bits are set (exponent value of 255) and a mantissa that is all zeroes is used to represent infinite numbers. The sign is used to determine if it is $-\infty$ or $+\infty$.

4. A number that contains an exponent with all bits set and a mantissa that is not zero is used to define a NaN (not a number). Trying to calculate the square root of a negative

number, for example, will produce a NaN. This is a special value used by the computer hardware in order to save time in unnecessary checks. Since any operation on a NaN produces a NaN, then it is faster to check if one operand is NaN, and then there is no need to carry out the calculation since the result will be a NaN as well.

Converting 754 Numbers

Converting decimal numbers to 754 floating-point numbers is done using the formula

$$(-1)^s * 1.M * 2^{e-127}$$

The conversion is a technical straightforward process that includes several structured steps:

1. Converting the decimal number to a binary fixed-point number.

2. Normalizing the binary number.

3. Calculating the floating-point exponent by adding the exponent of the normalized number to the bias. Assuming this is a 32-bit number, the bias is 127.

4. Converting the calculated exponent to a binary number.

5. Defining the sign of the floating-point number—this is the sign of the original decimal number.

6. Constructing the floating-point number by integrating all three fields. This involves starting with the sign (the leftmost bit—step 5 above) and then concatenating the 8 bits that represent the exponent (calculated in step 4 above) and then concatenating the 23 bits that represent only the fraction of the normalized number (step 2 above). If the fraction contains less than 23 bits, zeroes will be appended on the right side.

7. For clarity, the last step is to convert the binary number into a hexadecimal number. This reduces the number of digits from 32 bits to 8 hexadecimal digits. The conversion from binary to hexadecimal is done by grouping each 4 bits into the hexadecimal corresponding digit (see Table 2.3 for assistance).

For example, let us assume that we have to convert the decimal number (-0.75) into a floating-point number.

1. First we will convert the decimal number to a binary number:

$$0.75_{10} = 0.11_2$$

2. Then we have to normalize the binary number:

$$0.11_2 = 1.1_2 * 2^{-1}$$

3. From the normalized exponent, we will calculate the exponent of the 754 floating-point number by adding 127:

$$e = -1 + 127 = 126$$

4. The calculated exponent is a decimal number, so it has to be converted to a binary number:

$$126_{10} = 01111110_2$$

5. The sign is then defined according to the sign of the original decimal number. In this case, the number is negative, so

$$s = 1$$

6. With all parts defined, it is time to construct the floating-point number by integrating all the parts:

$$1\ 01111110\ 10000000000000000000000$$

The first bit, from the left side, is the sign bit.

The second field is the exponent.

The third field is the mantissa.

7. For simplification and to help the human eye comprehend the number, it is usually converted to hexadecimal. This involves arranging the binary numbers in groups and translating each group to its equivalent hexadecimal value:

$$1\ 01111110\ 10000000000000000000000_2 =$$

$$1011\ 1111\ 0100\ 0000\ 0000\ 0000\ 0000\ 0000_2 = BF400000_{16}$$

Converting a 754 floating-point number into a decimal number is the reverse process and includes similar structured steps:

1. Converting the hexadecimal 754 floating point to binary. This is done by replacing each hexadecimal digit with its binary equivalent (see Table 2.3).

2. Splitting the binary number into the three fields (sign, exponent, mantissa).

3. Converting the binary exponent to a decimal number.

4. Obtaining the real exponent by subtracting 127 from the exponent (step 3 above).

5. Constructing the real number by adding one (the significant digit that is not represented in the floating point format) to the mantissa.

6. Calculating the number by adding the exponent and sometimes denormalizing it.

7. Adding the sign.

For example, let us assume we need to convert the 754 floating-point number represented by C2F00000.

1. First we will convert the hexadecimal number to its binary equivalent:

$$C2F00000_{16} = 1100\ 0010\ 1111\ 0000\ 0000\ 0000\ 0000\ 0000_2$$

2. Then we will divide the number into the different groups:

$$1\ 1000\ 0101\ 1110\ 000....000_2$$

3. Now we have to convert the binary exponent into a decimal number:

$$1000\ 0101_2 = 133_{10}$$

4. Next we have to obtain the real exponent (by subtracting 127 from the decimal value calculated in step 3):

$$e = 133 - 127 = 6$$

5. Then we construct the number by adding the significant digit to the fraction in the number:

$$1 + 0.111_2 = 1.111_2$$

6. The next stage is to construct the whole number (including the exponent):

$$1.111_2 * 2^6 = 1111000_2 = 120_{10}$$

7. The last step consists of adding the sign, which in this case was negative:

$$C2F00000_{754} = -120_{10}$$

Adding Floating-Point Numbers

Floating-point numbers cannot be added directly like binary or decimal numbers because the fraction point in the two numbers may be in different locations. Therefore, before adding two floating-point numbers, the fraction points have to be aligned.

As with converting to floating point, adding such numbers is a structured process that follows several steps:

1. Converting the two hexadecimal numbers to binary numbers

2. Splitting the numbers into the three groups

3. Aligning the exponents of the two numbers by increasing the smaller exponent

4. Adding the fractions

5. Normalizing the result

6. Checking for overflow

For example, let us assume we have to add the two floating-point numbers BEE00000 and 3F000000.

1. First, we will convert the numbers to binary:

$$BEE00000_{16} = 1011\ 1110\ 1110\ 000...000_2$$

$$3F000000_{16} = 0011\ 1111\ 000...000_2$$

2. Next, we will extract the groups:

$$1011\ 1110\ 1110\ 000...000_2 = 1\ 0111\ 1101\ 1100\ 00...00_2 = -1.110 * 2^{-2}$$

$$0011\ 1111\ 000...000_2 = 0\ 0111\ 1110\ 000...000_2 = 1.0 * 2^{-1}$$

3. We then align the exponents by increasing the lower one:

$$-1.110 * 2^{-2} = -0.111 * 2^{-1}$$

4. Next, we have to add the fractions (a simple binary addition):

$$1.000 + (-0.111) = 0.001$$

5. The unnormalized result is

$$0.001 * 2^{-1}$$

6. Normalizing the result produces

$$0.001 * 2^{-1} = 1.0 * 2^{-4}$$

7. We then convert to 754:

$$1.0 * 2^{-4} = 3D800000_{754}$$

Just to verify the results, it is possible to add the numbers by converting to decimal, and then we'll get

$$3F000000_{754} = 0.5_{10}$$

$$BEE00000_{754} = -0.4375_{10}$$

$$0.5_{10} + (-0.4375_{10}) = 0.0625_{10}$$

In addition, when converting back, we will get

$$0.0625_{10} = 3D800000_{754}$$

Multiplying Floating-Point Numbers

Multiplying floating-point numbers is simpler than multiplying ordinary (decimal) numbers. As in the previous case, the process is based on several steps:

1. Converting the two hexadecimal numbers to binary numbers

2. Splitting the numbers into the three groups

3. Adding the exponents of the two numbers (simple integer addition)

4. Multiplying the fractions of the two numbers (simple binary multiplications)

5. Calculating the sign bit by performing a XOR* operation on the two sign bits. This means that when multiplying two positive or two negative numbers the result will be positive, while if one number is positive and the other is negative, the result will be negative.

6. Normalizing the result

For example, let us assume we have to multiply the two floating-point numbers BEE00000 and 3F000000.

---

* XOR or Exclusive OR is a Boolean function that returns "True" if the two input operands are different and "False" if the two input operands are identical.

1. First we will convert the numbers to binary:

$$BEE00000_{16} = 1011\ 1110\ 1110\ 000...000_2$$

$$3F000000_{16} = 0011\ 1111\ 000...000_2$$

2. Next we will extract the groups:

$$1011\ 1110\ 1110\ 000...000_2 = 1\ 0111\ 1101\ 1100\ 00...00_2 = -1.110 * 2^{-2}$$

$$0011\ 1111\ 000...000_2 = 0\ 0111\ 1110\ 000...000_2 = 1.0 * 2^{-1}$$

3. Next we have to add the exponents:

$$-1 + (-2) = -3$$

4. Then we have to multiply the fractions:

$$1.000 * 1.110 = 1.110$$

The fraction and the exponent are combined so the result is $-1.110 * 2^{-3}$

5. In this case, the result is normalized. In those cases when it is not, it will have to be normalized.

6. The two sign bits are different, so the XOR function will return "True" and thus the result will be negative.

7. When converting back to 754 format, we will get the result $BE600000_{754}$.

For verifying the result, we can multiply the numbers using the ordinary long way (converting the numbers to decimal, multiplying the decimal numbers, and then converting back to a 754 floating-point number):

$$3F000000_{754} = 0.5_{10}$$

$$BEE00000_{754} = -0.4375_{10}$$

$$0.5_{10} * (-0.4375_{10}) = -0.21875_{10}$$

In addition, when converting back, we will get that

$$-0.21875_{10} = BE600000_{754}$$

Decimal Numbers Representations

Decimal numbers are natural to human beings, and binary numbers are "natural" to computers. The migration between the two types is sometimes not as straightforward as might be anticipated. For that reason, over the years, additional intermediate formats have been defined, mainly for representing decimal numbers without the need for migration.

One of the most well-known formats is BCD (binary coded decimal), which uses four bits for representing a decimal digit. The format is sometimes referred to as 8421. These numbers are the weights of the binary digits in the migration process. The BCD value is calculated by multiplying each bit by its weight, and the weight is the appropriated power of 2. This is similar to the process of migrating binary numbers to decimal with the exception that BCD numbers have only 10 digits, so some of the combinations are illegal. Let us consider an example:

Migrating the binary number 0111_2 to a decimal number is performed by

$$0\ 1\ 1\ 1_2$$

$$2^3 2^2 2^1 2^0$$

or

$$0111_2 = 0*2^3 + 1*2^2 + 1*2^1 + 1*2^0$$

$$= 0+1+1+1 = 7$$

Unlike binary numbers, for which there exists a decimal value for each combination of the 4 bits, when using BCD, some values remain unused; 1010_2, 1011_2, 1100_2, 1101_2, 1110_2 and 1111_2, which represent the decimal values of 10, 11, 12, 13, 14, and 15, do not exist in BCD (see Table 2.4).

As far as efficiency is concerned, the binary codes are the most efficient due to the full usage of the possible values. BCD numbers, on the other hand, are less efficient since this format uses only 10 values out of the possible 16 (with 4 bits).

TABLE 2.4   Decimal Numbers' Representations

Decimal	BCD (8421)	2421	84-2-1	Excess-3
0	0000	0000	0000	0011
1	0001	0001	0111	0100
2	0010	0010	0110	0101
3	0011	0011	0101	0110
4	0100	0100	0100	0111
5	0101	1011	1011	1000
6	0110	1100	1011	1001
7	0111	1101	1001	1010
8	1000	1110	1000	1011
9	1001	1111	1111	1100

Migration between BCD and binary numbers is very easy and simple; however, using this format in calculation is quite complicated, and for that reason, the format is seldom used. The PC family of computers includes special instructions for supporting BCD mathematical operations.

The biggest problem associated with BCD numbers, however, is related to the fact that the complement value of a digit requires some thinking, and it cannot be obtained automatically as with binary numbers. For that reason, some other formats have been adopted. One such format is 2421. As with the previous format, in this case the digits represent the weights to be used in calculating the value of the number. An additional format is 84-2-1, and in this case, some of the weights are negative. In addition, there is the Excess-3 format, which is based on the 8421 calculation, but prior to the calculation the value is increased by 3. This means that the representation of an Excess-3 number is identical to the BCD representation of the number plus 3.

Key Takeaway

- *Numerical systems*: A numerical system is an order method for representing numbers using "digits" (or some agreed-upon symbols). When being used in calculations, such a system should include a limited number of digits and should support infinite numbers.

- *The decimal numbering system*: The standard system used by humans. It includes 10 symbols (digits), so its base is 10. The value of the number is obtained by multiplying each digit's value by a power of 10 designated by the location and summing up all values.

- *Other numbering systems*: It is possible to define additional numerical systems using any base. The digits participating in such a system for base n are 0, 1, 2,…, n-1.

- *The binary system*: The binary system is just an additional system; however, it is important in the computing context. Since computers use two values (on, off) the binary system uses two digits (called bits—binary digit).

- *The hexadecimal system*: The system that uses 16 digits (the ordinary 0–9 and A, B, C, D, E, F). It is important since 16 is a power of 2, so hexadecimal numbers can be used to represent binary numbers in such a way that they are more readable. This is especially true for large numbers.

- *Base conversion*: There are several cases in converting between the various systems:

  - *Binary to decimal*: Converted by calculating the value of the binary number.

  - *Decimal to any other base*: Converted by dividing the decimal number by the base in a repeated way, while collecting the remainder. The process stops when the result is 1.0. This can be an indefinite process.

  - *Binary to another base that is a power of two*: Converted by combining several binary bits together. The number of bits to be combined is the power of two.

- *Base that is a power of two to binary*: This is converted by translating each digit into its binary equivalence starting from the left.

- *Any base to any base*: The easiest way to do this is to convert to a decimal number as an intermediate step.

- *Negative binary numbers*: Contrary to the "−" (the minus sign) used in decimal notation, the sign in binary notation is actually part of the number. There are three ways to represent signed numbers:

  - *Sign and magnitude*, in which the first bit is the sign bit (one denotes a negative number) and the other bits are the value (or the magnitude of the number). This representation resembles the normal decimal notation of a sign followed by a number.

  - *One's complement*, in which the positive number is migrated to a negative one by flipping each bit.

  - *Two's complement*, in which the binary number is obtained by the one's complement plus adding a binary one.

  Most systems use the two's complement notation.

- *The number's range*: Refers to the understanding that binary numbers that are part of a byte (8 bits) are limited in range. When using the first two negative representations (sign and magnitude and one's complement), there are two possible values for zero. Two's complement has one zero, but the two sides of the number (positive and negative) are of different lengths (there is one additional negative value).

- *Standard IEEE 754*: A standard for representing real binary numbers. The standard resembles the scientific notation with some minor modifications. The binary number is divided into three parts:

  - The number's sign

  - A biased exponent

  - The mantissa

  The 32-bit floating-point format consists of one sign bit, 8 exponent bits, and 23 mantissa bits. When using 64 bits, the floating-point format consists of one sign bit, 11 exponent bits, and 52 mantissa bits.

CHAPTER 3

Hardware Architecture

HARDWARE ARCHITECTURE

As already described in the introduction and the chapter on the historic perspective, the role of computers in modern society is constantly changing. Nevertheless, in most cases, computers as well as computer-based appliances are designed to help their users. Originally, this help was intended mainly for tedious tasks, but slowly it moved to providing a better user experience. The first computers were designed to perform tasks that were impossible or practically impossible using manual labor. For example, the Electronic Numerical Integrator and Computer (ENIAC) (see the section, "The First Computers," in Chapter 1) was developed in order to help in complex calculations, which take a long time when performed by humans as well as potentially including human errors. Since then, computers have always been used to provide a technological solution to a known problem. In the case of information systems, the first significant contributions were related to manufacturing processes. Production planning, warehouse management, inventory control and management (both ingoing and outgoing), and so on cannot be achieved without a computerized system. As part of the production era (during the 1960s), various MRP (material requirements planning) systems were developed and sold. These systems help manage the whole production process, such as inventory control, bill of material, scheduling, and so on, and they support not only production but planning as well. It is this planning that is responsible for manufacturing what is required and exactly when it is required. Proper planning helps lower organizational overhead and leads to improved profitability. This elevated profitability was among the reasons so many manufacturing organizations started using expensive computers. In parallel, many other systems were developed for addressing scientific issues. Their contribution may be measured differently, but in many cases, these systems were responsible for advancing humanity in many ways (weather prediction, safer cars and airplanes, the human genome, etc.). At a later stage, with the development of communications, the whole supply chain was addressed, including new marketing strategies and new ways for distribution. Modern information systems added a new layer that addresses the customer and the tailored service provided for these customers.

This perceived role of information systems dominated the architectural development of computers. It was clear that for analyzing vast amounts of data, as is the case with many systems, some storage device is required. This led to the development of a large array of solutions, all intended for storing data so it will be available at a later stage.

The algorithms that are required for defining the business rules have to be translated into a set of instructions understood by the computer. This led to the development of various programming languages, each one with common basic capabilities but, in addition, some specific features. Over the years, hundreds of programming languages were developed, but only a handful of them were widely used (C, C++, C#, and Java, to name a few). One important part of the computer architecture is the processor (or the central processing unit), which resembles the human brain. It is responsible for accepting instructions, understanding their meaning, and acting on them. The developers are responsible for translating the business rules into an ordered list of instructions available as part of the programming language. Unlike the human brain, wherein most processes are intuitive unless we are engaged in a structured process such as a calculation, the processor follows the provided program, which is always structured. The electronic circuits within the processor are capable of reading the instructions and executing them.

In order to be executed, a program has to reside in a working space, just like the human short-term memory. In computers, it is the main memory that is used for storing the program to be executed as well as the data it requires.

Just as in the case of living creatures, the computer needs some devices that will serve as the outside interfaces. These devices have a dual role. Some are used as input devices (the various senses) and others are used as output devices (muscles). In addition to these two types, computers have hybrid devices that serve both as input and output devices, for example, communication lines or storage.

The rapid technological advancements made over the last centuries affected most of the electronic devices used, and especially computers and other computer-embedded appliances. This trend is made very clear by following the developments of the various mobile devices and the speed at which new, smaller, and more efficient devices emerge. To understand technological changes in the early stages of computing and how they affected computers, the term "computer generation" was used. Moving to a new generation implied using more dense electronic technologies, which allowed for higher speed and larger memory capacity, as predicted by Moore's law.

Computer Generations

- First-generation (1946–1957) computers used vacuum tubes and were physically very large, slow, and very expensive, and had reliability issues. The ENIAC (see the section in Chapter 1 on "The First Computers") was a first-generation computer. It represented an advancement over the Harvard Mark I; however, it was still slow and had high heat emission due to the use of vacuum tubes, which heated up just like ordinary (nonefficient) light bulbs. The ENIAC, for example, used 17,468[1] such tubes, which, in addition to the heat emission, required a lot of electricity. Other computers that belonged to the first generations are the EDVAC[2]—Electronic Discrete Variable Automatic Computer and the UNIVAC I[3]—Universal Computer.

The vacuum tube was invented in parallel to the electric bulb and used a similar concept. However, the vacuum tube possessed two important attributes required for their implementation in computers (and later in many other electronic devices). The tube could amplify the signals and be used as a switch. The switching capability, which is translated into turning on and off a particular bit, was the main reason for the important role the vacuum tubes played in early computers. However, the main problem associated with using the vacuum tube was the heat emission. In spite of efforts to cool the tubes, in many cases, they overheated and stopped working. This, combined with the large number of vacuum tubes in the system, severely affected the reliability of the system. The first-generation computers were also limited in the software development capabilities they provided. Only basic machine-programing languages were supported, and these languages were difficult to use. The systems executed only one task at a time (see the section "Historic Perspective" in Chapter 1) and were very limited in using input and output devices.

- Second-generation (1958–1964) computers were characterized by their use of the then newly invented replacement for the vacuum tube—the transistor. It was invented at AT&T labs in 1947, but its commercialization took several years. The transistor was faster, much smaller, highly reliable, and, especially, significantly cheaper. The transistor is made of silicon, which can be obtained from sand, so it is available and affordable. In contrast to vacuum tubes, the single transistor produces almost no heat, which contributed to the elevated reliability and lowered cost associated with cooling the system. The invention of the transistor had a tremendous effect, not only on computers but on the whole electronic industry as well. Even the rapid developments in space technology during the 1960s became possible due to the use of the transistor and the miniaturization processes that followed. However, in spite of the significant contribution of transistors to hardware implementations, the use of single transistors, as was the case with the second generation of computers, lasted only a couple of years.

The second-generation computers started using symbolic programming languages, which reduced the development time. In parallel, additional development activities were aimed at special-purpose programming languages such as COBOL—Common Business Oriented Language and FORTRAN—Formula Translator, which was tailored for scientific environments.

- Third generation (1965–1971) computers were characterized by the use of integrated circuits. Although the transistor provided a quantum leap in hardware development, the integrated circuit allowed for additional significant development. The integrated circuit, sometimes referred to as a semiconductor chip, was invented in parallel by two nonrelated persons: Robert Noyce, who worked for Fairchild Corporation; and Jack Kilby, who worked for Texas Instruments and received a Nobel Prize for his invention. The integrated circuit is a collection of transistors integrated and compacted into a single chip. Such a chip, which currently consists of hundreds of millions of transistors, significantly increases the system's performance while lowering the costs. Since its invention, the integrated circuit continues to advance, and about every 18 months, the number of transistors doubles while the price remains almost constant (see the section "Moore's Law" in Chapter 1 and Table 1.2).

Third-generation computers had the "known" input and output devices such as keyboards and mice, and they included more sophisticated operating systems capable of running several tasks in parallel. The most important benefit was that the lower price made possible by using integrated circuits increased computers' accessibility for a wider user community.

- Fourth-generation (starting from 1972) computers were characterized by a significant increase in the number of transistors integrated into a single chip and by the invention of the microprocessor. This is a fully functional processor implemented using a single chip. By integrating hundreds of millions of transistors into a single chip, the performance and speed increased as well. The smaller distance affects the time electrons have to spend moving within the processor, which in turn reduced the time even further. The wide distribution of computers as we all know it, and the fact that almost any human activity is done, managed, monitored, and even billed by some computer, is attributed to Ted Hoff, who worked for Intel (a company established by Noyce, the inventor of the integrated circuit, among others) and invented the microprocessor, which originally was no larger than a pencil sharpener. The aim of inventing the new processor was to use it for the development of calculators. However, as it turned out, it proved to be significantly more important by contributing to the wide spread of computers as we all know. The current computers belong to the fourth generation, and as a matter of fact, the term "generation" was replaced by measuring the transistor gate length in nanometers.

Computer Classification

The rapid technological development in the computing industry required a better definition of the types of computers or a better type of classification. In the early stages, however, there were only "computers" (see also the "Classification of Computers" section in Chapter 1).

- Mainframe was used to define and classify organizational computers that were responsible for back-end processing. As such, these systems had to provide a high degree of reliability, availability, and serviceability since all organizational processes depended on the outcome of this computer. The term mainframe came into existence only after other types of computers started to emerge, such as the departmental system.

- The minicomputer or departmental system originally was intended to support a single department. Digital Equipment Corporation* introduced the minicomputer, aiming at the organizational departments that suffered from lower priority on expensive organizational systems. This niche, which originally started as a marketing idea, proved to be extremely successful. Instead of spending huge amounts on an organizational system that provided bad service to the departments, departments could afford to buy their own system, which was significantly cheaper and provided superior service to individual departments.

- The personal computer, which was initially intended for a single user, was based on the microprocessor chip. Currently, microprocessor chip–based computers are not used only by a single user and are being used as the infrastructure for most systems, even the large ones like mainframes (which in some cases were replaced by a new term—servers).

The above mentioned classification based on usage is not accurate, and for that reason it is seldom used. Furthermore, due to the vast usage of computers in our daily lives, the classification had to be enhanced to include additional types:

- Supercomputers, which is a term used to define extremely fast and powerful computers capable of running large-scale complex programs such as weather forecasting, various simulations, molecular modeling, and so on. In the past, the dominant technology for addressing such needs was through the design and development of special-purpose systems such as vector processors.† Currently, all these requirements are fulfilled using parallel systems based on an array of microprocessors working together. The modern trend of cloud computing, which provides access to a virtual system that consists of a flexible number of processors and resides somewhere in the network, represents another implementation of high-performance systems.

- Servers, which in many organizations provide some partial replacement for the mainframes mainly for a specific functionality, for example, a mail server, file server, print server, and so on. In a sense, these servers are the "common denominator" between the mainframe and the departmental systems. On one hand, some part of the mainframe's workload migrated to the server (see Chapter 1, "Introduction and Historic Perspective"), which was better suited for the job. On the other hand, the departmental

---

* Digital Equipment Corporation (DEC) was a large American computers manufacturer. The company was active between from the 1960s to the 1990s and was very successful in the midrange computers market through its PDP and VAX computers. DEC was acquired In 1998 by Compaq, a large PC manufacturer, and four years later Compaq itself merged into Hewlett-Packard.

† Vector processors are special-purpose processors, which that implement vector instructions. Unlike the ordinary processors, in which a single instruction works on a single set of operands, the vector instructions work on multiple data. One instruction can add two vectors of numbers, creating a new vector of results. The vector computers provided a very fast computation engine, however but at a very high cost. These systems were operational from the 1970s to the 1990s and were gradually replaced by arrays of off-the-shelf microprocessors, which provided a superior price performance. Although vector processing is not widely used, some vector capabilities exist in modern implementations, and both Intel and AMD use vector capabilities, for example in the GPU (graphics processing unit).

systems were replaced by servers. For that reason, the once clear line that differentiated between mainframes and departmental systems does not exist anymore.

- Midrange computers, which are usually larger servers providing service to several departments or even to some of the organizational users. These were usually smaller than the mainframes but provided more functionality compared to ordinary servers.

- Workstations, which are various kinds of personal computers for a specific organizational task. The aim of the workstation defined the specific configuration and devices attached to the system. For example, workstations that were intended for CAD (computer aided design) had to be equipped with a faster processor and a larger memory capable of running engineering models. Furthermore, the graphics capabilities would be enhanced as well and the system usually required a bigger screen with a higher resolution. Currently, all workstations are some kind of a personal computer or even a tablet.

- Appliances, which in most cases are driven by a computer; these include most electrical and electronic devices, such as washing machines, television sets, alarm systems, watches, cameras, and many more. One special appliance deserves particular attention due to its popularity: the cellular phone, which has become the dominant device for accessing networks, an entertainment device, and a mobile information center.

Computer Systems

Every computer system (as described already in Chapter 1, "Introduction and Historic Perspective") consists of several components:

- Processor, responsible for executing the instructions (the brain in the human body)

- Memory, used as a temporary storage for instructions and data for the tasks being run (the various memories in the human body)

- Channels for transferring the data between the various components (the circulation and nervous systems in the human body)

- Input and output units, which connect the computer to the outer world or the users (in the human body, corresponding to the senses, which serve as input devices; and the muscles, which serve as output devices)

These components exist in every computer, and the specific type may affect the quantity or other attributes of the components. For example, a large server that is intended to support many concurrent active users will probably be equipped with more memory.

Figure 3.1 is a schematic representation of a computer system, including the above mentioned components. On the left side is the central processing unit (CPU) with the two units (the arithmetic and logic unit [ALU] and the control unit [CU], see Figure 1.5, as well as other components to be explained later). Additional system components are the memory and two boxes that represent input and output devices. The lines that connect all these components are a representation of the channels on which the data is transferred.

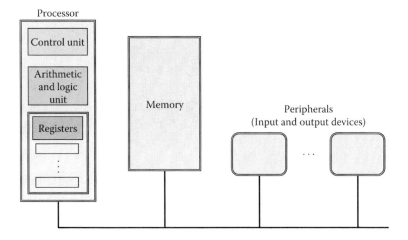

FIGURE 3.1   Schematic configuration.

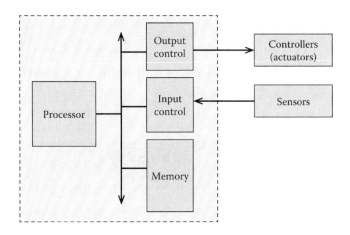

FIGURE 3.2   Embedded system.

Even the computers used as part of embedded systems have the same type of components, although, due to the different usage, their attributes may be different. Figure 3.2
describes such a configuration and, as can be seen, the input and output components may
need to be actuators and sensors (depending on the type of system). An alarm system,
for example, may need very limited memory and many connections to various sensors
(motion, volume, smoke, etc.)

Most modern computers still utilize the von Neumann architecture (see the section
in Chapter 1 titled "Von Neumann Architecture"). The idea of separating the processor
and memory was a breakthrough in architecture design. This separation led to the idea of
loading a program, that is, the concept that the computer can be used to perform various
tasks. This is one of the unique attributes of computers, and it derived from this separation.
The hardware remains unchanged, but by loading and executing different programs, the
computer behaves differently.

The architecture proposed included registers, which are small fast pieces of memory that reside inside the processor and are used to store information required during the processing; for example, there are registers that hold the next instruction to be executed, registers that hold the next instruction's address, registers for helping in arithmetic operations, and so on.

In parallel to the development of the von Neumann architecture (Figure 3.3), another slightly different architecture was developed at Harvard that was based on experience gathered from the development of the Mark I (see the section in Chapter 1 on "The First Computers").

In the Harvard architecture (Figure 3.4) a special emphasis was put on an additional separation between two types of memory. One type is the memory used for instructions, and the other type is used for data. This separation required additional channels capable of transferring data and instructions simultaneously. This additional level of parallelism provides better and more consistent performance. While the processor is fetching the next instruction, it can bring the operand needed for the executions. These two transfers can be performed simultaneously using two distinct channels.

Separating the memories, combined with the fact that each one has a different channel, provides additional capabilities. These can be heterogeneous channels with different

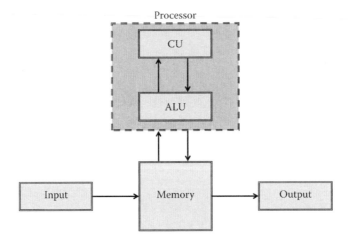

FIGURE 3.3 Von Neumann architecture.

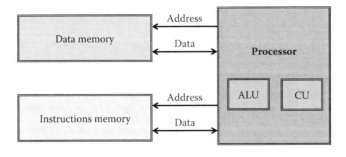

FIGURE 3.4 Harvard architecture.

attributes that may be useful when developing architectures better suited to specific needs. For that reason, many signal-processing systems are based on the Harvard architecture, which is more predictable in terms of performance. This is achieved due to less possible collisions on the channel. This higher predictability is one reason that this architecture is used for many real-time systems as well. Contrary to "ordinary" systems, real-time systems have to assure execution in a redefined timing window.

Processor

The processor is the heart of the system that executes the instructions. To simplify the execution process, the instructions are broken up into components or microinstructions. During execution, it is possible to dismantle the execution into several stages, which may increase speed though parallelism (this will be elaborated on in Chapter 4, "Central Processing Unit"). To understand the concept of microinstructions and to simplify the explanation, we will assume that each instruction is built from four microinstructions:

- *Fetch* is the stage in which the CU brings the instruction from the memory into the processor. Since the von Neumann architecture separates the processor and memory, the instruction has to be fetched before it can be executed.

- *Decode* is the stage in which the CU decodes the instruction in order to see if it is a valid instruction, to determine the type of instruction, and to work out the number of operands it requires and their locations. The ALU only executes the instructions and does not have the ability to fetch them or bring the required operands. For that reason, the CU has to do all the preparatory work. The CU fetches the instruction and stores it in a special register in the CPU, and then it brings the required operands and puts them in other special-purpose registers; only then does it signal to the ALU that it can start the execution. The decode stage is necessary since not all instructions are of the same length or require the same number of operands. For example, the JUMP instruction has only one operand (the address). Other instructions such as NOT have one operand, while arithmetic instructions usually have two operands and sometimes three.

- *Execute* is the stage in which the ALU executes the instruction using the operands that were brought by the CU.

- *Write back* is the stage in which the result of the instruction is written back to memory or into the destination register. Since the ALU cannot access its outer world (memory or devices), the CU is needed for this transfer.

Figure 3.5 outlines the four stages, and, as can be seen, the first two stages comprise the initiation phase, since they are performed by the CU; this phase is intended to prepare the instructions for execution. The second phase, which consists of the last two stages, is the execution since it contains the executions (performed by the ALU) and the storage of the result (performed by the CU).

Running a program is actually a continuous execution of the program's instructions one after the other. The processor never stops, and even if it does not have anything to do, it

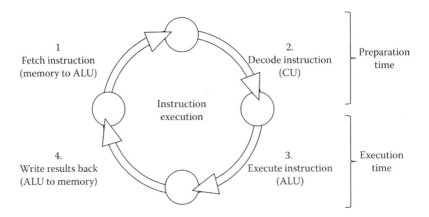

FIGURE 3.5   Stages in instruction execution.

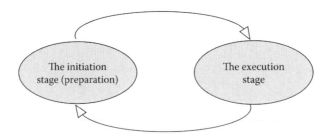

FIGURE 3.6   Phases in instruction execution.

runs an idle loop that also contains a list of instructions that do not carry out a meaningful task but are performed in an endless loop. For that reason, the execution of instructions is an endless process (as long as the system is up). This process moves between the two phases described previously, as represented in Figure 3.6.

Figure 3.7 elaborates on Figure 3.1, and it relates to a general architecture. It is a visual summary of this chapter, and it will be used in the following chapters of this book. Each chapter will address and elaborate on one specific component.

- The top left part represents the processor, which will be explained in Chapter 4, "Central Processing Unit."

- The bottom left part represents the memory, which will be explained in Chapter 5, "Memory."

- Between the memory and the processor (middle left) is the cache memory, which will be elaborated on in Chapter 6, "Cache Memory."

- The channels in the diagram are defined as lines with different widths. The channels are responsible for data transfer within the system. These transfers are performed using controllers, which are hardware and software devices designed to handle the various input–output components. These will be elaborated on in Chapter 7, "Bus."

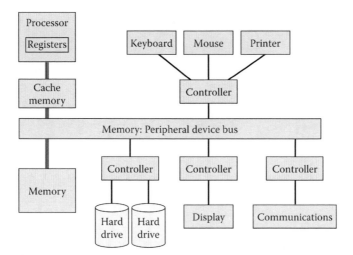

FIGURE 3.7   General hardware architecture.

- The most important input–output device is the magnetic disk, and this will be explained in Chapter 9, "Storage."

Key Takeaway

- *Computers' generation*: An old term that was used for classifying computers according to the hardware technology that was for their design. Modern terms relate to the specific role the computer plays in the organization rather than the hardware technology it uses, which, for the ordinary user, is irrelevant.

- *Computer systems*: Every computer system, regardless of its classification or type, has a common architecture that consists of a processor, memory, buses (or communication channels), and input–output (I/O) devices.

- *Harvard architecture*: An architecture that uses two separate memories, one for instructions and the other for data. This architecture can produce more predictable response times, so it is used in signal-processing and real-time systems.

- *Instruction execution*: There is a common set of activities that have to be performed as part of executing an instruction. The instruction has to be fetched from the memory. Then, it has to be decoded to realize the type of instruction as well as its operands. The third stage is execution, and in the fourth and last step, the result is stored back into its destination. Each of these steps can be further divided into additional substeps.

REFERENCES

1. PBS. (n.d.). ENIAC is built: 1945. Retrieved from http://www.pbs.org/wgbh/aso/databank/entries/dt45en.html.
2. Daintith, J. (2004). EDVAC. *A Dictionary of Computing*. Retrieved from http://www.encyclopedia.com/doc/1O11-EDVAC.html.
3. Michael, G. (n.d.). The Univac 1 computer. Retrieved from http://www.computer-history.info/Page4.dir/pages/Univac.dir/index.html.

CHAPTER 4

Central Processing Unit

PART I: CENTRAL PROCESSING UNIT

This chapter focuses on the various aspects of the processor (sometimes referred to as the central processing unit [CPU]). The processor is the core of the system, capable of executing the applications' instructions and performing the required tasks.

By relating to the general hardware architecture figure (Figure 4.1), we can see the exact location of the CPU.

The processor, through its electronic circuits, is capable of "understanding" and executing the instruction in the program. As already mentioned (see the section in Chapter 1 on the Von Neumann architecture and the processor) and due to implementing a modular approach, each processor is divided into additional components such as the control unit (CU), the arithmetic and logic unit (ALU), a special and dedicated internal fast memory, and so on.

- The CU is responsible for scheduling the instructions to be executed, by bringing each instruction from memory, decoding it to find out its operands, fetching these required operands, and then transferring it to the ALU for execution.

- The ALU executes the instruction using their operands.

- Registers are one kind of fast temporary memory, inside the processor. There are several types of registers: some are available for the developers, others are only available for the operating system, and a third type is used solely by the hardware itself (for additional elaboration see "Attributes of the First Computers" in Chapter 1). It should be noted that as part of software abstraction, accessing registers is available only by using the assembly language. Most high-level programming languages do not provide this capability and using the registers is left for the compiler only.

Registers

The idea of using registers was borne from the need to increase the speed of computers. Since even in the early days of computers, there was a need to overcome the architectural

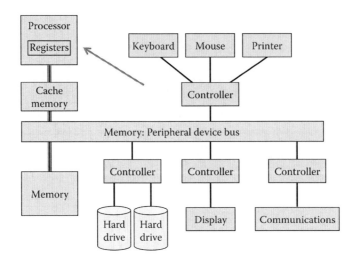

FIGURE 4.1 The CPU as part of the system.

built-in problem of the processor being significantly faster than the memory. For executing each instruction, the CU has to bring it and its operands from memory. This means that even the very fast processors will have to wait for the operands to be fetched from the relatively slow memory. Since most of the instructions use operands, the memory access became a significant limiting factor to speed. Over the years, various approaches were suggested to overcome this problem, such as *read ahead*, in which the CU reads the instruction that will be required in the near future (this will be elaborated as part of this chapter), or the introduction of cache memory (Chapter 6, "Cache Memory"), but the original and effective method was the implementation of registers.

A register is a very fast small memory that resides in the processor. By providing a very short access time to the information stored in the register, it speeds the execution of the program. In a sense, the registers resemble the human short-term memory. Like the short-term memory, registers have a fast access time, they are limited in space, and are used only for temporary data. Due to their speed, registers are considered as the top of the memory hierarchy (this term will be explained and elaborated in the next two chapters). Originally, the registers were developed in order to support the hardware operations; today's modern processors are using many registers as part of their normal operations. For example, every system should have an internal register (sometimes called program counter [PC]) that holds the address of the next instruction to be executed. When the CU has to fetch the next instruction for execution, it checks the PC to determine the address of that instruction. The PC can be seen as the queue number display often used by various service organizations. This register is maintained by the hardware and the software (applications or operating system) cannot modify it, although its content is changing according to the software behavior. For example, every loop in any application has a conditional branch* and

---

* A conditional branch instruction can be described as a switch. If a condition is met that execution will continue in a different location, which for the hardware means changing the content of the PC register. If the condition is false, execution continues to the following instruction and in this case, the PC will be increased so it points to the consecutive instruction.

holds the potential to indirectly change the content of the PC register. Furthermore, when executing the instructions, the ALU accesses only internal registers. This means that the CU that fetches the instruction's operands actually places the operands in these internal registers. After the ALU has finished the execution, the result is placed in another internal register and once again, the CU is responsible for copying its content to the required destination (as defined in the instruction).

For example, assuming the instruction to be executed is:

$$C = A + B$$

Regardless of the specific programming language, during compilation the instruction will be translated into a binary mnemonic that represents the ADD instruction. In this case A, B, and C are three variables and the intent of the instruction is to replace the content of variable C by the sum of A and B. The binary mnemonic will hold all relevant information needed for the execution, that is, the code for the ADD instruction, the address of the first operand (A), the address of the second operand (B), and the address of the result (C). The CU will fetch the instruction, decode it, and realize it is an ADD instruction. Since ADD has three parameters (or operands), it will fetch the first two and place them in the ALU internal registers. Only then will it signal to the ALU to perform the add operation. After the ALU finishes, the CU will copy the result that was stored in the internal output register of the ALU, to the third parameter defined in the instruction (the variable C).

As already mentioned, there are also registers designated to be used by the software. Due to their importance in enhancing performance, registers are widely used as part of computer architecture, and modern computers have large numbers of them. The idea of using registers did not emerge overnight; there were previously other technological solutions. The first computers worked without any registers, but were based on the idea of a stack.* The instructions assumed that the input operands as well as the result were put in the stack.

When the new computers that implemented registers started to emerge, the hardware instructions had to be changed in order to support and access this new type of temporary memory. The first implementation used just one register (sometimes referred to as the *accumulator* due to its usage in arithmetic instructions). Later, the usage increased with the addition of general registers as well as special purpose registers, such as data registers, address registers, and so on.

Stack-Based Architecture

The first computers, which were very simple (even primitive) compared with the current computers, were based on a stack architecture. This means that the instruction was just the mnemonic for the operation without any operands. This is the reason that sometimes this architecture is referred to as no-operand instructions' architecture. The convention

---

* Stack is a data type that acts as a container. It implements the LIFO (last-in first-out) mechanism which means that data elements are inserted and extracted only from the top of the stack. A stack can be demonstrated as a stack of books in which one can only add a book on top of the stack and extract a book that is on top of the stack. In this sense, the top of stack is the location where the next book will be placed or the location from where the next book will be extracted.

was that the operand (one or more) will be found at the top of the stack. This meant that the developer had to insert the data operands into the stack prior to initiating the instruction. In this case, the CU fetches the instruction, decodes it, and then decides the number of operands required. In the previous example, if the instruction is ADD, then there are two operands and the CU will use the two operands at the top of the stack. There are other cases in which only one operand is required, for example, an instruction such as

$$A = -A. \qquad \# \text{ Invert the sign of variable A}$$

In this case, the CU will use only one operand, the one that is in the top of the stack. When the ALU finishes executing the instruction, the CU will copy the result and insert it on top of the stack.

Going back to the previous example (C = A + B) and using stack-based architecture implies executing a sequence of instructions:

PUSH A	# Push variable A on TOS (Top Of Stack)
PUSH B	# Push variable B on TOS (A will be pushed further down)
ADD	# Add A + B; store result on TOS
POP C	# Move item at TOS to variable C

- The first instruction (PUSH A) inserts the first operand (A) on top of the stack. This operand (A), the other operand (B), and the result (C), are variables that reside in memory. By pushing the variable into the stack, all other elements in the stack are being pushed down, making space for the new element.

- The second instruction (PUSH B) inserts the second operand (B) on top of the stack. At this stage, the two entries at the top of the stack are the instruction's two operands.

- The third instruction (ADD) performs the addition. In stack-based architecture, the arithmetic instructions do not define their operands since the convention is that the operands are found in the stack (the two items on top of stack). In this case, the CU retrieves the two operands from the stack (by using an internal POP instruction). The ALU adds the two operands and then the CU enters the result into the stack by using an internal PUSH instruction.

- The fourth instruction (POP C) retrieves the top of stack that in this case contains the sum of the operands and stores it into the variable C.

Figures 4.2 through 4.6 provide a visual representation of the process.

Figure 4.2 depicts the initial state, prior to the execution of the first instruction. Elements are entered from above and each entered element pushes all existing stack items downward. In order to manage the stack, the hardware uses an internal register that points to the top of stack. This is the location of the last entered element. There are cases in which the top of the stack (TOS) register points to the next available location, which is

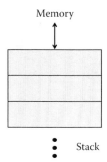

FIGURE 4.2   Stack architecture (initial state).

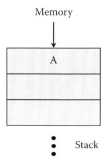

FIGURE 4.3   Stack architecture (after the first instruction).

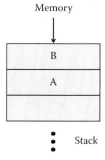

FIGURE 4.4   Stack architecture (after the second instruction).

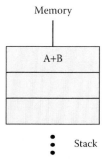

FIGURE 4.5   Stack architecture (after third instruction).

Memory

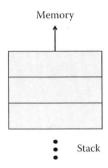

Stack

FIGURE 4.6   Stack architecture (after the fourth instructions).

one above the last entered item. In this example, we may assume the stack is still empty. At this stage, the first instruction is executed and it stores the variable on top of the empty stack.

Figure 4.3 depicts the stack after executing the first instruction. The first operand was moved from memory into the stack. At this stage, the second instruction is executed.

Figure 4.4 depicts the stack after the second instruction. The second operand was transferred from memory to the top of stack. At this stage, the stack contains the two operands, which will be used for the ADD instruction. These two operands are removed from the stack and moved into the internal registers. When the ADD instruction is completed, the result will be pushed into the stack (Figure 4.5).

As can be seen, the original operands are not in the stack anymore and all that is stored there is the result. There are two reasons for this behavior: (a) the CU can be simpler by using the standard POP circuitry, and (b) by removing the operands, the stack will not be flooded by unnecessary data. The last instruction in this set removes the result from the stack and copies it into the variable C. The arrow represents a data movement from the stack to memory, and the stack is empty once again (Figure 4.6).

The stack-based architecture was developed to support the Polish notation (sometimes called *prefix notation*) that was invented early in the twentieth century by Jan Lukasiewicz, a Polish philosopher. Polish notation defines logic or mathematical formulas in such a way that the operators are to the left of the operands. This is instead of the ordinary formulas in which the operators are between the operands.

For example, adding two numbers using the standard notation is written by:

$$A + B$$

By using Polish notation for the same formula, we will have to write:

$$+ A\ B$$

The Polish notation was very common in the early days of computing and it was even used by a family of programming languages (Lisp, for example); some of these are still available today. The Lisp programming language was among the first to define many important attributes related to computer science, such as recursion, trees (data structure), dynamic typing, and so on. The stack-based architecture was developed in order provide a simple infrastructure for supporting the Polish notation.

A mathematical formula that adds four numbers such as

$$R = A + B + C + D$$

when using Polish notation will change to

$$R = + + + D C B A$$

In addition, the stack-based architecture instruction will be

PUSH D	# Push variable D to TOS
PUSH C	# Push variable C to TOS
PUSH B	# Push variable B to TOS
PUSH A	# Push variable A to TOS
ADD	# Add the two items on TOS (A + B); store result on TOS
ADD	# Add the two items on TOS (A + B + C); store result on # TOS
ADD	# Add the two items on TOS (A + B + C + D); store result on # TOS
POP R	# Move TOS (A + B + C + D) into variable R

It can be seen that it is a straightforward translation. Although the stack-based architecture was replaced by other, more efficient architectures, it influenced the computer science discipline (e.g., by supporting software-based stacks and instructions to handle them).

Accumulator-Based Architecture

The next stage in the development of processors was intended to overcome inherent disadvantages and improve execution speed. As the processors speed increased, the differences between the processors' speed and the memories' speed increased as well. The stack, which was part of memory, imposed some speed limitations that had to be lifted. The solution was the implementation of a data register called the *accumulator*. As the accumulator was part of the processor, the access time was significantly shorter. All arithmetic operations in accumulator-based architecture were performed using the accumulator and the result was entered into the accumulator as well. The reason was that this way, the result could be ready as input for the next instruction. Contrary to the arithmetic instructions in the stack-based architecture that do not have any operands, in the accumulator architecture these instructions have one operand. The second operand is assumed to be in the accumulator. This implies that prior to executing an arithmetic instruction, one operand has to be in the accumulator. When writing assembly programs, it is the developer's responsibility to load the register with the operand. For higher-level programming languages, it is performed by the compiler. Since the result is stored in the accumulator, the previous content (one of the operands) is destroyed. Furthermore, the instruction's result has to be copied from the accumulator or it may be overwritten by the next instruction's operand or result. This is similar to the short-term memory behavior. The data stored in the short-term memory has to be transferred to the long-term memory (if it is important) otherwise it will be forgotten and overwritten by new data

Using the previous example (C = A + B) in an accumulator-based architecture requires a set of three instructions:

Load	A	# Load variable A into the accumulator
Add	B	# Add A + B; store result in the accumulator
Store	C	# Copy accumulator content to variable C

- The first instruction loads the accumulator. The content of the variable (A) is copied into the accumulator, overriding its previous content.

- The second instruction performs the add operation. Since in this architecture, always one operand is in the accumulator, we have only to provide the second operand, which in this case is the variable B. The ALU adds A to B and stores the result in the accumulator. As stated already, the result overrides the previous accumulator's content (the variable B). Now the content of the accumulator is A + B.

- The third and last instruction is used to copy the result from the accumulator to the variable C.

Figures 4.7 through 4.10 provide a visual representation of the process.

Figure 4.7 depicts the initial state. The rectangle represents the accumulator and the arrow represents the movement of data between the memory and the accumulator. It should be noted that the accumulator is never empty, but in this case, it may contain some previous data that is irrelevant to this set of instructions and for that reason is described as if it is empty.

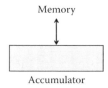

FIGURE 4.7 Accumulator architecture (initial state).

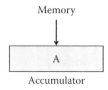

FIGURE 4.8 Accumulator architecture (after the first instruction).

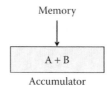

FIGURE 4.9   Accumulator architecture (after the second instruction).

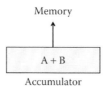

FIGURE 4.10   Accumulator architecture (after the last instruction).

Figure 4.8 depicts the situation after the execution of the first instruction (Load A). The first operand was copied from memory and now it resides in the accumulator as well.

Figure 4.9 depicts the situation after the execution of the second instruction (Add B). The CU fetched the second operand for the execution and then the ALU performed the addition. It used the operand that exists in the accumulator as the first operand. The result is stored back into the accumulator, overriding the content (variable A) that was there previously. The last instruction in this set is used to copy the result from the accumulator and save it in the required variable (C), as represented by Figure 4.10.

The accumulator-based architecture paved the way for more efficient and faster architectures; although it was invented decades ago, it is still used in small and cheap appliances. For example, many of the simple calculators adopted this architecture in which the display acts as the accumulator. Arithmetic operations done using a calculator supply only one operand and assume the other operand is in the display.

Memory–Register Architecture

The accumulator architecture was efficient for simple formulas with repeated similar arithmetic operations. For example the formula SUM = A + B + C + D could be translated into the following instructions:

Load	A	# Load variable A into the accumulator
Add	B	# Add A + B; store result in the accumulator
Add	C	# Add A + B + C; store result in the accumulator
Add	D	# Add A + B + C + D; store result in the accumulator
Store	SUM	# Copy accumulator content to variable SUM

Contrary to the previous set of instructions, where the result had to be copied from the accumulator and stored in memory, in this case the intermediate results can be used in the following instructions. In such an example, the accumulator proved very handy. Unfortunately, there are many cases in which the one accumulator becomes a limitation. For example, assuming the arithmetic formula: $NUM = A + B + C * D$

A straightforward translation of the formula into instructions may produce

Load	A	# Load A into the accumulator
Add	B	# Add A + B; store result in the accumulator
Add	C	# Add A + B + C; store result in the accumulator
Mult	D	# Multiply the result by C; store result in the accumulator
Store	NUM	# Copy accumulator content to variable NUM

Unfortunately, this is wrong! (Try figuring out why.)*

In this specific case, a smart compiler can fix the problem by temporarily saving the sum of A and B, or by changing the sequence of the instructions.

Temporarily saving:

Load	A	# Load variable A into the accumulator
Add	B	# Add A + B; store result in the accumulator
Store	Temp	# Copy accumulator content to variable Temp
Load	C	# Load variable C into the accumulator
Mult	D	# Multiply C * D; store result in the accumulator
Add	Temp	# Add Temp (A + B) + (C * D); store in the accumulator
Store	NUM	# Copy accumulator content to variable NUM

Changing the sequence:

Load	C	# Load variable C into the accumulator
Mult	D	# Multiply C * D; store result in the accumulator
Add	A	# Add A + (C * D); store result in the accumulator
Add	B	# Add A + B + (C * D); store result in the accumulator
Store	NUM	# Copy accumulator content to variable NUM

Changing the sequence of the instructions is preferable since it is more efficient (requires less instructions). However, there are cases in which changing the sequence is not possible. Assuming the arithmetic formula: $NUM = A * B - C * D$

In this case, the only possible solution will require saving temporary results during the calculation:

---

* The translation is wrong since the instructions will add all three operands (A, B, C) and then multiply the combined sum by D. That is, the execution of the instructions as written produces $NUM = (A + B + C) * D$.

Load	C	# Load variable C into the accumulator
Mult	D	# Multiply C * D; store result in the accumulator
Store	Temp	# Copy accumulator content to variable Temp
Load	A	# Load variable A into the accumulator
Mult	B	# Multiply A * B; store result in the accumulator
Sub	Temp	# Subtract Temp (A * B − C * D); store result in the #accumulator
Store	NUM	# Copy accumulator content to variable NUM

The extra two instructions that relate to the temp variable were due to the inherent limitation of this architecture that is based on only one register. In order to overcome this limitation, it was only natural to increase the number of registers. This change affected the arithmetic instructions as well. If in the accumulator-based architecture, the instruction had one operand (since the second one is always in the accumulator), when there are more registers, the instruction has to specify which register is to be used.

The memory–register architecture was just one small step forward since the arithmetic instructions were still using one operand in a register and the other in memory. As with the case of accumulator-based architecture, the result is stored in the register that was used as input. This means the content of this register is destroyed during the instruction's execution. As part of the technological advancement, the architecture designers had to define the number of registers and their names.

As in previous architectures, we will use a simple formula as an example:

$$C = A + B$$

The instructions required in this case include:

Load	R1, A	# Load variable A into R1 (register 1)
Add	R1, B	# Add A + B; store result in R1
Store	C, R1	# Copy the content of R1 into variable C

- The first instruction loads the operand A into a designated register. In this case, R1, which is the name of one of the registers, was used.

- The second instruction is the ADD that includes two operands. One operand resides in register R1 and the second is the variable B. After the add operation is done, the result will be stored into the input register.

- The third instruction copies the result (stored in R1) into the variable C.

Figures 4.11 through 4.14 provide a visual representation of the process.

Figure 4.11 depicts the initial stage, before the first instruction is executed. The figure is a schematic representation of a three-register system (although there might be many more additional registers). In addition, the figure contains the Adder, which is a component inside the ALU that is responsible for adding the numbers. In modern systems, the ALU is divided into separate units (components), where each one is responsible for a specific operation such

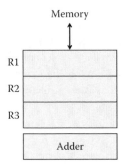

FIGURE 4.11 Memory–register architecture (initial stage).

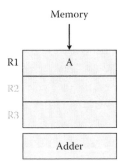

FIGURE 4.12 Memory–register architecture (after first instruction).

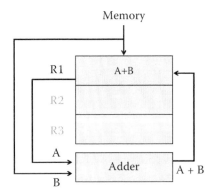

FIGURE 4.13 Memory–register architecture (after second instruction).

as adding, multiplying, shifting, and so on (this will be elaborated later in this chapter). In this case, for simplification reasons, only the Adder is included in the figure.

Figure 4.12 depicts the situation after completing the first instruction. The first operand (A) is copied into R1, while the content of the other registers is unchanged and irrelevant.

Figure 4.13 depicts the situation during and after the execution of the second instruction. The CU fetches the second operand (B) from memory and transfers it to the Adder. In parallel, the first operand (A) that is in R1 is transferred to the Adder. After both operands are available, the Adder performs the addition. The result is stored back into R1, overriding its original content.

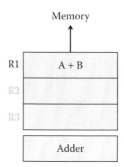

FIGURE 4.14   Memory–register architecture (after last instruction).

The last figure in this set depicts the situation after the last instruction. The result is copied from R1 into the variable. It should be noted that as in previous cases, the hardware uses a copy instruction, which means that the value remains in the register and a copy is stored into variable C.

Register–Register Architecture

The increase in the number of registers and the speed advantages they provide led to an additional architectural enhancement. The original idea behind implementing the accumulator and later the additional registers was to provide a fast temporary memory within the processor. The previous architectures (accumulator-based architecture and memory-register architecture) were using registers, but one operand was in memory, so the speed gains were limited. The next step in systems architecture design was utilizing only registers and not the memory for operands. In the register–register architecture, the arithmetic instructions' operands are located in registers minimizing the need to access memory. Such an instruction usually has three operands (registers). Two of the operands are the input registers and the third operand is the output register. This format of the instructions overcame the register–memory architecture's disadvantage that overrides the first operand. The register–register architecture does not store the result in the input register while overriding the previous value, and allows selecting a different destination register.

Relating to the simple formula as an example

$$C = A + B$$

The instructions required in this case include

Load R1, A	# Load variable A into R1
Load R2, B	# Load variable B into R2
Add R3, R2, R1	# Add R1 + R2; store the result in R3
Store C, R3	# Copy content of R3 into variable C

- The first instruction loads the operand A into a designated register. In this case, R1, which is the name of one of the registers, is used.

- The second instruction loads the second operand (B) into another designated register (R2).

- After the two operand registers are loaded, the third instruction is issued (the add operation). The instruction defines the two input registers as well as the output (or destination) register (R3). This means that the instruction will add the content of R1 to the content of R2 and store the sum in R3.

- The fourth instruction copies the result (stored in R3) into the variable C.

As with previous architectures, Figures 4.15 through 4.19 provide a visual representation of the process.

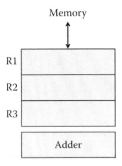

FIGURE 4.15   Register–register architecture (initial state).

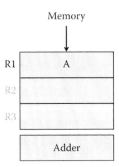

FIGURE 4.16   Register–register architecture (after first instruction).

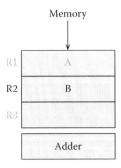

FIGURE 4.17   Register–register architecture (after second instruction).

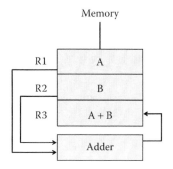

FIGURE 4.18   Register–register architecture (during third instruction execution).

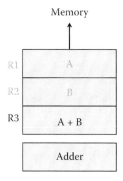

FIGURE 4.19   Register–register architecture (after fourth instruction).

Figure 4.15 depicts the initial situation. The figure schematically relates to only three registers although there might be many additional more registers. As with the previous example, the figure includes the Adder as well as the memory. In the initial stage, the registers contain no relevant information.

Figure 4.16 depicts the situation after the execution of the first instruction. The first operand (A) is transferred from memory and entered into R1.

Figure 4.17 depicts the situation after the second instruction that loads the second operand for the add operation

Figure 4.18 depicts the execution of the third instruction and the situation after it finished. The CU transfers the content of the two input registers (R1 and R2) into internal registers within the Adder and then issues the instruction. The Adder calculates the sum and then the CU copies it to the output register (R3). Briefly, this instruction demonstrates the benefits of the register–register architecture (minimizing memory access and using an output register in order to prevent overriding the input register). Retaining the value of the operand in the input registers may be handy in cases where a variable is used in several consecutive or close instructions. For example assuming the following formulas:

$$C = A * B$$

$$D = A + B$$

$$E = C - D$$

Using memory–register architecture, these formulas will be translated into

Load	R1, A	# Load variable A into R1
Mult	R1, B	# Multiply A * B store result in R1
Store	C, R1	# Copy content or R1 into variable C
Load	R1, A	# Load variable A into R1
Add	R1, B	# Add A + B store result in R1
Store	D, R1	# Copy content of R1 into variable D
Load	R1, C	# Load variable C into R1
Sub	R1, D	# Subtract C − D store result in R1
Store	E, R1	# Copy content of R1 into variable E

However, when using the register–register architecture the instruction needed will be

Load	R1, A	# Load variable A into R1
Load	R2, B	# Load variable B into R2
Mult	R3, R2, R1	# Multiply R1 * R2; store the result in R3
Add	R4, R2, R1	# Add R1 + R2; store the result in R4
Sub	R5, R3, R4	# Subtract R3 − R4; store the result in R5
Store	C, R3	# Copy content of R3 (A * B) into variable C
Store	D, R4	# Copy content of R4 (A + B) into variable D
Store	E, R5	# Copy content of R5 (A * B) − (A + B) into variable E

Figure 4.19 depicts the situation after the fourth instruction. The content of the output register was copied into the appropriate variable (C).

Architecture Summary

The architectures described in this chapter were developed over years, with each one intending to overcome existing limitations by providing new layers of understanding. Each new architecture required changes in the instructions formats.

Table 4.1 is a brief summary of the sequences of instructions to be executed for a specific formula (C = A + B). The sequences are defined in a chronological order.

- Stack-based architecture: The arithmetic instructions have no operands and the CU knows that the operands are the ones at the top of the stack. The instruction pops out the operands and inserts the result on top of the stack.

TABLE 4.1   Execution Sequences

Stack	Accumulator	Register–Memory	Register–Register
Push A	Load A	Load R1, A	Load R1, A
Push B	Add B	Add R1, B	Load R2, B
Add	Store C	Store C, R1	Add R3, R2, R1
Pop C			Store C, R3

- Accumulator-based architecture: The arithmetic instructions have one operand and the second one will be found in the accumulator. The result will be placed in the accumulator, overriding the previous value that was there.

- Memory–register architecture: This architecture utilizes more than one register. The arithmetic instructions have two operands. One will be in a register while the second operand resides in memory. The result will be placed in the input register and, as in previous case, it overrides the register's original value. It should be noted that there are variations in which the two operands may be placed in registers but even in these cases, the result will still be stored in the first register.

- Register–register architecture: This architecture usually has many registers. The arithmetic instructions have three operands and contrary to the previously described architectures, the result does not override one of the operands, unless explicitly requested by the programmer.

Since each one of the registers can be both the operand as well as the destination, an instruction such as

$$\text{ADD} \quad \text{R1, R1, R2}$$

is perfectly valid and it adds the content of R1 + R2 and stores the result in R1. In this case, the original content of R1 is destroyed. Furthermore, even the instruction:

$$\text{MULT} \quad \text{R2, R2, R2}$$

is valid.

The last two architectures (memory–register and register–register) are special enhancements to the general purpose register (GPR) architecture. It can be seen that the similarities between these two architectures are larger than the differences. Furthermore, the register–register architecture can be implemented in two ways. One implementation is the one described previously (see the section "Architecture Summary") and the second, simpler implementation that uses only two operands. The two operands are the registers to hold the inputs and the output that will be stored in the first register in the instruction. As with previous cases, it overrides the original content.

Most of the modern architectures developed during the last two decades are based on registers due to the speed enhancements gained.

Processor Paths

The processor contains several interconnected components (see Figure 3.1). The paths that connect all these components are used for transferring the required data before, during, and after execution of the instructions. These paths resemble a network of streets that are used for connecting places; however, instead of the cars, the computerized paths transfer data. Figure 4.20 provides a simplified example of the data communication required for

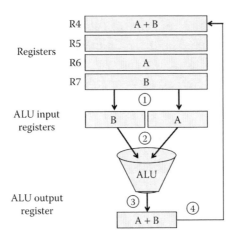

FIGURE 4.20 Processor's paths.

a simple ADD operation. This ADD instruction was described in the previous section as part of the register–register architecture. The upper part of the figure contains some of the general-purpose registers. Although the processor may have many such registers, the figure relates only to four of them. Prior to issuing the instruction, the operands have to be placed in the input registers. In this example the two operands, A and B, are in the appropriate registers (R6, R7). The instruction in this case was

ADD   R4, R6, R7

As part of preparing for the execution, the CU fetches the instruction, decodes it, and realizes it is using R6 and R7 as operands. The two operands are copied to internal registers inside the ALU and only then, provided the ALU has finished executing the previous instruction, is the ADD is initiated. After the ALU (which is drawn as a trapezoid cone), finishes execution, the output is stored in an internal register and from there transferred to the destination register (R4).

As already mentioned, the Von Neumann architecture separated the various computers' components and modern computers continue this trend of separation. The ALU is further divided into dedicated components (as will be further elaborated in this chapter). Each such component has its own internal registers. For that reason, the general-purpose registers that are also part of the processor are separated from the ALU itself, and the CU is responsible for the copy operations that are required. There are two types of registers presented in Figure 4.20. The general-purpose registers are located in the upper part, and the ALU internal registers, both for input and output, are located on the bottom part.

The figure relates to several types of paths:

- Paths that are intended for transferring the instruction's operands from the general-purpose registers to the ALU's internal registers (marked as 1 in the diagram). These paths are accessible only by the CU as part of the preparation for execution.

- Paths that are intended for transferring the content of the internal registers into the ALU itself (marked as 2 in the diagram). These paths are accessible only to the ALU and the transfers are performed as part of the instruction's execution.

- A path for transferring the output (the result) from the ALU into the ALU's internal register (marked as 3 in the diagram). This path is similar to the previously described path, only in this case the transfer is from the ALU into the internal register, while in the previous case it was from the internal registers into the ALU. As with the previous case, this path is only accessible by the ALU itself.

- A path for transferring the result from the ALU's internal output register to the general-purpose destination register (marked as 4 in the diagram). This type is similar to the aforementioned first type of paths; however, in this case the path is for the output, while the first type was for the input operands. This path is accessible only by the CU.

Instructions Execution

The computer system's capabilities are defined by the instructions the processor can perform. For that reason, as computers evolved, the instruction had to be changed to provide the additional capabilities required by software engineers. As previously described, the first computers used very simple instructions, for example with the stack-based architecture in which the instructions did not have any operands. However, as the technology advanced and more applications were developed, the requirements increased as well. Originally, these were very simple applications, but as time passed, the applications become more complex. End-user requirements for more functionality were driven by the demand for more sophisticated applications. In order to meet the shrinking deadlines imposed by the fluctuating market, developers sought more efficient and clever software tools to support the development process. At the bottom line, these requirements were translated into new, more robust hardware-supporting instructions with enhanced functionality. For that reason, the hardware manufacturers were constantly implementing new capabilities. Since inventing, designing, and implementing new instructions requires time and effort, most manufacturers have adopted the modular ideas represented by the von Neumann architecture. One aspect of modularity was implemented during the execution of the single instruction that was divided into several predefined steps (or building blocks):

- Fetching the instruction, which involves calculating the address in memory and bringing the appropriate bytes containing the instruction and its operands.

- Decoding the instruction to evaluate if it is a valid one; and if it is valid, figuring out how many operands it has.

- Copying the operands from their locations (memory and or general-purpose registers) into the internal ALU registers.

- Issuing the instruction to be executed, by signaling the ALU that all input data is available.

- Copying the result from the ALU internal register to the defined destination (memory or register).

For increasing the execution speeds, modern processors divide the execution into many more steps that allow for a higher degree of parallel execution (this will be discussed later in this chapter). However, splitting the instruction into these predefined stages provides an additional important capability. Each one of the stages can be considered as a building block resembling the Lego* construction games for children. By utilizing these existing building blocks, sometimes referred to as microinstructions, it is simpler to implement new instruction. This implementation actually provides the hardware engineers with capabilities similar to software development. The software engineer uses the hardware instructions as the building blocks for the application to be developed, and similarly the hardware engineer uses these microinstructions to form new instructions. Software engineers will probably find that this principle is similar to software development principles in which functions or methods are required to be very small and perform only one specific task. This is one of the better-known mechanisms for dealing with complexity, both in the development stage as well as during the later maintenance phase.

Performance

For a better understanding of the trends in processors' developments as well as the microinstructions technology, one has to briefly address the issue of performance. With the constantly increasing demands for new and more sophisticated applications, systems' engineers are continually looking for higher performance hardware. However, the meaning of performance it not accurately defined. As with many other technologies, when there are many implementations of the technology, there are also many definitions of the technology's performance. For example, when addressing cars, one type of performance defined is the total load the car can carry. Another type of performance may be driving speed, usually applicable for smaller family cars. Acceleration speed might also be applicable for special-purpose cars such as racing or sports cars. Of course, there might be additional metrics for measuring the cars' performance. The same problematic situation exists when trying to provide a common definition of computers' performance.

To better assess the performance issue, we have to define what is important for each type of user, since each type of user may have different needs. For example, a user working on the local personal computer that is connected to a remote server is interested in getting the best possible response time.† A computation center manager may define performance in a different way. Although the response time is important, however, the overall system throughput is important as well. The main reason being that, to justify the high costs associated with the center, the number of users using it has to be large in order to get a better price/performance ratio. With web-based applications and the hardware that

---

* Lego is a well-known company that manufactures plastic based interlocking bricks that are used by children to build their own worlds.
† Response time in this sense is the time that passed from entering the request and till the time the response was displayed on the screen.

supports them, the issue is even more complex. Slow response time in such a system, even for internal use, will result in more time wasted on waiting. Considering that in many service-oriented organizations, human resources represent a significant part of the budget, a slow responding system means lower productivity and a waste of expensive resources. Web systems that are intended for customers are even more problematic. In this case, it is not only the systems' response times, but the whole browsing experience, since the competitors' service or products are just several clicks away.

As with the car performance example, due to the various functionalities provided by the system, there is no agreed on definition of performance when it comes to computer systems. This is especially true with the many modern handheld devices (tablets, smartphones, etc.) that redefined performance to include user experience. This trend that was successfully marketed by Apple as an important differentiator and selling factor that revolutionized the term *systems' performance*. However, during the development of computing technology, especially given the high costs of computers, a method for comparing different systems was required. The methods manifested in several metrics that provided an agreed on basis for comparison. This resulted in several definitions:

- Millions of instructions per second (MIPS): This is a measurement based on the number of instructions a processor is capable of executing in one second. Although it is not accurate, it provides a rough comparison between different systems. It should be noted that instructions in this sense are machine instructions and not high-level programming language instructions. The high-level language instructions are translated by the compiler into machine language instructions. Usually one high-level instruction is translated into several machine-level instructions. From a software or systems-engineering point of view, MIPS metrics can be misleading, since it is not sure if the instruction executed during the test run can actually represent the mix of instructions used by the application.

- Millions of floating-point operations per second (MFLOPS): This is a measurement based only on the floating-point operations. This metric was developed in order to differentiate between the systems that are being used mainly for scientific purposes and thus need this type of instructions, and systems for general use, such as most of the management information systems (MIS).

- Megabytes per second (MB/sec): This measures data-transfer capabilities, such as the input and output devices or internal paths (buses). This, of course, is a special performance metric that is only indirectly involved with the speed of executing the application. The metric mainly measures the amounts of data that can be handled during one second. As will be discussed in the bus chapter, the longer the CU waits for the instruction or operands to be transferred from memory, due to a slower bus, the slower will be the execution. From a systems-engineering point of view, this is an accurate metric, since it is not important which type of data is transferred. The speed will be the same. Nevertheless, there is no direct correlation between the data transfer rates and the overall system's performance.

- Transactions per second (TPS): This measures the system's capability of handling transactions. This metric was developed in parallel to the development of online applications that support many concurrent users, such as banking transactions, shopping, reservations, and so on. For a reliable TPS measurement, the transactions have to be clearly defined (content and execution frequency). Contrary to the other three metrics, the TPS metric is a more holistic approach and for that reason, as far as systems' engineering is concerned, predications based on TPS are more reliable. The only thing to consider is the type of transactions performed, since query transactions are simpler and faster compared with transactions that update the database.

There are many additional metrics that were developed over the years, but even the small aforementioned sample is sufficient to understand the diversity and the many special needs. It should be noted that the metrics were developed by various vendors in an attempt to increase the probabilities of selling their systems. Not every customer had the abilities and possessed the expertise to measure the various systems' performances, so the metrics were aimed at helping in the decision-making process. If a specific vendor could demonstrate, for example, that its system had a higher TPS value, he or she had a better chance of selling it to interested customers.

Processor's Internal Clock

All the processor's activities are synchronized by an internal clock. This clock provides the monitoring capabilities required for executing the instructions and coordinating all components. For example, the CU has to be in synch with the ALU and provide all input before the ALU starts the execution. The clock frequency (or clock rate) defines the system's cycle time. These cycles are used to synchronize all processor's activities. The clock frequency and the cycle time have a similar meaning and one value is derived from the other since

$$\text{Cycles per Second} = \frac{1}{\text{Clock time}}$$

For example, if the cycle time of a specific system is one millionth of a second, this means that in this specific system the clock "beeps" one million times a second. These "beeps" define the clock frequency, or the cycles for second. The amount of time between two beeps is the clock cycle (Figure 4.21).

The clock frequency provides an accurate way of measuring the execution time of a specific application. This is done by counting the number of beeps during the execution. Using the previous example, if we divide the number of beeps by one million (number of beeps per second) we will get the time required for the application to run.

Figure 4.21 provides a visual explanation of the cycle time and the clock time. In early computers, an instruction required several cycles in order to execute. In modern computers, however, several instructions may be executed in a single cycle.

If we consider a processor that runs at a 1 GHz frequency, this means that the processor "beeps" one billion (10^9) times per second and the cycle time is one billionth of a

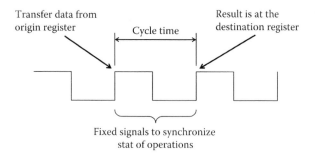

Transfer data from origin register

Cycle time

Result is at the destination register

Fixed signals to synchronize
stat of operations

FIGURE 4.21   Clock time.

second (10^{-9}). Due to the interchangeable nature of the number of beeps and time, it is possible to use the number of beeps for comparing the execution of two applications. It should be noted, however, that this measurement is applicable only to applications running on the same system. If the applications are executed on different systems, the number of beeps is insufficient for an accurate measurement. When the applications are executed on different systems, it is possible that each system has a different clock frequency. In such a case, considering only the number of cycles (number of beeps) is wrong. When assessing execution times, we cannot relate only to the number of cycles; we also have to multiply the number of beeps by the cycle time.

Since the clock frequency is a hardware attribute, it does not change between different applications' executions. So for measuring or comparing execution times of different applications that were run on the same system, the number of cycles (or the number of beeps) is sufficient, since in all these cases it is the same clock frequency .

This understanding can be easily proved mathematically. The processor time is defined by the number of seconds required to run the application. This time is calculated by the number of cycles required for running the application multiplied by the cycle time

$$\text{Processor time} = \text{Seconds per application} \left(\frac{\text{Seconds}}{\text{Application}} \right)$$

$$\frac{\text{Seconds}}{\text{Application}} = \frac{\text{Cycles}}{\text{Application}} * \frac{\text{Seconds}}{\text{Cycle}}$$

Table 4.2 is provided for better understanding the time names. The left side refers to the clock rate while the right side refers to the appropriate number of cycles.

"Iron Law" of Processor Performance

Although for various users, the term *performance* may have different meanings, the most common definition relates to the response time obtained by the system. However, this time includes the time required to perform the specific task (execute the program) as well as other time-consuming activities that might be needed, such as input, output, and

TABLE 4.2 Time Names

Name	Duration	Number of Cycles	Name
Millisecond	10^{-3} s	10^3	Kilo
Microsecond	10^{-6} s	10^6	Mega
Nanosecond	10^{-9} s	10^9	Giga
Picosecond	10^{-12} s	10^{12}	Terra

communication. In this section, we will concentrate only on the processor performance, that is, the amount of time required by the processor to perform a specific task (or program). In this case, we will define that

$$\text{Processor performance} = \text{time per program}$$

However, the time per task (or program) is calculated based on three parameters:

- The program size or the number of instructions executed in this specific run of the program

- Cycles per instruction (CPI): The average number of cycles required for executing one instruction

- Cycle time: The amount of time for each processor cycle

As such, the formula ("Iron Law") to calculate the processors performance is:

$$\frac{\text{Time}}{\text{Program}} = \left(\frac{\text{Instructions}}{\text{Program}} * \frac{\text{Cycles}}{\text{Instruction}} * \frac{\text{Time}}{\text{Cycle}} \right)$$

$$\text{Time} = \left(\text{Program size} * \text{CPI} * \text{Cycle time} \right)$$

The first value in the formula defines the size of the program, that is, the number of instruction to be executed. This value is driven from the program written by the developers, and cannot be changed by the hardware. In this sense, the hardware assumes that the number of instructions to be executed is a constant number. Of course, for a different input, the number of instructions executed may differ. If there is a need to decrease this number, for example, due to long execution times, the program will have to be analyzed and the time-consuming portion will have to be rewritten using a more efficient algorithm. Alternatively, using a more sophisticated compiler may produce a shorter code, in terms of number of instructions executed. The compiler that is responsible for converting the high-level programming language instructions to machine-level instructions may sometimes speed up the times, for example, by eliminating redundant pieces of code or a better registers usage.

The second value in the formula (CPI ratio) is an important enhancement factor that has changed over the years in order to increase execution speed. Reducing the number of cycles required for a single instruction has a direct effect on the processor's performance. During the 1980s, the average CPI was five; that is, for executing a single machine instruction, five cycles were required. Modern processors, on the other hand, have a CPI of less than one, which means the processor is capable of running several instructions in parallel during the same cycle.

The third value (cycle time) is another important enhancement factor addressed by many computer manufacturers. During the past three decades, the clock rate increase is over three orders of magnitude. In the last decade, however, the trend of reducing the cycle time was replaced by the trend of increasing the number of processors or cores. Combined with the software engineering trends of using threads,* the multiple execution units provide much better performance enhancements.

Following this brief explanation of performance, we can proceed to a more general discussion.

If processor X is said to be n times faster than processor Y, it means that the performance of X is n times the performance of Y. However, since performance and execution times are inversely proportional, the execution time on processor Y will be n times the execution time of processor X.

Unfortunately, there are some limitations to this simple extrapolation. If a specific program runs on processor X for 10 s and on processor Y for 20 s, will it be correct to assume that processor X is twice as fast compared with processor Y?

Without any hesitations, some of the students will probably answer "yes;" however, the answer is no! The information obtained from running a single program is not sufficient to determine the processor's performance. For example, if this test program does not use any floating-point instructions, it provides no information on the processor's floating-point performance. The correct answer is that when running this specific test program, processor X was twice as fast, but we cannot assess its speed regarding other programs.

The lack of a common standard and acceptable metrics for assessing a processor's performance led to the definition of a variety of methods. These methods that were invented by various manufacturers provided the means to present their systems in a better way.

For example, assuming we have two programs (1 and 2) and two systems (A and B) and the execution times as defined in Table 4.3.

The question is which system is faster?

---

* A thread is an important principle in modern computer science and a mandatory method in developing application and especially web based applications. Thread is a sequence of executing instructions as part of a program (or process). The threads share the same address space as the process they belong too. This sharing makes the communication between the process and its threads very simple and straight forward. The operating system scheduler can manage the thread independently although it is part of the process. As such if the process is divided into several threads, and the system has several execution units (processors or cores), several threads can run in parallel. A very simple example that demonstrates thread usage is for example a text editor, such as Microsoft's Word. While typing data in, there is one thread that is responsible for collecting the input characters. Another thread that runs in parallel is checking for spelling errors. A third thread is responsible for formatting and pagination and another is responsible for auto saving the file. All these threads are executed in parallel without any interference to the user. Another example relates to Microsoft's Excel. When the spread sheet is large and it contains many calculations, sometimes the spread sheet may use several threads for computing. If the system contains several execution units, these computations will be done in parallel.

TABLE 4.3   Execution Times

System	Time to Run Program 1	Time to Run Program 2
A	10	40
B	40	10

TABLE 4.4   Average Performance

System	Time to Run Program 1	Time to Run Program 2	Average Performance
A	10	40	$(10+40)/2=25$
B	40	10	$(40+10)/2=25$

TABLE 4.5   Average Ratio (to System B)

System	Program 1 Time Ratio (to System B)	Program 2 Time Ratio (to System B)	Average Ratio
A	0.25	4.0	$(0.25+4.0)/2=2.125$
B	1.0	1.0	$(1.0+1.0)/2=1.0$

There might be various different answers based on the ways to calculate the execution times. If we want to measure the average response time, then the answer will be that the performance is identical as demonstrated by Table 4.4.

However, the results can be deviated by calculating the average performance ratio. This was done by a vendor that used number tricks as a way to persuade that its system is faster.

Table 4.5 was prepared with the intention to convince the naïve, inexperienced user that system B is superior. In this case, there are only two programs, so it is quite obvious that this representation is misleading. However, when there are many programs, it might be more difficult to realize the error. Of course, using the same calculation but relative to system A will reveal that A is faster. The fact that the truth can be arithmetically manipulated in order to influence the inexperienced user requires an effort to define a measurement standard and agreed on metrics.

It should be noted, however, that at present most of the systems are based on personal computers, which are being used by a single user. These systems are relatively cheap, so there is no real need in the evaluations metrics. In the past, when there were many vendors that provided a variety of very expensive systems, the decisions were much more significant in terms of the performance to be achieved and the price to be paid. As with many other cases, even if the earlier metrics and methods are seldom used, if the need arises, they are readily available.

CYCLES PER INSTRUCTION-BASED METRIC

The processor architecture defines the number of cycles that are required for executing every instruction. Simple instructions will require a smaller number of cycles, while complex instructions, such as division, will require more cycles. Since the CPI is constant (per each instruction), it can be used as a more accurate metric in assessing the anticipated system's performance.

When using a CPI-based metric, we have to estimate the mix of instructions used in a specific program. This mix will include the types of instructions and their occurrences. By using such a mix, it is possible to calculate an average CPI. Contrary to the CPI that is a constant value for each instruction (the number of cycles that are required for executing it), the average CPI is a dynamic value that is directly derived from the instructions' mix. As such, the average CPI provides a more accurate assessment for the specific run. The total execution time can still be calculated by using the "Iron Law":

$$\text{Time} = \text{Average CPI} * \text{Number of Instructions} * \text{Cycle Time}$$

The advantage of using this metric is that it is accurate for the specific run and reflects the actual usage of the system. On the other hand, it is quite complicated to estimate the instructions' mix and if the estimate is not accurate it will hamper the results obtained.
Example:

- Assuming a program was run on two processors (A and B), using the same compiler.

- The cycle time of processor A is 1 ns (10^{-9} s). While running the program the average CPI obtained was 2.4.

- The cycle time of processor B is 1.5 ns and the CPI measured was 2.

Which processor is faster? And by how much?
In solving the question, we'll have to use the "Iron Law":

$$\frac{\text{Time}}{\text{Program}} = \left(\frac{\text{Instructions}}{\text{Program}} * \frac{\text{Cycles}}{\text{Instruction}} * \frac{\text{Time}}{\text{Cycle}} \right)$$

$$\text{Time} = \left(\text{Program size} * \text{CPI} * \text{Cycle time} \right)$$

In this specific case, the number of instructions that were executed is unknown, but since it is the same program and the same compiler, it is safe to assume that the number of instructions executed was roughly the same. We will mark the number of instructions by N and then

$$\text{Time}_A = N * 2.4 * 1 = 2.4N$$

$$\text{Time}_B = N * 2.0 * 1.5 = 3.0N$$

And then

$$\frac{\text{Time}_B}{\text{Time}_A} = \frac{3.0N}{2.4N} = 1.25$$

This means that the time required for running the program on processor B is larger than the time required for running the program on processor A by 25%. So for this specific program, processor A is faster by 25% compared with processor B.

The previous example is relevant for systems engineers in assessing relative processors' performance. However, the CPI metric can be used not only to compare the relative performance of different processors, but also to assess what hardware changes will be required for one processor to perform like the other processor. These required changes are mainly related to hardware engineers and are included here for completeness.

Consider the previous example: what should be the CPI on processor A so the performance of the two processors will be identical?

Once again, we will use the "Iron Law" and figure out the new CPI_A:

$$\frac{Time_A}{Time_B} = 1$$

$$\frac{Time_A}{Time_B} = \frac{(N*CPI_A*1)}{(N*2.0*1.5)}$$

$$CPI_A = 3.0$$

Therefore, if the average CPI on processor A will be 3.0, the performance of the two systems will be identical.

It should be noted that for identical performance, there are additional alternative possible changes. CPI_B can be altered as well as the cycle time of each of the two processors.

Therefore, if we want to change CPI_B instead of CPI_A, we will use the above formula, but change the unknown.

$$\frac{Time_A}{Time_B} = 1$$

$$\frac{Time_A}{Time_B} = \frac{(N*2.4*1)}{(N*CPI_B*1.5)}$$

$$CPI_B = 1.6$$

This means that in getting the same performance, we can change the CPI on processor B to 1.6.

Similarly, we can calculate the required changes to the cycle times and find out if identical performance can be obtained by changing the cycle time of processor A to 1.25,[*] or alternatively changing the cycle time of processor B to 1.2.[†]

---

[*] This is obtained by using the "Iron Law" with a different unknown.

$$Time_A/Time_B = 1$$

$$Time_A/Time_B = (N*2.4*Cycle_A)/(N*2.0*1.5)$$

$$Cycle_A = 1.25$$

[†] This value is obtained once again by using the "Iron Law" formula

$$Time_A/Time_B = 1$$

$$Time_A/Time_B = (N*2.4*1)/(N*2.0*Cycle_B)$$

$$Cycle_B = 1.2$$

Performance Estimation

As already mentioned, the variety of computer systems (servers, desktops, laptops, tablets, smartphones, various appliances, etc.), makes it extremely difficult to define a reliable and agreed on standard metric for measuring performance. Without such a standard, and especially when computer systems were extremely expensive, various vendors invented all kinds of metrics that could provide them some advantage. The main idea was to provide only part of the information, which delivered a slightly different picture (see the section "Cycles Per Instruction-Based Metric"). For example, during the late 1980s, the author was working on a benchmark* for a large customer. There were only two vendors that participated. The results were that vendor A was better, both in terms of performance and price/performance. Due to its importance and possible effects on future sales, the marketing people working for system B's vendor defined the benchmark's results in a very creative way.

> "In a recent benchmark, computer B's performance was rated in second place, while computer A's performance was one before last"

This true example demonstrates that although the statement was 100% true, it was very misleading.

Currently, due to the significant decrease in computer prices, benchmarks are not run anymore, but the vendors still use various creative descriptions to try to differentiate their solution. This is evident with smartphones, which provide a wide range of functionality besides being a phone. This functionality is used as a selling gimmick, since in most cases the majority of users really do not need, for example, a super high-resolution camera.

In trying to provide some standard, various metrics were suggested (MIPS, MFLOPS, etc.); see the section "Processor's Internal Clock." However, even these metrics had severe disadvantages that could have been exploited by the vendors. For example, a 100 MIPS computer is capable of executing 100 million instructions per second. Unfortunately, the MIPS metric does not define which instructions are measured. Theoretically, therefore, it is possible to choose the fastest instruction, even though this makes no sense. For example, assuming a specific system's fastest instruction is NOP (No Operation),† then it can be used for calculating the systems speed even though it is a nonpractical example that provides no information on the real system's performance.

These "standard" metrics may be used to indicate the peak performance of the system. Unfortunately, peak performance is an imaginary figure that the processor will never surpass. As such, peak performance provides no valid information regarding the performance of real life programs since the difference between peak performance and real performance

---

* Benchmark is a process in which a customer gets access to a computer system for assessing its performance. During the 1980's due to the very high costs of computers this was a common practice. The customer will get to the vendor's benchmark lab and run various typical programs and/or simulations. Usually it was done using several vendors' labs so the best decision can be made.

† NOP is an instruction that does nothing. It is sometimes used by the compiler for various timing issues that are related to the hardware architecture

cannot be predicted. Peak performance, however, can be useful when comparing the same program on two processors that share a similar architecture, such as Intel core i7* processors. If, for the case of comparison, the program uses the same compiler, the binary execution file will be identical, which means that there will be the same number of instructions. In such a case, when the peak performances of the two systems are known, then the difference between the peak performance figures and the actual performance measured on one system can provide a better indication of the performance of the second system (by using the simple rule of three).

For example, assuming the peak performance for system A is 50 MIPS, and for system B is 60 MIPS. A specific program was run on system A and achieved 40 MIPS. If system A and system B have the same hardware architecture, we can assume that the anticipated performance on system B will be 48 MIPS.

The problematic situation regarding the assessment of systems performance provides numerous opportunities for companies to offer new, unbiased services. However, before proceeding, some definitions are required.

- Elapsed time: This is the amount of time that is required to run the program. This time includes the processor time as well as any other time needed, such as reading the information from the hard drive, accessing memory, and so on. If we need to assess the amount of time needed by the processor, we cannot use the elapsed time since is includes additional irrelevant components. The elapsed time is sometimes referred to as Wall Clock Time since it relates to the total time from the start of the program to its finish. From a systems-engineering perspective, the elapsed time is the time from pressing the Enter key and up to the results being displayed on the screen.

- CPU (or processor) time: This is the amount of the time the processor worked on the program. This is not the response time, since it does not include other time-related components. Some operating systems, such as Windows, do not report the amount of CPU time consumed by the program. Other operating systems that provide the CPU time, such as UNIX and Linux, sometimes differentiate between User CPU time, which is the amount of time the processor worked on the specific program, and System CPU time, which is the amount of time the processor worked on operating system's functions connected to the program. The sum of the User CPU time and the System CPU time provides the program's CPU time.

The expensive, earlier systems required a thorough investigation into their anticipated performance before the proper decision could be made. In some cases, the computer department personnel did not possess the required qualifications for such tests and simulations. In other cases, the costs associated with such benchmarks were significant. This led to the development of various benchmark programs that provided a standard model for assessing and evaluation of systems performance. This was provided as a service at a fraction of the

---

* Intel Core is a brand name used by Intel Corporation for several microprocessors implemented in various computers.

cost associated with real benchmarks. The service provided information about a variety of systems, including detailed comparisons with publicly available formulas, contrary to the arithmetic manipulations of some of the vendors.

Benchmark Programs

Benchmark programs for assessing performance (system as well as processor) evolved over the years. Each generation was trying to overcome previous limitations and provide additional functionality based on the gathered experience. The main idea was to develop a set of tools that will provide the required information applicable to wide range of computing departments. An important aspect of developing such a set of programs is the validity and relevancy the results. For example, a program that uses mainly integer calculations cannot be relevant to sites that usually perform floating-point calculations. Furthermore, a useful set of benchmark programs should provide additional flexibility, for example, a parameter that will define the proportion of integer and floating-point calculations. There are cases, however, when even this flexibility is not sufficient, since the site cannot define its own mix. For example, an interactive site that supports end users with constantly changing programs.

The first generation of test programs were real life simple toy benchmarks that included tens of instructions.

Some of these simple programs were:

- Hanoi Towers: This is a small game that uses three towers and some disks. All disks are of different size. The game starts when all disks are on one tower arranged by size where the biggest is at the bottom. The player has to move the stack of disks to a different tower; however, only the top disk can be moved, and the rule is that no disk can be placed on top of a smaller disk. The game, which is sometimes used as an exercise in the study of computer science recursion, was invented by Edouard Lucas, a French mathematician toward the end of the nineteenth century.

- Sieve of Eratosthenes: This is an algorithm for finding prime numbers. Eratosthenes, who lived around 200 B.C., invented several algorithms (estimating the circumference of the earth, the distance to the sun and moon, etc.). His algorithm for finding prime numbers is based on writing down all numbers in a predefined range and crossing out all multiplications of the prime numbers. For example, assuming one wants to find all prime numbers below n (for simplicity, we will choose n = 20 in this example).

The first step will be to write down the whole range:

1 2 3 4 5 6 7 8 9 10 11 12 13 14 15 16 17 18 19 20

Then the first step is crossing out the one, which is not a prime number.

1̶ 2 3 4 5 6 7 8 9 10 11 12 13 14 15 16 17 18 19 20

The next step is to define 2 as a prime and cross out all its multiples:

~~1~~ 2 3 ~~4~~ 5 ~~6~~ 7 ~~8~~ 9 ~~10~~ 11 ~~12~~ 13 ~~14~~ 15 ~~16~~ 17 ~~18~~ 19 ~~20~~

Then the next available number (3) is defined as a prime number and all its multiples are crossed out:

~~1~~ 2 3 ~~4~~ 5 ~~6~~ 7 ~~8~~ ~~9~~ ~~10~~ 11 ~~12~~ 13 ~~14~~ ~~15~~ ~~16~~ 17 ~~18~~ 19 ~~20~~

This process repeats until the next available number is larger than the square of n (20 in this case) and all numbers that remain uncrossed are primes: 2, 3, 5, 7, 11, 13, 17, and 19.

- A third type of benchmark programs consists of various sorts of algorithms, and so on.

All these aforementioned benchmark programs were real life programs, and therefore easily available. It was easy to run them on a variety of platforms and obtain the required measurements. Unfortunately, the results were relevant only for computer centers, which run a mix similar to the toy benchmark. For example, the results obtained by the Hanoi Towers benchmark were relevant for a mix that makes heavy usage of recursion and stack.

Due to these inherent limitations, it was clear that in order to provide better and more valid information regarding the systems' performance, more robust benchmark test programs were required. The next generation of benchmark programs grew out of the limitations of the toy benchmarks and involved mainly synthetic programs that were developed solely for the measurement process. The advantage of such synthetic programs is the fact that they can be modified as needed, so various aspects of the processor performance can be assessed. This possibility is not available with real life existing programs. Over the years, many such benchmark programs were developed, but we will relate only to two of them:

- Whetstone benchmark: This program was developed in 1970s in the United Kingdom by Harold Curnow. The program was originally written using ALGOL* and was used to measure the performance of a computer system developed in the United Kingdom in those days. Later versions of the program were translated into a variety of other programming languages. The results of the program were measured in kilo whetstone instructions per second (KWIPS) that provided some standard way of comparing the performance of different systems. Most calculations were performed using floating-point arithmetic.

- Dhrystone benchmark: This was another synthetic program, which was developed during the 1980s by Reinhold P. Weicker. Unlike Whetstone, which mainly measured floating-point arithmetic performance, Dhrystone put more emphasis on

---

* ALGOL (ALGOrithmic Language) is a set of programming languages that were developed in the early days of computers (1950s). The importance of ALGOL is mainly in the foundations it laid for other more modern languages such as Pascal, PL/I and C.

integer arithmetic, procedure calls, pointers calculations, and so on. The program was translated into C and became very popular among UNIX users. Its popularity stems from the many UNIX-based workstations that flooded the computer industry during the 1990s. The result obtained is the number of Dhrystone loops per second. Another standard that derived from using Dhrystone was Dhrystone MIPS (DMIPS). This was achieved by dividing the number of Dhrystone loops by 1757. The VAX computer, which was designed by Digital Equipment Corporation (DEC), was considered a 1 MIPS computer and when running the Dhrystone benchmark it obtained 1757 Dhrystone loops.

In parallel to the development of the synthetic benchmark programs, there was a trend of using real life larger programs that could be indicative to a site's workload. The main idea was to provide a benchmark mainly for systems engineers. The benchmark will resemble the users' activities instead of spending time and money on developing synthetic programs that are difficult to compare. Although the synthetic programs measure various aspects of the system, it is unclear how much of these aspects are relevant to the actual work. One such program was SPICE, which is a circuit simulation program.

A significant development in attempts to standardize performance measurement was when the Standard Performance Evaluations Corporation (SPEC) was formed. This nonprofit organization develops, maintains, and strengthens the usage of standard measurement tools. The organization, which still exists, provided several generations of benchmarking tools following the technological developments in the computing industry. The idea was to provide the programs to any vendor. The vendor ran the benchmark and sent back the results. The SPEC organization maintained the list that is available for the public.

- The first generation (1989) of SPEC's based benchmarking programs contained ten programs that produced a metric called SPECmark. The main problem associated with this benchmark is due to the usage of ten different programs. Some programs used mainly integer arithmetic and others used mainly floating-point arithmetic, but there was no way to weigh the two types.

- The second generation (1992) was designed to overcome the limitations of the first generation's programs by defining two different metrics for integer and floating-point calculations. There were 6 programs that used integer arithmetic that produced the SPECInt92 metric and 14 programs that used floating-point arithmetic and produced the SPECFp92 metric. To ensure consistency between various systems, vendors were allowed to use any flags the compiler supported, but not to change the programs' source code.

- The third generation (1995) included additional modifications and enhancements. All the benchmark programs were rewritten. Due to the importance of the SPEC standards and the wide popularity it gained, many purchasing decisions were directly linked to the marks obtained. As a result, some vendors have modified their compilers and added various flags for recognizing the benchmark programs and produce better (faster) results. Unfortunately, although these were real results, they provide no real indication of the performance to be achieved on site. In this generation, there were the two types of metrics—SPECInt95 was calculated by using eight integer benchmark programs and SPECFp95 was calculated by 10 floating-point benchmark programs. All the programs have to be run using the similar compiler settings. The benchmark programs continued to evolve and new versions were released in 2000 (CPU2000) and in 2006 (CPU2006).

- The following generations focused on special and unique aspects of computing. Mainly due to the rapid changes in the computing industry and the diversity of the computing environments. As of 2014, SPEC provides tens of benchmark results relating to CPU performance, graphics and workstation performance, handheld, high-performance computing, client/server, mail servers, and so on.

In parallel to the establishment of SPEC, which originally aimed to define a standard metric for processor performance, another organization was formed with the aim to measure the overall system performance. The Transaction Processing Performance Council (TPC) is another nonprofit organization that focuses on defining and disseminating performance data regarding transaction processing and database performance. The main difference between the two organizations is that while SPEC started by measuring the hardware performance, TPC was looking at the business transactions. This may be considered a more holistic approach, since the measurements relate to the processor performance as well as reading and writing the hard drive, database performance, and the transfer of information. The TPC benchmark programs reflect the maturity processes in the computing industry and the understanding that although the processor performance is important, other possible bottlenecks also need to be addressed to achieve optimal performance. As with SPEC, these benchmark programs evolved over the years:

- TPC-A was the original program that was introduced during 1989. It was intended for measuring system performance in a simple online transaction processing (OLTP) environment. It was discontinued in 1995.

- TPC-B was developed in 1990 and was intended for measuring the systems performance in terms of transactions per second. It was a stress test since it simulated the maximum load the system can support. It too was discontinued in 1995.

- TPC-C was developed in 1992, continued to evolve, and is in still in use today. The program simulates a complex OLTP environment that uses a variety of databases and many types of queries. TPC-C is used to simulate a real life environment.

- Other benchmarks: Over the years, TPC published additional benchmarks such as TPC-D that was aimed at decision-support systems, which usually are based on more complex transactions and use complex data structures. This benchmark was discontinued in 1999. TPC-R was intended for report generation environments and it was discontinued in 2005. TPC-W was intended for an Internet-based e-commerce environment and it was discontinued in 2005.

As of 2014, TPC maintains a list of benchmarks (in addition to TPC-C) for decision-support environments (TPC-DS), a new OLTP benchmark (TPC-E), and others.

It should be noted that in parallel to the establishment of TPC, SPEC understood that there is a need for real measurements that reflect the users' observed performance and not only the processor's relative performance. For that reason, SPEC offers a wide range of benchmark programs that are designed to measure various system configurations.

Calculating and Presenting the Results Obtained

Usually, when performing a specific benchmark, the programs are run several times in order to eliminate some external and unrelated noise, such as delays in the communication networks or some operating system's processes, and so on. Furthermore, many benchmarks consist of a variety of programs, each one runs for a different duration of time. Therefore, after receiving several and sometimes different times, the question is how to form a single average, coherent, and especially useful result.

Usually there are three main simple ways for calculating this average:

- Arithmetic mean that is defined by the formula

$$AM = \left(\frac{\sum Time_i}{n} \right)$$

where $Time_i$ is the various times obtained and n in the number of runs or programs.

The problem associated with this type of calculation appears if the set of timing results obtained contains a large variance. In such a case, the longer times tend to affect the average and produce misleading results. For example, assuming most programs run in an organization are small ones, but once a month there is a long process. If an appropriate mix will be built, one cannot ignore the long run and it has to be represented in the mix. However, including a program with very different attributes may produce wrong results.

For example, assuming the mix contains 99 programs, each one runs one second and one program that runs 1000 s. The simple average that represents the small programs is one second however when calculating the combined average (including the long run), it changes to 10.99 s $(1000 + 99 * 1) / 100 = 10.99$

The result obtained is misleading because it does not provide meaningful information. This is an artificial number that does represent neither the short runs nor the long run.

- Weighted arithmetic mean that is defined by the formula

$$WAM = \frac{\left(\sum Weight_i * Time_i \right)}{\sum Weight_i}$$

This formula provides a mechanism for correcting the distortion associated with the arithmetic mean by providing a weight of each result obtained. Using the previous example, if the weight of each short run will be 1 and the weight of the long run will be 0.01, then the weighted average will be 1 s. This is a true estimate for the time that represents the short runs. On the other hand, if the weight of the long run will be set to 0.1 the average calculated will be 2 s, which again is distorting reality. As can be seen from this example the weighted arithmetic mean holds the potential to provide the right result, however it depends on selecting the correct weight values. This process is not simple even when trying to assess the relative importance or frequency of the programs. In many cases, these weights depend on the system itself and cannot be easily changed for a different system. It becomes significantly more complex when the same set of weight values has to be used in evaluating different computer system. In such a case, the weighted average mean may prove to be less objective and therefore unreliable.

- Geometric mean that is defined by the nth root of the product of the results (multiplying all the n timing results and then calculating the nth root). This mean is useful when there is a large variance between the results; however, it does not provide a useful estimate of the correct average. In the previous example, using a geometric mean produced the result of 1.07, which is far better than the result obtained by the arithmetic mean calculations. The variance in this case is 9980.* However, if we choose a set of 100 runs, whose time increments by a constant—for example if the times are defined by {1, 2, 3, 4, 5 . . . 100}—then the arithmetic mean will be 51 and the geometric mean will be 37. The variance in his case is 842.

The bottom line is that defining a proper benchmarking capability is quite complex. Not only do the programs have to reflect the real life mix used by the site, there is also a problem in interpreting the obtained results, since each of the averaging methods described has some inherent limitations.

Key Takeaway

- *Registers*: Are small memory buffers inside the processor that are used for storing data. Compared with the memory, the registers are much faster and smaller.

- *Stack-based architecture*: A computer system that uses instructions without operands. The operands are stored in the stack. Design based on the Polish notation.

---

* The variance was calculated using the Excel VAR function.

For adding two numbers, for example, the numbers have to be pushed into the stack and only then the ADD instruction is issued. The results will be on top of the stack.

- *Accumulator-based architecture*: An architecture that uses one register called accumulator. Resembles the common calculator. For adding two numbers, for example, one number is stored in the accumulator and the second number is part of the ADD instruction. The result will be stored in the accumulator.

- *Memory–register based architecture*: An architecture in which there are several registers. However, the instructions use just one register and other operands, if they exist, are in memory.

- *Register–register architecture*: Architecture with several registers; the instructions are performed on operands that reside in registers.

- *Processor's paths*: Relates to the data communication links that exist inside the processor. The paths are responsible for transferring the data between the various processor's internal components, for example, transferring the content of the input register into the ALU where the ADD instruction is performed.

- *Instruction execution*: Involves several steps (this is an elaboration to the explanation in Chapter 3, "Hardware Architecture"):

  - Fetching the instruction, which involves calculating the address in memory and bringing the appropriate bytes containing the instruction and its operands.

  - Decoding the instruction for evaluating if it is a valid one and if it is valid, figuring out how many operands it has.

  - Copying the operands from their locations (memory and or general-purpose registers) into the internal ALU registers.

  - Issuing the instruction to be executed, by signaling the ALU that all input data is available.

  - Copying the result from the ALU internal register to the defined destination (memory or register).

- *System performance*: Refers to a set of measurements, benchmarks, and tools that were developed over the years for assessing systems' performance, such as:

  - Millions of instructions per second (MIPS): Measures the number of instruction the processor executes per second.

  - Millions of floating-point operations per second (MFLOPS): Measures the number of floating-point instruction the processor executes per second.

  - Megabytes per second (MB/sec): Measures data-transfer capabilities, such as the input and output devices or internal paths (buses).

- Transactions per second (TPS). Measures the system's capability of handling transactions.

- *The processor's internal clock*: A clock inside the processor that synchronizes all instruction executions.

- *The "Iron Law" of processor performance*: Defines that the time required to run a program is a product of the number of instruction to be executed, the cycles required per instruction and the cycle time.

- *Cycles per instruction* (CPI): Measures how many cycles are required to execute one instruction. Since different instructions may require different number of cycles, CPI is usually an average number, or is provided per a specific instruction. CPI is one of the performance indicators. While two or three decades ago executing an instruction required several cycles, modern system can execute (on average) several instructions per cycle.

- *CPI-based metric*: A performance metric intended to estimate the execution time based on CPI. In order to use a CPI-based metric, we will have to estimate the mix of instructions used in a specific program. Each instruction has its CPI and the total execution time will be given in cycles.

- *Benchmark programs*: Refers to a large set of existing as well as artificial programs that were used for assessing the processors performance.

PART II: CENTRAL PROCESSING UNIT

Amdahl's Law

Gene Myron Amdahl, who was one of the architects of the mainframe computers including the famous IBM System 360, defined a phenomenon that over the years became a cornerstone in processors' performance evaluation. However, it can be applied to other disciplines as well, such as systems engineering at large.

Amdahl's law states that the performance enhancements to be gained by some component is limited by the percentage of time the component is being used. This law is commonly used in situations where we have to estimate the performance improvements to be achieved by adding additional processors to the system, or in the modern systems using several cores. However, the law is not confined only to computers and it is possible to use it in other, noncomputer-related settings as well.

The formula that represents the law is:

Assuming:

F_E is the fraction of time the enhancement (or improvement) can be used

P_E is the performance gained by the enhancement

then the new execution time expected is given by:

$$\text{Execution Time}_{new} = \text{Execution Time}_{old} * \left((1 - F_E) + \frac{F_E}{P_E} \right)$$

Using this formula, is it fairly simple to extract the speedup

$$\text{Speedup} = \frac{\text{Execution Time}_{old}}{\text{Execution Tine}_{new}}$$

$$= \frac{1}{\left((1 - F_E) + F_E / P_E \right)}$$

For example, assuming a program consists of two parts, the first part is executed for 70% of the time and the second part runs during 30% of the time. In an effort to reduce the execution time, the second part was rewritten and now it executes five times faster. What is the overall time for the programs after introducing this change?

By using Amdahl's law, we will define

$$F_E = 30\%$$

$$P_E = 5$$

And then

$$\text{Speedup} = \frac{1}{\left((1 - 0.3) + \frac{0.3}{5} \right)}$$

$$= 1.32$$

This means that the overall improvement will be 32%, although the improvement for the second part was five times.

The law is useful not only for software estimates. For example, it can also be applied when there is a need to increase the speed of a computer system. One group of engineers that designed the ALU proposes a change that will yield 10% speed increase. Another group that designed the memory access proposes a change that will increase the access speed by a factor of eight. It is known that the ALU accounts for 93% of the execution time and memory access accounts for 7%. Assuming only one of these modifications can be implemented, which one has the greater impact?

Once again, we will use Amdahl's law twice: first, we will use it for calculating the ALU improvement contribution, and then we will use it to calculate the memory improvement contribution.

ALU contribution:

$$F_E = 93\%$$

$$P_E = 110\%$$

Using the formula will produce an improvement of 9.2%
Memory contribution

$$F_E = 7\%$$

$$P_E = 8$$

Using the formula once again will produce an improvement of 6.5%.

This means that the ALU modification is the more effective and this is the one that will be chosen. Furthermore, using the formula on various theoretical improvements reveals that due to its limited usage (7%) the memory improvement will never be more efficient than the ALU improvement. This can be seen in Figure 4.22 that depicts various theoretical and probably unrealistic improvements, but even with an improvement of seven orders of magnitude, the overall speedup is less than 7.6%.

One of the most useful usages of the law, related to systems engineers is in regard to the anticipated performance increase that can be gained from using multiple core processors. Figure 4.23 depicts a hypothetical task that runs 140 s on a single core. The task consists of three parts. The first and third parts that run 20 s each are sequential by nature and cannot be parallelized. The second part that runs for 100 s can be parallelized, so it may benefit from rewriting it using threads and running them on several cores. When running the task on one processor and one core, it runs for a total of 140 s

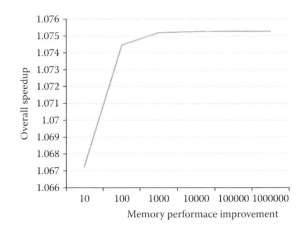

FIGURE 4.22 Memory performance improvement.

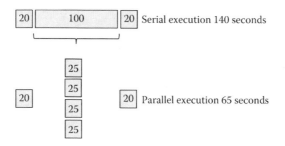

20 | 100 | 20 | Serial execution 140 seconds

20 | 25 / 25 / 25 / 25 | 20 | Parallel execution 65 seconds

FIGURE 4.23   Amdahl's law visualized.

(20 + 100 + 20). Assuming it runs on four cores, the speedup gained can be calculated using Amdahl's law:

$$F_E = \frac{100}{140}$$

$$P_E = 4$$

$$\text{Speedup} = 1/((1-100/140)+100/140/4) = 2.15$$

This means that the gain is 115% and the total time will be reduced to 65 s. Figure 4.23, demonstrates this visually.

The upper part is related to the run on a single core and the lower part is the run on four cores. As can be seen, the first and third part were not influenced by the additional cores; however, the second part ran in parallel so the overall time used by this part is just 25 s. The total time required for completing the task is 65 s (20 + 25 + 20).

According to the definition of Amdahl's law, the gains are limited by the percentage of using the improvement. In this example, even if theoretically it will be possible to use an indefinite number of cores, the overall time will never be less than 40 s—the time required by the two serial parts.

The law can be used for decisions regarding performance improvement of user code as well. Assume there is a program that consists of a total of 150 lines of code; 120 lines are being run for 80% of the time and the remaining 30 lines are executed during 20% of the time. To reduce the time, it is possible to improve the first part so it will run 50% faster or it is possible to improve the second part so it will run 100 times faster. Assuming it is possible to implement only one change, which is the most effective?

As in previous cases, we will have to use Amdahl's law for each one of the cases.

Improving part one:

$$F_E = 80\%$$

$$P_E = 1.5$$

$$\text{Speedup} = 1.364 \left(\text{or } 36.4\%\right)$$

Improving part two:

$$F_E = 20$$

$$P_E = 100$$

$$\text{Speedup} = 1.247 \left(\text{or } 24.7\%\right)$$

This means that the most effective route is by implementing the change proposed for the first part.

Amdahl's law is not confined only to computer (hardware and software) related performance assessment and it can be used in other environments as well, for example, a transatlantic flight. In the past, there were two alternatives to flying from London to New York. Using a standard (subsonic) airliner that flies for 7 h or using a supersonic airliner (the Concorde) that flies for 3.5 h. There was a significant difference in the fares, which sometimes may have been justified. However, one has to take into account that the flight time is halved, the total trip is not. Usually, such a trip includes additional time required for security checks and check-in as well as waiting for the luggage after landing. If we assume that besides the flight time an additional 4 h are needed, then we can use Amdahl's law for calculating the supersonic contribution in the trip overall time reduction.

$$FE = 63.6\% \left(\text{the flight is just 7 hours of the total 11 hours trip}\right)$$

$$PE = 2$$

$$\text{Speedup} = 46.7\%$$

This means that although the flight's time is halved, the overall trip time was reduced from 11 h to 7.5 h. It should be noted that in this simple example, it is possible to get to the result without using the formula. The 4 h of nonflying time remain unchanged while the 7 h of flying became 3.5. The total trip time is 7.5 (4 + 3.5).

Processors' Types

Although the abstraction used in processors' design that aims to reduce costs while maintaining capabilities, the financial resources still required for designing a new generation of processors are enormous. This means that surviving in this highly competitive market is not easy and manufacturers had to look for ways to sell as many processors as possible in order to get a return on their investments. This is one of the main reasons that many of the old mainframe companies disappeared and the ones that still exist use off-the-shelf processors.

For a better understanding these trends, we must follow the technological developments since the 1990s. During the first years of that decade, there was an increase in the number of newly emerging computing companies. Many designed and sold UNIX-based workstations that were based on processors designed using a "new" technology called reduced instructions set computer (RISC; which will be discussed in the two next sections). The innovation introduced by RISC is mainly the capability to design and develop alternative processors that are fast but simple, and relatively cheap to design.

Although there were tens of such companies during the 1990s, each one trying to concentrate on some other specific part of the market, the dominant players were:

- IBM, which designed and manufactured the PowerPC* that currently is part of the Power architecture, but originally was intended to run UNIX-based systems. The chip was designed in collaboration between Apple, IBM, and Motorola. It was used in systems designed and manufactured by the three companies. Unfortunately, the main personal computing market was dominated by Intel processors and the new chip did not succeed in obtaining a significant share. Nevertheless, the Apple Macintosh system used the chip until 2006 (when Apple switched to Intel's processors). Currently the chip is implemented mainly in various high-performance embedded appliances.

- Digital Equipment Corporation (known as DEC or Digital) was a successful computer company that introduced the concept of minicomputers. DEC was acquired by Compaq (a large producer of personal computers: IBM PC compatible systems) in 1998. Prior to that acquisition, DEC designed and developed a fast 64-bit chip called Alpha. It was mainly used by DEC systems and there were no significant collaborations with other computer systems manufacturers. This meant that the high-design costs could not be shared with other manufacturers, which may have contributed to DEC's financial problems. Compaq itself was acquired by HP in 2002, which still maintains the brand name mainly for the low-end systems. Prior to that, due to Compaq's being an Intel customer, the Alpha technology and the intellectual property rights were sold to Intel, which marked the end of the technology.

- MIPS Computer Systems was a company that designed a family of processors' chips that were intended both for commercial systems as well as for various embedded devices. The company's processors were used by SGI (Silicon Graphics, Inc.) a company that manufactured high-performance 3D-graphics computing solutions. As a result, in 1992 SGI acquired MIPS. Unfortunately, several years later, SGI decided to switch to Intel processors as the engine for their systems and MIPS was spun out. In 2013, it was acquired by Imagination a UK company that offers embedded processors.

---

* The PowerPC was an acronym for Performance Optimization With Enhanced RISC—Performance Computing.

- Sun Microsystems, Inc. was another successful company that paved the computing industry. Sun Microsystems was a significant player in producing some of the currently heavily used technologies such as UNIX, the Java programming concept,* the Network File System (NFS),† Virtualization,‡ and so on. Despite its successful contribution, Sun Microsystems was acquired by Oracle Corporation to provide a high-end integrated (hardware/software) system optimized for large enterprises as well as cloud-based systems.

- Intel is a semiconductor company that invented the x86 family of microprocessors (see Table 1.2), which is the heart of most of the 32-bit personal computers worldwide. The fast technological development in the personal computing industry and Intel's presence in hardware part-influenced its dramatic success. Although there were several competitors, such as AMD, during the 1990s, Intel established itself as the leading supplier of processors.

- Hewlett-Packard (HP) is a computer systems and peripherals manufacturer founded in 1939. Although the company had its own line of processors, it decided to team-up with Intel for a new line of processors (Itanium).

In the very early stages, the hardware design and manufacturing companies understood that strategic cooperation with other manufacturers is a must for achieving large volume sales. The revenues from these sales could produce the high costs associated with the technological developments. This is the reason that most of the 1990s chip manufacturers entered into partnerships and strategic cooperation.

- IBM's PowerPC was used by RS/6000§, and integrated into Motorola's systems and computing devices. It is also used by IBM in many of its controllers and was used by Apple until 2006.

- The MIPS chip was used by Silicon Graphics as well as several gaming console manufacturers.

- Intel and other manufacturers of the personal computer processors enjoyed the high demand of these systems, which provided their streams of revenue.

---

* Java is a class based, object oriented programming language that was developed by James Gosling of Sun Microsystems. However, Java through its compilation process is more than a programming language. After compilation a bytecode is produced and this bytecode can be executed on any system that has a JVM (Java Virtual Machine). This means that every embedded device that have an available JVM can execute the Java application. This idea opened a vast array of possibilities to develop applications for any appliance, as is currently happening with various smart phones.

† NFS is a distributed file system that was originally developed by Sun Microsystems. The main idea is to support seamless access to distributed files. Any user, assuming can access files that reside on other interconnected systems. The access is done over the standard network provided the user has the appropriate rights.

‡ Virtualization is the capability to create virtual system. It is possible to split a physical system into several virtual systems or to define a virtual system that is built from several physical systems.

§ IBM's line of UNIX based workstations and servers.

- Only DEC did not succeed in its efforts to attract strategic partners that could provide the necessary funds required for future enhancements. This could have been an alarming sign to the company's ability to continue and strive. So in 1998, Compaq computers, which was mainly a personal computer manufacturer, acquired DEC. The main value was not the Alpha chip, but DEC's worldwide marketing, distribution, and support organization. Unfortunately, the combined Compaq-DEC company did not survive and in 2002 it was acquired by HP.

This brief historic overview of processors developed over the last two decades is important mainly because of the lessons that can be learned. In a fast-paced technological advancements, even large and successful companies have to constantly develop new solutions. These new developments require significant funds and the only way to return the investment is by increasing the market share and through strategic partnerships and cooperation. Currently, with even faster technological developments, a market that is constantly changing, and the introduction of more standards in the industry, these cooperations become even more necessary.

During the 1990s, there were two technologies used for designing processors:

- Most mainframes as well as the personal computers used a technology called CISC (Complex Instructions Set Computer) that was relatively slow and expensive. The personal computers' processors however were cheap due to their manufacturing volumes.

- The emerging (at that time) UNIX-based workstations used the RISC technology, which was significantly faster, even compared with the large mainframes. The technology, although simpler, was still expensive due to the relative small numbers of workstations, compared with PCs.

By the end of the 1990s, Intel as well as other PC processor manufacturers started implementing the RISC technology, which reduced its price and provided a performance boost to personal computers.

The processors' map during the second decade of the twenty-first century is of course different due to the changes in the computing industry. The number of the various handheld appliances (smartphones, tablets, gadgets, etc.) sold each year surpasses the number of personal computers and these new appliances have different processing requirements. This led to new companies that offer new types of processors better aimed for the new market requirements. For example, new processors characterized by lower energy consumption and less heat dispersion.

The next two sections elaborate on the two technologies in explaining the RISC contribution to the computing industry performance enhancements.

CISC Technology

The CISC technology was the dominant technology during the first stages of computing. The implementation of microinstructions (see the section "Performance" in this chapter) provided an easy way of defining and implementing additional new instructions. Some of these instructions were quite complicated. The convention at that time was that such complex instructions will make it easier for the compiler when translating the high-level programming instructions to the machine-level instructions. As it was clear that as time passes, applications will become more and more complex and the developers will need more robust instructions, the microinstruction concept proved useful. For that reason, many manufacturers were implementing complex and sometimes unnecessary instructions, based on the assumption that it will help the developers and the compiler. As a matter of fact, these complex instructions provided a better support for high-level programming languages. Due to the relative simplicity in defining new instructions, the CISC-based computers had hundreds of different machine instructions and many addressing modes. These addressing modes that define the way the instructions address memory are one of the main contributors to the instruction's complexity. Table 4.6 provides a partial list of some of the addressing modes that were used by CISC-based computers.

The meaning of these addressing modes is as follows:

- Register: The instructions using this addressing mode are using only registers. In this example, the instruction adds the contents of registers R5 and R3 and the result is stored in R5. This is an example of a register–register-based architecture (see the section "Architecture Summary").

- Immediate: This addressing mode is used for instructions that use a register and an immediate value that is stored in the instruction itself. In this case, the constant 3 is added to the value in R2 and the sum is placed back into R2. It is important to notice that instructions that contain immediate values require more space (in terms of bytes in memory). In this specific case the value 3 is small enough to fit even in 4 bits (half a byte), but the developer can use large immediate values that may require more bits. This means that these instructions will have to use variable lengths or alternatively use a predefined length that may limit the values used. For example, if one byte is dedicated to holding the immediate value, it will limit the possible values to be used in such an instruction to 1024 values $[-511 < \times < 512]$.

TABLE 4.6   Addressing Modes Example

Addressing Mode	Example	Meaning
Register	Add R5, R3	$R5 <= R5 + R3$
Immediate	Add R2, 3	$R2 <= R2 + 3$
Displacement	Add R3,100(R1)	$R3 <= R3 + Mem[100 + R1]$
Register Indirect	Add R2, (R1)	$R2 <= R2 + Mem[R1]$
Indexed/Based	Add R3, (R1 + R2)	$R3 <= R3 + Mem[R1 + R2]$
Direct or Absolute	Add R3, (1001)	$R1 <= R3 + Mem[1001]$
Memory Indirect	Add R1, @R4	$R1 <= R1 + Mem[Mem[R4]]$
Auto-increment	Add R3, (R2)+	$R3 <= R3 + Mem[R2]; R2 <= R2 + d$
Auto-decrement	Add R1, −(R2)	$R2 <= R2 − d; R1 <= R1 + Mem[R2]$
Scaled	Add R1, 100 (R2)[R3]	$R1 <= R1 + Mem[100 + R2 + R3 * d]$

- Displacement: Although instructions are performed between registers, in this addressing mode the register can be in parentheses, and this means the register acts as a pointer (the value in that register is the address in memory). Furthermore, the instruction includes a displacement to be added to the address in the register. In this example, the content of R1 is increased by 100 (the displacement) and the new value obtained is the address in memory. The content of this address is then added to the content in R3 and the sum is stored back in R3. Like with the previous addressing mode, the displacement increases the length of the instruction.

- Register indirect: This is a simpler version of the previous addressing mode. In this case, the second register is used as a pointer, without the ability to add a displacement. The content of R1 points to a specific memory location. The content of this memory location is then added to the content of R2 and the result is placed in R2. Due to the missing displacement in this addressing mode, this is a shorter instruction compared with the previous one.

- Indexed based: Instructions that are executed using registers, some of which are used as pointers. A register that is put in parentheses is considered to be a pointer. This addressing mode is similar to the previous one with a small addition. The pointer can be calculated as the sum of the content of two registers. In the example, the content of R1 is added to the content of R2 and the sum represents an address in memory. The content of this memory cell is added to the content of R3 and the sum is stored in R3. This addressing mode extends the previous addressing mode by providing a mechanism for handling tables and two-dimensional arrays. One register holds the address of a specific row in the table while the second register holds the address of the field (the displacement in the row).

- Direct or absolute: This addressing mode supports instructions that are performed between registers or registers and memory locations. In the example, the instructions add the contents of cell 1001 to the content in R3 and the sum is stored in R3. Similar to previous cases where the instruction contains a constant value, the length of the instruction will have to be longer. This is an example of the memory–register-based architecture (see the section "Memory–Register Architecture").

- Memory indirect: In this addressing mode, the instructions are executed using operands that are in registers and in memory. In the example, the instruction adds the content of a memory location whose address is in R4 and the content of R1. As with previous cases, the sum is stored in R1.

- Auto increment: This addressing mode is an extension to previous defined addressing modes. One operand is in memory in the location pointed by R2. The second operand is in R1. The instruction adds the two numbers and the sum is stored in R1. In addition, the instruction automatically increments the value in R2, so it will point to the next value. This is very useful for a loop since it eliminates the need to manually increment the pointer. This is an example of an instruction and the appropriate addressing mode that were designed to support higher-level programming languages' instructions.

- Auto decrement: This is an instruction that is very similar to the previous one with a minor difference. The auto increment increases the value of the register (moving the pointer forward), while the auto decrement decreases the value (moving the pointer backward).

- Scaled: This is a more complex addressing mode. It is used to add the content of a register to the content of a memory location. In this case, the memory location is determined by the content in R3 multiplied by a constant plus the value in R2 and the displacement 100. The intention of this addressing mode is to support more complex data structures and, as with previous cases, in terms of memory usage, the instruction will have to be longer.

Implementing the CISC technology provided a better path from the high-level programming languages' instructions to the machine instructions and provided the means for designing simpler compilers. These complex instructions offered a more compact code and as a result, the amount of memory needed for the program was reduced. This was a significant benefit when memory prices were very high. As memory costs reduced sharply, this was no advantage at all. On the other hand, CISC produces some serious problems, both in terms of costs and in preventing the required fast technological advancement.

As already noted, the processor contains two major parts. The ALU that is responsible for executing the instruction and the CU that is responsible for control and scheduling. The CU fetches the instruction from memory, decodes it, brings the necessary operands and only then sends it for execution to the ALU. With CISC, the CU has to know all the instructions and the various addressing modes as well as knowing the amount of time needed to execute each instruction, since the next instruction cannot be initiated before the previous instruction is finished. Although CISC provided some advantages at the time, the complex nature of the instructions and their addressing modes led to the CU itself becoming very complex. Most of the processors' logic was in the CU and each new instruction implemented added new layers of complexity. Even the instructions' lengths, in terms of memory usage, caused some degree of complexity. An instruction that uses registers as operands can be very short (2–3 bytes only), while instructions that contain an immediate operand (that is stored as part of the instruction) need to be longer. Furthermore, some instructions, such as the Scaled instruction, contain two immediate operands so by definition will have to be even longer. This means that the CU has to figure out the number of bytes each instruction needs. It starts reading the instruction, decodes it, and only after the decode stage is finished, the CU knows the instruction's format and how many bytes it requires. The same process repeats itself with preparing the required operands. Sometimes the operands were in registers, and in such cases, the fetch is simple and straightforward. However, in some other times, the operands were in memory and the CU had to calculate their locations. This contradicted the original idea that the ALU is responsible for the calculations and the CU controls the operations, since the CU had to have simple calculations capabilities as well. It turns out that most of the CISC processors' logic and complexity was in the CU. This complexity manifested itself in higher costs that were associated with design of new processors, which slowed down the technological developments. These problems triggered the development of a new computing technology—RISC.

RISC Technology

RISC technology has been discussed for a long time and some of the 1960s mainframes used it in a partial way. However, it only flourished during the 1990s. The trigger for using this "new" technology was mainly due to the problems associated with CISC and the understanding that the CISC complex instructions were seldom used. Furthermore, due to the overhead incurred by these complex instructions, it was not clear if they are really faster compared with a loop of simpler instructions.

The RISC technology is based on several principles:

- There is a limited number of instructions (several tens)

- The instructions are simple

- All instructions are of the same length (bytes in memory)

- The execution times of all instructions are identical

- There are many registers to minimize the relatively slower memory access

- There are only a few minimal addressing modes

- The compilers have to be more sophisticated for performing code optimizations and using the registers in a clever way

The idea that pushed the RISC technology forward was that software provides a much faster development path. Although hardware designers have borrowed principles used by software engineers, such as modular design and simplicity, it is usually faster to handle some of these issues with software. When it was clear that the CU became complex and it slowed down the technological development, it was time for a change. New developments in software engineering enabled simplifying the architecture, especially the CU, and enhancing the compiler's flexibility and sophistications. Implementing RISC technology produces more instructions per program compiled. This means that the program will require more memory. However, the design of the processors is simpler and cheaper, especially regarding the CU. The uniform execution times provide a mechanism for executing the instruction in a pipeline (as will be explained later). The pipeline concept is an important performance booster, which provides the possibility to execute one instruction every cycle. Unfortunately, due to objective reasons, there is a gap between the planned principles and their implementation. For example, it is impossible to have similar execution times when some instructions are very simple like IF or integer ADD and others are more complicated like DIVIDE. These problems were

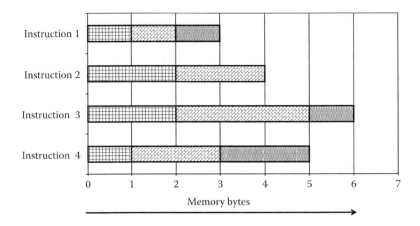

FIGURE 4.24   CISC instructions' lengths.

overcome by splitting the longer executing instructions into several segments to achieve the same result.

Figure 4.24 is a schematic visual representation of the CISC instruction lengths. The first part is the Opcode (Operation Code, which is a binary code that represents the instruction). In the schematic figure, the Opcode of the first instruction is one byte while for the second and third instructions it is two bytes. The next field or fields are the instructions' operands. In the first instructions, both operands occupy one byte each. In the second instruction, there is just one operand that requires two bytes. In the third instruction, there are two operands, the first needs three bytes and the second just one byte. This is an example and there are of course other situations in which an instruction will have three and even four operands, such as with the Scaled instructions. Nevertheless, even this example demonstrates the problems associated with the CISC technology's complex instructions, which directly influence the complexity of the CU.

Figure 4.25 depicts the schematic RISC technology principles. There are four different instructions in which the Opcode is always one byte and each instruction has two operands each one occupies two bytes.

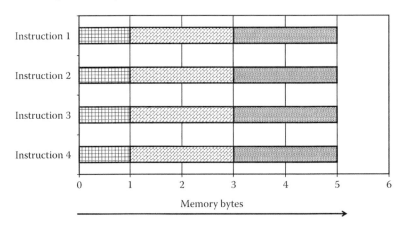

FIGURE 4.25   RISC instructions' lengths.

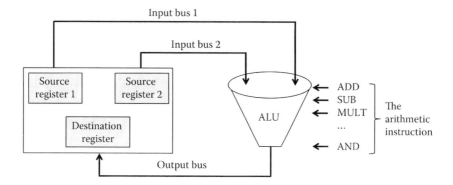

FIGURE 4.26   Micro instruction execution.

As already stated (see the section "Performance"), machine instructions are built from standard execution components (microinstructions). Integrating these microinstructions provides the means for implementing new capabilities and new instructions. These building blocks are being used in RISC technology as well.

Figure 4.26 depicts the processor with its two main components. The left side represents part of the ALU, which among other things contains three (or more) registers to hold the operands as well as the result. Before executing the instruction, the CU copies the operands from their location (register, or memory) to these internal registers. The ALU gets the operands by using special input buses and then gets the specific operation to be performed. After the instruction completes, the result is stored in the special destination register (using an output bus) and it is the CU's responsibility to copy the result to its destinations as defined by the instruction.

Various implementations of RISC may use different microinstructions (or execution stages), but usually as part of the execution there should be:

- Calculating of the address of the next instruction to be executed

- Fetching the instruction from memory

- Decoding the instruction to determine if it is valid, has operands, and how many

- Calculating the addresses of the operands

- Fetching the operands

- Executing the instruction

- Calculating the result's address

- Copying the result from the internal register to the destination register or memory location

Various processors may augment some of these stages and others may divide some stages into substages, however these stages (or microinstructions) are an important building block in the instruction-level parallelism (ILP; this will be explained in this chapter).

CISC versus RISC

In order to compare CISC and RISC and highlight the advantages and disadvantages of each, we will check the execution of a specific instruction and how it is performed by each technology. The von Neumann architecture, which defined the foundations for the modern computers, distinguished between the CPU that executes the instructions and the memory that holds the data and the instructions. For accessing the data stored in memory, each location has an address. The ALU executes the instruction only after the operands were stored in internal registers, so the ALU does not have to access memory—this is done by the CU. Assuming we have to multiply two numbers, one that is in address 1058* and the other that is in address 2076. The result will be stored in address 2076.

The CISC technology was designed to minimize the number of instructions, and as a result the program as a whole will required less memory, the main reason being the (then) high costs of memory (tens of thousands of dollars for 32 KB). This means that the hardware was designed in a way that would support complex instructions. In this simple example, the compiler will use the MULT instruction that will first load the ALU internal registers with the two operands and after the multiplication is finished, the result that resides in another internal register will be stored in the proper location in memory (2076 in this example).

The format of the instruction in this case will be:

$$\text{MULT} \quad 2076, \quad 1058$$

This is an additional architecture that was not discussed earlier and can be classified as memory–memory based architecture.

The fact that the instruction is working with memory resident operands (since the CU copies the operands from memory to the internal registers), means it is a direct translation to a similar instruction available in high-level programming languages. If, for example, the variable in location 1058 is called A and the variable in location 2076 is called B, then the previously described instruction is the equivalence of the instruction:

$$B = B * A$$

This instruction is available in most of the higher-level programming languages. The compiler in this case did not have to be too sophisticated and just replaced the high-level instruction (B = B * A) by its machine-level instruction (MULT 2076, 1058).

As such, the advantages of using the CISC technology can be summarized by:

- The compiler does not have to be too clever in translating the program code into machine-level instructions.

- The complex instructions are better suited for the program code so the whole implementation requires less memory cells.

---

* The addresses in memory, like any other value is expressed as a binary number, or for large number it is expressed as a hexadecimal number. However, for clarity reason, this example uses decimal numbers.

The RISC technology on the other hand uses simple instructions with the aim to execute each one in one cycle. Therefore, the complex MULT instruction that was implemented using one CISC machine instruction will have to be split into several instructions:

- Load the first operand into a register

- Load the second operand into another register

- Multiply the contents of the two registers

- Store the result back into memory

So for translating the instruction (B = B * A) the compiler (or the developer that is using assembly or machine-level instructions) will have to use four instructions (in this example R1, R2 represent registers):

LOAD	R1, 2076	# Load cell 2076 unto Register R1
LOAD	R2, 1058	# Load cell 1058 into Register R2
MULT	R1, R2	# Multiply R1 * R2; store result in R1
STORE	2076, R1	# Move result to cell 2076

The first impression is that the RISC implementation is wasteful regarding memory needs, since it requires four instructions compared with the single instruction used in the CISC implementation. In addition, due to the difference between the RISC machine language instructions and the higher-level instructions, the compiler will have to do more work during compilation. However, the RISC implementation has some other significant advantages. The similar execution times of most of the instructions provide the possibility to create a pipeline. Such a pipeline holds a potential of increasing the execution speed by utilizing ILP (Instruction Level Parallelism will be explained in the following section). For that reason, as far as execution times are concerned it is possible that the four RISC instructions will require almost the same amount of time as the single CISC instruction. However, since the RISC implementation is much simpler it reduces the resources and time required for the design of new processors' generations. Furthermore, the simpler CU implies that less transistors to be implemented on the chip, which provides the space for additional registers, even without the technological minimization.

Actually, splitting the LOAD and STORE operations from the execution itself simplifies the processor's work as well. In the first implementations of the CISC technology, the CU had to load the internal registers for each instruction, even if due to the previous instruction the value is in one of the registers already. This means an additional unnecessary memory access. In the RISC implementation, the values are in registers and they stay there until deliberately replaced by another value.

For example, assuming A, B, C are three variables that reside in memory in addresses 1058, 2076, 2086, respectively, and the two high-level instructions to be performed are

$$B = B * A$$

$$C = C * A$$

When implementing the CISC technology, the CU will have to load the content of A (address 1058) as part of the second instruction, although it was loaded already as part of the first instruction while implementing these two instructions with RISC-based machine instructions includes

LOAD	R1, 1058	# Load cell 1058 into R1
LOAD	R2, 2076	# Load cell 2076 into R2
MULT	R2, R1	# Multiply R2 * R1; store result in R2
STORE	2076, R2	# Copy result to cell 2076
LOAD	R2, 2086	# Load cell 2086 into R2
MULT	R2, R1	# Multiply R2 * R1; store result in R2
STORE	2086, R2	# Copy result to cell 2086

It can be seen that the value in register R1 (the variable A) remained unchanged and there was no need to load it once again.

Relating to the "Iron Law" (see the section "CPI-Based Metric"), the CISC technology tries to minimize the number of machine-level instructions ignoring the number of cycles required for each instruction. The RISC implementation on the other hand tries to improve the CPI, ignoring the increase in the number of instructions.

Despite the inherent advantages in the RISC technology, it took quite some time before it was widely implemented in commercial systems. One of the reasons was the lack of software suited for the technology. Significant performance gains were achieved by sophisticated compilers that optimize the code to the architecture. Using a nonfitted compiler will not provide the anticipated benefits.

Instruction-Level Parallelism

One of the important principles of the RISC technology is the fixed duration execution instructions, because this feature enables parallelism on the single instruction level. The parallelism is made possible by using a pipeline mechanism that splits the single instruction into its microinstructions and executing these in parallel.

As already stated, each instruction when executed is split into several distinct stages as described by Figure 4.27.

- Compute the instruction's address. This is necessary when the instruction occupies a different number of bytes or when the previous instruction was a branch.

- IF: Instruction fetch which brings the instruction from memory into the CPU.

- ID: Instruction Decode including determining the instruction's operands.

- Compute operand addresses. After the instruction was decoded, it is possible it addresses some memory resident variables. This stage calculates the addresses of these operands.

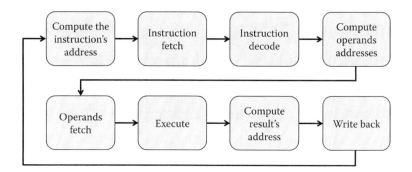

FIGURE 4.27   Instruction execution steps.

- Operands fetch which brings the operands from memory or registers.

- Execute the instruction.

- Compute the results address.

- Write back to store the result into its destination.

Then, it starts all over again for the next instruction.

To simplify the issue and to better explain the principle of pipelining, we will assume a pipeline with four stages. Therefore, in this specific case each instruction is split into:

- IF: Instruction Fetch, which brings the instruction from memory into the CPU.

- ID: Instruction Decode, including fetching all the instruction's operands.

- EX: Execute.

- WB: Write Back to store the result into its destination.

In the standard (serial or nonpipelined) execution mode, assuming each such microinstruction executes in one cycle, it will take four cycles to complete each instruction (as seen on Figure 4.28). There are five instructions, each one divided into the four abovementioned stages. The first instruction will be executed during four cycles; when it finishes, the next instruction will start. It too will require four cycles to complete, and then the third instruction will start and so on. The total amount of time required to complete the five instructions (in this specific example) is 20 cycles.

Since RISC technology strives to have similar execution times for instructions, but sometimes objectively, it is impossible, the attempt is to have fixed duration microinstructions, as described in the previous example. By using RISC technology, the hardware is designed and built in such a way that each one of the stages can be executed in a different component (or unit) of the CPU. Each such unit should be self-sufficient and does not share any resources with other units. This means that the instructions can be executed in parallel in a stepwise way as described by Figure 4.29.

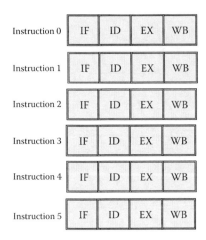

FIGURE 4.28   Execution stages (example).

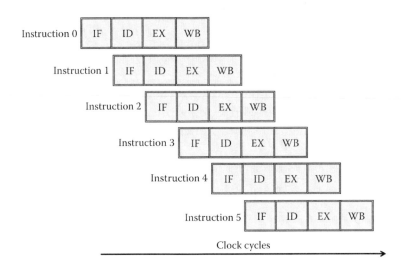

FIGURE 4.29   Pipelines executions stages.

The first instruction starts executing and as in the previous (standard) case, it needs four cycles in order to complete. During the first cycle, the instruction is fetched from memory. During the second cycle, the instruction undergoes through the decode stage. However, since the decoding is done in a separate autonomous hardware unit, it means that during this second cycle the fetch unit is idle. Therefore, instead of being idle and waiting its turn, the fetch unit starts fetching the second instruction although the first instruction is still in the process of execution. This means that during the second cycle, the CPU is decoding the first instruction and fetching the second instruction. This logic repeats itself in the next cycle as well. In the third cycle, the first instruction is being executed, the second instruction is in its decoding stage and the third instruction is being fetched from memory. Because in this example the instruction's execution was split into four stages, at any specific time, there are four instructions that are being executed in a stepwise parallelism.

It should be noted that this parallelism does not affect a single instruction's execution time and in the above example it remains four cycles, however it provides a mechanism in which the CPU performance is enhanced. This is clearly demonstrated by the last example. Executing the five instructions the standard way required 20 cycles, while implementing the pipeline mechanism it required only 8 cycles.

The performance improvement (or speedup) can be defined by a ratio between the original execution time and the enhanced (pipelined) execution time. In this specific example, the speedup is 2.5 (20/8 = 2.5). In general, the performance improvement can be calculated by

Assuming

- s: The number of stages in the pipeline

- t: Time required to execute one stage (the cycle time, or the time required by the slowest stage in a nonbalanced pipeline, which will be explained later)

- n: The number of instructions to be executed

In such a case, the standard or serial execution time will be calculated by

$$\text{Serial Time} = n * s * t$$

For calculating the time in the pipelined execution, we will distinguish between two cases. Execution of the first instruction required $s * t$ cycles. All other instructions require just one additional cycle per instruction (or t time per instruction) and then

$$\text{Parallel Time} = s * t + (n - 1) * t$$

The speedup will be

$$\text{Speedup} = \frac{\text{Serial Time}}{\text{Parallel Time}}$$

$$= \frac{n * s * t}{(s * t) + (n - 1) * t}$$

$$= \frac{n * s}{(s + n + 1)}$$

This means that for a very large n the speedup approaches s (the number of stages in the pipeline).

Instruction-Level Parallelism Problems

Although ILP does not improve the execution time of a single instruction, this does not represent a problem since there is no meaning in running a single instruction. What matters is the application's executing time, which is made of running millions of instructions. The theoretical possible speedup is the number of stages in the pipeline, but these stages are not always balanced, which hampers the maximum speedup obtained.

A pipeline is considered balanced when the execution times of all stages are identical (as shown in Figure 4.30). There are three stages, which are executed from left to right. The amount of time required for each stage is fixed (10 ns).

An unbalanced pipeline refers to a situation in which the time required for executing each stage might be different (as is shown in Figure 4.31).

As with the previous figure, the stages are performed from left to right, but the time required for each stage is different from the time required by the other stages. In such a case and for the pipeline to work properly, the time will have to be defined as the time that represents the longest stage. This means that although the first stage finishes in 5 ns, the stage will wait idle for additional 10 ns until the following stage will finish. This behavior repeats itself with the third stage as well, but in this case, the waiting time will be additional 5 ns.

Unbalanced stages in the pipeline is an example of problems that limit the possible speedup and for that reason, these problems are usually dealt with by the hardware systems' designers. One simple solution for the situation described in Figure 4.31 is adding stages. It is possible to split the second stage into three 5 ns stages and split the third stage into two 5 ns stages and then the three stages unbalanced pipeline will become a six stages balanced pipeline as described by Figure 4.32.

The processor's internal clock was already explained (see the section "Iron Law" of processor performance); however, the intention and explanations were related to the internal

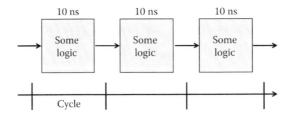

FIGURE 4.30   A balanced pipeline.

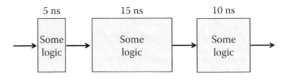

FIGURE 4.31   A nonbalanced pipeline.

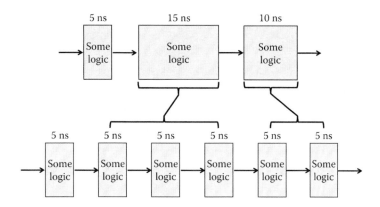

FIGURE 4.32   Balancing the unbalanced pipeline.

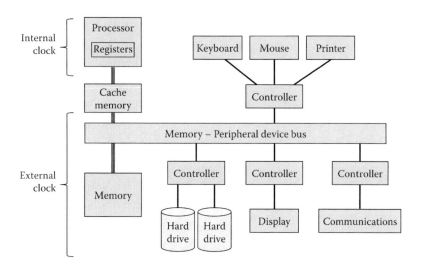

FIGURE 4.33   Internal and external clocks.

clock that synchronizes the processor. Each system has several clocks (at least two) that utilize different frequencies. The internal clock defines the processor's cycle and affects the instructions' execution times. The external clock defines the speed at which the processor communicates with other external devices, such as memory, or input and output devices. Figure 4.33 describes the general architecture (as in Figure 4.1) but with the devices affected by the two (or more) different clocks.

For example, the Intel Atom processor C2750 runs at a 2.4 GHz frequency, while the memory speed is 1.6 GHz. This is because the internal clock is used for synchronizing the instructions, or parts of the instructions, so it has to be faster, while the memory is an external device that although it is a part of the system, it is not part of the processor as defined by the von Neumann modular architecture. The procedure of fetching data from memory includes several stages. First, the memory controller is instructed to "bring" the required data from memory. The controller accesses the memory, finds the required data, and sends it to the processor. All the data movement is done using buses (that will be explained later in the bus chapter) which can be viewed as pipes responsible for data movement between the various devices.

The gap between the processor's speed and the memory speed that manifests itself into delays in the processor's work each time data has to be brought or sent to the memory, was among the reasons for implementing RISC-based systems, since RISC architecture emphasizes heavy usage of registers in an attempt to reduce the number of memory accesses. It should be noted, however, that RISC architecture, even with its many registers, cannot eliminate memory access. When it happens, usually the instruction pipeline is halted, which increases the execution overhead and reduces the speed (as will be explained in the following section).

Instruction-Level Parallelism Hazards

ILP hazards are special dynamic conditions that prevent the pipeline from executing smoothly. In software development, there might be situations in which one instruction is using an operand that is the result of a previous instruction. This can also happen in cases where a single higher-level programming language instruction has to be translated into several machine language instructions. For example,

Assuming A, B, C, and D are all variables in the program and the developer wrote the higher-level instruction:

$$A = B + C + D$$

Since in most systems the machine instruction ADD accepts only two operands, the compiler will have to split the higher-level instruction into two machine instructions.

$$R0 = R1 + R2$$

$$R0 = R0 + R4$$

Prior to the ADD instructions, the compiler will have to load the variables B, C, and D into registers, for example into R1, R2, and R4.

For CISC-based systems or systems that do not implement a pipeline, there is no problem since the second instruction starts execution only after the first instruction is completed. For pipelined systems, in which the instructions are executed in parallel, this is a problem. When the second instruction will try to fetch the first operand (R0) it will have to wait since R0 is the result of the previous instruction, which is still executing.

Relating to a four-stage pipeline (as described in the section "Instruction-Level Parallelism"):

- In the first cycle, the first instruction is fetched.

- In the second cycle, the first instruction is decoded and its operands (R1 and R2) are fetched. In parallel, the second instruction is fetched.

- In the third cycle, the first instruction is being executed and in parallel the second instruction is being decoded and there is an attempt to fetch its operands (R0 and R4). While R4 is available, the content of R0 is invalid since the first instruction that calculates its value is still executing.

This means that the pipeline will have to stop and wait for the first instruction to complete before it could fetch the required operand. Although the hardware can sometimes override this kind of hazard, it is better if the developer understands the way the hardware works and is aware of the consequences of the high-level programming instructions.

Data Hazards

The problem described earlier is a special case of data hazards. These are hazards that are caused by the fact that required data are not available on time. Usually there are three possible data hazards:

- Read after write (RAW) occurs when a later instruction is trying to access an operand calculated by a previous instruction, but the operand is not available since the previous instruction did not write it yet. The example on the previous section is an RAW hazard.

- Write after read (WAR) occurs when one instruction reads an operand after a later instruction has already changed it. For example

$$R3 = R1 + R2$$

$$R1 = R5 + R4$$

Apparently it is impossible that the first instruction will fetch R1 after the following instruction modified it. However, as will be explained later, one of the techniques used by modern processors for increasing execution speeds is execution out of order. If the technique is applied in this case and the second instruction in executed before the first one, this hazard will materialize. Furthermore, sometimes the pipeline is not balanced (see the section "Level Parallelism Problems") and then the microinstructions used require different times. There are also instructions that require more time to be executed, for example the DIV (divide) instruction compared with ADD. For trying to balance the pipeline in such cases, usually the execution stage will be split into several segments (Figure 4.34).

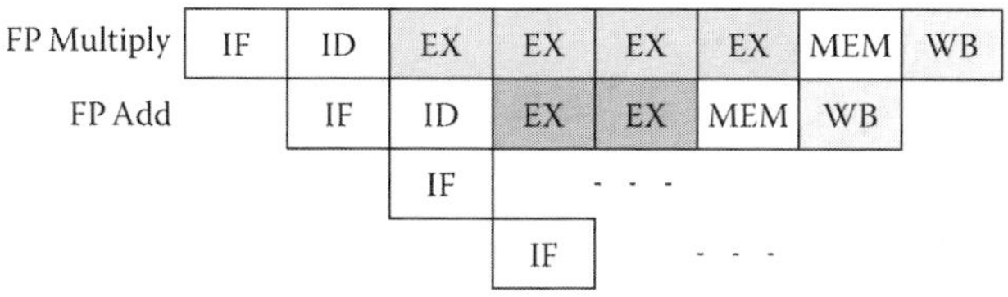

FP Multiply	IF	ID	EX	EX	EX	EX	MEM	WB
FP Add		IF	ID	EX	EX	MEM	WB	
			IF		- - -			
				IF		- - -		

FIGURE 4.34 Different execution stages.

In this case, the pipeline has five stages, but the execution stage may require several additional cycles. In this theoretical system, the floating-point MULT (multiply) execution segment is divided into four, one-cycle subsegments, while the floating-point ADD instruction is simpler to perform so its execution stage is divided into only two segments.

The WAR hazard can easily happen if the example will be slightly modified to:

$$R3 = R1 * R2$$

$$R1 = R5 + R4$$

In most cases it is the compiler's responsibility to avoid the problem. This can easily be achieved by changing the registers in use. Since the RISC architecture implements many registers, replacing the registers used, by other registers has no real overhead. The solution in this case will be to replace the R1 by another register, for example R8, and the code will change accordingly:

$$R3 = R1 * R2$$

$$R8 = R5 + R4$$

Due to the different register to be used, this solution is sometimes called register renaming.

- Write after write (WAW) occurs when a later instruction is writing its result and a previous instruction modifies it. This means that two instructions are changing the content of the same register, so it does not make sense to write it this way. Nevertheless, if it happens, the hardware will notice and make sure it executes correctly.

  An example may be

$$R3 = R1 * R2$$

$$R3 = R5 + R4$$

  Dealing with this hazard, as was the case with the previous one is the compiler responsibility.

Resources' Access Conflicts Hazards

A common hazard that impacts the pipeline performance is due to conflicts in accessing the various resources (or pipeline stages). The ILP was made possible by providing different and separate units of execution (resources) for each stage in the pipeline. In most cases, there will be just one unit for each stage, that is, if there is a five-stage pipeline there will be five different such resources. Access conflicts are possible when two instructions attempt to access the same resource during the same cycle.

For example, we will check the execution of the following instructions:

$$R0 = R1 + R2$$

$$R0 = R0 + R4$$

$$R5 = R1 + R6$$

Relating to a higher-level language and assuming that A, B, C, D are four variables, then the instruction that produced the aforementioned machine instructions are

$$\text{Sum } 1 = A + B + C$$

$$\text{Sum } 2 = A + D$$

In order to evaluate the execution of the machine instructions, we will build an execution table in which each column represents one cycle and each line represents one instruction. For simplicity we will use a four-stage pipeline (fetch, decode, execute, and write back). Figure 4.35 represents a normal and standard execution when no hazards occur and then the pipeline is executed without any interrupts.

Unfortunately, this is not the case with the code presented. The second instruction is using an operand that is not ready at the time it is required (data hazard). This means that in the third cycle, the first instruction is executing the ADD operation, the second instruction is in the decoding stage and tried to obtain the operands, and the third instruction is in the fetch stage. The problem arises because the second instruction cannot fetch one operand (R0) since it is not ready yet, and it will have to retry the fetch in the following cycle. This means that the assumption that each stage will be executed in one cycle does not materialize. The ID unit will have to wait for an additional cycle and then try once again to fetch the required input operand. This means that at least for the second instruction, the ID stage will require more than one cycle as represented by Figure 4.36.

However, the data hazard in executing the second instruction influences the execution of the third instruction as well. In a normal (hazardless) situation, in the fourth cycle, the third instruction was intended to be in the second stage (decode the instruction and fetch its operands). But since each stage consists of just one unit (resource), and since the decode unit is still being used by the second instruction, then the third instruction cannot execute the third stage and will have to wait for one cycle before retrying. Actually, in this specific

IF	ID	EX	WB			
	IF	ID	EX	WB		
		IF	ID	EX	WB	

FIGURE 4.35 A standard pipeline.

IF	ID	EX	WB			
	IF	ID	ID			
		IF	..			

FIGURE 4.36 The fourth cycle.

IF	ID	EX	WB				
	IF	ID	ID	ID	EX		
		IF	..	..	ID		

FIGURE 4.37 The sixth cycle.

example, the situation is even worse. The input operand required by the second instruction will be available only after the first instruction completes. This means that the second instruction will have to wait for an additional cycle before it can obtain the operand. This affects the execution of the third instruction as well since it will have to wait until the decoding unit will be available. Figure 4.37 represents the situation during the sixth cycle.

The delay in executing the third instruction was caused because of the conflicts in accessing the limited resources (the single decoding unit).

It should be noted that in this example of a four-stage pipeline, the operand fetch was done as part of the decode cycle. There might be implementations in which obtaining the operands is performed as part of the execution stage. In such cases, the problem still exists and the data hazard will manifest itself in delaying the executions stage and the conflict will be on the execution unit.

The pipeline mechanism works fine and delivers a significant performance improvement provided there are no hazards. Unfortunately, these hazards may always exist and have a negative impact on the pipeline execution. In the previous example, the data hazard of the second instruction created a resource conflict hazard in the third instruction and if there were additional instructions to be executed, it would have affected all of them. Figure 4.38 represents the real situation (as it was executed).

The penalty, or delay in execution caused by these hazards can be easily calculated. Executing these three instructions in a nonpipelined architecture requires twelve cycles. In a standard and optimal situation, the pipelined execution of the three instructions should have required six cycles (Figure 4.35). This is a significant improvement, since it reduces the time by half. However, with the hazards, the execution requires eight cycles, and this significantly hampers the potential pipeline improvements. Instead of a 50% potential improvement, the real improvement was only 30%.

Due to the execution times penalty caused by the various hazards, and due to the fact that sometimes this penalty may be severe, efforts were spent in trying to prevent or reduce the penalty's impact. Originally, the ideal was that the ALU should be divided into separate functional units. This means that there will be a unit for example for ADD, a unit for MULT, DIV (divide), and so on (see Figure 4.26 the right side of the ALU). Although there is one ALU, it was divided into different functional units. However, even with this division, there are still situations in which hazards may occur. Therefore, the next step

IF	ID	EX	WB				
	IF	ID	ID	ID	EX	WB	
		IF	..	.	ID	EX	WB

FIGURE 4.38 Real execution.

was the introduction of multiple functional units. When relating to the resource conflict hazard example, then two decoding units could minimize the negative impact. This line of thinking led to the understanding that a system can be designed based on the tasks it has to perform. For example, a computer system that is intended mainly for floating-point calculation may benefit from multiple floating-point units.

The duplication of functional units can be designed in many forms as described in Figures 4.39 and 4.40.

Figure 4.39 represents a five-stage pipelined system in which all except the first unit are duplicated. The underlining assumption is that the Instruction Fetch unit is fast enough to support the two pipelines without causing any delay. When a specific stage is executed, it is the CU's responsibility to transfer the execution to the next available functional unit. Usually it will use a simple flip-flop mechanism in which the two similar functional units are allocated alternatively. For example, all odd instructions will be directed to unit zero and all even instructions will be directed to unit one. In this implementation, the allocation is static. Once a pipeline was allocated for an instruction, there is no way to switch to the other pipeline. It is also possible to design a dynamic allocation in which the instructions are dynamically allocated in each stage.

The architecture described in Figure 4.40 uses a different approach. In this case, as in the previous example, it is a five-stage pipeline system. However, in this example only the ALU functionality was divided into different functional units. The assumption in this example is that all other functional units, except the ALU, are fast enough to support the system without any delays. This example is relevant in cases when the bottleneck is caused by the execution (in the ALU) and not by the preparations stages performed by the CU (see Figure 3.6).

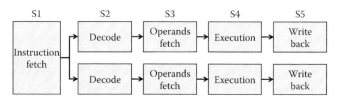

FIGURE 4.39   Multiple functional units example.

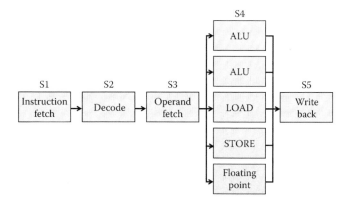

FIGURE 4.40   Multiple arithmetic and logical functional units.

Dynamic Scheduling

Although the RISC-based pipeline was widely accepted during the 1990's, it was implemented in some systems several decades prior to that. Control Data Corporation (CDC), an American computer company that was active during the second half of the twentieth century, used a technology similar to the modern RISC. The CDC 6600* computer was designed in the early 1960s by Seymour Cray,[†] and it used a pipeline mechanism. Instead of the Instruction Decode stage used in RISC technology, the CDC computer had two distinct stages. One was dedicated to decoding the instructions and wait (if there are any access conflicts) and the second was used for fetching the operands. The main idea behind this design was that access conflicts and collisions are normal in parallel execution and there is a need for a stage that will wait and synchronize the activities. The CDC 6600 used ten functional units as part of the ALU (roughly resembling Figure 4.40 with additional functional units). These 10 functional units were among the main contributors to the execution speed obtained by the machine compared with other computers available at that time (1964).

As can be seen from Figure 4.41, the RISC-decoding stage was divided into two different stages:

- Stage I, which decodes the instruction, identifies the operands that are required and checks if there are any access problems (data or access conflicts hazards). If such a hazard (one or more) was found, the stage will initiate a delay for one cycle. In the next cycle, a new check will be performed and so on until no hazards exist and it is possible to fetch the operands. The execution can start only after all operands are available. The mechanism for assessing the availability of the operands that was originally developed in the 1960s is still used by many processors, and it will be explained in the next section.

- Stage R, which fetches the operands. There is no need to check their availability since it was performed by the previous stage and if the operands were not available, the previous stage would have been still waiting. The fetched operands are transferred to the execution unit.

In addition to the special pipeline, the CDC 6600 implemented dynamic scheduling that was intended to overcome some hazards and enhance execution speeds. Dynamic execution means executing the instructions in an order that is different from the order they were written by the developer. It should be noted that this is a mechanism implemented by the hardware with no intervention of the developer or the compiler. For that reason, in addition to the hardware algorithms that decide on order changes, the system should include sophisticated mechanisms for ensuring the correct result in spite the changes.

---

* The CDC 6600 was a breakthrough system that was introduced in 1964. Since it was roughly ten times faster than any system available at that time it was names a supercomputer.

† Seymour Cray was an American electrical engineer better known for his contribution to the design of superfast computers.

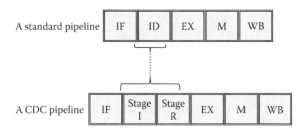

FIGURE 4.41   The CDC 6600 pipeline.

F	I	R	X	X	X	X	X	M	W							
	F	I	.	.	.	.	.	.	.	R	X	X	M	W		
		F	I	.	.	.	.	.	.	.	.	.	.	R	X	.

FIGURE 4.42   Fixed scheduling pipeline.

For example, assuming there are three instructions:

$$R2 = \frac{R4}{R6}$$

$$R10 = R2 + R4$$

$$R12 = R6 - R4$$

For that example, we will assume that add and subtract operations require two execution cycles, multiply requires three cycles, and divide requires five cycles. Figure 4.42 depicts the execution using the CDC 6600 pipeline and a fixed scheduling (executing the instruction exactly as written).

The first instruction starts execution and it includes the stages:

- F: Fetching the instruction.

- I: Decoding the instruction and checking for hazards. If there are hazards, the stage waits for one cycle and then rechecks once again. Only after there are no hazards, it will proceed to the next stage.

- R: Fetching the required operands and transferring them into the internal ALU registers.

- X: Executing the instruction. For the first instruction, this stage will require five cycles since the divide operation lasts five cycles.

- M: Memory access, which in this case is not needed. Since memory access is relatively slow, it was given a separate stage.

- W: Writing the result into the destination register. It is a copy of the result from the internal output register in the ALU to the external destination register in the instruction.

Similarly, the second instruction starts executing. Although the divide in the first instruction and the addition in the second instructions are performed in different functional units, there is a data hazard so the I stage has to wait until R2 will become available. One may notice that the third instruction has nothing to do with the first two. It uses other registers and needs a different functional unit. Despite all this, the third instruction, which has to be executed after the second instruction finished, is waiting.

This and similar situations led to the understanding that a dynamic scheduling may benefit twice. The third instruction will not have to wait and it will be possible to use the idle subtract function unit. Figure 4.43 depicts the dynamic scheduling pipeline.

As can be seen from Figure 4.43, in this specific case, the dynamic scheduling was highly effective and the third instruction was executed in parallel to the first two instructions with no extra time. However, in spite the greater efficiency of the dynamic scheduling, a special attention has to be paid to additional hazard, as can be seen in the example:

$$R2 = R\,4*R6$$

$$R8 = R10*R12$$

$$R8 = \frac{R14}{R6}$$

Implementing dynamic scheduling in this case creates a new hazard as can be seen by pipeline depicted in Figure 4.44.

In this case, as with the previous example, the dynamic scheduling executes the third instruction out of its order, which increases the execution speed. However, this created a new hazard that is not available in the sequential execution. Due to the dynamic scheduling, the third instruction finished prior to the second instruction. This means that when the system finished executing the three instructions, the value in R8 is not the value the developer was expecting. Although the dynamic scheduling increased the execution speed, it cannot be applied here because it created a WAW hazard and the results are wrong. It should be noted, however, that a compiler that knows the execution target computer can change the output register (Register Renaming) of the third instruction and overcome the problem.

F	I	R	X	X	X	X	X	M	W					
	F	I	.	.	.	.	.	.	.	R	X	X	M	W
		F	I	R	X	X	M	W						

FIGURE 4.43 Dynamic scheduling pipeline.

F	I	R	X	X	X	M	W					
	F	I	.	.	.	.	R	X	X	X	M	W
		F	I	R	X	X	X	X	X	M	W	

FIGURE 4.44 Hazards in dynamic scheduling.

Dynamic scheduling can create other hazards and not just WAW. The following example demonstrates a WAR hazard.

$$R12 = R4/R6$$

$$R8 = \frac{R10}{R12}$$

$$R10 = R14 + R6$$

The appropriate pipeline execution cycles is provided in Figure 4.45.

Due to the dynamic scheduling, the second instruction retrieves its operands after the third instruction finished its execution. This means that the second instruction intended to use R10 as the operand, assuming it get the register's old version. However, due to the dynamic scheduling when the second instruction retrieves R10, its content was changed already.

Once again the dynamic scheduling increases speed, but if not properly checked, holds the potential to produce wrong results. As in the previous case, the compiler can address these new hazards and fix them quite easily.

It should be noted that the main reason for developing the dynamic scheduling was to increase execution speed. As was demonstrated by the two examples, during execution, there are many functional units that are idle since there are no instructions that require their functionality. The dynamic scheduling attempts to use the system's resources (functional unit) in a more efficient way. However, using dynamic scheduling may cause new hazards that do not exist in sequential execution. These new potential problems do not prevent using the dynamic scheduling; it is being used more and in parallel with new solutions developed that allow using the dynamic scheduling safely. One of the methods that originate in the CDC 6600 days is Scoreboarding.

Scoreboarding

Scoreboarding is a mechanism that is intended to delay the execution of an instruction in cases where its operands are not ready since they are a result of prior instructions that are still being executed. As part of the mechanism, there is a validity bit for each register and an algorithm that is performed by the hardware. The algorithm includes the following steps:

1. During the decode stage, all participating registers are identified and their validity bits are checked.

F	I	R	X	X	X	X	X	M	W					
	F	I	.	.	.	.	.	.	.	R	X	X	M	W
		F	I	R	X	X	M	W						

FIGURE 4.45   WAR hazard due to dynamic scheduling.

2. If the validity bits of all the registers are set, it means that the registers are valid and their content can be read and transferred to the execution unit.

   a. The validity bit of the destination register is turned off meaning that the current content is not valid anymore (it is going to be changed once the instruction completes).

   b. Executing the instruction.

3. If one or more of the participating registers is not valid, it means that there is an instruction under execution and it will change the content of the register, the hardware waits for one cycle and then retries the check.

4. When the instruction finishes execution.

   a. The result is entered to the destination register.

   b. The register's validity bit is set (it is valid).

For explaining the algorithm, we will use it on a piece of high-level programming code translated to machine language. Assuming there are four variables (A, B, C, and D) and the developer wants to calculate the value:

$$E = A * A * B + A * C + D$$

The compiler loads the variables into registers as follows:

$$R2 = A$$

$$R6 = B$$

$$R5 = C$$

$$R7 = D$$

Then the following machine-level language code represents the instructions to be performed:

$$R3 = R2 * R2$$

$$R3 = R6 * R3$$

$$R4 = R2 * R5$$

$$R4 = R4 + R7$$

$$R4 = R3 + R4$$

For evaluating the execution of the code, we will use a simple balanced four-stage pipeline in which each operation (addition or multiplications) is executed in one cycle. In an ideal situation execution of five instructions required eight cycles (four cycles for the first instruction and one cycle for each additional instruction). In this specific example, however, there are some hazards so the execution will require eleven cycles (or 37.5% penalty) as outlined in Figure 4.46.

After analyzing the execution, one may notice that there are some hazards in all but the first instruction:

- The second instruction has to wait for its input operand (R3).

- The third instruction experiences resource conflict since it has to wait for the execution unit.

- The fourth instruction has to wait for its input operand (R4).

- The fifth instruction has to wait for its input operand (R4).

Due to the hazards, the hardware may decide to change the order of instructions two and three by executing instruction three before executing instruction two.

The new code for execution will be

$$R3 = R2 * R2$$

$$R4 = R2 * R5$$

$$R3 = R6 * R3$$

$$R4 = R4 + R7$$

$$R4 = R3 + R4$$

This change managed to eliminate most of the hazards and the code executes in nine cycles as can be seen from Figure 4.47.

After analyzing the new execution, we may notice that

- The second instruction that now became the third one does not have to wait for its input operand (R3). By the time it started executing, the first instruction finished already and the operand is valid.

F	D	E	W							
	F	D	.	E	W					
		F	D	.	E	W				
			F	D	.	.	E	W		
				F	D	.	.	.	E	W

FIGURE 4.46   Original code pipelined.

F	D	E	W					
	F	D	E	W				
		F	D	E	W			
			F	D	E	W		
				F	D	.	E	W

FIGURE 4.47   Modified code pipelined.

- The third instruction, which in the modified version became the second instruction, does not have to wait for the resource (the execution unit), which in this case is available.

- The fourth instruction does not have to wait for its input operand (R4), which is the result of the original third instruction, but in the modified version it finished already since it was moved to second place.

- The fifth instruction is the only one that still has to wait for its input operand (R4) that is the result of the previous instruction's execution.

Although the dynamic execution did not succeed in eliminating the last hazard caused by the dependency between the last two instructions, the example demonstrates once more the importance of the dynamic scheduling for execution times.

For a more detailed explanation regarding scoreboarding, we will use the modified code and run it through the algorithm as performed by the hardware. In every step, the relevant instruction will be addressed as well as the relevant registers' validity bits. For simplification reasons, not all registers will be included in the example. For each stage, the left side represents the registers' validity bits before executing the instruction, and the right side defines the situation after the instruction was executed. We may assume that when the code starts executing all relevant registers are valid.

- First stage: Executing the first instruction

$$R3 = R2 * R2$$

$$R4 = R2 * R5$$

$$R3 = R6 * R3$$

$$R4 = R4 + R7$$

$$R4 = R3 + R4$$

The content of the validity bits is as follows:

2: 1	2: 1
3: 1	3: 0
4: 1	4: 1
5: 1	5: 1
6: 1	6: 1
7: 1	7: 1

The only operand required for the first instruction is R2, Since R2.Valid = 1 this means that the register is valid. R2 is copied to the internal execution unit register (actually it is copied to the two internal input registers). The validity of the output register (R3) is set to no (by executing Set R3.Valid = 0) and the system can proceed to the execution stage.

- Second stage: Executing the second instruction

$$R3 = R2 * R2$$

$$\mathbf{R4 = R2 * R5}$$

$$R3 = R6 * R3$$

$$R4 = R4 + R7$$

$$R4 = R3 + R4$$

The content of the validity bits is as follows:

2: 1	2: 1
3: 0	3: 0
4: 1	4: 0
5: 1	5: 1
6: 1	6: 1
7: 1	7: 1

The validity bits of the input operands are checked (R2.Valid = 1, R5.Valid = 1) and since both are valid, their contents are copied to the internal execution unit's registers, the output register validity is turned off (by executing Set R4.Valid = 0), and the system can proceed to the next stage.

- Third stage: Executing the third instruction

$$R3 = R2 * R2$$

$$R4 = R2 * R5$$

$$R3 = R6 * R3$$

$$R4 = R4 + R7$$

$$R4 = R3 + R4$$

The content of the validity bits is as follows:

2: 1	2: 1
3: 0	3: 0
4: 0	4: 0
5: 1	5: 1
6: 1	6: 1
7: 1	7: 1

The validity bits of the input operands are checked (R6.Valid = 1, R3.Valid = 0). Although R6 is valid, R3 is not since the instruction that modifies its content is still executing. This means that execution has to be delayed for one cycle. No changes are introduced to the validity bits since the system is still in the same stage.

- Fourth stage: The execution of the first instruction has finished.

$$R3 = R2 * R2$$

$$R4 = R2 * R5$$

$$R3 = R6 * R3$$

$$R4 = R4 + R7$$

$$R4 = R3 + R4$$

The instruction to be executed next is still the third instruction. However, this stage does not initiate a new instruction, but finalizes the execution of a previous instruction. The content of the validity bits is as follows:

2: 1	2: 1
3: 0	3: 1
4: 0	4: 0
5: 1	5: 1
6: 1	6: 1
7: 1	7: 1

When the first instruction finished executing, it means that the content of R3 is updated so it is time to set its validity bit (Set R3.Valid = 1). This is done in order to signal to other instruction, which may be waiting for the content of that register.

- Fifth stage: Another attempt to try executing the third instruction, which was put on hold due to the input register being not available.

$$R3 = R2 * R2$$

$$R4 = R2 * R5$$

$$\mathbf{R3 = R6 * R3}$$

$$R4 = R4 + R7$$

$$R4 = R3 + R4$$

As already stated, this instruction waits for the validity of its input registers (R3 and R6), As long as these registers (one or both) are not valid the instruction will remain on hold. The content of the validity bits is

2: 1	2: 1
3: 1	3: 0
4: 0	4: 0
5: 1	5: 1
6: 1	6: 1
7: 1	7: 1

Once again the input registers' validity bits are checked (R6.Valid = 1, R3.Valid = 1). Since both are valid, the instruction can start executing. The content of the two input registers in copied to the internal input registers, the validity of the output register is set to no (Set R3.Valid = 0) and the instruction execution stage may start.

- Sixth stage: Executing the fourth instruction:

$$R3 = R2 * R2$$

$$R4 = R2 * R5$$

$$R3 = R6 * R3$$

$$\mathbf{R4 = R4 + R7}$$

$$R4 = R3 + R4$$

The content of the validity bits is as follows:

2: 1	2: 1
3: 0	3: 0
4: 0	4: 0
5: 1	5: 1
6: 1	6: 1
7: 1	7: 1

The validity bits of the input operands are checked (R7.Valid = 1, R4.Valid = 0). R7 is valid, but R4 is not, since the instruction that modifies its content (the second instruction) is still executing. This means that execution has to be delayed for one cycle. No changes are introduced to the validity bits since the system is still in the same stage.

- Seventh stage: Another attempt to try and execute the fourth instruction:

$$R3 = R2 * R2$$

$$R4 = R2 * R5$$

$$R3 = R6 * R3$$

$$R4 = R4 + R7$$

$$R4 = R3 + R4$$

The content of the validity bits is as follows:

2: 1	2: 1
3: 0	3: 0
4: 0	4: 0
5: 1	5: 1
6: 1	6: 1
7: 1	7: 1

The validity bits of the input operands are checked once again (R7.Valid = 1, R4.Valid = 0). R7 is valid, but R4 is not, since the second instruction that modifies its content is still executing. This means that execution has to be delayed for one additional cycle. No changes are introduced to the validity bits since the system is still in the same stage. It should be noted that these are dynamic events and it may be that the execution of the second instruction was delayed for some reason and this caused the two cycles of delay in executing the fourth instruction.

- Eighth stage: The execution of the second instruction has finished.

$$R3 = R2 * R2$$

$$\mathbf{R4 = R2 * R5}$$

$$R3 = R6 * R3$$

$$R4 = R4 + R7$$

$$R4 = R3 + R4$$

The instruction to be executed next is still the fourth instruction however; this stage does not initiate a new instruction, but finalizes the execution of a previous instruction. The content of the validity bits is as follows:

2: 1	2: 1
3: 0	3: 0
4: 0	4: 1
5: 1	5: 1
6: 1	6: 1
7: 1	7: 1

When the second instruction finished executing, it means that the content of R4 is updated so it is time to set its validity bit (Set R4.Valid = 1). This acts as a signal to other instruction, which may be waiting for the content of that register.

- Ninth stage: The execution of the third instruction was finished.

$$R3 = R2 * R2$$

$$R4 = R2 * R5$$

$$\mathbf{R3 = R6 * R3}$$

$$R4 = R4 + R7$$

$$R4 = R3 + R4$$

The instruction to be executed next is still the fourth instruction. However, this stage does not initiate a new instruction; rather, it finalizes the execution of a previous instruction. The content of the validity bits is as follows:

2: 1	2: 1
3: 0	3: 1
4: 1	4: 1
5: 1	5: 1
6: 1	6: 1
7: 1	7: 1

When the third instruction finishes executing, it means that the content of R3 is updated so it is time to set its validity bit (Set R3.Valid = 1) and signal to other instructions which may be waiting for the content of that register that it is valid.

- Tenth stage: Another attempt to try executing the fourth instruction, which was put on hold due to the input register being not available.

$$R3 = R2 * R2$$

$$R4 = R2 * R5$$

$$R3 = R6 * R3$$

$$\mathbf{R4 = R4 + R7}$$

$$R4 = R3 + R4$$

As already stated, this instruction waits for the validity of its input registers, As long as these registers (one or both) are not valid, the instruction will remain on hold. The content of the validity bits is as follows:

2: 1	2: 1
3: 1	3: 1
4: 1	4: 0
5: 1	5: 1
6: 1	6: 1
7: 1	7: 1

Once again the input registers' validity bits are checked (R7.Valid = 1, R4.Valid = 1). Since both are valid, the instruction can start executing. The content of the two input registers are copied to the internal input registers, the validity of the output register is set to no (Set R4.Valid = 0), and the instruction execution stage may start.

- Eleventh stage: Executing the fifth instruction:

$$R3 = R2 * R2$$

$$R4 = R2 * R5$$

$$R3 = R6 * R3$$

$$R4 = R4 + R7$$

$$\mathbf{R4 = R3 + R4}$$

The content of the validity bits is as follows:

2: 1	2: 1
3: 1	3: 1
4: 0	4: 0
5: 1	5: 1
6: 1	6: 1
7: 1	7: 1

Once again the input registers' validity bits are checked (R3.Valid = 1, R4.Valid = 0). Since R4 is not valid, the instruction is put on hold.

- Twelfth stage: The execution of the fourth instruction was finished

$$R3 = R2 * R2$$

$$R4 = R2 * R5$$

$$R3 = R6 * R3$$

$$\mathbf{R4 = R4 + R7}$$

$$R4 = R3 + R4$$

The instruction to be executed next is still the fifth instruction. However, this stage does not initiate a new instruction; rather, it finalizes the execution of a previous instruction. The content of the validity bits is as follows:

2: 1	2: 1
3: 1	3: 1
4: 0	4: 1
5: 1	5: 1
6: 1	6: 1
7: 1	7: 1

When the fourth instruction finishes executing, it means that the content of R4 is updated so it is time to set its validity bit (Set R4.Valid = 1) and signal to other instructions which may be waiting for the content of that register that it is valid.

- Thirteenth stage: Executing the fifth instruction, which was put on hold due to the input register being not available.

$$R3 = R2 * R2$$

$$R4 = R2 * R5$$

$$R3 = R6 * R3$$

$$R4 = R4 + R7$$

$$\mathbf{R4 = R3 + R4}$$

The instruction waits for the validity of its input registers. The content of the validity bits is as follows:

2: 1	2: 1
3: 1	3: 1
4: 1	4: 0
5: 1	5: 1
6: 1	6: 1
7: 1	7: 1

Once again, the input registers' validity bits are checked (R3.Valid = 1, R4.Valid = 1). Since both are valid, the instruction can start executing. The content of the two input registers are copied to the internal input registers, the validity of the output register is set to no (Set R4.Valid = 0), and the instruction execution stage may start.

- Fourteenth stage: The execution of the fifth instruction was finished

$$R3 = R2 * R2$$

$$R4 = R2 * R5$$

$$R3 = R6 * R3$$

$$R4 = R4 + R7$$

$$\mathbf{R4 = R3 + R4}$$

There are no additional instructions in this example and this stage is intended to finalize the execution of a previous instruction. The content of the validity bits is as follows:

2: 1	2: 1
3: 1	3: 1
4: 0	4: 1
5: 1	5: 1
6: 1	6: 1
7: 1	7: 1

When the fifth instruction finished executing, it means that the content of R4 is updated so it is time to set its validity bit (Set R4.Valid = 1) and signal to other instructions which may be waiting for the content of that register that it is valid.

Performance Enhancements

Many of the hazards previously described were introduced by the performance enhancements tactics used by the processors' designers. Nevertheless, these enhancements are implemented in most of the modern processors, which in addition to pipeline use two other improvements:

- Super-pipeline which improves the performance obtained by a pipeline by increasing the number of stages (usually n > 5). Since the possible enhancement is driven by the number of stages (see the section "Instruction-Level Parallelism") then increasing the number of stages holds the potential to increase performance.

- Super-scalar refers to a processor that has multiple identical functional units. For example, instead of one addition unit and one multiplication unit, the designers may choose to include two addition units and two multiplication units. Figures 4.39 and 4.40 are examples of super-scalar. A processor that implements super-scalar improves its CPI, since at any stage in the pipeline there might be more instructions and the processor is capable of producing more than one result per cycle. While in a regular pipeline, there are several instructions executing, each one in a different stage, with super-scalar it is possible to create real parallelism.

It should be noted, however, that in addition to the enhanced performance, there are additional new hazards and the penalty becomes more significant. Stopping a four-stage pipeline and reloading it with new content, as may be that case with a conditional branch instruction, produces some penalty that is significantly lower that the penalty of a twenty-stage pipeline.

For that reason, as part of enhancing performance, a special emphasis was put on controlling and minimizing the new potential hazards.

Branch Prediction

The pipeline mechanism works fine and manages to enhance the processor's performance as long as the instructions are executed in a sequential manner. For example, in a four-stage pipeline the instruction execution occurs in the third stage. At this point, the next two instructions are already in the pipeline in various stages of execution. If the code to be executed is not sequential, the pipeline may be inefficient. Nonsequential code refers to a sequence of execution instructions that contain conditional branches as part of the sequence (e.g., a loop). The reason is that branch is performed during execution of the instruction and is based on data that is available only at run time. However, the pipeline mechanism has loaded and partially executed the following, sometimes unneeded, instructions. Figure 4.48 provides a visual example of the aforementioned situation.

1		F	D	E	W					
2			F	D	E	W				
3				F	D	E	W			
4					F	D	E	W		
5						F	D			
6							F			
7								F	D	E	W
8									F	D	E
9										F	D

FIGURE 4.48   Nonsequential code pipeline.

For clarity reasons, the table includes on the left side a column number that defines the instruction's number. This is a simple four-stage pipeline. In the example, the first three instructions are executed sequentially. The fourth instruction is a conditional branch (such as a condition to end a loop). Only when the processor gets to the third stage (E), it knows if to continue execution of the following instructions (assuming the loop ended) or branch back to the start of the loop for an additional iteration. Unfortunately, at this stage, instructions 5 and 6 have already been partially executed. If the following instructions are not the ones that follow, the processor has to purge these two instructions and reload the instructions in the new location.

The penalty in this case is the lost time in which the pipeline was stopped for reloading the correct instructions. It should be noted that is some cases the processor will also have to undo changes introduced into the scoreboard that are not relevant anymore.

In order to minimize this type of penalty, many processors have implemented a mechanism of dynamic branch prediction. Although this mechanism exists for decades, as the number of stages in the pipeline increased, the importance of the branch prediction increased as well.

There are several mechanisms for predicting branch behaviors:

- Static arbitrary decision, which was used by various proprietary companies. The idea was to design the processor in a way that it always acts in a similar fashion. For example, the VAX computer that was designed by DEC used to bring the following instructions. The idea behind this behavior was that the compiler that is familiar with the processor behavior will use the appropriate machine instructions to assure optimum performance. For example, since in most cases loops are used for repeating calculations and not just for one cycle, at the end of the loop the processor will be required to load different instructions and not the following ones. In such a case, the compiler will use a JUMP instruction. This is not a conditional branch and the processor will be able to handle it properly. Other proprietary systems designers used the opposite approach and the pipeline loaded the instructions at the branch destination, instead of the following ones. In this case too, it was left for the compiler to provide the additional level of optimization.

- Dynamic history-based decision, which required a small hardware table that maintains a history log about specific branches. The assumption was that programs are usually consistent and if a specific branch was taken, it will be taken in the next time as well. For example, a loop that executes one hundred times. The first time a cycle of the loop ends, the processor does not know if the following instruction will be needed or the ones at the branch destination. However, during the next 98 loops, the branch behaves similarly. The last iteration of the loop is once again different. This mechanism is implemented using a hardware table sometimes called branch history table (BHT) that maintains information about the branch behavior in the past. If it is a conditional branch instruction, during the fetch stage the fetch functional unit will access the table and decide accordingly as explained in Figure 4.49. On the left side of the figure, there are two internal registers: instruction register (IR) that contains the instruction to be executed and the program counter (PC) that holds the address of the next instruction to be executed. If the current instruction is a branch or a conditional branch, the destination address is defined as the signed magnitude to be added to the current address, in order to produce the branch target address. In parallel, the current branch address is used as a pointer to the BHT to check prior behavior of the branch. If in the past the branch was taken, the address used is the one previously calculated, otherwise, the PC will be increased so it points to the following instruction. The PC will be updated so the pipeline can bring the next instruction to be executed.

There are several ways for implementing the history log table based on the accuracy required and the additional cost associated with the implementation. For comparing two implementations, we will use a simple pseudo code:

$$\text{For } (i = 10, \ i > 0, \ i = i - 1)$$

$$x = x + 1$$

Figure 4.50 is a flowchart that visualizes the small loop:

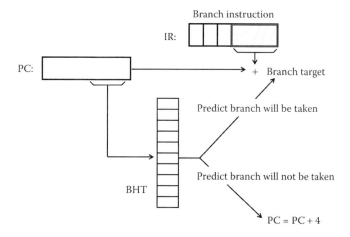

FIGURE 4.49   Branch prediction mechanism.

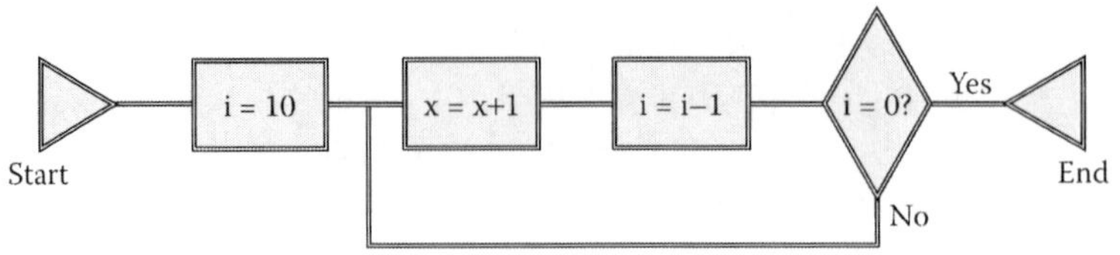

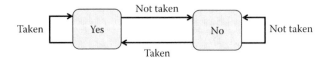

FIGURE 4.50 The example's flowchart.

Taken ⟶ Yes — Not taken ⟶ No ⟵ Not taken
Yes ⟵ Taken ⟵ No

FIGURE 4.51 One-bit prediction algorithm.

The first implementation defines one bit for each entry in the BHT. The algorithm in this case was very simple and it provided history only about the last execution of the branch. If the bit is on (Yes) it means that in the last time the branch was taken so the assumption is that it will be taken once again. If this was the case and the current branch was also taken, the bit will be left as it is. However, if the branch was not taken, despite the prediction, the bit will be turn off (No) in order to signal the next time the instruction will be executed. Figure 4.51 depicts the algorithm in a visual way.

- If the bit is set (Yes).
  - If the branch was taken, the bit remains unchanged.
  - If the branch was not taken, the bit will be zeroed (No).
- If the bit is zero (No).
  - If the branch was not taken, the bit will remain unchanged.
  - If the branch was taken the bit will be set (Yes).

If the example code was executed, using the one-bit prediction algorithm the success sequence is given by

$$F,T,T,T,T,T,T,T,T,F,F,T,T,T,T,T,T,T,T,F\ldots$$

F means the prediction failed while T means the prediction succeeded. The algorithm fails in the first and last iterations of the executed loop. The overall prediction success rate is 80%.

For increasing the prediction's accuracy, it is possible to use two bits for each entry in the BHT. The algorithm in this case is defined by Figure 4.52.

Due to the fact that this algorithm uses two bits per entry, it can be more accurate by providing more information about the historic behavior of the branch.

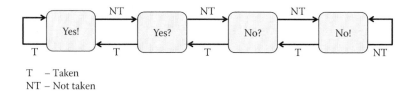

T – Taken
NT – Not taken

FIGURE 4.52 Two bits prediction algorithm.

For explaining the algorithm, we will start on the left side.

- If the two bits are set (a binary value of 11 that designates Yes!), this means that in the past the branch was taken more than once and for that reason the processor is "certain" the branch will be taken once again.

- If the binary value of the two bits is 10 (Yes? or probably the branch will be taken).

- If the binary value of the two bits is 01 (No? or probably not taken).

- If the two bits are zero (No!).

- If the branch was taken, there is no change, and the binary value remains 11 (Yes!).
- If the branch was not taken, the binary value will change to 10 (Yes?). This means that the algorithm predicts the branch will be taken, but it is not certain about it.
- If the branch was taken, the binary value will be change to 11 (Yes!), meaning that the next time the branch will be taken for certain.
- If the branch was not taken, the binary value will be changed to 01 (No?) meaning that probably the next time the branch will not be taken.
- If the branch was taken, the binary value will be changed to 10 (Yes?) meaning probably next time the branch will be taken.
- If the branch was not taken, the binary value will be changed to 00 (No!) meaning that the next branch will certainly not be taken.
- If the branch was not taken, there will be no change and the two bits will remain zero.
- If the branch was taken, the binary value will be changed to 01 (No?).

The basic idea is that two values (00, 01) represent the prediction of not taken and two values (10, 11) represent the prediction of taken. Each time a branch is taken, the binary value is increased by one (up to the upper limit of 11) and each time the branch is not taken the value is decreased by one (down to the lower value of 00).

The accuracy of this algorithm on the code previously defined is given by:

$$F,F,T,T,T,T,T,T,T,F,T,T,T,T,T,T,T,T,T,T,F,T\ldots$$

Using this algorithm, the efficiency tends to get to 90%, slightly better that the one-bit prediction algorithm.

Loop Buffer

One of the most common hazards, the data hazard, usually appears when one instruction is using the result of the previous instruction. One of the ways to avoid it is dynamic execution, or executing the instructions in a different order than they were written. However, there is another mechanism introduced in the Cray supercomputers during the 1970s. The mechanism is called Loop Buffer or Forwarding. The basic idea was quite simple. The output of the previous instruction is in the execution unit and the hazard occurs due to the need to write it back into the destination defined in the instruction. Instead of waiting while it is copied to the destination and then copied again to the internal register in the execution unit, it is simpler to copy (forwarding) it from the output register in the execution unit to its input register. The CU that is responsible for fetching the operands has to check if the required operand is the result of a previous instruction. If this is the case, the operand does not have to be loaded since it is already in the execution unit and the ALU can use it.

For example, we will use the following instructions:

$$R0 = R1 + R2$$

$$R0 = R0 + R4$$

$$R5 = R1 + R6$$

For visualizing the pipeline cycles, we will use a simple four-stage pipeline. Figure 4.53 represents the execution sequence.

The data hazard occurs during the decode stage of the second instruction since the instruction has to wait for R0. During the execution stage of the third instruction, a resource conflict occurs, since the execution unit is executing the second instruction so the third instruction has to wait for its turn.

When using Loop Buffer, the second instruction does not have to wait since the input operand is already in the execution unit. If the data hazard was eliminated, then the

F	D	E	W			
	F	D	.	E	W	
		F	D	.	E	W

FIGURE 4.53 Standard pipeline (no loop buffer).

F	D	E	W		
	F	D	E	W	
		F	D	E	W

FIGURE 4.54   Pipeline with loop buffer.

resource conflict does not exist as well (Figure 4.54). The Loop Buffer implementation managed to eliminate the hazards and explore the full potential of the pipeline.

Key Takeaway

- *Amdahl's law*: Defined by Gene Amdahl and states that the performance enhancements to be gained by some component is limited by the percentage of time the component is being used.

- *Microinstructions*: A concept in which the basic stages of executing an instruction (fetch, decode, execute, write back) are divided into additional substages. These substages can be used as building blocks for defining new instructions.

- *Complex instruction set computer (CISC)*: That uses many addressing modes, many instructions with varying lengths and execution times. The variety of instructions was made possible by using the microinstructions. The main problem associated with the CISC technology is that the CU is extremely complex, which slows down the development of new processors.

- *Addressing modes*: Refers to the way instructions can access variables that are stored in memory. CISC computer implement many such modes that may include, immediate (the address is in the instruction), pointer (the address is in a register), displacement (a fixed number specified in the instruction is added to a pointer or an immediate address), memory indirect (in which the memory address is a pointer to the real address), and many others.

- *Reduced instruction set computer (RISC) technology* that refers to computers that were designed using a limited number of instructions and a few addressing modes. On the other hand, they use registers extensively to avoid excessive memory access.

- *Instruction-level parallelism (ILP)*: A pipeline mechanism that splits the single instruction into its microinstructions and executes these in parallel.

- *ILP hazards*: Refers to a list of possible hazards that may stop or delay the pipeline, such as an unbalanced pipeline, read after write (RAW), write after read (WAR), and writer after write (WAW).

- *Resource conflict*: Refers to a situation in which two instructions are trying to execute the same microinstruction on the same cycle. Due to resource limitations, one instruction only will continue executing, while the other will have to wait for one cycle.

- *Dynamic scheduling*: Refers to hardware mechanism that changes the order of the instructions executed in order to minimize hazards.

- *Scoreboarding*: Is a hardware mechanism that analyzes the registers used by the instruction for deciding if it can start execution or it has to be delayed since its operands (one or two) are still not ready.

- *Branch prediction*: Is a hardware mechanism that tries to predict the behavior of conditional instructions based on their previous execution.

- *Loop buffer (or forwarding)*: Is another hardware mechanism that is intended to reduce delays. In cases, the next instruction needs an operand that is the output of the previous instruction, the mechanism copies the content of the internal output register into the internal input register.

CHAPTER 5

Memory

MEMORY

This chapter focuses on computers' memory. By using the general architecture figure, we can relate to the memory and its contribution to systems' performance (Figure 5.1).

The memory is an integral and essential part of the system. Just as one cannot execute instructions without the processor, it is impossible to run a program without having a memory for storing its instructions and data. In the first computers, the memory was integrated seamlessly with the processor so the computer was capable of running just one program at a time. Loading a program into the memory was a lengthy tedious task. Only after a program was loaded into memory was the computer able to execute it. This procedure still currently exists, and a program has to be loaded (at least partially) in memory in order to be able to run. However, in modern systems, the memory is a different modular component, as suggested by the von Neumann architecture. The first computers supported a relatively small memory, which limited the maximum size of the programs that could be executed as well as the number of programs that could run in parallel.

As already stated, a major step in the development of computers was the introduction of the Von Neumann architecture (see the section "Von Neumann Architecture" in Chapter 1). The architecture (Figure 5.2) divides the system into several different components, so that future developments related to one component will have only minimal effects on other components. This type of modularity is currently used in many other industries, but for computers it was made possible due von Neumann's ideas. Prior to von Neumann, the computer's logic was tightly integrated, and each changed introduced affected other parts as well. Relating to a different industry, it is like a driver that has replaced a car's tires and has to modify the engine as well. When the modularity that stems from von Neumann's ideas was introduced to computer systems, it enabled reduced complexity and supported fast technological developments. For example, increasing the memory capacity and capabilities was easily implemented without any required change to other system components.

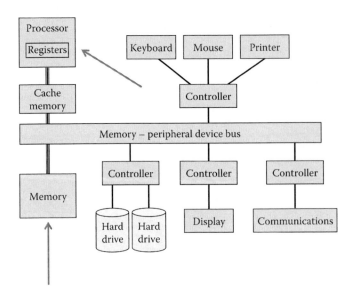

FIGURE 5.1   Memory as part of the system.

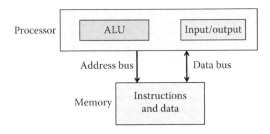

FIGURE 5.2   Von Neumann architecture.

One of the most important developments was to increase the capacity of computer memory, which manifested itself in the ability to better utilize the system. This improved utilization was achieved by enabling the central processing unit (CPU) to run more than one program at a time. This way, during the input and output (I/O) activities of one program, the CPU did not have to wait idle for I/O operations to complete. As several programs can reside in the memory, even if one or more are waiting for input or output, the CPU can still be kept busy.

One of the consequences of dividing the system into distinct components was the need to design a common mechanism for data transfers between the different components. The mechanism, which will be explained later in this book, is called a *bus*. As it relates to the memory activities, the bus is responsible for transferring instructions and data from the memory to the CPU as well as for transferring some of the data back to be stored in the memory.

It should be noted that when there is just one bus, as is the case with the von Neumann architecture, the instructions and data have to compete in accessing the bus. The usual and standard solution is implementing a wider and faster bus that will be able to support all requests without becoming a bottleneck (see the explanation in Chapter 7, "Bus").

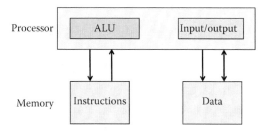

FIGURE 5.3   Harvard architecture.

Another approach to release the possible bus bottleneck was suggested by the Harvard architecture (see the section "Computer Systems" in Chapter 3), which utilizes a dual memory/bus concept (Figure 5.3).

The main idea of eliminating contingencies and preventing data-transfer bottlenecks is achieved by using two different memories, one for instructions and the other for data. Each such memory has its own bus, so the potential bus access conflicts do not develop. While the control unit fetches the next instruction, it can fetch the operands without interfering with the other arithmetic and logic unit (ALU)—memory activities.

Memory Sizes

The memory sizes used in modern computers, as well as in other digital appliances such as smartphones, cameras, smart TVs, and so on, follow Moore's law, and memory size is constantly increasing. The first computers, even prior to the appearance of the personal computer (PC), used several thousands of memory cells. The first PC used 640 KB, and since then, memory capacity has been increasing at a rapid pace. On the one hand, the applications have become more sophisticated, using tools that require larger memories; and on the other hand, as predicted by Moore's law, memory prices are plunging. The net result is systems with constantly increasing memory sizes.

Table 5.1 provides a list of memory sizes (past, current, and future) as well as their meaning both in decimal and binary notations.

Although the higher-end sizes in the table are not relevant for memories (yet), since the current amount of memory in a single system is measured in gigabytes, larger memories are used by various virtual machines that comprise of many systems working in parallel, as is the case with cloud computing, for example.

TABLE 5.1   Memory Sizes

Name	Mnemonic	Binary Size	Decimal Size
Kilobyte	KB	2^{10}	1,024
Megabyte	MB	2^{20}	1,048,576
Gigabyte	GB	2^{30}	1,073,741,824
Terabyte	TB	2^{40}	1,099,511,627,776
Petabyte	PB	2^{50}	1,125,899,906,842,624
Exabyte	EB	2^{60}	1,152,921,504,606,846,976
Zettabyte	ZB	2^{70}	1,180,591,620,717,411,303,424
Yottabyte	YB	2^{80}	1,208,925,819,614,629,174,706,176

Memory Organization

Technically speaking, memory is a digital device that is used to store data. Based on this general definition, hard drives, CD-ROMs, disk-on keys, and so on are all various types of memory devices. In this chapter, the emphasis will be on the computer's memory (random access memory [RAM]), which, unlike most other devices, is used only for temporary data storage. After turning the system off and on again, or just rebooting (restarting) the computer, all the data that was stored in the memory is gone. For that reason, memory is referred to as volatile in contrast to other storage devices that maintain the data even after the electricity is turned off, which are referred to as nonvolatile.

The computer memory can be described as a one-dimensional matrix of cells used to store and retrieve data. Each cell has an address, which provides a unique mechanism for accessing the data it stores. As with a matrix, the address is used as the index to the cell. In various computers' implementations, the memory cell may have different sizes. Sometimes, it is one byte (8 bits), and other times it may be a word of various sizes. If the cell's size is a byte, the memory is described as *byte addressable*, or each address refers to 1 byte. This is also the minimal piece of information to be accessed (brought from the memory or sent to the memory). The cell is an atomic unit, so if its size is 1 byte, all memory accesses will be in multiples of 1 byte. On the other hand, if its size is one word, all memory accesses will be in multiples of one word. When there is a need to access a smaller portion of the byte, the whole byte will be brought from memory and the irrelevant parts will be masked out. Consider the example of a byte used to hold eight different binary switches. When the need arises to check, for example, bit number five, the whole byte will be loaded from memory, and the CPU will use an AND* instruction with the constant $0000\ 0100_2$. If the result is zero, it means that bit number five was zero or "False"; otherwise it would be "True."

The first generations of computers referred to memory as RAM in order to differentiate it from serial devices such as magnetic tapes. The name was chosen to describe the important feature of being able to directly access any cell without the need to read all previous ones. This direct access implies that the access time is constant and does not depend on the cell's location. Although all memories provide direct access, the name RAM is still being used several decades after it was coined. Figure 5.4 provides a visual representation of the memory organization (partial view).

In systems such as PCs, in which the memory is byte addressable, the registers are usually larger and are based on words. It should be noted, however, that the term *word* has different meanings, and various systems use different sizes for their words. In some systems, it may represent 16 bits; in others, like the x86† based architecture, it is 32 bits; and in modern PCs, it is 64 bits. A larger register implies that a register includes several bytes. However, regardless of the size of the register or the number of bytes it contains, the memory is still byte addressable.

---

* AND is a bitwise logical operation that produced "True" (or a binary "1") if, and only if, the two operands were "True."

† x86 is a family of PC architectures based on the Intel 8086 processor. This architecture was initially introduced in the late 1970s, and the first systems used 16-bit words. Although the architecture developed over the years with systems such as the 80286, 80386, and 80486 (see Table 1.2), it maintained a backward compatibility.

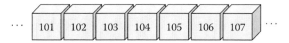

FIGURE 5.4 Memory organization.

One important register for understanding memory operations is the memory address register (MAR), which holds the address of the bytes to be read from or written to the memory. Like other registers in the x86-based systems, this register is a 32-bit register. This means that the largest address supported is $2^{32}-1$ (or 4 GB of memory). During the 1990s, it became evident that, due to this limitation, word size would have to be increased to 64 bits. It should be noted that there were other systems that used 64-bit words; however, for the PC market with its vast amounts of software packages, the change was significantly slower, and the 64-bit versions only started to appear during the first decade of the twenty-first century. As already mentioned in Chapter 2, "Data Representation," the larger word size provides a higher degree of accuracy when performing arithmetic calculations. Nevertheless, the main contributor to the switch to a 64-bit architecture was the memory limitation imposed by 32-bit architectures. During the 1990s, it became evident that unless the maximum supported memory was increased, the PC platform would not be able to develop further.

There are many types of memory, for example, volatile and nonvolatile, but there is an additional important distinction that is based on speed. The software developer sees the memory as part of the hardware platform and as such prefers to get as much memory as possible as well as the fastest memory available. This, of course, is possible, but it is associated with high costs. For that reason, most computer systems implement a hierarchy of memories. Memory close to the processor is faster and costs more, and, for that reason, its quantity is smaller. As it gets further away from the processor, it becomes slower, cheaper, and larger (Figure 5.5).

In addition to the registers—which are a type of temporary, limited, and very fast memory that resides within the processor—in most cases, systems include several cache memories (to be elaborated on in subsequent chapters) that increase the access speed to frequently used data and instructions. On the other hand, the disks (hard drives, to be discussed in Chapter 9, "Storage") are sometimes considered an additional type of memory since at run

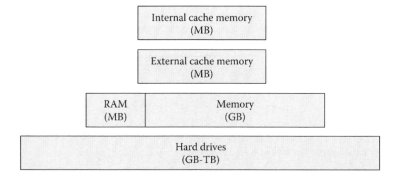

FIGURE 5.5 Memory hierarchy.

time, only parts of the executing program reside in memory and other, nonused parts are stored on disk. As such, the disk acts as an extension of the memory.

The main memory (RAM) is usually implemented using the dynamic RAM (DRAM) technology, which is characterized by the need to refresh the data every couple of milliseconds. This type of memory requires only one transistor* and one capacitor[†] for each bit. The fact that these components are extremely small, and that as technology proceeds, they become even smaller, provides the capability of designing systems with billions of bytes.

The cache memory, on the other hand, is implemented using a faster technology (static RAM [SRAM]), which does not have to be refreshed but requires between four and six transistors for each bit. This is the reason that cache memory is also more expensive compared with standard memory.

Schematically, the memory access in byte-addressable PCs uses two internal registers:

- Memory address register (MAR), used to hold the relevant memory address to read from or write into

- Memory data register (MDR), used to hold the data to be written into the memory or the data read from memory

A simplified version of memory access can be described by the following steps. If the processor needs to read data from address 1000, it has to put the value 1000 into the MAR and issue a read command. The memory controller will fetch the content and place it in the MDR, where it will be available for the processor. On the other hand, if the processor needs to store data in memory, for example, due to an instruction in the program that is being executed, the processor places the data in the MDR, places the appropriate address in the MAR, and issues a write command. It is the memory controller's task to actually perform the required operation.

The memory's read and write procedures previously described were initially intended for a single byte. The memory is byte addressable and the registers were of a byte size. When the word size increased, for example to 16 bits (or 2 bytes), the memory controller had to read or write 2 bytes at a time. This was implemented in different ways by various hardware manufacturers. The PC, for example, used a mechanism in which the low-order byte was stored in the leftmost location and the high-order byte was stored in the next byte location. For that reason, a 16-bit word is written into memory in an inverse order. For example, the 16-bit word that contains the characters "AB" is written in memory as "BA," the first byte is the leftmost character, and the second is the rightmost character. Due to compatibility reasons, this was also true when the word increased in size, and a 32-bit word that contains "ABCD" is written into memory as "DCBA."

---

* A transistor is a semiconductor component used to amplify and switch electrical signals. It is an important building block of all electronic devices.

[†] A capacitor is an electrical component that is used to store energy and is thus used, among other things, as a mechanism for storing data.

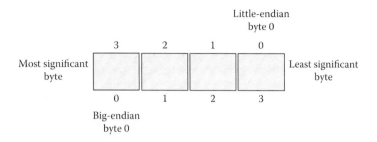

FIGURE 5.6   Big- and little-endian.

This method, which is called *little-endian*, was implemented mainly by the various PCs, while many other computers used the *big-endian* method, which is more intuitive and understandable (Figure 5.6).

Explanation

In a "standard" way, the 32-bit word that is represented in Figure 5.6 is written from left to right (big-endian), which means that the most significant byte is on the left and the least significant byte is on the right. With the little-endian method, the most significant byte is on the right and the least significant byte is on the left.

The big-endian method is considered more "natural" since numbers are written from left to right, which means that the most significant digit is on the left, and when reading numbers one usually starts with the most significant digit first. For example, the number 57 is called fifty-seven (it starts with the five). It should be noted, however, that there are languages (German, Danish, Dutch, etc.) in which the number is pronounced using the little-endian method, starting with the seven in the last example.

The little-endian method remained due to the compatibility maintained in PC architecture. Originally, when the word size increased from 1 byte to 2 bytes, the memory controller had to transfer the 2 bytes one at a time. Implementing the little-endian method was simpler, and it remained, although currently the memory controller transfers a whole word at a time.

Due to the wide spread of PCs and the fact they use a little-endian method, some vendors implemented a dual method (bi-endian). This means that the system supported both methods (big- and little-endian), and it was possible to switch from one method to the other at boot time. Later versions provided a software-based mechanism for switching between the methods.

For the accuracy of this description, it should be noted that there was another method that integrated the two methods. The PDP computer, designed by DEC, used a 32-bit word. A word that contains "ABCD" was written in memory as "BADC." This means that the word was divided into two halves. The halves were written in order (big-endian); however, the bytes in each half were written using little-endian. For that reason, this method was call mixed-endian or middle-endian.

Despite the little-endian method's popularity among PCs, it should be noted that most networks use the big-endian method. Systems and software engineers do not have to bother

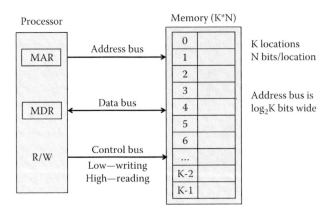

FIGURE 5.7 Memory buses.

about the data migration from one method to the other since this is done automatically by the hardware.

In a byte addressable–based architecture, the memory is organized in bytes, and all data transfer to and from the memory is done in blocks containing several bytes. It is possible to access several bytes in one access cycle; however, it is not possible to read or write less than a whole byte. As previously explained, even if the program has to access one bit, it will have to read a byte and mask off all other nonrelevant bits. The mechanism for transferring data between the memory and the processor is based on buses (this issue will be elaborated in the coming chapters). Logically, the bus is divided into three distinct buses with a different functionality. One is responsible for sending the relevant address that was put in the MAR. The second bus is responsible for transferring the data. This bus has to be wide enough to accommodate the full width of the register. The third bus is intended for signaling the data direction if it has to be read from the memory or written to the memory (Figure 5.7).

The width* of each of the buses should be suitable for transferring the required data. For that reason, the address bus should be wide enough to represent the address of the last cell in memory. In other words, if k is the last physical address, the width of the address bus should be $Log_2 k$. The data bus should be wide enough to accommodate the size of the memory cell. In a byte-addressable architecture, it should be at least 1 byte wide. However, in cases where the registers are wider, for example 32 bits, then the bus should be wider as well. Otherwise, for transferring the data into the register, the bus will require four cycles, which will slow down the transfer rate as well as the execution. In modern computers, the data bus width is significantly larger than the memory cells, so several bytes will be transferred in one cycle. The third bus is used as a control signal so it can be very narrow (one bit to signal if it is a read or a write operation).

---

* *Bus width* is a term that defines the amount of data to be transferred by the bus during a predefined period of time. In this case, the intention is the amount of data (bits) that can be transferred in one cycle. Usually, the bus width is defined by bits, bytes, or megabytes per time. For example, a 100 MB/sec bus can transfer 100 MB of data every second. In the above case, the intention is the number of bytes or bits the bus can transfer in a single cycle.

The corresponding internal registers should be of the same size. The MDR that holds the data will have the same width as the data bus, and the MAR that holds the address will have the same width as the address bus.

The memory and the memory buses are significantly slower compared with the processor. This was one of the reasons for implementing the memory hierarchy as well as increasing the bus width. However, in order to prevent or minimize possible memory bottlenecks, additional tactics were developed. The reduced instruction set computer (RISC) architecture (see the section in Chapter 4 on RISC technology) was developed with the intention of minimizing memory access by using many registers, which augments the memory hierarchy. Virtual operating systems (to be explained later in this chapter) provide an additional software-based contribution to the problem. Nevertheless, with all the tactics used, there are still cases in which memory access can significantly hamper the systems' performance. One such example is parallel systems with a shared memory. In these cases, several and sometimes many processors are trying to access the memory, and the total bandwidth may not be sufficient. In such cases not only is the bus width increased but sometimes additional buses are also added to the memory (Figure 5.8).

Figure 5.8 depicts a dual-processor system, which implements a separate set of buses for each processor. This means that if one bus is busy transferring data to one processor, the other processor does not have to wait, and it can use its own bus. This solution is called a dual-port memory since there are two buses capable of working in parallel. Similarly, it is possible to increase the number of buses connecting the memory to the processors (Figure 5.9).

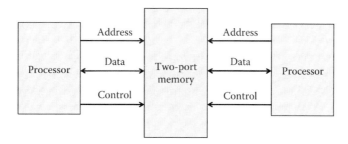

FIGURE 5.8   Dual-port memory.

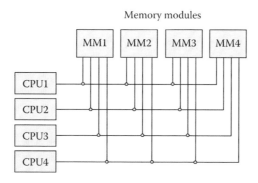

FIGURE 5.9   Multiport memory.

Implementing additional ports (or buses) implies additional cost, which sometimes may be significant. The main cost contributor is not related to hardware (the cable) but rather to the required synchronization mechanisms that have to be put in place to prevent writing in parallel from two processors to the same location, or the reading of data before it has been updated by a different processor (very similar to the pipeline hazards available in the CPU).

Figure 5.9 depicts a four-processor system with a shared memory and with multiple parallel buses. To enhance the memory speed, it was divided into four different parts, each capable of working in parallel with the others.

Running Programs

The way programs run on the system and their memory utilization has changed in the years following the technological developments (see Chapter 1, "Introduction and Historic Perspective"). The first computers and the operating systems that supported them were capable of running just one program at a time. It was the operating system's responsibility to load the program prior to the execution. The physical memory had to be large enough to accommodate the whole program as well as the system utilities it may have needed. If the available memory was not large enough, the program could not be loaded and could not be run. This mode of operation was called monoprogramming, since only one program was executing at a given time.

This mode of operation was extremely inefficient, since it did not provide the means to adequately utilize the system. It should be noted that at that time computer systems were very expensive, so there was an economic pressure to utilize the system in the best way possible. If the price of a computer system was several millions of dollars and it was not fully utilized, it meant wasting large amounts of money. However, since the first systems ran just one program at a time, this inherently created a utilization problem. When the program was waiting for input or output, which was, and still is, significantly slower than the processor, it meant that the processor was waiting idle (Figure 5.10).

Figure 5.10 depicts the situation in which some of the time the processor executes the program, but during other times it is just waiting.

Another side effect of the monoprogramming method was that since the whole program had to be loaded into memory, the physical memory size should have been large enough to accommodate the largest possible program. For many other small programs, parts of the memory remained unused (Figure 5.11).

Figure 5.11 depicts four different situations. The leftmost diagram is of the system waiting to execute a program, for example, just after the system was booted. Part of the memory is used by the operating system and another part is used by the various device drivers. The unused part or the program area is for loading the program to be run. The other

FIGURE 5.10 Monoprogramming.

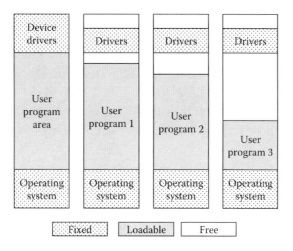

FIGURE 5.11 Monoprogramming: Memory content.

three diagrams represent three programs that are being executed. Each program needs a different memory size, so in all these cases, some part of the memory is not being used.

The high costs associated with purchasing a computer system, on the one hand, and, on the other, the monoprogramming method that does not allow full utilization of the system, called for an urgent change. The improvement included some hardware changes as well as some operating system modifications to allow more than one program to be run at a time. In addition to a better utilization of the costly resources, the move from monoprogramming also provided additional benefits:

- Dividing the program into smaller programs: Instead of running one long program, it is better and more efficient to run several programs one after the other. It should be noted that the first computers had some reliability problems (problems with hardware and operating systems and even bugs in the application), so if a problem occurred during a long program run, it had to be restarted.* This change in the way people develop their programs became very important with the introduction of interactive programs as well as modern architectures that use several processors and several cores. Furthermore, with the development of the software engineering discipline, once-huge programs were replaced by a modular approach in order to ease the development process as well as allow for future easier maintenance.

- Better and fairer resource management: With the monoprogramming methods, a program can use all computer resources for the duration of its run, and no other programs can run. When there are several programs that run in parallel, the operating system is responsible for defining mechanisms for priority setting, so the resources can be divided among several identical priority programs.

---

* For accuracy reasons, it should be stated that for dealing with reliability problems, another method was developed, in which the programs save some checkpoints and, in the event of a problem, the program could be restarted from the last checkpoint.

- Support for interactive programs: Support for interactive usage was developed at a later stage, but before it can be implemented, the system has to be able to support the execution of more than one program at a time. It should be noted, and it will be explained later, that the term *in parallel* is not accurate. Since there was just one processor, it means that only one program/task was executing; however, when one program was waiting for input or output, another program could proceed. The interactive user has the impression that his/her job is the only one executing.

The idea of changing the system so it would be able to support multiple programs stems from the understanding that the computer is fast enough to run several task, so that each such task will not be aware of the existence of the other tasks and will "feel" as if it is running by itself. As part of the new features, the new term *time sharing* was coined, which represents the system behavior during the execution of several tasks. The processor shares its time among all available tasks or processes. The processor works on one task for a predefined amount of time, as defined by the operating system, and then it moves to the next task, which gets its time, and so on. Over the years, many scheduling algorithms were developed for handling the amount of time each task gets; however, these are part of the operating system and will not be discussed here.*

Task scheduling includes decisions on the next task to be executed, the amount of time it runs, setting priorities, and so on, and it is performed by the operating system. Additional hardware features were required in order to provide the required capabilities, such as protecting the integrity of the tasks and preventing a situation in which a task is trying to access data that belongs to some other task or to the operating system. In addition, the hardware had to support the context switching, which means saving the whole execution environment of a task while it is waiting for its turn to run. This execution environment includes the content of the hardware registers at the moment of preemption, the content of the stack, the status of the open files that are being used, and so on.

Figure 5.12 depicts and emphasizes that in a single-processor system, although we refer to programs/tasks running in parallel, a better term would be *time sharing*, since the processor shares the time between the various tasks. The figure depicts three tasks that are in the process of executing, sharing the system's resources, and using the single available processor.

To better understand the technological advancements, we will use an example. From a monoprogramming mode (see Figure 5.10) in which each program/task works by itself,

---

* For completeness, some of the most famous scheduling algorithms are
  - *FCFS* (first come first served), in which the processor works on the tasks as they were introduced. Each task gets the full amount of processor time it needs, and only after it finishes does the processor move to the next task.
  - *SJF* (shortest job first), in which the task has to declare the amount of time it requires and then, if a short task enters (shorter than the time remaining to the current executing task), the system will switch to the new task.
  - *Priority*, in which the operating system assigns a priority to each task to be executed, or alternatively the task can define its priority. The order of execution is defined by that priority.
  - *Round Robin*, in which the processor executes all available tasks in a circular manner. Each task waits for its turn, and then gets a predefined amount of time. If it did not finish, it will wait for its next turn.

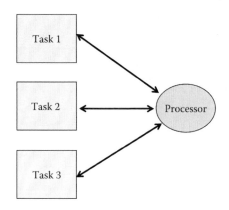

FIGURE 5.12   Time sharing.

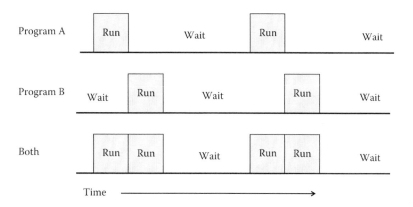

FIGURE 5.13   Dual programming.

the system moved to dual programming, which provided the capabilities for running two tasks "in parallel" (Figure 5.13).

The upper part of the diagram depicts the situation when only task A is executing. The middle part refers to the execution of task B, and the lower part depicts the system when the two tasks are running. It is clear that the two tasks do not execute in parallel (this is a single-processor system, so there are no resources to run two tasks in parallel). One task runs only when the system is idle, that is, when the other task is not running.

The important issue, however, is that the processor's idle time decreased. This means that the utilization of the system's resources increased and the computer system was more productive, which improved its price/performance ratio. It should be noted that it is possible that the second task (B) will not arrive exactly after task A has finished (as is the case in the figure). In such a case, it will have to wait for its turn, which may result in some increase in the response time, but the processor's idle time will decrease anyhow.

Based on the success of dual programming, a natural development was to enhance the method so it would accommodate a larger number of tasks executing "in parallel." This is the multiprogramming method (see Figure 5.14, which depicts three tasks).

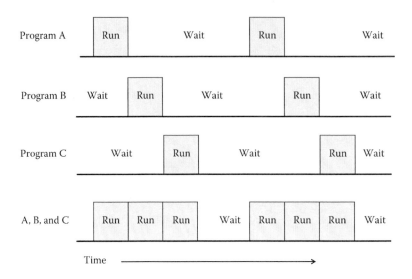

FIGURE 5.14   Three tasks "in parallel."

As with dual programming, the processor's idle time continues to decrease. It should be noted, however, that the figure is very simplistic. In real life, no one can ensure that the tasks will arrive at the processor's idle windows. However, as previously explained (in the dual-programming example), even if the tasks arrive at the same time, it is the operating system's responsibility to run them, but the increased workload will allow a better system utilization, which will improve the price/performance ratio.

The number of tasks executed concurrently is not, of course, limited to three, and in most modern computers, this number is significantly larger; this is mainly due to the virtual memory concept, which does not require the whole program to reside in memory, just the running parts (this will be elaborated on in this chapter).

The number of concurrently executing tasks can be increased as long as the available resources can support it. The underlying assumption for increasing the number of tasks stems from several understandings:

- Most programs do not use just the processor and need additional resources. In many cases, especially with interactive programs, some input data will be needed and output will be generated. Furthermore, during execution, the program may need data that is stored on the disk (hard drive). Such devices are very slow compared with the processor speed. When human beings are involved in providing the input, it may take a very long time; that is, the program is waiting for input, but the user is talking on the phone or has even left for lunch. In all these examples, if the system uses a monoprogramming approach, the system utilization will be very low.

- The memory in the first computers was limited and very expensive. Although in modern computers, this is not an issue any more as memory capacity has increased dramatically and its price is insignificant (one of the consequences of Moore's law), we still enjoy the developments that were required to address past problems. This is not the only case in which technological advances were required to fix a problem that does not exist anymore.

- The processor, as well as the whole computer system, was very expensive, and special emphasis was placed on using it in the best and most efficient way. This too is a past problem, since computer systems today are relatively cheap. Furthermore, with the PC revolution, the price/performance issue is not important any more. Due to its low price, people buy a PC and use it only for a fraction of the day. Overutilization was replaced by a better response time as well as a better user experience.

- Another historic issue was the understanding that exchanging between tasks is sometimes impossible and, if it is possible, it is time consuming. Since then the hardware has been modified, new context-switching* instructions have been added, and the overhead associated with task switching has been lowered. Nevertheless, every such context switching still involves some degree of overhead that should be considered. For example, in modern architectures that employ many registers, the overhead is larger since the system, among other things, has to store the contents of these registers and then reload them with new content.

Estimating the Processor's Utilization

It is possible to estimate the processor's utilization when running a specific load, but to do so we will have to estimate the percentage of time the tasks/processes are waiting for input or output. The processor's utilization can come in handy in cases where a system's engineer has to figure out the exact required architecture. On the one hand, the decreasing cost of hardware makes it possible to decide on a much larger configuration; on the other, however, if the system is to be used by users and there are thousands of such systems to be installed, more reliable decision making is required.

The estimate is given by the formula

$$CPU\_Utilization = 1 - p^n$$

where

  p   is the average percentage of time processes are waiting for I/O
  n   is the number of processes executing in the system

More specifically, the detailed formula is

$$CPU\_Utilization = 1 - \left(p_1^* \ p_2^* \ p_3^* \cdots \ p_n \right)$$

---

* Context switching is the process that changes the process that is being executed by the processor. Before the processor can switch to a different process, all the registers' content has to be saved, as well as other running variables. Then the registers' running environment for the new process has to be loaded (including reloading the registers with their original content).

where

p₁   is the percentage of time the first process is waiting for I/O

p₂   is the percentage of time the second process is waiting for I/O, and so on

n   is the number of processes

For example, assuming

p = 0.8 (on average the processes are waiting for I/O 80% of the time)

n = 4 (there are four processes executing)

the processor's utilization will be

$$CPU\_Utilization = 1 - 0.8^4$$

$$= 1 - 0.4096$$

$$= 0.59$$

In this example, and assuming there are no additional bottlenecks, such as memory for instance, the processor's utilization will be 59%.

Using the CPU utilization formula can provide an effective mechanism in decision-making regarding upgrading a system, assuming the memory size of a given system limits its CPU utilization. This happens when the free and available memory size provides the space for a limited number of tasks. Since the memory upgrade cost is known, it is simple to calculate the effect of this upgrade. This is shown in Figure 5.15.

The figure depicts three configurations:

- The leftmost diagram depicts the system just after the boot process has been completed. The system consists of 1 GB memory; part is used by the operating system while the other part is empty and will be used for user processes.

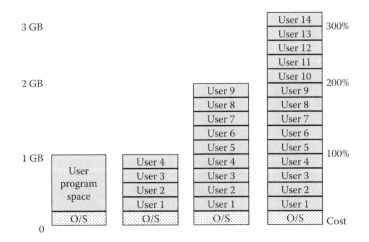

FIGURE 5.15   Example of calculating CPU utilization.

- The next (to the right) diagram is the same system, but in this case the memory holds four user processes. For the sake of this example, we assume that the empty part of the memory can accommodate four processes considering the average size of each process.

- The next possible diagram depicts an upgraded system in which the memory size was doubled. Instead of the original 1 GB, this system has 2 GB. In this system, the number of processes executed concurrently increased as well, and instead of the four processes in the 1 GB architecture, there are now nine user processes.

- The last (rightmost) diagram depicts the original system after it has been upgraded twice, and instead of the original 1 GB, the memory size is now 3 GB. Once again, the number of user processes increases as well, and instead of the four processes in the original architecture and the nine processes in the 2 GB system, the system is now capable of running 14 processes concurrently.

- The rightmost scale does not relate to the cost of the system but to the memory size and the costs associated only with the memory.

If on average each such process is waiting for I/O 80% of the time, then the processor's utilization of the original configuration will be 59%. Upgrading the system by adding 1 GB of memory increases the number of processors as well as the processor's utilization. Using the formula for $n = 9$ reveals that the processor's utilization climbs to 87%. Since the upgrade cost is known, it is simple to assess if the additional added performance gained by increasing the CPU utilization by 28% (87% − 59% = 28%) can be justified by the additional cost.

The same assessment can be repeated for the third architecture. When the memory size increases to 3 GB, there are 14 concurrent processes. The processor's utilization will increase to 96% and once again, since the upgrade cost is known, its merit can be judged based on the increased performance of the system. In this specific case, the first upgrade yields a 28% performance increase, while the second upgrade yields just an additional 9%, so it may be that the best course of action would be to use a 2 GB system.

The important issue regarding the processor's utilization is the fact that all these calculations and assessments can be performed without the real upgrade, so it is possible for the system's engineer to achieve the right solution without spending money on the real upgrade or using any of the available benchmarks. However, all these calculations are based on the assumption that the site's processes behavior is known. Actually, it is extremely difficult to estimate the percentage of time a process is waiting for I/O.

In addition, the abovementioned formula does not take into account the user's point of view. If the described system is used for interactive tasks, one has to consider that a CPU utilization of 96% may provide an improved price/performance, but the response time will probably be very high. In such a case, the money saved by the improved utilization may have a negative impact considering the time wasted by users while waiting for the system's response.

Partitions

It is possible to implement multiprogramming by using a variety of mechanisms. The first and most simple approach is by defining and using partitions. A partition is a defined area in memory that stores a program to be executed. It is a type of running environment. Originally, the partitions were defined during the boot process. Each partition had a different size, which could not be changed until the next boot. The total size of the partitions is the free memory available on the system for user processes. The partition size defined the processes that could execute in the specific partition. Since at that time, prior to the virtual memory concept being developed, the whole process had to be loaded, only some of the partitions were applicable. The number of partitions defined determined the number of processes that could be run concurrently. Managing the partitions and deciding which program would be loaded to which partition was the operating system's responsibility. The partition idea tried to mimic the first monoprogramming computers, and the intention was to divide the computer into several predefined working environments, each one resembling a monoprogramming system. As such, the first implementations of partitions used a fixed-size partition, in which the total free available memory was divided by the number of partitions. Only at a later stage did the designers understand that the problems associated with monoprogramming exist with fixed- and identical-size partitions. The next stage was to define partitions with variable sizes. By using this idea, the partitions continued to mimic the monoprogramming concept but with some improvement. It was the operating system's role to handle the partitions and to decide, based on the processes' memory requirements, which partition provided the best fit. To implement these changes, the operating system had to be aware of the number of partitions and their sizes as well as the size of each process to be executed. Each process/program to be executed had to specify its memory requirements, and this parameter was used by the operating system in its allocations decisions, as shown in Figure 5.16.

The figure relates to fixed partitions. The term *fixed* in this context does not define the fixed size of the partitions but rather the fact that the number of partitions is determined at boot time. This means that the number of partitions remains fixed and cannot be changed until the next boot process.

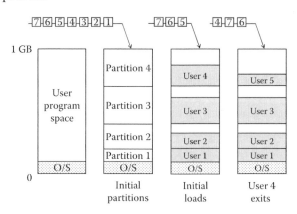

FIGURE 5.16   Fixed partitions.

The figure consists of four connected diagrams:

- The leftmost diagram defines the memory characteristics of the system. In this case, it is a 1 GB system, and the diagram depicts the free memory available for the user processes. To simplify the diagram, the device drivers, which should have been loaded at the higher addresses of memory, were not included.

- The next (to the right) diagram relates to the system after the free memory space was divided into four distinct parts (partitions) with different sizes. As previously stated, with fixed partitions, changing the number of partitions or altering their sizes requires a new boot of the system. At the top of the diagram is a list (queue) of priority processes (marked as 1–7) that are waiting to be executed.

- The next diagram depicts the situation after the operating system has started allocating the partitions to the available and waiting processes. The operating system allocates each one of the first four to the best fitted partition, even though it can be seen that, in most cases, the process's memory requirements are lower than the partition size, which yields unused memory.

- The next diagram depicts a situation some time later. At some time, Process 4 finishes executing and then the operating system has to allocate the next process in line. Unfortunately, Process 5 requires very little memory, but the only available partition is a large one. The scheduler* allocates the large partition to the small task, wasting a large part of the partition's memory. It should be noted that modern operating systems may have elevated wisdom regarding the scheduling process, for example, making decisions based on some additional parameters; however, in this example, the scheduler decisions are based on one parameter only, the next process in line (this is an example of a simple first come first served [FCFS] algorithm—see the footnote in the section "Running Programs" in this chapter).

The fixed-partitions mechanism, although not optimal, provided the required possibility of running several processes in parallel. However, its most important contribution was that it paved the way for a more sophisticated mechanism—the dynamic partitions.

The understanding that fixed partitions still waste memory resources pushed for new developments. The dynamic partitions are based on the fixed partitions with one step forward. The concept of dynamic partitions is based on the idea that the number of partitions and their sizes can be changed by the operating system during normal operations. This was intended to provide better memory management and better processor utilization by increasing the number of processes being executed concurrently. Unfortunately, there are also some disadvantages; since the operating system's overhead increases, there needs to be a new mechanism for handling "holes," which are parts of unallocated memory that has to be maintained, moved, and combined, as shown in Figure 5.17.

---

* A scheduler is the part of the operating system that is responsible for scheduling the processes and deciding which one will be executed next. In the partitions example, the scheduler decides on the applicable partition.

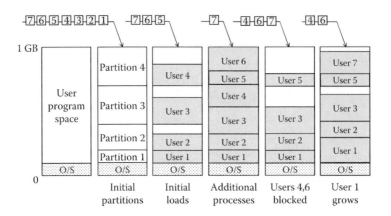

FIGURE 5.17   Dynamic partitions.

This figure is based on Figure 5.16, and the first three (leftmost) diagrams are identical:

- The leftmost diagram defines the memory characteristics of the system. Once again, it is a 1 GB system, and the diagram depicts the free memory available for the user processes.

- The next (to the right) diagram relates to the system after the free memory space was divided into four partitions with different sizes. At the top of the diagram is the queue of processes waiting to be executed.

- The next diagram depicts the situation after the operating system has allocated a partition for each process. In this case, since there are only four partitions, then four processes are loaded into memory.

- After allocating the four processes, the operating system realizes that there are holes at the end of some of the partitions. Furthermore, the next process in line (Process 5) is very small, and the amount of memory it requires can be obtained by combining the remaining holes. The operating system moves the two upper partitions in such a way that all the holes are combined to create a continuous segment of memory. The operating system then defines a new partition to be used for the new memory segments and allocates it to Process 5. Furthermore, the available memory is sufficient to load Process 6 as well, so the operating system creates an additional partition and loads Process 6 into it. The diagram depicts the situation after all six processes have been loaded.

- At some point in time, Processes 4 and 6 finish executing and the memory allocated for these processes is marked as free. Regarding holes that are being created, the operating systems use various approaches. The basic rule is not to perform extra work if it is not needed. For that reason, in most cases the operating system will not use dynamic holes management. The dynamic holes management implies that the operating system will move the partitions in order to create a larger continuous segment. The common behavior is holes management by demand, in which only if a process requires a larger chunk of memory will the operating system move the partitions in order to create it. In this specific example, the memory holes management is per demand. It should be noted that holes management is an overhead to the system, so for dynamic holes management, the operating system increases the system's overhead, but it is ready for future memory requirements. With holes management per demand, the overhead is lower, but when a request arrives, it will take longer to fulfill it.

- At a later stage, Process 1 requests additional memory. As part of the improvements to the operating system, some new functions were added to help the user better manage the process's memory requirements. One of these functions is memory allocation (MALLOC).* Unfortunately, Process 1 is in a partition and it is using its entire size. It may even be that the process was placed in a larger partition and the operating system deallocated the unnecessary memory, which was assigned to a different partition. TO provide the requested memory, the operating system can roll out Process 1 until a larger partition becomes available. When the memory is available, Process 1 will be rolled in again so it can resume working. In the case depicted, the operating system checks if it can fulfill the request and realizes that there is a large hole after partition 3. Then the operating system moves partitions 2 and 3 upward and creates the newly requested chunk that is combined with partition 1.

Virtual Memory

The solutions described in the previous sections were intended to provide the possibility to run several tasks concurrently. However, as the applications' sizes increased, even larger memories were able to store only a limited number of tasks, which introduced new problems.

As already stated, the main motivational factor for the technological improvements was economical. The first computers were extremely expensive and for justifying the expense the computer center manager had to make sure the system was being used as much as possible. Computer vendors provided the mechanisms for multiprogramming in an effort to provide a better price/performance ratio. However, the then existing technology, which was based on loading the whole program into memory, hampered these efforts. Although the memory size could be increased, the price associated with such a move was significant. Furthermore, after carefully analyzing the executing program's behavior, it became clear that each program has large parts that are only rarely being used and other parts that are not being used at all. For example, some parts of the program are used for error handling, and it may be that in a specific run, there are no errors to be handled. This behavior led to the understanding that it is not necessary to load whole programs into memory, provided

---

* MALLOC is an operating system function intended for dynamic allocation of memory to the running process. Usually, there two types of variables: static variables, which reside in the program and exist as long as the program is running; and automatic variables, which can be stored in the process stack every time the program calls a new function (or method). There are cases in which these two types of variables are not flexible enough and then the software developer can use a third type to be stored in a newly acquired piece of memory. The program uses the MALLOC function to get these additional memory cells, and when they are no longer required, the memory will be returned to the operating system.

other mechanisms may be developed that will load the missing parts on demand. Another important motivator was the development of the off-the-shelf applications' market. Such applications should be able to run on each system, even if its physical memory size is limited. In such cases, it may perhaps run slower, but it should be able to run.

There are several solutions that provide the means to run a program that needs more memory than the physical memory available. One simple solution was to have the developers deal with the issue. The developer of course is familiar with the program and understands its patterns of execution, so a tailored solution can be developed. Unfortunately, such solutions are sometimes limited to a specific system. An example of such an approach is to use an overlay mechanism. The underlying assumption is that the program can be divided into different parts (overlays) and each such part can be executed independently from the other parts. Alternatively, the program can be developed in such a way that it uses different parts executed one after the other. When using a limited memory system, only one part at a time will be loaded into memory, and when it finishes, it will be unloaded, making space for the next part to be loaded and executed. Although modern computers have adopted other more efficient and sophisticated methods, the overlay mechanism is used by some appliances as well as by cellular phones.

For example, let us assume a specific program is divided into six parts, each one responsible for a different activity. The first three parts work independently; that is, when part one is working it will never interact with parts two and three, or when part two is running is does not call or relate to data that resides in parts one and three. Similarity, parts five and six work independently. Part four, on the other hand, is a common framework that runs throughout the whole program, and it provides services required by all other parts. The old and simple solution was to load all parts into memory, which represents an inefficient move. A better approach would be to define three overlays as described in Figure 5.18. The first overlay would be used for loading part one, two, or three. The second overlay would be used for loading the common infrastructure (part four), and the third overlay would be used for loading part five or six.

For further clarification, we will use a real example. Assuming that for running the application in some embedded system, 63 KB of memory is required (see the upper part of Figure 5.19). Due to some constraints, this embedded device accommodates only 32 KB of

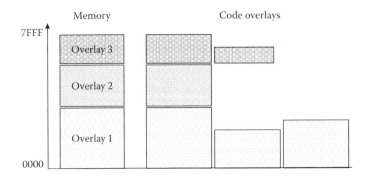

FIGURE 5.18   Example of overlay.

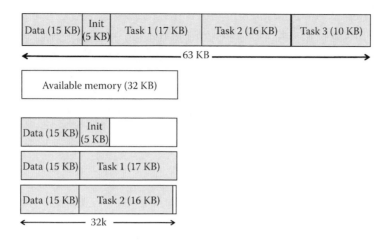

FIGURE 5.19   Example of overlay-based embedded system.

memory. For bridging the gap between the physical limitations and the software memory requirements, overlays were used. The system works with common tables and variables that require 15 KB. This common part has to be available to all other parts, and for that reason this part will be loaded throughout the whole duration. The program itself was divided into four independent parts:

- The first part requires 5 KB for initializing the system and for that reason is being used only at the beginning of the run.

- The second part requires 17 KB.

- The third part requires 16 KB.

- The fourth part requires 10 KB.

Parts two, three, and four work independently but need access to the common parts. This means that the parts do not call each other and do not access data stored in another part.

For reducing the amount of memory required, the available 32 KB of memory were divided into two chunks. The first is a static chunk of 15 KB that was intended for the common data. In addition, a second chunk of 17 KB will be used for the code. The second chunk should, of course, be large enough to accommodate the largest available code overlay (the second part in this example). During the initialization phase, the first part is loaded into the second chunk. After the initialization is finished, the same chunk will be used for loading the other code parts based on the behavior of the program (Figure 5.19).

It should be noted that the overlay mechanism is possible only in cases where the program can be divided into different executing parts and there is a complete separation between these parts. Sometimes, it is necessary to have similar functions/methods duplicated to achieve the required separation. This duplication, of course, contradicts one of the basic and important principles of good programming practices. The redundant code replication as well as the understanding that manual optimization is not the way to go convinced the industry to look for a different approach.

Currently, running a program even when the physical memory is insufficient is done automatically by utilizing a mechanism called *virtual memory*. The underlying and proven assumption is that programs contain many parts for dealing with various situations and cases; however, when the program runs, it uses only a small fraction of the code. For example, if during the execution of a banking application that handles checking accounts, all withdrawals are valid, the application does not have to run the code that handles all possible invalid situations (invalid date, insufficient funds in the account, etc.). These specific parts of the application do not have to be in memory, thus freeing space for other more useful purposes.

Implementing virtual memory implies developing a mechanism that will load only parts of the running applications, while other parts will be loaded on demand. This of course is applicable provided the system can load the missing parts reasonably fast. The parts that are not required will remain on the disks (hard drives) and for that reason, when relating to memory hierarchy (Figure 5.5), the disks are part of the memory organization. If we freeze the system while an application is running, we will be able to see some parts of that application that reside in memory, while other parts are still on the disk.

The mechanism is called virtual memory since the memory organization is very different from the ordinary understanding. As stated earlier (see the section "Memory Organization" in this chapter), the memory is a one-dimensional matrix of consecutive cells. The virtual memory's used cells, however, are not in consecutive order. For translating the virtual memory addresses to real addresses, a special hardware mechanism is required. The program represents the developers' view of the system in which the memory is a continuous array of cells, while physically these cells may reside in the memory in different and probably not continuous locations. The translation between the virtual and physical addresses is performed on the fly during execution for each memory access.

For a more elaborated explanation, we will define the virtual and physical addresses:

- A virtual address is created by the program at execution time by accessing a variable or calling a function or a method. After compilation, the address where the method or the variables reside becomes part of the instruction. This address may be considered as a virtual address since it is possible that the required content is not in memory because it was not loaded yet.

- The physical address is where the specific cell or method resides in memory. During execution, when the program tries to access a specific virtual location, the hardware has to translate the virtual address to a physical address. As part of the translation, the hardware also checks if the required address is in memory. In this case, the access will be performed. If the address is not in memory, the hardware will issue an interrupt that will be caught by the operating system. It is the operating system's responsibility to load the required content. During the load process, the program is put on hold and other programs can use the processor. Only after the content in the address has been loaded will the interrupted program be able to continue its execution.

The virtual memory mechanism is based on the overlays concept but it includes a significant improvement. There are two major differences between the two mechanisms. With virtual memory, the program is divided into fixed-size parts, and handling these parts is done automatically by the hardware and the operating system.

For example, let us assume there is a program that requires 5 MB of memory. The program is divided into fixed-length parts called pages.* For this example, we will use 64 KB pages.† This means that the program contains 80 pages. As already mentioned, not all of these pages have to be in memory during execution. The physical memory is also divided into segments of 64 KB called *frames*. Each such frame is intended to store one page. In determining the page/frame size, the designers are trying to balance between two contradicting trends. On the one hand, the smaller the page/frame size, the better utilization of memory (less unneeded parts that are loaded). On the other hand, a small page/frame size requires more input and output operations for loading the pages. In addition, the operating system maintains a table containing the pages' addresses, and with the trend of increasing the memory size, this table gets very large. A large page table increases the system's overhead and decreases the amount of memory available for the users' programs. For that reason, some manufacturers are considering doubling the page/frame's size, which halves this table's size.

In the past, when computers were significantly more expensive and systems were in use for a longer duration, some systems supported different page sizes. This means that the page size was determined at boot time and could be changed only at the next boot. Currently, most systems no longer provide this capability, and the page/frame size is fixed. The page size is usually a number that is a power of two.

Figure 5.20 depicts the previous example; the left side is dedicated to the application and its pages, and the right side represents a system with a limited amount of memory. The application's addresses are virtual addresses since, as can be seen in the figure, not all pages are loaded into the physical memory. Furthermore, the pages of the application that are loaded reside in different locations in the physical memory. When the program starts running, we will assume it executes instructions that are on page zero. This means that page zero will be loaded into the next available frame. In this specific case, the first available frame was frame zero, so the page was loaded into frame zero. The program continues its execution, and at some point, it accesses or calls a method that resides on page four. Since this page was not in memory, the hardware cannot complete the address translation, and it issues an interrupt. The operating system realizes the type of interrupt and puts the program on hold. Then it locates the missing page and loads it into the next available frame. In this specific case, the page is loaded into frame one. Only after the page is loaded will the program be allowed to continue its execution. The program continues as per this example, and at some point in time the program accesses page zero once

---

* A page is an atomic unit that is loaded and stored in memory consecutively. The program is split into pages, and the memory is also divided into same length segments. The fixed-size implementation makes it very simple to handle and manage.

† It should be noted that the amount 64 KB per page is used just to simplify the example. In reality, the pages' sizes are significantly smaller.

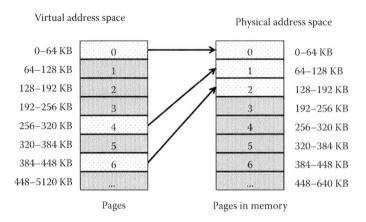

FIGURE 5.20 Pages and frames example.

again. The page is in memory, so the hardware translates the virtual address to the real address and the program continues without knowing it is working on a different location in memory. Some time later, the programs access page six. Once again, the page is not in memory, so the hardware signals the operating system, which loads the page, and so on until the program finishes.

The operating system that loads the required pages handles all the frames in the system, and it uses various algorithms to optimize programs execution. For example, it is responsible for preventing situations in which one program dominates the system and uses all available memory. In other cases when frames are not readily available, the operating system may preempt frames from another program that is running in the system. There are many algorithms used by the operating system in handling the frames, but these are beyond the scope of this book. There is, however, another issue that is relevant for systems engineers. As part of good software development practice, the developed program should be modular and divided into function or class and methods. Each function or method should be relatively small, which reduces complexity and eases development and future maintenance. Understanding the virtual memory mechanism provides an additional reason for keeping the functions and methods relatively small. With such small chunks of code, there is a greater chance the whole function or method will reside on one page, which will lower the number of pages loaded during execution.

For handling the address translation, the processor has a special unit (memory management unit [MMU]). This is in addition to previously mentioned ALU and CU (Figure 5.21).

Figure 5.21 depicts the MMU, which is responsible for handling the communication to and from memory as well as translating the virtual addresses stored in the instructions into real addresses in the memory. A program that is being executed by the processor needs to access some virtual address. The address may contain a variable needed by the executing instruction, or the next instruction to be executed. The program relates to its address space as a contiguous array of cells using virtual addresses. The CU, which is responsible for fetching the next instruction as well as fetching the required operands,

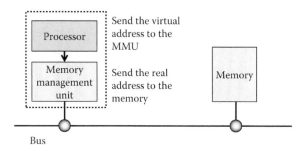

FIGURE 5.21   Address translation.

sends the virtual address to the MMU. There it is translated to find out its real location. As part of the translation, the MMU also checks if the page is in memory. Assuming it is in memory, the required cell will be transferred from the memory to the CU.

To better understand the translation process, we will use a simplified example based on a theoretical system. Assuming this theoretical system works with 8-byte pages and each program can use no more than four pages, this means that the largest possible address supported by this system is 31 (addresses starting from zero to 31). This means the address space in this system is based on 5 bits.* These 5 bits will be divided into two groups. The first group will be used for defining the page number, and since the program can use no more than four pages, this part will use 2 bits. The second part will be used to define the displacement in the page. Since the page size is 8 bytes, the address space will need 3 bits (Figure 5.22). A very simple real example may be the system used for catalog numbers in a warehouse. Let us assume that each component has a unique five-digit number that can be viewed as a concatenation of two values. One value (two digits) defines the room where the component is located, and the second value (three digits) defines the relevant shelf. By examining the catalog number, it is very clear where the specific component is located. Since the virtual address space is consecutive, the program address are sequential and even so, the address can be split into two numbers.

Figure 5.22 depicts a theoretical program that uses 13 bytes. The addresses required by the program are 00000–01100. The left side of the figure describes the program bytes. The leftmost two columns represent the address, while the right column includes a different character so it will be easy to differentiate between the different bytes. The virtual address is the concatenation of the two leftmost columns. For example, the character "a" is in address 00000, while the character "k" is in address 01010.

The next part of the diagram (the middle of the figure) is the page table. This is a major component of the address translation, since it holds the mapping information. For each page, the table contains its real location in memory, as well as information if it is in memory or not. In this specific case, page zero of the program is located in frame six (binary 0110) in memory, while page one of the program is located in frame number four (binary 0100) in memory. Other pages are not loaded yet.

---

* Using 5 bits for addressing provides the possibility to access 2^5 locations or 32 bytes.

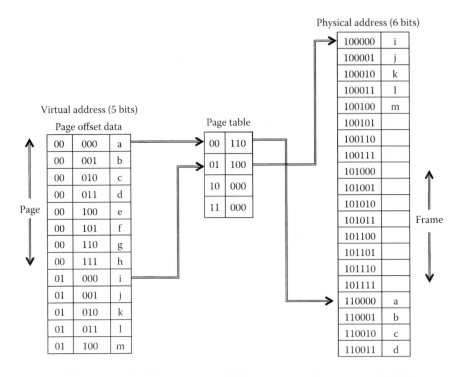

FIGURE 5.22 Translation process.

The right side of the figure is the real memory layout with the loaded pages as well as the empty frames. It can be seen, as was evident from the page table, that page zero of the program is actually in frame six (110), and page one of the program is located in frame four.

The memory translation performed by the hardware consists of several simple steps:

- Extract the page number from the virtual address

- Use the page number as the index to the page table

- Pull out the page's new location

- If the page is not in memory, issue an interrupt

- Concatenate the new page address with the displacement from the virtual address

- The combined value represents the real memory location

Dividing the address into two parts (page number and the displacement within the page) is the reason behind the requirement that the page size will be a power of two. In real systems where the address space is large, for example, 4 GB (assuming a 32-bit architecture), the MMU splits the address into these two groups. The number of bits allocated for the displacement is driven by the page size. Currently, the common page size is 4 KB, but other figures such as 8 KB are also available. Therefore, if a 4 GB system uses a 1 KB page (1024 bytes), then the page size will require 10 bits and the remaining 22 bits will be used for the page number. When using 4 KB pages, the same system will have 12 bits assigned for the page displacement and 20 bits for the number of page.

Because each and every address has to be translated and the translation has to access the page table, most operating systems have added some functionality to the page table entries. Each such entry includes additional information that can be used for added security and a more efficient operation. For example, it is possible to add an access control mechanism that will provide information about the processes that can access this page and about others that are not allowed. Another functionality is a ready or available bit that, when set, means that the page was loaded. On the other hand, if the bit is clear, it means that it is still in the process of being loaded but it is not available yet, even though the frame was already allocated to the program. Another example is when a page is loaded but for some reason the operating system decided to preempt it because the space was required by another program. In such a case, although the page may still be there, it is not available since it can be overwritten by other content.

This added functionality can be used not only for access control but also for defining the type of access. It is possible to assign a bit in order to signal if the page can be written by the program, or if it may only be read. In such a case, if the accessing program is trying to write or modify the page, the hardware will issue an interrupt and the operating system will have to decide about the situation.

Figure 5.23 depicts the page table, which is being used as part of the address translation. It contains for each virtual page its physical address (PA), but in addition, each entry includes information about access rights as well as a validity bit (V). In this specific example, the page size is 1 KB. (Why? See answer at the bottom of the page.*)

Each program, and actually each process running in the system, has its own page table. It resides in the memory, and a special register points to its beginning. By adding the virtual page number to the content of this register, a pointer is created. This pointer is used to find the page's real location (PA).

In addition to the many benefits of the virtual memory mechanism, it is important to add that such a system does not create "holes" in memory. This means that the virtual memory

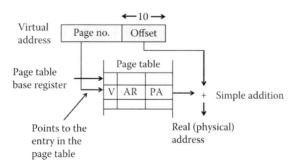

FIGURE 5.23   Page table.

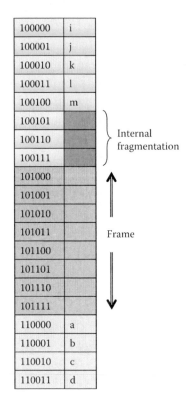

FIGURE 5.24   Internal fragments.

system does not need a mechanism for managing the holes by moving and compacting (see the section "Partitions" in this chapter). When all frames are of the same size, there are no more external fragments.* However, there still might be internal fragments† (Figure 5.24).

The figure depicts the real memory when the theoretical program is loaded. In this example, each page contains 8 bytes, but the second page needs only 5 bytes. For that reason, the frame that contains this page (frame zero) will have 3 bytes that are not being used (holes).

Understanding the way the memory is organized is very important for software developers as well. Let us assume that a two-dimensional matrix has to be initialized. It is usually done by two nested loops that access all of the matrix elements. From a simple programming point of view, it makes little difference which of the indexes will be in the inner loop and which will be in the outer loop. In other words, the following pseudo code

$$\text{for } \left(i = 0; \; i < n; \; i++\right)$$

$$\text{for } \left(j = 0; \; j < m; \; j++\right)$$

$$a\left[i, j\right] = i * j$$

---

* External fragments are holes between fragments.
† Internal fragments are holes within a frame, usually in the last frame of the program.

is equivalent to the following code:

$$\text{for } (=0;\ j<m;\ j++)$$
$$\text{for } (i=0;\ i<n;\ i++)$$
$$a[i,\ j] = i*j$$

Both of these loops will produce the same result. However, if we consider the locality of reference and the fact that the virtual memory (and cache) is organized in pages, then there will be a difference in the execution times of these two codes. This depends on the specific programming language and the way it allocates the arrays in the matrix, but usually it is better to have the second index in the inner loop. In this specific case, the first code will result in a faster execution due to a more sequential access of the data elements. It should be noted, however, that some modern compilers will detect if the code is not optimized. In such cases, the compiler will interchange the order of the loops automatically.

Paging

The virtual memory mechanism was intended, among other things, to allow the running of large programs that are larger than the physical memory and better utilize the system resources. This increased efficiency is achieved by loading only the pages that are required by the program and not "wasting" parts of memory for pages that are not needed. Due to the large difference between the processor and the memory, more pages are required by the program, so its speed will be decreased. Usually, all operating systems use an allocation window, which defines the amount of frames to be allocated for the process. If the process needs significantly more pages, the new ones will be loaded but others will be released.

During the virtual address translation, when the MMU realizes that a specific required page is not in memory and it has to be brought from disk, it issues a "Page Fault" interrupt. However, despite its name, this is not a fault caused by the user's program but a natural side effect of the virtual memory mechanism. Since the pages are loaded on demand, then by definition some of the pages will not be in memory when requested and will have to be loaded. This process of loading the pages is called *paging*. As with all other interrupts, the control is transferred to the operating system, which has to act accordingly. The user process that caused the page fault is put on hold until the page is loaded. In the meantime, another process enters execution. This is done mainly due to the large speed difference between the disk and the processor and to better utilize the system while the running process is waiting for its page.

During a page fault interrupt, the operating system has to

- Find a frame in memory where this page will be loaded. It can be achieved by allocating a new frame from a pool of empty frames or by preempting pages belonging to another running process, including the one that requested the page.

- Find the page, which is usually part of the execution file of the running program, but the operating system has to find out its location.

- Issue the instructions to load the page.

- During the time the page is being loaded, which may require several tens of milliseconds, the running process is put on hold and the operating system lets another process use the processor.

- When the page finishes loading, the disk driver, which is part of the operating system responsible for handling the disk activity, will issue an interrupt. The operating system will then put the process back on the running queue* so it will enter execution when its turn arrives.

There are cases in which, on the one hand, the number of free frames is limited; and on the other hand, many processes are running concurrently and then a competition for the frames will occur. This situation can be described by a process that enters into execution and, through a series of interrupts, loads all the required pages. Since there are no free frames, some of these pages were loaded into frames preempted from other processes waiting for their turn. Since the system runs many processes concurrently, at some point the operating system will switch to another process. It is possible that during the time the new assigned process was waiting to run, its frames were allocated to another process. This means that the new process will have to go through a series of interrupts before its pages will be loaded. Due to the limited number of free frames, some of the process's page will be loaded into frames preempted from another running process, and so on.

The bottom line is a situation wherein each process that starts running has to fulfill its requirements for pages by using frames preempted from another process. This creates a problem in which the system spends most of its time loading pages with very little work being done. To better explain this situation, we will use a visual example. Let us assume the system (Figure 5.25) has a small predefined number of frames and that there are four processes to be executed. The left side depicts the four running processes (the four rectangles); the scheduler,† which periodically enters a process into execution; and the address translation, which initiates loading the requested and missing pages into memory. The large rectangle divided into cells represents memory, and each cell is a frame. On the right, there is the disk from which the pages are loaded.

---

* A running queue is one of the queues maintained by the operating system in managing the processes that are waiting to be executed. There are many algorithms for process scheduling, however, when a process is ready for execution, for example, when the missing page was loaded, or the required input from the user was entered, the process is put on the queue and the operating system scheduler will put it to run when its turn arrives.

† The scheduler is part of the operating system that schedules the processes. There are several scheduling algorithms implemented by the different operating systems, but in all cases the scheduler tries to divide the system's resources among the waiting processes in an objective and fair manner. This means that each process gets a share of the processor and executes for a predefined amount of time. After this time has elapsed, the scheduler will stop the running process, put the process on hold, and run another process that has been waiting for its turn. The second process will run, and if it does not finish it will be stopped and put on hold; the third process will then enter execution, and so on.

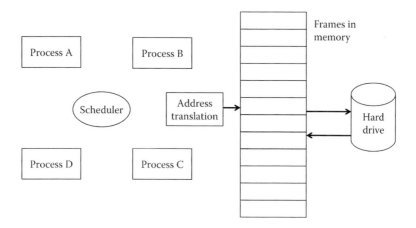

FIGURE 5.25   System's initial stage.

Figure 5.25 is the initial stage of the system with four processes waiting to be executed, and all frames are still empty. For this example, we will assume that the scheduler decides to enter Process A into execution. This process needs several pages, so through a series of interrupts initiated by the MMU, these pages will be loaded. For identifying the frames/pages in memory, the process identification will be used, so frames that belong to Process A will be identified by the letter A. Process A runs, but since it does not finish, at some point the scheduler decides it is time for another process to run. Figure 5.26 depicts the situation at the point where Process A is put on hold.

It can be seen that when Process A starts running, there are 12 empty frames. During execution, Process A needs some pages that were loaded, and when it is stopped, eight of the frames are used by Process A, leaving only four free frames. Assuming the scheduler decides it is Process B's turn after Process A is put on hold, Process B is loaded. As with the previous case, when Process B starts (or continues) running, it needs some pages. So, after a series of interrupts initiated by the MMU, the missing pages are loaded.

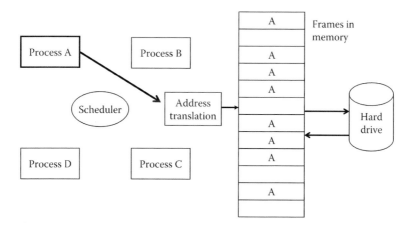

FIGURE 5.26   System after Process A stopped.

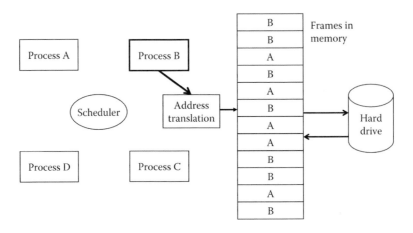

FIGURE 5.27   System after Process B stopped.

For each page that is required, the operating system will have to find a free frame. Since when Process A is stopped there are four empty frames, the operating system will allocate these. However, when Process B needs additional frames, the operating system will have to preempt these from Process A.

At some point in time, since Process B did not finish, the scheduler decides to put Process B on hold so that other waiting processes can run as well. Figure 5.27 depicts the situation when Process B is stopped.

As can be seen, when Process B is stopped that there are no empty frames at all; furthermore, from the eight frames that were originally allocated to Process A, only five remain.

At this stage, the scheduler decides it is Process C's turn, so it initiates it. As usual, the process needs some pages to be loaded so the MMU will issue several interrupts so the missing pages can be loaded by the operating system. Unlike the previous situation in which, at least at first, the operating system could allocate free frames, now there are no free frames, so the allocation process has first to preempt frames that belong to existing processes. There are of course several algorithms for finding a candidate frame, but usually the intention will be to free the frames that have not been used for the longest period of time. This means that to satisfy Process C's demand, the frames to be used belonged to Process A. In this specific example, the requests can be fulfilled by Process A's frames, and there is no need to preempt any of the frames that belong to Process B. In other cases, of course, it may not be sufficient, and then Process B frames will have to be reassigned as well.

At some point in time, the scheduler decides that Process C has used its time slice,* and it is time for the next process that is waiting to be executed. The last process that is still waiting for its turn is Process D, so the scheduler will put Process C on hold and initiate Process D.

---

* *Time slice* or *time slot* is a term used by the operating system to define the amount of time a process will use the processor before it is put back to wait. Multiprocessing systems usually share the resources between the running processes, and the time slice defines the amount of time the processes use at one shot.

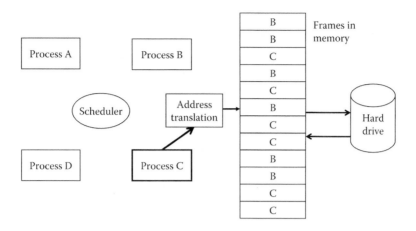

FIGURE 5.28   System after Process C stopped.

As with the previous case, when Process D enters into execution, it needs some pages. Unfortunately, there are no free frames, so the operating system will have to preempt pages that belong to other processes. Figure 5.28 depicts the situation after Process C is stopped, and it can be seen that the only frames available belong to Processes B and C.

The Process D missing pages will be loaded after freeing existing frames. Once again, at some point in time and after Process D uses its time slice and does not finish, the scheduler will decide it is time for the next process in line to be executed. Process D will be put on hold. Figure 5.29 depicts the situation after Process D is stopped.

In this example, there are just four processes, so after all of them have run and did not finish, the scheduler selects Process A once again. At this stage, there are no empty frames at all, and furthermore none of the frames that belonged to Process A are still in memory. This means that the system will have to load these pages once again. Although it was demonstrated for Process A, it actually happens with every process that will be executed. Not only does the process have to load additional pages that are required, even the pages

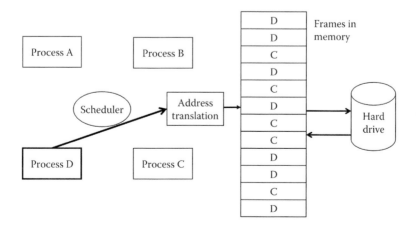

FIGURE 5.29   System after Process D stopped.

that were loaded do not exist anymore. Usually, the time slices used are several tens of milliseconds, so in this example, when there are four processes running, the system will load many pages and the processor will wait most of its time.

It should be noted that paging is a normal behavior of the system due to the on-demand page loading; however, the situation previously described is called *thrashing* since the processor is idly waiting and the disk is constantly loading pages.

It is the operating system's responsibility to realize this situation and try to avoid it. Some operating systems have configuration parameters to avoid it, but in general the solution in such cases may be to either decrease the number of processes running concurrently (to lower the competition on frames) or increase the size of memory (so the operating system will not need to preempt useful frames).

It should be noted that the example is intended to explain the thrashing phenomenon so it is extremely exaggerated, for example, when relating to the number of free frames.

Segments

As part of architectural developments after the partition (fixed and dynamic) stage and before virtual memory was implemented, there was a stage in which segments were developed. Some of these segments are used as part of the 32-bit architecture even when virtual memory is being used. As with many other developments, the main idea behind segments is rooted in the need to be more efficient.

Every time an instruction has to access memory, either for reading or writing, the address has to be calculated, so the simplest way is to relate to the absolute address. However, the rapid developments in memory technology and the fact that memory address space increased dramatically posed a new problem. Let us assume an instruction to add two numbers located in memory and store the result in another memory location. The instruction, assuming absolute addressing is used, may look like

ADD   2210176,993288,1576761

As part of executing the instruction, the CU will fetch the operands in addresses 993288 and 1576761. The ALU will add the two operands and then the result will be stored in memory address 2210176. The problem associated with this mechanism is the addresses that are part of the instruction. For a memory size of 4 GB, the required address occupies 32 bits. This means that such an ADD instruction, which has three operands, will have to be quite long—over 100 bits, since 96 of these bits are dedicated just to the operands and the result addresses. In addition, some extra bits will be required for the operation code (ADD in this example). In such a case when the instruction has to be very long, the added memory capacity will be wasted by the increased size of the instructions. Since each program has many instructions, this means that increasing the memory size will have a marginal effect, if any. Further increasing the memory size will increase the instructions size even more, creating a vicious loop. The understanding that this architectural limitation prevents the technology from advancing led to some proposed solutions.

One such solution was to change the arithmetic instruction. These instructions, which sometimes require three operands that reside in memory, were changed so that one, two, and even all three operands will have to be registers. It should be noted that the ×86 architecture used only four registers (AX, BX, CX, DX), which could have been split into the left (high) side and the right (low) side to form eight registers (AH, AL, BH, BL, CH, CL, DH, DL). When there are only eight registers, then each operand requires just 3 bits. Therefore, the ADD instruction from the above example, which required over 100 bits, will need just 16 bits when the allowed operands are registers.* This solution was very effective in reducing the arithmetic instruction size; however, one has to take into account that there are other instructions that remain very long, such as the instructions to load the registers or store their content into memory and the various branch instructions, which change the address of the next instruction to be executed.

Another way, already discussed, to minimize the length of the instructions was by using fixed definitions. The accumulator architecture is just one example. The idea was to define the instruction in such a way that it uses a predefined register. The ADD instruction will always use the AX register as one of its operands. This way, the developer knows that one of the operands has to be placed in AX and the instruction has only two operands (the second input and the output). This convention was partially used by the ×86 architecture. The multiplication instruction in this architecture has just one operand, while the other two are always fixed and predefined. The assumption in word-wide multiplications is that one of the multipliers (input operands) is in AX and the result will be found in the two registers DX and AX. The only operand can of course be another register or a memory location. If it is a memory location, then the instruction should be long enough to hold it.

These two approaches for minimizing the instruction's size were problematic since there was a constant need to increase the instructions' size each time the memory capacity was increased, or alternatively to use the maximum allowed, which for the 64 bits architecture means 48 bits for addressing. The example previously described, of an instruction that supports three memory resident operands, will require 19 bytes (48 bits for each operand and 6 bits for the Opcode). It was clear that a different approach was required.

The idea proposed was to use relative addresses. This means that the address mechanism will combine two addresses to form the real memory location. There will be a base address and a displacement. Practically, it is very similar to addresses used in reality. Due to the large number of houses, we do not use a sequential number for each one but use street names as well as house numbers. The idea of base address and displacement mimics the house addresses in which each address has two parts. The base address is known and kept in a special register so the instruction has to use only the displacement. Before a program

---

* The ADD instruction needs three operands. When it works with memory resident operands, each operand requires 32 bits (assuming a 4 GB system). If the system supports 64 different instructions, the Opcode, which defines the instruction, will require an additional 6 bits. This means that the ADD instruction will require 102 bits (three operands of 32 bits each and an Opcode of 6 bits). Since the instructions occupy full bytes, this means that the ADD will require 104 bits or 13 bytes. On the other hand, when the instruction is using only registers as operands, there are 3 bits for each operand and 6 bits for the Opcode, or a total of 15 bits. Once again, since the instructions occupy full bytes, the ADD instruction in this case will need 16 bits or 2 bytes.

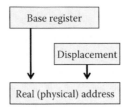

FIGURE 5.30   Calculating the real address.

starts execution, the operating system loads the base register, and each memory access is calculated by adding the content of the register to the displacement defined in the instruction. In this way, it is possible to access a very large address space and to maintain control of the instruction sizes.

Calculating the real address is done by the MMU for each memory access, and it includes a simple addition of the logical address that appears in the instruction and the base register (Figure 5.30).

The principle that led to this addressing mode is locality of reference, which is also responsible for the hierarchical memory architecture already discussed. This locality of reference, which will be further elaborated on in Chapter 6, "Cache Memory," means that when a program is executed, most of the time it will use items of data that are close to each other and the instructions for which are in close proximity. For example, when entering a method or a function, all the executed instructions belong to the same method so they reside very close to each other. The same happens when the program is working on a data record or is analyzing an array. The data items to be addressed belong to the same record or array and thus are relatively close.

The PC convention for these memory chunks is a segment, and in general, there are three types of segments with a base register for each one:

- *Code segment*, used for the program's instructions. The register that holds the code base address is CS (code segment). To reinforce the system's data integrity, the content of the code segment cannot be accessed (read or written) by other processes, and only the operating system and the MMU can access its content.

- *Data segment*, used for storing the program's data. The register that holds the data-base address is the DS (data segment). Due to the need of some programs to use very large data address spaces, sometimes the program may have two data segments. In this case, the base address of the second segment will be in a different register called ES (extra segment). For obvious reasons, all data stored in the data segments can be read and written.

- *Stack segment*, which is a dynamic memory used during execution to hold special program attributes; for example, when calling a new method, the stack maintains the full working environments before the call, so when the called method finishes, the program can continue as if it was never interrupted. The register that holds the stack base address is the SS (stack segment).

The first PCs used 16-bit registers, which can support an address space of only 64 KB.* The systems' memory capacity was larger, up to 1 million bytes. Therefore, to overcome the problem, system designers came up with the idea of increasing the address space without increasing the register size. It was decided that a segment will start on a paragraph† boundary. Due to the four 0 bits on the right side of the paragraph address, the designers decided that the segments' base registers would contain the address without these 4 bits. This means that, unlike all other pieces of data stored in memory, in which their addressing mode is based on byte addressing, the segments' base registers use paragraph addressing. The practical meaning of this decision is to increase the address space from 64 KB to one million bytes. This is also the reason that in Figure 5.30, the segment base register is shifted to the left. This is done in order to accommodate the missing four bits on the right side.

For example, the address defined by

$$1000:1FFF$$

relates a real memory location calculated by the two parts of the address. The left side is the content of the base register, and the right side is the displacement. In this specific case, the meaning is displacement $1FFF_{16}$. The real address in this case will be

$$1000_{16} * 10_{16} + 1FFF_{16} = 11FFF_{16}$$

Figure 5.31 depicts the address calculation process in which two 16-bit registers form a 20-bit address.

The segments approach provided a solution to the increasing size of the instructions; however, it was not efficient in dealing with many processes that run in parallel. The segment is a continuous address space, and usually segments have different sizes. This means that memory management became difficult due to fragmentations and the required holes management. The original 16-bit registers defined the size of the segments (64 KB). Since the total memory size was larger, during execution the memory was filled with many segments of various sizes. To manage the processes that are being executed concurrently, the operating system had to spend a lot of resources. Each time a program finished execution, its three, and sometimes four, segments had to be freed, so the holes management activities increased the systems overhead. Not only was the processor busy for part of the time moving the segments that reside in memory, but also sometimes the segments of a running program had to be written to the disk until enough space would be made available.

In the first PCs with 16-bit registers, the segments were small (up to 64 KB), so the movement was fast. With the introduction of the 80386 and 32-bit registers, the maximum theoretical segment size increased to 4 GB. This change provided support for the larger real memories that were required and increased the number of programs that could run

* The maximum address space is calculated by 2^n, where n is the number of bits in the address register. For 16-bit registers the maximum supported address is $2^{16} = 64KB$.
† A paragraph in the ×86 architecture is a sequence of 16 bytes. A paragraph always starts on the boundary of a paragraph, that is, 0, 16, 32, 64,..., which means that paragraph addresses always will have four 0 bits on their right side.

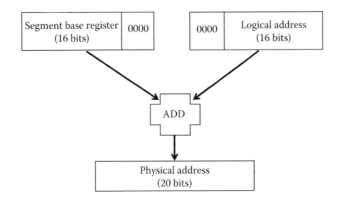

FIGURE 5.31   Real address calculation (PC).

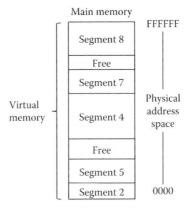

FIGURE 5.32   Segment-based memory.

concurrently, but copying these larger segments required much more time. So, in addition to the previously described problems and increased overhead associated with using segments, the increased sizes posed an additional and more severe problem.

Figure 5.32 depicts the real memory of a segment-based system. On the left side appears the logical (or virtual) memory with its relative addresses; each one includes a base address and the displacement, which starts from zero for each segment and continues up to the maximum size of that segment. It should be noted that the maximum size is 4 GB; however, the real size is dependent on the program as developed. On the right side appears the real memory with addresses starting from zero up to the highest address in the system. As in real situations, part of the memory is unassigned, representing free space or holes.

Figure 5.33 provides an additional elaboration, and it depicts the memory structure as well as the address translation. On the right side appears the memory, similar to the description in Figure 5.32. The left side describes the address translation. The virtual (or logical) address defines just the displacement. The assumption is that the processor knows which base register is to be used. For example, if the address is taken from the instruction

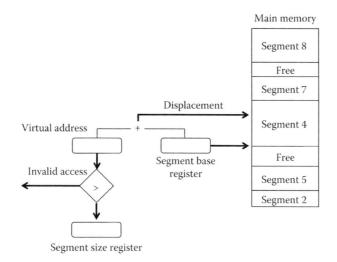

FIGURE 5.33 Segment-based memory and the translation process.

pointer (IP),* the hardware knows it is related to the code, so the CS register will be used. If the address is related to the stack, the SS register will be used, and so on.

The translation process is initiated by the virtual address that arrives from the processor. It is transferred in parallel to two hardware processes. On the one hand, as shown by the lower arrow, it is checked against the segment's size register.† When the segment is created or loaded into memory, the operating system stores its size in the register. The content of this register is used by the hardware to ensure the displacement is within the boundaries of the segment. If the program tries to access an address beyond the segment, the hardware will issue an interrupt. The operating system will be called on to decide what to do. In most cases, it will end with aborting the running program with an address violation error. This check, which ensures the validity of the address, is performed in parallel to the translation process, but it has a higher priority. If the check fails, the translation will be stopped, since it is not needed any more.

The address is always positive, and for that reason there is no need to check that the program is attempting to access a negative address or one that is lower than the start of segment. If the address is valid, the MMU will add the displacement to the content of the base register after shifting this content right by four bits. This shift is required for changing the paragraph addressing used by the base registers to byte addressing.

Swap

Modern operating systems manage the system's many aspects with a special emphasis on ensuring proper and efficient operations. One such activity is related to identifying

---

* IP is an internal register used by the hardware, and it holds the address of the next instruction to be executed. During sequential execution, the register will point to the next instruction. In cases of branches, it may point to a different address and not the next one based on the evaluation of the executing instruction.

† The segment's size register is an internal register available only for the operating system, and it holds the size of the segment. It is used in order to ensure that, when accessing a segment, the displacement is not larger than the segment size, which will give the program the possibility of accessing areas that belong to some other process.

thrashing situations and taking the necessary steps to correct them. As previously explained (see the section "Paging" in this chapter), thrashing occurs when various processes are competing for a small number of available frames. In its turn, each process loads the pages required for its execution; however, besides constantly loading pages, the system performs very little real work since most of the system's resources are tied up with page loading. Some operating systems can identify these patterns, locate the one or more problematic processes, and temporarily suspend one or more of these processes. The suspension is achieved by rolling the process out of memory and writing all of its pages (or segments) on the disk. If it is a segment-based system, although the program uses more memory, usually this rolling out will be quite simple since the segment is a continuous chunk of memory. If it is a page-based system, the program uses less memory; however, the operating system will have to "collect" the pages that are spread all over the memory. After some time, the operating system will bring back the program that was rolled out, assuming the conflicts on the available frames will be minimal. In many cases, the situation is caused by the mix of the programs run in parallel. If most of the programs load many pages, it may cause the situation, while if some of the programs do not need frequent loading, the situation may be controlled.

This process of rolling out the whole program is called *swap out* (or roll out), and the process of rolling the program back into memory is called *swap in* (or roll in).

There is a significant difference between the standard execution, for example, of a page-based system and swapping. When a program is running, several pages are requested, and since these pages are not in memory, a page fault occurs. The process is put on hold and another process is allowed to work. The operating system loads the required page, and only after it is loaded will the process be put in the queue of processes waiting to run. In some cases, when a frame has to be assigned, the operating system will have to preempt a frame that belongs to some other process. If it is a data page with content that has changed, the operating system will have to write the content back to the disk before the frame is freed. This is the normal situation when processes are executed in the system. When a process is swapped out, all its pages are on disk, and it does not exist in any of the processes' queues* that are waiting for the processor or for an event. The system, of course, knows about these processes that were swapped out and when the situation will change. It may be that the number of processes running in parallel will decrease or the mix of running processes will change, which will increase the number of free frames.

Figure 5.34 depicts the swapping process, in which the whole process is written to disk (swapped out) or loaded from disk (swapped in).

Memory Performance

Moore's law (see the section "Moore's Law" in Chapter 1), which predicts the evolution of technology, relates to the number of transistors in the chip. Since memory is implemented

---

* Usually, operating systems manage their processes by using several queues. One important queue is the one that holds information about processes ready for execution. The only reason these processes do not run is because there are insufficient resources; for example, there is one processor and several processes waiting. Another queue is the processes that wait for an event, such as an input or output operation.

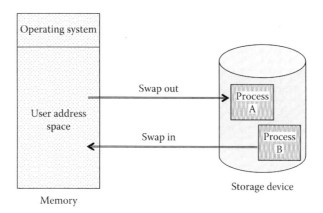

FIGURE 5.34   Swap in and swap out.

using transistors, then the law provides a good prediction regarding memory sizes in the future. Many current PCs are based on a 64-bit architecture in which 48 bits are used for addressing memory. This represents a huge address space that, even with Moore's prediction, will be sufficient for a long time.*

However, the memory size is not the real and most important problem, mainly due to the developments that addressed this issue back when memory was very expensive. Virtual memory is the best example of a solution devised to increase memory utilization and allow the running of large applications while loading only the relevant parts. While Moore's law can be used to predict memory size, it fails to predict memory access time, which was and still is a bottleneck. A proposed solution is the development of RISC technology, which tried to minimize memory access by promoting register usage; this provided many registers and register-based instructions.

In order to cope better with the continuous requests for additional larger and faster memories, large efforts were put into advancing technology. One of these developments was the introduction of synchronous dynamic random access memory (SDRAM), which, in addition to the standard DRAM, provided a mechanism of synchronization with the computer bus.† The speed increase is achieved by implementing a pipeline, similar to pipelines implemented in the processor. The memory can accept a new request while the previous request is still being processed. The next development in memory technology was double data rate SDRAM (DDR SDRAM), which is characterized by the fact that it can transfer two data elements on each cycle, thereby providing almost twice the bandwidth of the previous generation SDRAM. Further developments in memory technology produced the next generation DDR, called DDR2 SDRAM. The main characteristics of DDR2 compared with DDR are that it doubles the bandwidth while lowering power consumption. As can be imagined, the technology did not stop at DDR2, and since 2007 a new DDR3

---

* 48 bit represents an address space of 2^{48}, which is $2.8 * 10^{14}$. Assuming the currently available processors support 32 GB (or $3.2 * 10^{10}$), then it will require at least an additional 20 years to achieve this limit, provided the technology, as well as minimization, is able to continue at the current pace.
† The bus is the mechanism that is responsible for data transfers between the various components of the system. The mechanism will be described in subsequent chapters.

standard has been used. As with its predecessors, DDR3 doubles the bandwidth achieved by DDR2. As of 2015, the next generation DDR4 is starting to appear.

It should be noted, however, that all these developments relate just to enhancing the speed of the main memory, which is one part of the memory hierarchy used in computer systems. The idea behind the memory hierarchy stems from similar ideas that drove the development of virtual memory. Most parts of the running program reside on disk, and only the ones that are required for running will be in the memory. The same concept can be further applied by providing several levels of memory. The ones that are close to the processor can be smaller but have to be extremely fast, while the levels that are far from the processor have to be large to accommodate more data but can also be slower (Figure 5.35).

The figure depicts several memory components arranged according to order and speed:

- The first smaller and fastest type of memory is the registers. They reside in the processor itself so the access time is extremely fast (one cycle); however, their capacity is limited. Even with the 64-bit architectures that implement a register file, there are many more general-purpose as well as special-purpose registers; their number is in the tens of registers compared with gigabytes of memory.

- Usually, there are several levels of cache memory, a concept that will be addressed in the next chapter.

- The next level comprises the memory (RAM) itself.

- The last level is the disks, which are very slow compared with all other levels but on the other hand provide almost endless capacity. It should be noted that this level is also changing, and in the last decade parts of the disks have transformed into electronic devices without any moving parts, such as a disk on key, for example. These technological advancements change the traditional memory hierarchy by adding new levels and changing the order of the existing ones.

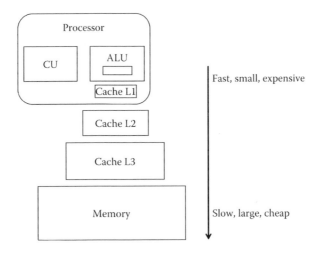

FIGURE 5.35 Memory hierarchy.

Parallelism and pipelining are concepts that were introduced as a mechanism for increasing speed and memory bandwidth. Most memories, especially the DRAM type, use a technology that needs to be refreshed, so the data stored has to be periodically rewritten. This means that the memory uses two different timing schemes:

- *Access time*, which defines the time elapsed from the moment the request was sent up to the moment the data was received. This time can be seen as the memory response time. Response time defines the amount of time that passes between sending the request (pressing the Enter key) and the time the results are displayed on the screen. In the case of memory, the access time measures the memory response time.

- *Cycle time*, which defines the time between two consecutive requests or the amount of time that passes between two consecutive requests made to the memory. In order to reduce costs, the memory (DRAM) uses a "destructive" technology that, for maintaining the data, needs to be refreshed. This means that during reading the cell from memory, its content is destroyed. Before the memory can become available once again, it has to reconstruct the destroyed cell. During this time, the memory is locked and cannot process additional requests. In most cases, the memory cycle time is significantly higher than the memory access time.

To better explain the two timing schemes, we may use a real example. Let us assume that a person's salary is transferred to his or her bank account. If such a person tries to withdraw the full salary amount by using an ATM or a check, the transaction will be instantaneous. This represents the access time (accessing the money in the account). However, if the person tries to withdraw the sum again (assuming no additional funds are available in the account), he or she will have to wait for the next payment cycle. This represents the cycle time, which defines the amount of time between two withdrawal cycles.

Figure 5.36 depicts the two timing schemes. Figure 5.37 provides additional explanation and shows two consecutive memory accesses. D1 is requested and delivered. Before D2 can be requested, the cycle time has to elapse.

Although in modern implementations the difference between the memory access time and the memory cycle time is not very large, in the past it was significant. Ratios of 1:4 or 1:5 were quite common, which led to additional developments in that area. One such development is based on parallel access. In general, the concept divides the memory into different parts, called *banks*, each one with its own access possibilities. After a cell's content has been sent to the processor, only the bank in which the cell resides is locked, while all other banks are ready to accept requests. In a sense, this approach actually splits

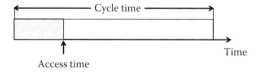

FIGURE 5.36   Memory timing schemes.

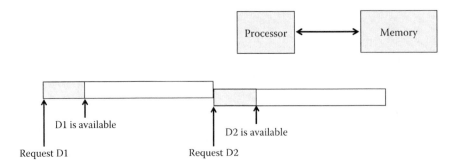

FIGURE 5.37 "Standard" access pattern.

the memory into several independent parts in order to minimize the time-based cost associated with memory access. The processor, of course, sees just one memory, and it is the MMU's responsibility to maintain and manage the access.

If the program is reading the data from memory, the assumption is that after reading one cell, its bank will be locked. The program will be able to read the next cell that belongs to another bank. After this read, the second bank will be locked as well, but the program will be able to read another cell from an unlocked bank.

This method is sometimes referred to as *interleaving*, since consecutive cells in memory are divided and belong to different banks. Figure 5.38 depicts a system with four memory banks.

Using this architecture and assuming the program accesses the memory in a serial fashion, the access time achieved is described in Figure 5.39. If the ratio between the memory access time and the memory cycle time is 1:4, it means that four banks will be required to ensure sequential reading without delays.

Unlike Figure 5.38, which describes architectural aspects of the multibank memory, Figure 5.39 depicts the timing aspects of reading sequential cells. Every empty rectangle represents the cycle time. Let us assume that the program reads the first address that belongs to bank 0. The processor requests the content of the cell and after some time (the access time) gets the required data. This is represented by the small rectangle on the left. However, after delivery of the data, the bank is locked for some additional

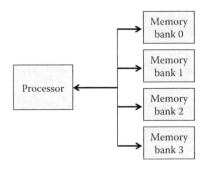

FIGURE 5.38 Four banks memory architecture.

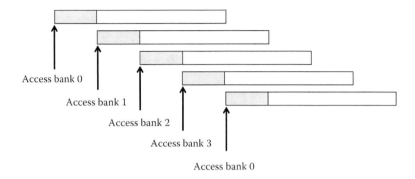

FIGURE 5.39   Memory access time (four banks).

time (the cycle time minus the access time). If the program, like in many cases in reality, needs the next consecutive cell, the processor will address the memory, asking for the next cell's content. Once again, after a short period of time (the access time), the date will be available; however, the bank will be locked for additional reads. This process continues with the third and fourth cells. When the program needs the content of the fifth cell, which resides in the same bank as the first cell, the bank is unlocked once again since it managed to restore the data. As previously stated, the timing ratio defines the number of banks that have to be implemented in order to ensure sequential reads without delays. In this specific case, the memory cycle is four times the memory access time, which means that after reading four cells, the first bank is ready once again. In addition, in implementing the bank mechanism, each bank has to be self-sufficient in a way done in the CPU, where the instruction is executed by several independent autonomous units (such as IF, ID, EX, WB).

Figure 5.40 describes the memory organization in which consecutive cells belong to different banks.

Memory Organization

The memory can be organized using various methods, and this section will concentrate on three of those. For completeness, the explanation related to cache memory will be addressed in the next chapter.

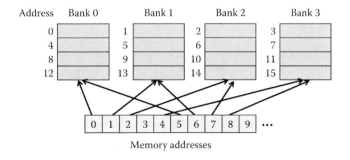

FIGURE 5.40   Banks' organization.

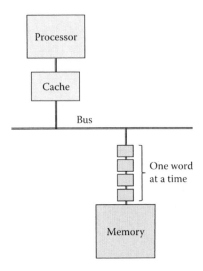

FIGURE 5.41   One word at a time.

- A memory architecture in which the MMU transfers one word* at a time (Figure 5.41). Usually, this is a very simple and cheap approach since the word is sent on the bus so that in each bus cycle† just one word is transferred. The negative side effect is the relative slow memory bandwidth.

- A memory architecture that transfers a block (several words) at a time (Figure 5.42). This type of memory requires a wider bandwidth, which is more expensive; however, it is capable of transferring more data in each cycle.

- Memory built using the interleaving method (Figure 5.43), which provides a better bandwidth due to the internal division.

Memory Technologies

As already stated in this chapter, the memory is used for storing the programs to be executed as well as the data required for execution. For that reason, the memory speed is directly linked to the system's performance. Although in the first decades, most technological efforts were spent on enhancing the processor's performance, in the last two decades some efforts have been aimed at improving the memory's performance as well.

At present, cache memory (explained in the next chapter) is implemented using fast static memory (SRAM), and the main memory is implemented using dynamic RAM (DRAM). Each memory chip contains millions of cells and is connected to a memory bus, which is a cable with many wires running in parallel and is used to transfer several bytes

---

* In this case, we refer to a virtual word. In various systems, "word" has different meanings ; moreover, the bus width may be different. Some systems use a 16-bit word while others use 32 or 64 bits.

† A bus, like the processor and memory, is synchronized by an internal clock cycle. This cycle defines the number of transfers it can perform in a unit of time. A bus with a cycle of one millionth of a second can transfer one million chunks of data per second. The other parameter that defines the bus capacity is its transfer unit (or width). If a bus is working with 32-bit words, it means that with each cycle it will transfer 32 bits.

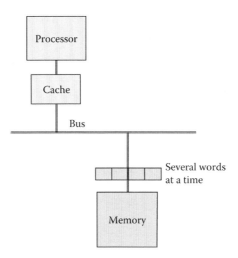

FIGURE 5.42   Several words at a time.

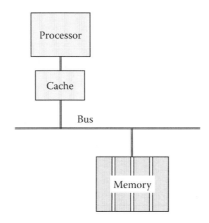

FIGURE 5.43   Interleaving.

in one cycle. The bus width, or the number of wires it has, defines the number of bits to be transferred in parallel. In a sense, it resembles the number of lanes in a highway. Modern PCs use a 64-bit bus, which means that in each cycle, 8 bytes are transferred.

In addition to the increase in memory capacity, its structure has changed as well. While the first memories' structure was a one-dimensional array of cells, modern memories are based on a two-dimensional matrix. The MAR (see Figure 5.7) in modern systems is divided into two registers: the row address strobe (RAS) and the column address strobe (CAS). Combined together, they provide the required two-dimensional addresses.

The technological miniaturization trends that affected the whole electronic industry have impacted memory technologies as well. If, four decades ago, a memory chip included 1000 bits, the currently used memories are based on 4 GB. Another important factor is the electricity required. In the past, the memory needed 5 V, and currently the requirement is a little over 1 V. This lower electricity consumption provides many new usages for memory, especially for appliances that are not constantly connected to an electric outlet.

All systems operations are synchronized by an internal clock. The various buses, which are intended for bridging the systems devices and transfer the data between them, have to be synchronized as well. Usually, synchronous devices are faster than asynchronous devices. If an asynchronous device needs to transfer data, either it has to wait for the other devices or the other devices have to wait for it. This delay does not exist in the case of synchronous devices. This was the reason that a new standard was developed* for synchronous DRAM (SDRAM). The main aim was to minimize the waiting cycles that exist in asynchronous transfers. The standard used a 100 MHz channel, which means transferring a block of eight bytes 100 million times a second (or a transfer rate of 800 MB/sec).

As with other technologies, the next generation, which addressed the issue from a different angle, closely followed. By the end of the 1990s, the Rambus DRAM (RDRAM) technology had been introduced. The main idea behind this technology was the bus that was used. Instead of one bus that connected all memory components, RDRAM used a network of connections, which provided better performance. The main disadvantage was the increased price and the fact it required a different memory bus that was not compatible with the existing ones.

The limitations associated with the implementation of Rambus led to the definition of a new SDRAM standard: the DDR (double data rate) SDRAM. The first version (DDR1) used improvements borrowed from processor technology, such as a dual pipeline that connects the memory components to the bus. This allowed the doubling of the data rate by transferring 2 bits during the same time unit (at the beginning and end of the cycle). The second version (DDR2) improved the bus speed by doubling the cycle time and, in particular, it lowered the electricity consumption to 1.8 V. The next version (DDR3) further improved the bandwidth and lowered the power consumption even more. This was required due to the variety of new mobile devices that, despite developments in battery manufacturing technologies, still needed longer operating times. It is anticipated that during 2016 a wide dispersion of DDR4 will begin, which, as with other versions, will increase performance while lowering power consumption. One point to be considered relates to compatibility. Due to the need to lower power consumption so the designed memory will be able to accommodate various mobile devices' requirements, the various DDR versions are not compatible. This means that systems that use one technology will not be able to upgrade to the next one, since it may require a different motherboard. This, of course, decreases the life span of the modern system, which is a known phenomenon of the modern society as can be observed regarding other appliances as well.

Key Takeaway

- *Memory organization*: The memory may be organized using various methods; however, in all cases the developer view is of a one-dimensional array of cells.

---

* The organization that is responsible for developing the new standard is the Joint Electronic Device Engineering Council (JEDEC), which is an international body of hundreds of companies working together to define and implement open standards that will allow the development of various devices where each one can work with all the others.

- *Memory hierarchy*: Defines the actual memory organization used by modern computers. Usually there are several levels of memory, and data may be moved between them automatically without any involvement on the part of the developer or the application that is being executed.

- *Big- and little-endian*: Refers to the direction in which the bits are transferred to and from memory. Big-endian starts with the most significant bit first, while little-endian starts with the least significant bit first. In both cases, it has no effect on the running program/application.

- *Single, dual, and multiple port memory*: Usually when the system consists of one processor, the memory will use one port (entry point for data communications). When there are two processors, they will have to compete on the single port, and for that reason the memory may have a dual port. When there are more processors, the memory may use multiple ports.

- *Partitions*: Refers to executing areas within the memory, which hold programs to be executed. Originally the number of partitions was fixed (determined at boot time), while later the operating system could change their number and size.

- *Virtual memory*: Refers to a concept used by most modern computers. The virtual (or logical) addresses used by the program are mapped into physical locations. This is done automatically by the hardware every time a memory location is accessed. The program is automatically divided into pages, and the physical memory is divided into frames. The pages and frames are of the same size. If a page is not in memory, it is the operating system's responsibility to load it.

- *Page table*: This is a table in memory that is being used by the hardware to translate the logical address to a physical one. In addition, entries in the table hold security and access bits.

- *Paging*: Refers to the situation in which a page is requested but it is not in the memory. The hardware detects the problem and signals the operating system by issuing an interrupt. The operating system will put the process on hold until the request page is loaded from disk. Only then will the program continue running.

- *Swap*: Refers to swapping the whole program from memory to the disk. It may be done to improve the system's performance, for example, when there are many programs competing for a relatively small pool of pages.

- *Memory performance*: This is important to the overall performance of the system and is enhanced using several techniques: technology that improves the memory speed, increased memory hierarchy levels, interleaving, and a wider bus.

CHAPTER 6

Cache Memory

CACHE MEMORY

This chapter focuses on cache memory. By using the general architecture figure, we can relate to the cache memory and its contribution to system performance (Figure 6.1).

As stated in the previous chapter, cache memory is an important layer in the memory hierarchy, and its main contribution is in improving the execution speed. The memory hierarchy is depicted once again in Figure 6.2, but this time the emphasis is on the sizes of the various levels of the hierarchy. The slowest and largest level (as far as capacity is concerned) is the disks. Currently, the standard disks used in personal computers (PCs) have a capacity that starts with several hundreds of gigabytes and goes up to several terabytes. Furthermore, utilizing cloud computing, in which the system's resources reside on remote servers, the disk capacity increases significantly. The main memory (random access memory [RAM]), which represents the second level, has a standard capacity ranging from several gigabytes up to hundreds of gigabytes. The cache memory, which is the next level, is usually divided into several components, each with a different purpose and a different size. The last level of the memory hierarchy is the registers which usually are very limited.

The RAM described in the previous chapter is used for storing programs and data. There is another memory component called read-only memory (ROM), which is used by the operating system and the hardware and is intended for components (programs and/ or data) that do not change frequently. Despite its name, some of the currently available ROMs can be changed; sometimes, a special recording device is required. Even so, their main use remains for special operating systems or hardware functions. As such, ROM is not available for standard computer programs.

One of the important attributes of ROM is the fact it is a nonvolatile memory, which means it retains its content even if the power is switched off. For that reason, ROM is used, for example, by the boot programs that are responsible for bringing the system up. Other components stored in the ROM are programs or data required for managing some input and output devices. Usually, these types of data will not be modified during the life span of the device. In modern computers, some of the ROM is replaced by flash memory, which is a nonvolatile device that can be rewritten if the need arises.

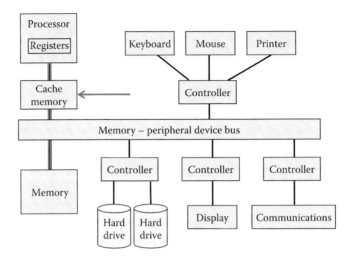

FIGURE 6.1   Cache memory.

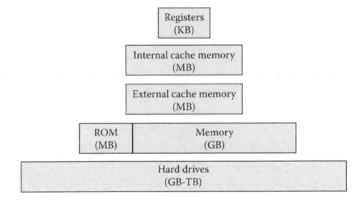

FIGURE 6.2   Memory hierarchy—size.

Figure 6.3 depicts the memory hierarchy but includes the additional average access times of each level. In various systems, the number of cycles may vary; however, it still provides a good base for comparison. By observing the figure, the very large differences between the access times of the various levels become clear and realistic. Only by realizing these differences can one understand the contribution of the cache memory to the system's performance.

To better understand the need for the cache memory, we will use a visual example. Let us assume that a processor implements a classic unbalanced* five-stage pipeline:

---

* This is an unbalanced pipeline, since the amount of time required for each step is different. In a balanced pipeline, since all times are identical, in every cycle the pipeline proceeds to the next stage. When the pipeline is unbalanced, the shorter stages will have to wait idle for the longer stage to finish. In Chapter 4, "Central Processing Unit," there were some examples of unbalanced pipelines, but these were taken care of by the processors' designers. In this case, we can assume that the problem exists in order to demonstrate its effect on performance.

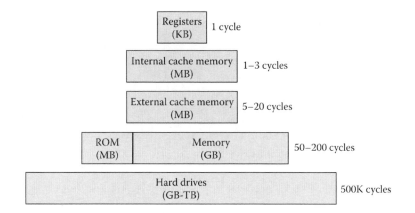

FIGURE 6.3   Memory hierarchy—access time.

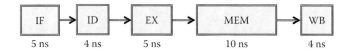

FIGURE 6.4   Pipeline execution times.

- Instruction fetch (IF) requires 5 ns

- Instruction decode (ID) requires 4 ns

- Execute (EX) requires 5 ns

- Memory access (MEM) requires 10 ns

- Write back (WB) requires 4 ns

Figure 6.4 depicts the scaled execution times of the various stages.

We will start by computing the pipeline performance and the latency* of a single instruction. This performance is important for assessing the pipeline's efficiency. However, the time required to execute one instruction cannot be an indication of efficiency, and the system's performance is calculated by the number of instructions performed during a single unit of time.

Theoretically, calculating the performance is simple. Assuming the pipeline works without hazards or delays, we have to figure out the maximum amount of time required for one stage. Due to the pipeline's mechanism, the longer stage dominates the execution time since the shorter stages have to wait for its completion.

Since in a pipelined execution, the processor completes another instruction with every cycle, the systems' cycle time is indicative of the instruction execution time.

The time required for one instruction as part of the pipelined execution is given by[†]

---

* Latency is the amount of time required to complete just one instruction or one step.
† The function LAT designates the latency of the stage.

$$\text{Instruction time: MAX}\left(\text{LAT}(\text{IF}),\ \text{LAT}(\text{ID}),\ \text{LAT}(\text{EX}),\ \text{LAT}(\text{MEM}),\ \text{LAT}(\text{WB})\right)$$

$$\text{Instruction time} = \text{MAX}\left(5\text{ ns},\ 4\text{ ns},\ 5\text{ ns},\ 10\text{ ns},\ 4\text{ ns}\right)$$

$$\text{Instruction time} = 10\text{ ns}$$

The meaning of an instruction being executed every 10 ns is that the system is capable of executing 10^8 instructions per second, assuming, of course, that the pipeline works without any delays or hazards.

The instruction latency can be calculated in a similar way:

$$\text{Instruction latency} = \text{LAT}(\text{IF}) + \text{LAT}(\text{ID}) + \text{LAT}(\text{EX}) + \text{LAT}(\text{MEM}) + \text{LAT}(\text{WB})$$

$$\text{Instruction latency} = 5\text{ ns} + 4\text{ ns} + 5\text{ ns} + 10\text{ ns} + 4\text{ ns}$$

$$\text{Instruction latency} = 28\text{ ns}$$

The calculation reveals that the amount of time required for executing one instruction, regardless of the pipeline, is 28 ns. Unfortunately, this result is only true for an isolated execution of just one instruction. Not only is this an impossible situation, since we never execute just one single instruction, but also the result obtained is worthless. In this case, due to the unbalanced pipeline, there is a hazard that the previous calculation ignores. This hazard is related to memory access.

When building the execution sequence with all its stages, it becomes evident that the hazard severely impacts the system's performance (Figure 6.5).

Although the first instruction executes in 28 ns (as calculated), this is not the case with the following instructions. The second instruction will have to wait during the fourth execution stage, so instead of 28 ns it will require 33 ns. The memory hazard continues and intensifies with every additional instruction executed. Each such additional instruction increases the amount of time required by 5 ns. This means that the third instruction will require 38 ns, the fourth will require 43 ns, and so forth.

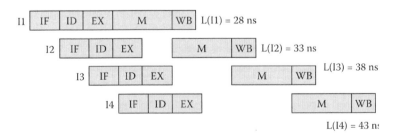

FIGURE 6.5 Execution table.

This problem occurred due to the differences between the processor and the memory. The longest stage in the pipeline is the one where the instruction tries to access memory and has to wait due to its slowness.

The solution can be achieved by implementing a memory hierarchy in which an additional level of fast memory is added. This is a relatively small-capacity memory used for storing just the instructions and data that are currently within the processor or that will be required for execution. Since it is usually a smaller memory (in terms of capacity), it can be more expensive. The added cost it inflicts will have a very marginal effect on the overall system's price. This combination provides the better of the two solutions: on the one hand, a fast memory that will enhance performance; and on the other hand, a meaningless increase in price. Every time the processor needs data or instructions, it will look first in the cache memory. If it is found, then the access time will be very fast. If it is not in the cache, it will have to be brought from memory, and then the time will be longer (Figure 6.6).

To better understand the concept of cache memory, we will use a more realistic and known example. Let us assume that a student has to write a seminar paper and for that reason he or she is working in the library. The student has a limited-sized desk on which only one book can be used. Every time he or she has to refer to or cite various bibliographic sources, he or she has to return the book to the shelf, take the new book that is needed, and bring it to the working desk. It should be noted that sometimes it is a very large library, and the books needed may be on a different floor. Furthermore, the working space and the desk may be located in a special area far away from the shelves and sometimes even in a different building. Due to library rules that permit only one book on the desk, before using a new book, the current one has to be returned. Even if the previous book that he or she used several minutes ago is needed once more, it does not shorten the time, and the student has to return the current book and bring out the previous one once again. The only benefit

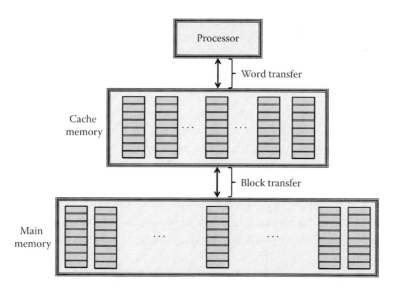

FIGURE 6.6 Cache data transfer.

here is that maybe the student remembers where the book is located and does not have to search for it.

To improve the students' work and prevent heavy movements of students between the working area and the library, it was decided to add an additional working space (cart) near each desk. The working space can accommodate several books, and the working procedures are changed accordingly. Each student is not limited to one book only and can take and use several books locally in the working area. This change enhances the students' work, which becomes significantly more efficient. Each time the student needs to work on some subject, he or she goes to the library and fetches several relevant books. The books are placed in the new working space. Each time a book is needed, it is moved from the working space to the desk. Since the desk is still limited and can hold just one book, if there is a book on the desk, then first it is moved to the cart and then the new book is brought to the desk. In this mode of operation, if the student needs a book that was previously used, it is still in the working space and can easily be found and used. The significant improvement in the new method is that it eliminates the need to go back and forth to the library. If the student can evaluate his or her needs and bring the relevant books, the "trips" to the library can be minimized.

The underlying assumption in adding the working space is that students need several books when working on their papers and that each of these books is used more than once. When the student finishes the current subject, he or she will return all books to the library and take a new batch of books that are needed for the next subject.

This way, the student has to go to the library only if a new book that is not in the working space is needed or when he or she switches to a new subject and all the currently available books are not needed; however, the space is required for the new books. Another idea implemented here is that if the student goes to the library, it might be a good idea to bring back several books at a time and not just one book each time. The number of books that the student can bring from the library depends on the amount of space available or on his or her ability to carry the books. On the other hand, when the student is working on paper and all the relevant books are easily reachable, he or she may feel that the whole library is easily accessible.

Although this visual example relates to a different area, it provides a very good representation of the memory's work. In a system without any cache memory, the processor has to get the operands from memory, exactly as happens in the library. This mode of operation causes a lot of data to be moved on the bus. These transfers and the fact that the memory is significantly slower than the processor slows the execution speed. When the working space is added, which in the computer is implemented as cache memory, the work is more efficient. Less data is transferred through the bus. The processor that requests some data causes the memory management unit (MMU) to bring additional cells that may be required—exactly as the student brings additional books that might be required later. When the processor asks for this additional data, the access is fast since the data is already in the cache.

The computer implementation is based on a similar procedure. The processor checks the cache for the required data or instructions. If the information is not in the cache, it has

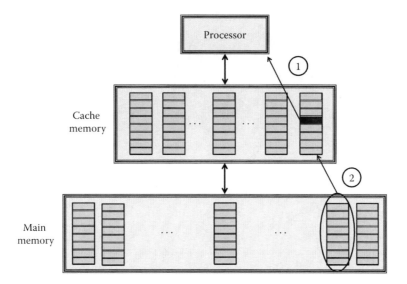

FIGURE 6.7   Cache memory—miss.

to be brought from memory. However, the transfer between the cache and the memory is done in blocks that contain several words. The assumption is that words in close proximity to the required word will be required as well (locality of reference). This is the case when instructions are fetched, since in many cases, the execution is serial; after the current instructions, the following ones will be needed as well. This is also the case when a program is accessing an array of data. The program will probably want to access other data items in the same array. In both cases, the next processor's request will be fulfilled rapidly since the data already resides in the cache.

Figure 6.7 depicts the abovementioned process. During execution, the processor needs some data or the next instruction (depicted as the dark cell in the cache). It accesses the cache memory in the hope that it will be found. Unfortunately, the required cell or cache element is not in the cache, so it has to be brought from memory (Stage 2 in the diagram). The MMU that gets the request fetches not only the required cell but also the whole row. A row in this sense is a block of cells, such as a paragraph, that includes the requested cell. The whole row is transferred to the cache, and only then can the required cell be sent to the processor as requested (Stage 1 in the diagram). The assumption in this case is that the additional cells might be needed, as in the case of the student's books, especially considering that the memory access overhead was paid already.

Hit Rate

To evaluate the efficiency and effectiveness of the cache memory for the system's performance, we will use the following definitions:

- *Hit*: This is the situation in which the data requested by the processor is found in the cache. Since the cache is faster, then each time the data is found, the execution will be fast (no need to bring the data from main memory).

- *Miss*: This is the situation in which the requested data is not in the cache. This situation, which is the inverse of hit, requires the data to be brought from memory. In such a case, the instruction execution will be slowed down until the required data is transferred from memory.

- *Hit rate*: This is the percentage of cases in which the requested data is found in the cache.

- *Miss rate*: This is the percentage of the cases in which the requested data is not found in the cache.

- *Miss penalty*: This is the amount of extra time needed to receive the requested data (see the section "Miss Penalty" in this chapter for elaboration).

For the cache memory to be effective, it is essential that the hit rate will be as high as possible. The success of the cache is driven by two assumptions:

- Temporal: It is reasonable to assume that the instructions and data that were requested in the near past will be requested once again, for example, the instructions in a loop that are repeated every cycle of the loop.

- Spatial: It is reasonable to assume that the data that is close to the address requested in the near past will be needed soon, for example, variables in an array or fields in a record that are being accessed sequentially.

When the requested data is not in the cache, the processor has to wait. If the missing data is an operand, the instruction is delayed until the operand is brought from memory. If the missing data is an instruction, the processor stops and it will reissue the instruction when it arrives from memory. In both cases, the additional waiting time is part of the miss penalty.

To better understand the meaning of the terms, we may use Figure 6.8.

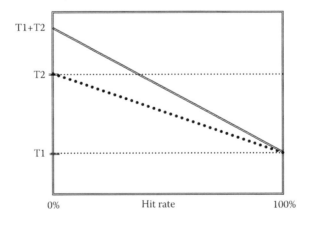

FIGURE 6.8   Average access time as a function of the hit rate.

Let us assume that the time required for accessing the cache is defined by T1, and the time required for accessing the memory is T2. T2 is, of course, significantly larger than T1.

The horizontal axis represents the hit rate, and the vertical axis represents the access time. If the hit rate is high (close to 100%) then the access time is close to T1. This means that in many cases, the data is in the cache and the access time required is close to the cache access time. On the other hand, if the hit rate is low (close to 0%), then the access time may be T2 or even T1 + T2. This means that the requested data is not in the cache so it has to be brought from memory. There are systems in which every time the processor tries to fetch data from the cache, in parallel it requests the same data from the memory. This is done in order to save time in case the data is not in the cache. In these systems, when the hit rate is low, then the access time will be T2. Other systems work in a serial mode. First, the cache is checked and only if the data is not in the cache will the memory be accessed. In these cases, a low hit rate will result in an access time of T1 + T2.

Figure 6.9 depicts the abovementioned process. It starts with a request issued by the processor. It might be sent to the cache by itself (the arrow at the middle of the diagram). If it is found in the cache, it is sent to the processor. On the other hand, if it is not in the cache, the cache will issue a request to the memory for the missing data. When is it brought from the memory, it is placed in the cache (along with the whole row) and in parallel it is sent to the processor. In this case, the miss penalty is T1 + T2. All additional requests for data in the same row will be fulfilled by the cache. Alternatively, the processor can send the initial request not only to the cache but to both the cache and to the memory. The memory request is done as a precaution in case the data is not in the cache and it intended to lower the miss penalty to T2. As with the previous case, once it is brought from the memory, the whole row is placed in the cache so future requests to data in the same row will produce a high hit rate.

The hit rate defines the probability of finding the requested data in the cache. If a variable is accessed k times during a short duration of time (such as the index of a loop), then in the first case the access time will be longer since it has to be brought from the memory, but in all other $k - 1$ cases, the access times will be short. In this example, the hit rate will be calculated by

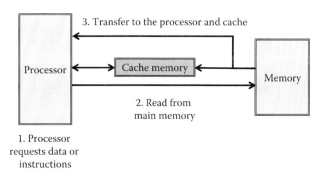

FIGURE 6.9 Cache and memory access.

$$\text{Hit rate} = \frac{(k-1)}{k}$$

assuming:

    c   is the cache access time

    m is the memory access time

    h is the hit rate

Then the average access time will be calculated by

$$t = c + (1-h) * m$$

In other words, the processor will always try the cache memory first, and if it misses, it will have to access the main memory as well. If all requested data is found in the cache, then the hit rate will be 100%, so there will not be any access to the main memory. In these cases, the access time will be c (the cache memory access time). On the other hand, if none of the data is in the cache, then the hit rate will be 0, which means that each time there is a need to access both the cache and the main memory. The access time in these cases will be c + m. It should be noted that in this case, the processor first accesses the cache and only if the data is not found will it access the main memory. If the mechanism used is based on a parallel access, then the memory access time overlaps the cache access time. In such a case, when the data is not found in cache, the access time will be just m.

Over time, the memory access tends to concentrate on locations in close proximity. A program accesses data, for example, in a specific record and only after finishing the process of this record will it access and process the next one. The program usually does not access fields in random records. Another example already addressed is a loop. The instructions that comprise the loop are repeated, and the number of repetitions increases as the loop contains more cycles. This behavior ensures that, even for small cache memories, the hit rate will be high. For example, we will address the following loop:

$$\text{sum} = 0\ ;$$

$$\text{for } (i = 0;\ i < n,\ i++)$$

$$\text{sum} += a[i];$$

$$v = \text{sum};$$

The temporal aspect of the environment is due to the repeating instructions. The loop repeats n times and each cycle it adds the next cell in the array (a), increases the loop index and checks for the end of loop. In the first cycle, the instructions are loaded from the main memory into the cache, but in all subsequent n−1 cycles, the instructions are already in the cache so their access time will be fast.

Another aspect of the performance gained by using the cache is because the loop adds the next consecutive items of the array. When the processor accesses the first item, the whole row containing the item will be loaded into cache. This ensures that when the next items are required, they will be found in cache as well. It should be noted that modern systems sometimes implement a read-ahead mechanism, which uses some kind of artificial intelligence. Each time the processor accesses an item that is close to the end of a block in cache memory, the MMU will automatically issue a read instruction for the following block, even though it has not yet been requested. This way the hardware manages to understand the mode of operation used by the program, and by loading the future cells, it improves the hit rate.

Miss Penalty

The miss penalty is the amount of time that will be wasted when the data is not found in cache. There are cases when this penalty might be severe, since it includes several required activities:

- Understanding that it is a miss: This the amount of time that elapses before the processor understands that the data has not been found in cache.

- Locating space: This is the amount of time that the hardware spends locating the least recently used block (or row). This block will be overwritten by the new block that will be brought from memory.

- Writing the block if "dirty": This the time taken to write the content of the block to be overwritten back to memory, if needed. In modern computers, the code cannot be modified. This means that if the block to be overwritten contains code, there is no need to save its content. However, if the block contains data, it may be that some of this data was changed by the processor. To identify the blocks that were changed, the hardware maintains a "dirty" bit, which is set with every modification made to cells in the block. Before the hardware can override the block's content, the dirty bit is checked. If it is set, then the content is copied back to memory and only then can the block's space be released.

- Request the block from the lower level in the hierarchy: This is the time that is needed to transfer the request.

- Transferring the block: This is the time needed for the block's transfer.

- Fetching the operand: This is the time needed for transferring the operand into the processor, as is usually done by the control unit (CU).

- Initiating the instruction that was suspended when it was found that some data is missing.

The penalty for such a cache miss can be several cycles, but it may also be several hundred cycles. In extreme situations, if the hardware does not have a page and the read ahead mechanism did not bring it in advance, the penalty may be hundreds of thousands of cycles. In such a case, the processor will not wait for the missing data but will continue executing a different process.

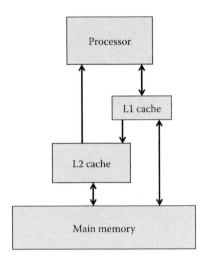

FIGURE 6.10   Two levels of cache memory.

In an attempt to minimize the potential penalty, modern systems have several levels of cache memory. The first level is usually intended to lower the access time, and for that reason this level can be relatively small. The second level is usually aimed at increasing the hit rate, so this type of cache will be larger (Figure 6.10).

Figure 6.10 depicts a system that is using two levels of cache memory, Level 1 (L1) and Level 2 (L2). Although it is not always the case, the search for data is hierarchical. In the first stage, the processor is looking for the data in the faster cache (L1). If it is found, then the access time will be the shortest. If it is not found, then the processor will look in the second level (L2). It is found, the whole block will be copied to L1, so the next time the processor tries to access the block, it will be found in the faster cache. If the data is not found in the second level, it will have to be brought from the main memory. In this case, once again the block will be copied into L1.

The performance gains from adding cache memory were significant, so modern systems have multilevel cache mechanisms. Furthermore, the cache itself can be split into two different types (Figure 6.11).

Figure 6.11 depicts a two-level cache in which L1 is divided into two separate caches. The idea stems from the Harvard architecture (see Figure 3.4). The intention behind this division is the different attributes of the content. Since instruction cannot be modified, the L1 instruction cache's blocks do not need a dirty bit and will never require saving, while the L1 data cache's blocks have to be checked before their space is released. In addition, this division can ensure that there will never be any conflicts between instructions and data when it comes to cache blocks. In a sense, this type of architecture provides additional credibility to the ideas defined and used by the Harvard architecture.

Figure 6.12 is an additional possible configuration that employs three levels of cache, two of which are located very close to the processor while the third is an external cache. As with the previous cases, the added level does not change the process, and every data item

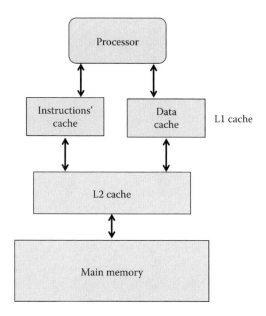

FIGURE 6.11   Two-level cache including split (instructions and data).

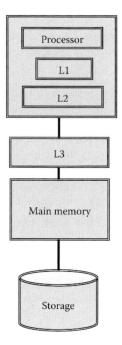

FIGURE 6.12   Additional cache level.

that is required by the processor is looked for in all the hierarchy levels. As with the previous cases, the processor may use a serial approach in which the L1 cache will be searched first and, if the item is not found, L2 will be searched, and so on. Or alternatively, the processor may issue the request to all four levels (the three cache levels and the memory). Once it has been found in a higher level, all the lower levels' requests will be stopped.

Address Translation

As already stated, programs use virtual addresses that are relevant to the program itself. In many cases (at least with PCs), these addresses are actually a displacement to the beginning of the relevant segment. When the program executes, there is a need to translate these virtual addresses into real addresses, since the MMU works only with real addresses (see Figure 5.22). The real addresses are physical addresses that relate to the main memory. However, since the cache memory is a reflection of the main memory, the real address is sent to the cache as well to check if the required data is there. Only if it is not in the cache will it be brought from the main memory.

Figure 6.13 depicts the address translation process. It starts from the left upper corner when the processor sends the virtual address (VA) obtained for the instruction. The address is translated into a physical address (PA), as explained in the previous chapter. The translated PA is then sent to the cache. If it is found, it is a hit, and the requested data is sent back to the processor. If it is not found (miss), the address is sent to the main memory. To simplify the process, the figure assumes a single level of cache and a serial search. In addition, the underlying assumption of the figure is that the data is found in memory (it is not a virtual page that has to be loaded from disk). The data that is found in memory is sent to the processor, and in parallel it is also sent to the cache (the lower line in the diagram). The two addresses are transferred on the upper bus, while the data is transferred on the lower bus, which has a higher speed and a larger bandwidth.

This translation process hides a severe performance problem that became evident to hardware designers. To translate the addresses, the hardware uses the page table. This table resides in the main memory and this makes no sense. The hardware has to access the relatively slow main memory in order to calculate the address of the data that is stored in the high-speed cache. This means that to access the data in the cache, the hardware has to go through memory. All the efforts spent in lowering the access time will be worthless if the translation process depends on the main memory.

The solution adopted by most systems is a special high-speed buffer (implemented using static RAM [SRAM], just like the cache) called TLB (translation lookaside buffer). It is being used as a cache for the page table itself. During a program's execution, the TLB contains part of the page table. As with the cache, the addresses located in the TLB are the addresses of the pages that have recently been used.

Figure 6.14 depicts the translation process including the usage of TLB. It is very similar to Figure 6.13 with some minor additions: the addition of the TLB translation as well as the addition of the relative access times.

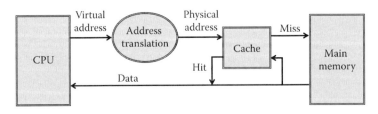

FIGURE 6.13   Address translation process.

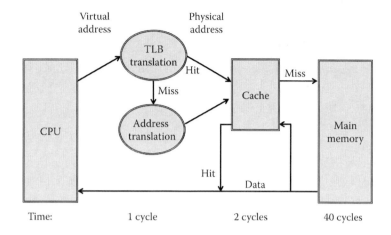

FIGURE 6.14   Address translation including TLB.

As with the previous figure, the process starts from the left upper corner, which depicts the virtual address being sent by the processor. The address is translated using the pages' information obtained from the TLB. If the page information is in the TLB, the virtual address is translated to the physical address, which is then transferred to the cache, and the rest is exactly as was previously described in Figure 6.13. If the page information is not found in the TLB, an ordinary translation will be performed using the page information obtained from the memory resident page table.

The lower part of the figure relates to timing information. If the page information is found in the TLB, it will take one cycle. Checking if the data is in the cache will require an additional two cycles. However, if it is not in cache and it will have to be brought from memory, an additional 40 cycles will be required. If the page information is not found in the TLB and it has to be brought from the memory resident page table, it will require an additional 40 cycles. The significant timing differences between the various implementations led to the development of multilevel caches (Figure 6.15).

Figure 6.15 is a more elaborated variation of the previous configurations (Figures 6.10 and 6.11). In this case, the memory hierarchy includes

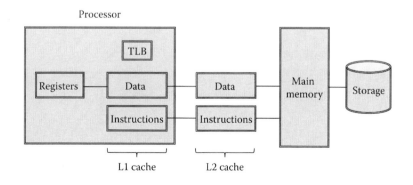

FIGURE 6.15   Multilevel caches.

- Registers

- Two cache memories as part of the first level, one for instructions and one for data

- Two cache memories in the second level split into instruction and data

- Main memory

- Disks

The figure describes the TLB, although it is not a memory storage that is available for the system processes and it is used only by the hardware; nevertheless, it has been included for completeness. It should be noted that the content of the various caches is maintained by only the hardware and the user program or the operating system cannot directly change or manage this content.

For better understanding the cache memory contribution, we will use a numeric example. Let us assume that the system has two levels of cache and a specific program with various characteristics:

- During execution, 30% of the instructions access memory. This means that 70% of the instructions are performed between registers and do not need the memory.

- The first-level cache contains 4 KB and its access time is 1 ns. The miss rate when running the program is 10%. In other words, in 90% of cases the information is found in this cache.

- The second-level cache is of size 128 KB and its access time is 5 ns. The miss rate of this case when running the program is 1%.

- The main memory has an access time of 50 ns, and it has no miss or hit rate since in that example we assume all required information is found in memory. Some of this information may be in one or two of the caches as well. The system uses a serial (or hierarchical) access mechanism in which first L1 is checked. If the information is not found, L2 is checked and if the information is still not found, the main memory will be accessed.

Now we will calculate the changes in the cycles per instruction (CPI) (see section "'Iron Law' of Processor Performance" in Chapter 4) value in each case.

- If we use just the main memory without any of the caches:

$$CPI_{new} = CPI_{old} + 30\% * 50 = CPI_{old} + 15$$

The new CPI is based on the CPI as calculated in Chapter 4, "Central Processing Unit," but in that case, it was a pure processor's calculation without any external impact. Here, the memory access is taken into account, and it can be seen that with all the efforts to lower the CPI as much as possible, the memory access adds 15 ns for each instruction.

- If we use the main memory and the first-level cache,

$$CPI_{new} = CPI_{old} + 30\% * \left(10\% * 50 + 90\% * 1\right) = CPI_{old} + 1.77$$

As with the previous case, here the program accesses memory only in 30% of the instructions. Among these accesses, 90% are found in the cache so their access time is 1 ns, and the other 10% will have to access memory so their access time will be 50 ns. The combination of both types of memory increases the original CPI by 1.77 ns (significantly better compared with memory only).

- If we use the main memory and the second-level cache,

$$CPI_{new} = CPI_{old} + 30\% * \left(1\% * 50 + 99\% * 5\right) = CPI_{old} + 1.64$$

In this case, the 30% memory accesses are divided into 90% that are found in the L2 case, so their access time is 5 ns; the access time of the additional 1% that has to access memory is 50 ns. It can be seen that the performance in this case is slightly better than the performance of the main memory with the first-level cache. This means that the L2 cache, although it is five times slower compared with L1, provides better performance. This due to its elevated hit rate (99% compared with 90% for L1).

- If we use all three memories (the main memory and the two levels of cache),

$$CPI_{new} = CPI_{old} + 30\% * \left(1\% * 50 + 9\% * 5 + 90\% * 1\right) = CPI_{old} + 0.55$$

In this case, there are three levels of memory: main memory, L1, and L2. As with previous cases, only 30% of the instructions access memory. The first attempt is to find the data in L1. In 90% of the cases, it is found and then the access time is 1 ns. When it is not found, L2 is searched, and an additional 9% is found in L2 with an access time of 5 ns. The last 1% will have to be brought from memory and then the access time will be 50 ns. In this case, when all three memory levels are working combined, the CPI is increased only by 0.55 ns.

Multiple Processor Architectures

One of the most widely used methods for increasing systems' performance is by adding processors. This technology was implemented as early as the 1960s, but in the last decade it has advanced rapidly and has become the main performance booster (see later chapters). Generally speaking, a multiprocessor system will include several processors that share a common memory. (Figure 6.16). If the main memory is divided, then usually these will be different systems.

There are several ways of implementing a multiprocessor system, but the most common ones are uniform memory access (UMA) and nonuniform memory access (NUMA).

UMA will usually have a common memory, while any of the processors will have its own cache memory (Figure 6.17). The problem associated with this configuration is data integrity. When the system has just one memory and one cache memory, then each data element can be—but does not have to be—in the cache memory. If there are many processors, each

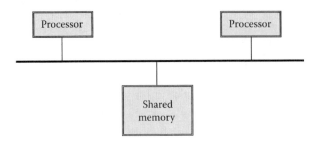

FIGURE 6.16   Multiple processors.

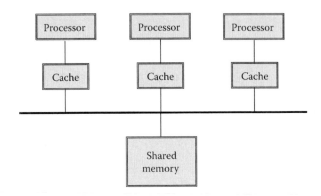

FIGURE 6.17   Uniform memory access (UMA).

one with its own cache memory, a data element can be in multiple locations. When such an element is changed, the hardware has to make sure all the possibly available copies are marked as invalid so no other process may use an outdated value.

NUMA, on the other hand (Figure 6.18), resembles different systems that are connected using a fast bus. Each processor has its own cache memory and its own memory, and, as part of the modern architecture, it even may have several cores, which elevates the complexity as well as the data consistency.

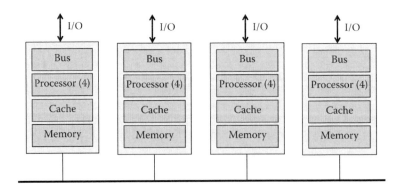

FIGURE 6.18   Nonuniform memory access (NUMA).

On the other hand, the NUMA architecture may be simpler, since each cache memory accesses only its memory. Therefore, changing a data element in memory requires checking just one cache memory.

Key Takeaway

- *Unbalanced pipeline*: Refers to a pipeline in which the various stages require different times. This hampers the instruction-level parallelism (ILP) (see section "Instruction-Level Parallelism" in Chapter 4) mechanism and may have a severe impact on performance. One slow stage not only increases the time of the single instruction's execution but it may also increase the time it takes for future instructions to be executed.

- *Cache hit*: The situation in which the required data is found in the cache.

- *Cache miss*: The situation in which the data is not in the cache and has to be brought from the lower memory level.

- *Miss penalty*: Refers to the actions to be performed when a miss occurs and to the time penalty it costs.

- *Address translation*: The process that translates the virtual addresses used by the running programs into the real location (physical) in memory. The MMU is responsible for the address translation. After the translation, the physical address is checked against the cache. If it is found, it is a hit; otherwise, it is a miss.

- *TLB (translation lookaside buffer)*: This is a special high-speed buffer used for caching the page table in order to speed up the address translation process.

CHAPTER 7

Bus

BUS

This chapter focuses and elaborates on various aspects of buses, which are the infrastructure for data transfer in the system. By using the general architecture figure, we can relate to the buses in the system (Figure 7.1). A bus, sometimes called a channel, is the mechanism for connecting various functional units in the system. We have discussed already some units that connect and transfer data, for example, the processor, which needs the data from the memory, both for instructions and their operands. Another similar example is the various types of memories that have to be connected for transferring the data seamlessly (without the running program or the operating system's control). The concept of modularity, emphasized by the von Neumann architecture, needs a mechanism for data transfer, and this is implemented using various buses.

The bus is a collection of parallel electrical wires used for transferring data. Each such wire transfers one bit. The collection of wires is capable of transferring a byte or a word at a time as a function of its width. The bus uses some protocols or rules that define its behavior, such as ownership, who can send data and in what order, priority, and so on.

Figure 7.2 depicts two types of buses that connect five different functional units (devices) represented as ellipses. The diagram on the right is of a mechanism that provides a network of connections, and each device is directly connected to all other devices. This type provides very good transfer rates since one transfer between two devices does not affect the transfer of data between other devices. On the left side, there is one bus that connects all the devices. In this case, all the connected devices will have to share the same protocol. Compared with a network of connections, the single bus approach is usually cheaper and slower and requires a higher degree of management. Each device that needs to transfer data will have to acquire access to the bus and then act according to the governing rules.

Since it is a common bus that at any specific moment can transfer just one block of data, each device has to ask for permission before it starts to use the bus. A realistic example for working with a bus is a train system. Let us assume there is just one railroad between two points and trains that travel in both directions. Each train that leaves the station where there is just one railroad has to make sure, before it starts its journey, that no other train is

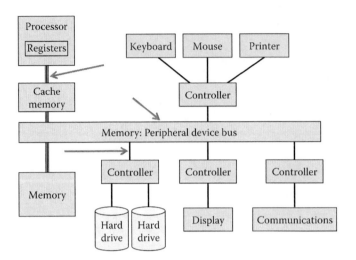

FIGURE 7.1   Buses as part of the architecture.

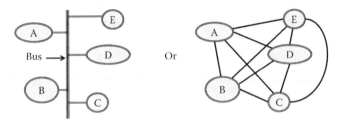

FIGURE 7.2   Types of buses.

using the railroad. The same is applicable to each device that needs to use the bus. First, it has to ask for permission to use the bus, and only after this permission is granted can the device start the data transfer. The transfer itself is actually used for

- Sending commands (read, write, etc.)

- Sending the address of the device on the other end (just like calling a number when using the telephone system)

- Transferring the data itself (after communication has been established)

A bus can be managed from a central location (central arbitration), or alternatively it can use a distributed arbitration.

Central arbitration (Figure 7.3) is characterized by one central unit (arbitrator) that manages the bus transfers. Every device that wants to use the bus will first ask the arbitrator for permission, and only after the permission is granted can the device use the bus for its purposes.

Due to the different types of transfers possible on the bus, it is logically divided into three different channels:

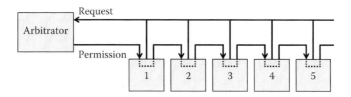

FIGURE 7.3   Central arbitration.

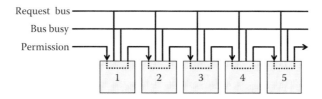

FIGURE 7.4   Distributed arbitration.

- One is used for control, and the device uses it for sending the commands.

- The second is used for addresses.

- The third is used for data transfers.

All the devices are serially connected and are listening to the address channel. When the device's specific address is broadcasted, the device answers. All other devices continue listening, but if it is not their number, they ignore it. In a sense, it is just like cellular phones, which listen to the network and respond only if their number is called.

Distributed arbitration (Figure 7.4) is characterized by the fact that there is no central management for the bus's activities. Instead of the central unit, the management is done collaboratively by all the devices by following the defined protocol. In a distributed arbitration, the device still has to ask permission to use the bus; however, the confirmation process is somewhat different. In addition to the three parts of the bus (channels), there is an additional one used for signaling if the bus is used or free. Each device checks the free/busy signal and waits until the bus becomes free. Only then does it send its request. The other devices on the bus receive the requests, and they answer based on a predefined priority mechanism. When the transfer is finished, the device is responsible for changing the bus signal back to free so other devices can use it. It is important to note that this is a very basic definition of the priority algorithms, and in reality there are additional algorithms for ensuring smooth communications, including priority management and preventing starvation.*

When a device is transferring data, it can use one of two methods:

- *Full transaction*: This means that the device asks for the bus, and once it is granted, the device holds it for the whole duration of the communication. This means that

---

* *Starvation* is a term used by the operating system during process management, and it refers to a situation in which a lower priority process is waiting endlessly for its turn.

during this time, several blocks can be sent back and forth. The requesting device sends the address and then the other device replies. In the next stage, the requesting device sends the request and the other device replies, and this goes on until all required data has been received. Only when the whole communication is finished will the requesting device release the bus. This mode of operation is similar to line communication, in which the calling telephone holds the line for the whole call duration, even if nothing is actually transferred on the line. This type of communication is applicable only to very fast devices and short communications, since during this transaction the bus is busy and all other devices that need it will have to wait.

- *Split transaction*: This means that the device asks for the bus and, when permission is granted, the device will send a command, address, or data and immediately afterward it will release the bus. Split transaction is the preferred type when there is a delay between the operations. For example, let us assume the cache memory needs a block of data from the main memory. The cache memory controller will ask permission to use the bus. When the permission is granted, the cache controller will send the command to the main memory, asking for the block. Following this command transfer, the cache memory controller will release the bus. This is done since the main memory controller needs time to process the request. It is possible that it has several requests already waiting, which will have to be processed before the current request is processed. Even if the current request is the first in line, it will take time for the main memory controller to access memory and fetch the required block. Only when the data is available will the main memory controller ask permission to use the bus, and when permission is granted, it will transfer the block to the cache memory controller. This mode of operation is similar to the one used by modern cellular networks, in which the channel is shared by many phones. Each pair (assuming no conference calls) of phones establishes a virtual channel using the bus. This bus supports several such virtual channels working concurrently in a time-sharing fashion. The main idea of the split-transaction method is that if there is nothing to transfer, the virtual channel will relinquish the bus so it can be used by someone else.

Transferring the data over the bus can be done in two ways based on the bus type:

- One type is a synchronous bus that is synchronized by a clock. The control channel includes a constant signal that is being used by all devices connected to the bus. Every operation on the bus such as sending data is synchronized to the beginning of the signal. The event (sending a command, address, or data) will last one or two bus cycles (Figure 7.5).

  The first (upper) line describes the synchronization signal, and it can be seen in the following lines that all other operations (read, confirmation, write, etc.) are synchronized and start at the beginning of a cycle.

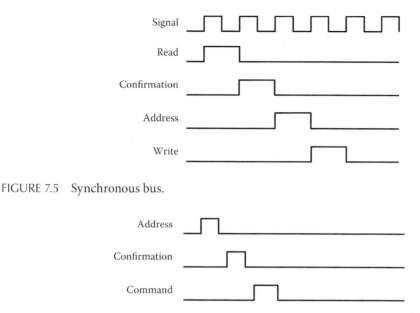

FIGURE 7.5   Synchronous bus.

FIGURE 7.6   Asynchronous bus.

- The other type is an asynchronous bus, which is not synchronized, and each operation follows the previous one. The device that sends the data defines the rate. On the one hand, this approach is more complicated, but on the other hand, it allows the connection of various devices that work at different speeds (Figure 7.6).

Bus Principle

The bus first appeared in 1964 in a computer called a programmed data processor (PDP),[*] which was designed and built by Digital Equipment Corporation (DEC). The computing industry at that time was characterized by large computers that were very expensive and used special cooling systems. The PDP, later called a minicomputer, was very different. It was cheap compared with mainframes (costing tens of thousands of dollars compared with hundreds of thousands and even millions). It had implemented several revolutionary ideas; for example, it could work in an ordinary air-conditioned room without special cooling facilities. Another idea implemented was a common bus (called *omnibus*). Prior to the introduction of the bus, the computer systems used channels that formed a matrix of connections in which each device is connected to all other devices using a dedicated cable (very similar to the diagram on the right in Figure 7.2). By using a common bus that all devices could share, the cost could be lowered; however, this caused some other bottleneck problems as will be discussed in the following sections.

Figure 7.7 depicts the PDP architecture with its common bus.

---

[*] PDP was a mini computer developed by DEC. The intention was to build a simple and, most importantly, affordable machine that could compete with extremely expensive mainframes at that time. For that reason, the system used a simple approach aimed at lowering costs.

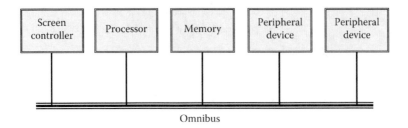

FIGURE 7.7   PDP 8 architecture.

As already stated, the bus is logically divided into three channels with different functionalities (Figure 7.8):

- The control channel, used for sending the commands and requests

- The address channel, used for sending the device addresses

- The data channels, used for sending the data

It should be noted that physically, the bus consists of a group of wires in which this logical division is maintained.

The bus principle was a significant and important contributor to the development of the computing industry. Prior to the appearance of the personal computer (PC), the computing world was dominated by several vendors that manufactured and sold turnkey systems. As such, the buses and channels used were proprietary, so other companies could not provide any devices or components to connect to these proprietary systems. Contrary to this approach, PCs were developed using standard buses that provide endless components and devices that can seamlessly be connected to the system. The once closed environment is currently very open, providing many vendors, even small ones, with access to the market—assuming their solution is better. This open environment managed to lower prices due to fierce competition, as we all know. A PC manufactured by any vendor can connect to memory manufactured by other vendors as well as disks that were manufactured by yet other vendors and so on.

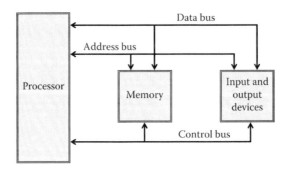

FIGURE 7.8   Channel types.

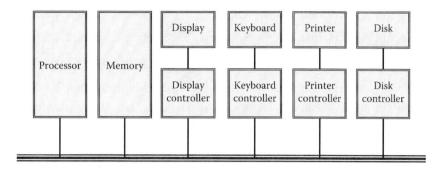

FIGURE 7.9   Architecture of the first PCs.

The standard bus that was originally implemented in the PC was initially intended to lower the PC's cost, as was the case with the PDP 20 years earlier. As a matter of fact, the first PCs implemented an architecture that resembles the PDP architecture (Figure 7.9).

The controllers that are part of the architecture were mainly used for bridging between the bus protocol and the devices (keyboard, display, disk, etc.). Since each device works differently, there is a need to translate and integrate the devices so they will be able to function in the bus environment. Usually, the device manufacturer is the one that develops the controller, unless the device is a standard device, which may have already an off-the-shelf controller.

In addition to the economic advantages associated with using a bus, it also allows the easy replacement of devices as well as the transfer of a device from one system to another (assuming the two systems use the same bus). Unfortunately, some of the advantages turned into disadvantages as the hardware advanced. As more devices were connected to the bus, especially devices with varying speeds and transfer rates, the bus became a bottleneck. For example, there might be cases where the processor is waiting for data to be transferred from memory just because the bus is busy transferring a character typed on the keyboard. The solution that was adopted, as in the case of memory, was to create a hierarchy of buses based on their required functionality:

- A processor-memory bus, which has to provide the maximum possible transfer rate. In many cases, this is a proprietary bus implemented by the motherboard* manufacturer. As seen already in previous chapters on memory and cache memory, the bus that connects the processor to the memory can become a severe bottleneck, which will have a negative impact on performance (e.g., by increasing the CPI (see section "'Iron Law' of Processor Performance" in Chapter 4)). For that reason, the bus speed and bandwidth are very important. In addition, due to the close proximity of the processor and memory, the length of the processor-memory bus is usually very small. This short distance is an additional factor in enhancing performance. In the modern speeds, the length the electrons are moving starts to be a relevant timing factor.

---

* A motherboard, sometimes called the *mainboard*, is a printed circuit board that is used for holding most of the system components. As such, it has a socket for connecting the central processing unit (CPU), sockets for memory, various connectors for peripheral devices' controllers, and expansion capabilities as well as the required communications.

- An input and output (I/O) bus, which is usually a standard off-the-shelf bus. This is used in order to increase the potential I/O devices that can be connected to the system. This bus is usually longer than the processor-memory bus in order to provide the space for connecting the various devices, especially considering that some of these devices are physically large and cannot be very close. In addition, the I/O bus supports not only a variety of devices but also devices that work at different speeds. In some cases, the differences in speed are several orders of magnitude. The I/O bus usually connects to the processor-memory bus or to the system bus if it exists. In modern systems, the I/O bus is implemented as a hierarchy of buses (as will be explained later in this chapter).

- A system bus, which can be a standard or a proprietary bus that is located on the motherboard. In some implementations, there is no system bus, and then the I/O bus and the processor-memory bus are connected. On the other hand, if the system bus exists, the other two buses will be connected to the system bus. Like with the I/O bus, the system bus is sometimes also implemented as a hierarchy of buses.

Bus Evolution

As already stated, the first implementations of buses (in the PDP in the 1960s and in PCs in the early 1980s) used a single bus, and all the system's devices were connected to this (Figure 7.10). The advantages in using a single bus were obvious (simplicity, which led to a lower cost). The bus that is responsible for all data transfers in the system (processor, memory, disks, keyboard, etc.) became a limiting factor. The many diverse devices that were connected to the bus not only slowed it down but also severely impacted the processor's speed. A single bus has to be longer, which affects its timing. Even in cases where a bus works efficiently, the volume of data transferred by all the different devices is close to its maximum capacity. Furthermore, the various devices' speeds represent a large spectrum of values. For example, the keyboard that depends on human clicks can produce less than 10 key strokes a second. Each such keystroke is translated into an eight-bit character or a maximum bandwidth of 80 bits per second. On the higher end, the processor that works at a 3 GHz clock rate needs tens of billions of bits per second.

In a system with two buses, there will be a fast processor-memory bus and an I/O bus, and both will be connected using a special adapter to bridge the two (Figure 7.11).

A system that has more than one bus will always utilize some hierarchy among the buses. For example, in Figure 7.11 the fast bus connects the processor and memory. Other buses will connect to the processor-memory bus. The adapter is some kind of controller that connects and synchronizes between the two buses and their protocols. Such an

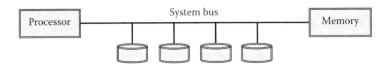

FIGURE 7.10   A system with a single bus.

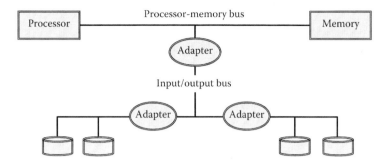

FIGURE 7.11   A system with two buses.

adapter usually includes several internal buffers that are used for temporarily collecting data on the slower bus. Only after the buffer is full will the adapter send the data as a single block over the faster bus. This way, although the data was collected from slow devices, the processor-memory bus was not interrupted until the whole block was ready for transfer. Although this mechanism minimizes the impact of the slower devices on the processor-memory bus, some systems use more buses to further reduce the possible negative impact (Figure 7.12).

Figure 7.12 depicts a system with three buses, and in such a system, the processor-memory bus is used just for communications between the processor and the memory. Although the processor-memory bus is connected to the system bus, this connection is used only in cases in which the processor has to access an input or output device, or in cases in which a device has to transfer an input block into memory. The main bus in such a system is the system bus, which serves as a connection for the other buses. The system bus can be connected to several slower I/O buses based on the devices connected and their attributes.

There are many standards for I/O buses. The standard provides the flexibility of connecting a variety of standard devices (that use the same standard), which leads to an open architecture. This type of architecture lays the foundation for integrating various components

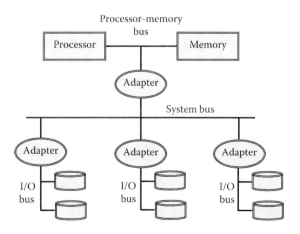

FIGURE 7.12   A system with three buses.

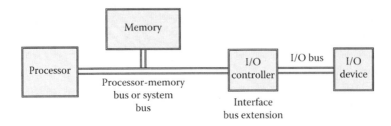

FIGURE 7.13   An extension bus.

manufactured by many different suppliers. Most modern systems support several buses as well as additional interfaces that provide the means to extend these buses. The additional interfaces or adapters are used for connecting yet other additional standard buses. Such adapters are acting as protocol converters. On the one hand, the adapter connects to one bus, and on the other hand, it connects to an extension bus, as shown in Figure 7.13. The extension bus is an ordinary bus, which implies that it can be connected to an additional adapter, which is connected to another bus. The bus hierarchy that is established can form various architectures for maximum flexibility in connecting a variety of I/O devices.

In the example depicted in Figure 7.13, the I/O controller acts as a protocol converter. On one end, there is the bus to which the adapter is connected, and on the other end is the specific I/O device. The controller (as will be explained later) not only manages and monitors the I/O device but also provides the capability of connecting the device to a variety of standard buses (at least the one the specific controller supports). In most cases, the controller is developed and sold by the device manufacturer in an attempt to have the device working on a variety of buses. In some cases, for example with hard drives, the controller is an integral part of the disk and is sold as part of the disk itself.

In most PCs, some of the buses are located on the motherboard, and connecting the controller is done by inserting it into special slots as shown in Figure 7.14.

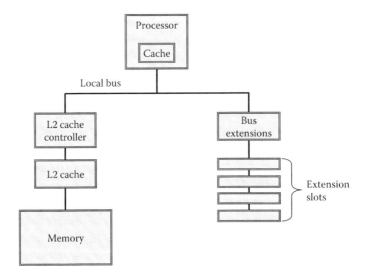

FIGURE 7.14   Extension slots.

There is a large variety of standard buses and their number continues to grow. Some of these standard buses and protocols are

- Industry Standard Architecture (ISA)*

- Extended ISA (EISA)†

- Micro Channel Architecture (MCA) ‡

- Personal Computer Interconnect (PCI)§

- Single Inline Memory Module (SIMM)¶

- Dual Inline Memory Module (DIMM)**

- Accelerated Graphics Port (AGP)††

- Personal Computer Memory Card International Association (PCMCIA)‡‡

- Universal Serial Bus (USB)§§

These standards are just several examples of the wealth of solutions devised and the fact that these solutions continue to evolve as technology develops.

In addition to the elevated flexibility in connecting the many I/O peripheral devices, the variety of standards supports the buses' hierarchy. This means that the connection provides an efficient way to use the fast buses at their maximum speed with very little interference caused by the slower buses. The initial idea was to support the data required for the processor without delays while providing a common infrastructure for transferring data between all the system components. Furthermore, the ability to reuse old devices and their controllers provides an additional economic benefit. Keyboards, for example, underwent

---

* ISA is an old bus developed for the IBM PC/AT during the 1980s. It was a 16-bit bus with backward compatibility.

† The EISA was developed by several personal computer vendors (AST, Compaq, Epson, Hewlett-Packard, NEC, Olivetti, Tandy, Wyse, and Zenith) and was a 32-bit bus that extended the standard AT bus. The EISA was developed in an attempt to compete with IBM, which was trying to promote its proprietary bus (the Micro Channel Architecture).

‡ MCA was an IBM proprietary bus that was used in their PS/2 systems as well as other computers. It was later replaced by PCI.

§ PCI was a bus that was introduced by Intel with the intention of connecting various hardware devices. The bus stems from the Peripheral Components Interconnect, which aimed to provide a standard infrastructure for computer peripherals.

¶ Contrary to the previous examples, SIMM is not a bus but a standard method of connecting memory modules. The standard provides the capability of connecting any memory modules to any system. It supports transfers of 32 bits per cycle.

** DIMM is another standard for connecting memory modules that doubles the SIMM's capabilities by supporting the transfer of 64 bits per cycle.

†† The AGP is yet another example relevant for connecting graphics controllers to the system, and it represents just one example of graphics controllers.

‡‡ PCMCIA is an organization made up of over 500 manufacturers that defined a common standard for devices and controllers, which are very common in laptops and other handheld and mobile appliances.

§§ USB is yet another industry standard developed around the mid-1990s and is still being developed further. The standard defines the protocols for connecting devices as well as providing the power supply. Although it was originally designed for connecting several devices, it gradually replaced many of the previous standards, and currently it is widely used to connect peripheral devices not only in the computer industry.

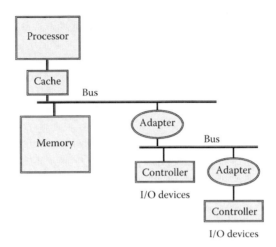

FIGURE 7.15 Bus hierarchy.

almost no change over the years. By using a proper adapter, there is no need to design new keyboards that are capable of working with the new buses.

Figure 7.15 depicts a system that supports a hierarchy of buses. At the upper left corner is the processor with its cache memory. There is a direct connection between the two (not a standard bus) since there are no additional devices connected to this bus. Usually, this will be a very fast connection. The cache memory is connected to the memory using a fast bus (such as the processor-memory bus). The only devices connected to this bus are the cache memory, the main memory, and an adapter that connects the lower-level buses. Every time the data required by the processor is not in the cache memory, this bus will be used to transfer the data from the memory to the cache memory and the processor. From time to time, the adapter will use the bus for transferring data, but it happens relatively rarely, and when it happens, the adapter works at the bus speed. The lower bus is the I/O bus, which connects a variety of controllers. These controllers connect the peripheral devices, or they can be used to bridge to further lower and slower buses, for example, as with the slow communications controller that connects to the bus and which, on the other end, may connect to a variety of devices or even additional communication buses (these are not part of the figure).

The most important need that led to the development of the bus hierarchy was to minimize as much as possible delays in transferring data to the processor. This was an important issue in designing the memory architecture and hierarchy. The bus hierarchy should, on the one hand, provide open access, in which data from a slower device can get to the processor; and on the other hand, the slower devices should never slow down the processor. Figure 7.16 is an example of a design that is far from being optimal.

As can be seen in Figure 7.16, the designer provided a very fast bus between the processor and the cache memory (a backdoor channel that is reserved just for communication between the two), but the processor, on the other hand, is connected to the north bus. The processor-memory bus is also connected to the north bus. In this way, the north bus is actually a system bus, and most of the data transfers in the system go through it.

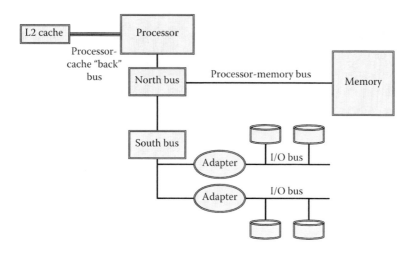

FIGURE 7.16   Bus conflicts.

The problem associated with this configuration is because the processor and the cache memory have to go through the north bus instead of a direct connection that is not shared by slower devices. Furthermore, the cache memory has to be directly connected to the memory to provide the required fast communication, and in this example, it is missing.

Figure 7.17 provides an example of the bus architecture in one of the Pentium-based systems. At the right upper corner, we may find the processor with its on-chip cache Level 1. A dedicated fast communication channel connects the two caches (Level 1 and Level 2).

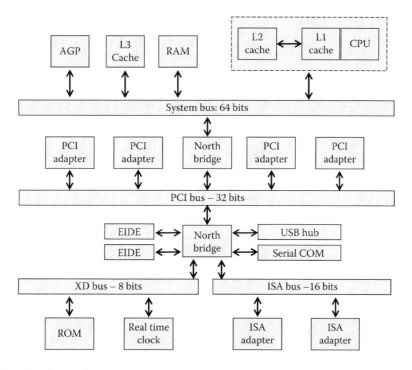

FIGURE 7.17   Pentium architecture.

This component (comprising the processor and the two caches) is connected to a fast 64-bit system bus. This bus is used for connecting the main memory, the graphics adapter, and the Level 3 cache. The graphics adapter is part of this bus to support very fast graphic displays, for example, for gamers. If the system does not require these superfast displays, then the ordinary monitors will be connected using a slower USB. As already stated in this chapter, the memory speed is influenced by two major aspects: the bus speed and its width. The speed defines how many units of data can be transferred every cycle, and the width defines the unit of data (byte, word, etc.). For example, if this bus speed is 800 MHz, it means that the bus is capable of transferring 800 million blocks every second. Each of these blocks is 64 bits wide. Although wider buses are more expensive (they require more wires in the cable as well as a larger connector that occupies more space on the motherboard), designers use them in order to achieve better transfer rates.

The fast system bus is connected (by the north bridge) to a 32-bit PCI bus. The north bridge is used for connecting the two buses, adjusting the speeds and block sizes, and translating the protocols. In addition, the PCI bus includes an additional four adapters that can be used for connecting PCI devices or for adapters/bridges that will allow the connection of other slower buses. On its lower side, the PCI bus is connected to the south bridge, which connects additional even slower buses. One of the important features and contributors to the success of the PC line of computers is its backward compatibility. Modern computers still support some of the old and even outdated peripherals, such as keyboards, floppy disks, and so on. For that reason, the south bridge, which on one side connects the PCI bus and on the other connects to modern buses such as USB, provides also backward compatibility by connecting to other old 16-bit and even 8-bit buses. This allows the reuse of some peripherals that, while working relatively slowly, do not need to be replaced, such as a real-time clock that synchronizes the system's activities but involves a minimal amount of data being sent over the bus.

Figure 7.18 elaborates on the timing aspects of the buses close to the processor. It can be seen that accessing the internal (Level 1) cache requires one cycle, similar to accessing registers. When the data has to be brought for the second-level cache, it requires two or three cycles depending on the implementation and the proximity. In cases in which the data is not found in Level 1 and Level 2, it has to be brought from the memory. In this case, the "cost" can be 50–200 cycles (up to two orders of magnitude) based on the specific

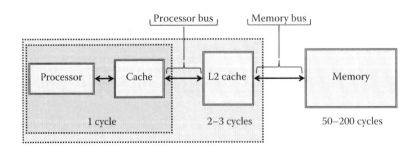

FIGURE 7.18   Faster bus access time.

implementation, bus conflicts, and so on. The figure addresses once again the importance of cache memory to the system's performance.

Hard Drive Buses

Disks, especially hard drives as well as optical disks, solid-state disks, and disks-on-key, are among the most important devices that were developed in parallel to the processors and memory. Many manufacturers concentrate on disks and provide a large spectrum of devices to be integrated into many systems (computers, handheld appliances, mobile phones, cameras, etc.). To provide the required connectivity, many standards for connecting explicitly disks were developed. Since the disks have different and sometimes unique attributes, there was a need for dedicated buses. As with ordinary buses, the buses that were designed specifically for disks were developed over time in an evolutionary process that closely followed technological developments. Due to the rapid developments in recent years, some of the more important improvements are relatively new.

A partial list of past and current disk buses includes

- AT Attachment (ATA)*
- Integrated Drive Electronics (IDE)†
- Enhanced IDE (EIDE)‡
- Small Computer Systems Interface (SCSI)§

Some of these standards do not exist anymore, having been replaced due to some of their inherent limitations. The constantly growing demand for faster and high-capacity disks takes its toll on the standard buses, which have to be enhanced in order to accommodate the new features and capabilities. It should be noted that the variety of buses represents the fierce competition between various manufacturers, in which each one tries to "push" its products and gain a larger market acceptance. Usually, hard-drive manufacturers are not interested in just developing new standards; this is done in order to promote their products. In the twenty-first century, the computing industry prefers open standards that allow sharing devices from many manufacturers. In most cases, the user prefers a standard product even if a different proprietary product is superior.

One of the buses that was widely used for high-performance systems and is currently being used mainly for servers is SCSI. Its name reflects the market position its designers were hoping to acquire. This bus, which was developed several decades ago, has been

---

* ATA was a standard for connecting disks or other ATA-compatible devices to the computer. This is an old standard that was mainly available for PCs. This is a general name that includes several other standards such as IDE, DMA, EIDE, and so on.
† IDE is a different name for ATA.
‡ Enhanced IDE, which encompasses several older standards (ST-506/ST-412, IDE, ESDI, ATA-2, ATA-3, ATA-4), is actually an advanced version of the IDE bus. The reason that there were several names for the same standard is due to ownership constraints. The two names IDE and EIDE were owned by Western Digital (one of the large hard-drive manufacturers). Other manufacturers were not allowed to use these names, so they came up with their own name or used the generic term ATA.
§ SCSI is a set of standards for connecting various peripheral devices to the system.

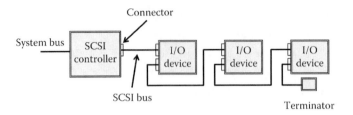

FIGURE 7.19 The SCSI bus.

widely used by IBM to try to differentiate its products and provide superior performance. It is a parallel channel that connects and concatenates several devices (Figure 7.19).

Generally speaking, the bus is no different from other buses. It has an adapter (SCSI controller) that converts and bridges between the buses (such as PCMCIA or USB and SCSI). One of its advantages is its ability to concatenate several devices on the bus. The last device is connected to a terminator that identifies the end of the bus (Figure 7.19, right bottom corner). The bus was successful due to its relative high throughput compared with other available buses. As with other devices and buses in the PC market, the standard went through a series of improvements, and over the years, many variations were developed. In most cases, the variations were for accommodating features such as faster transfer rates, increasing the maximum number of devices on the bus, and so on.

The process of defining and developing special buses for connecting mass storage (hard drives) was not confined only to disks and was done in order to connect a variety of other devices as well. The more common buses, interfaces, and protocols used in PCs are

- Parallel (line printer or LPT)*
- Serial (typically RS232C)†
- PS/2 (for keyboards and mice)‡
- Universal Serial Bus (USB)§

---

* LPT (line printer) was a general name for the parallel bus used in PCs. It was originally designed to connect line printers, thus its name. This bus was used as a de jure standard until it became standard IEEE 1284 by the end of the 1990s. The standard was developed by Centronics, a company that developed dot-matrix printers in the early 1970s. Additional developments were done by Epson, which is also very active in the market.

† The serial port or serial bus is an interface that transfers one bit at a time, compared to a parallel bus that transfers a byte, a word, or some other quantity of bits in each transfer. It can be said that the serial bus has a width of one bit.

‡ PS/2 was a bus designed by IBM as part of a proprietary PC it tried to introduce to the market in the early 1990s. The system was call PS/2 and it represented IBM's efforts to increase its presence in the PC market segment. The system had its own operating system called OS/2. The PS/2 bus was intended mainly for connecting keyboards and mice. Although IBM's efforts were unsuccessful and the PS/2 systems disappeared, the bus was used as a standard for quite some time until it was replaced by the USB. The PS/2 connectors were physically different compared with other connectors (being round connectors instead of the usual rectangle connectors).

§ USB is a serial bus that was designed to connect a large variety of devices to the system. One of the most important advantages of this bus is its support for plug and play. USB supports the connection and disconnection of devices on the fly without the need to reboot. An additional advantage is that the electricity required for the device is provided through the bus. Due to its advantages, USB has gradually replaced many of the older buses (serial and parallel). As with other buses, USB continues to evolve with additional enhancements mainly related to its speed; for example, USB2 supports up to 480 Mbits/sec and USB3 supports 5 Gbits/sec.

- Infrared Data Association (IrDA)*

- Bluetooth (wireless communication)†

- FireWire, or IEEE standard 1394‡

- WiFi (Wireless Fidelity)§

As with the previous example, the intention was to provide a partial list of technologies that were and still are being used in order to explain the rapid changes associated not only with the processor's or memory technologies but also with all devices connected to the system as well as their connection infrastructure. As an example, a more elaborated explanation of the connections and the protocol is provided for the very simple serial bus.

Serial Bus

The serial bus was implemented in early models of PCs. The idea behind the serial bus is based on transferring the data one bit at a time. If a 1-byte datum has to be transferred, then on every bus cycle, one bit will be sent. Sending the whole byte will require eight bus cycles. This, of course, is a very slow way of communication, but it is simple and provides a good explanation of the PC's communication principles.

PC communication was performed using one of the communication (COM) ports. The first computers included four such ports, to which the peripheral devices were connected. The protocol used for communicating on the serial ports was called RS-232. It was developed by the Electronic Industry Association (EIA) in order to promote connecting and using electronic equipment. One early example was using a modem¶ that serves as an adapter between the computer and the telephone network. The modem and the telephone line are responsible for connecting a remote piece of data communication equipment (DCE) with the data terminal equipment (DTE). The DCE represents the computer while the DTE represents the terminal, as can be seen in Figure 7.20. The main idea, which is currently achieved in a very simple way and at much higher speeds, was to create the first networks, which paved the way for current offerings.

---

* IrDA is an interest group that promotes the use of infrared devices for computers and other handheld devices. It was popular during the early 2000s, but is has been phased out by other wireless technologies (Bluetooth and WiFi).
† Bluetooth is a standard for defining a private area network (PAN), and it is capable of wirelessly connecting a large variety of devices as well as systems. The standard was developed by a group of electronic appliance manufacturers that formed in the late 1990s. As with other successful communication protocols, Bluetooth has evolved over the years (versions 1, 2, 3, and 4), and currently it is being used to connect a wide variety of devices and appliances not directly related to computers.
‡ FireWire was originally developed by Apple Computers and is used on most of its products. As of 2014, it is being replaced by the newer Thunderbolt (developed by Intel). The FireWire (or IEEE 1394 standard) is comparable to USB with several differences, although the USB market share is significantly larger.
§ WiFi is a wireless local area network that provides an infrastructure for connecting devices and appliances and exchanging data between them. It is widely used in mobile devices for connecting to the Internet.
¶ Modem (modulator–demodulator) is a device that modulates signals produced by the computer so the signal can be sent over a different media (e.g., analog telephone lines). On the other end, an additional device demodulates the signal back to digital signals understood by the computer.

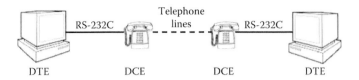

FIGURE 7.20 Serial communication.

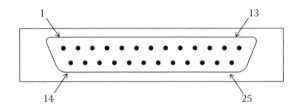

FIGURE 7.21 RS-232C connector.

The serial bus, like any other bus, could work synchronously, in which the transfer is synchronized by an external signal; or asynchronously by transferring the bits one after the other at the bus speed. The devices were connected using a standard connector used for the RS-232C* protocol (Figure 7.21).

It should be noted that the serial bus on the PC works in full duplex, and this means that the bus can simultaneously send and receive data. To enable the parallel communication, two separate lines are used for transmitting and receiving data. There are cases in which the bus works in a half-duplex mode, which means it is capable of sending or receiving, and then only one set of wires is sufficient. When the first PCs started using telephone lines, due to the lines' limitation (a twisted pair of wires), the communication was half duplex.

In addition to using a standard connector, the protocol defines the various connection lines and the way they have to be connected on both sides, as can be seen in Figure 7.22.

For half duplex, only bits 2 and 7 are being used. The serial bus, which was intended for connecting various devices and provided the beginning of communication using the

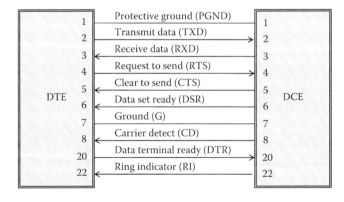

FIGURE 7.22 RS-232 connection meaning.

---

* The meaning of the name RS-232C is Recommended Standard 232 Version C.

telephone network, was capable of connecting to computers. It allowed a simple (primitive) way of connecting two computers without a telephone line. The proximity, of course, was very limited, and it was even smaller when the speed of the transfers increased.

The meaning of the various bits (signals) sent on the bus is as follows:

- Protective ground (PGND) is a reference signal used to synchronize the voltage between the two sides. The other signals are compared with this reference in order to determine if they are set or off. In some connectors, the PGND is connected to the ground (G).

- Transmit data (TXD) is a signal that is being used for transmitting the data (bits) from the DTE (computer) to the device. While there is no communication, the signal is set to "ON" (logical 1). It should be noted that for the DCE (the peripheral), this line signals the input, so it will be connected to the RXD signal.

- Receive data (RXD) is the signal used for receiving the data (bits). It is connected to the TXD on the other side.

- Request to send (RTS) is a control line that is used to communicate with the other side and to request the bus for the transmission of data.

- Clear to send (CTS) is an additional control line that is used to signal to the other end that this device is ready for receiving the communication. The two lines (RTS and CTS) are used as part of the hardware flow control. When one device wants to transmit data, it has to raise the RTS signal. The device on the other end picks the request, and when it is ready to receive the data it will raise the CTS signal. Only after the sending device gets the CTS from the second side will it start sending the data. If the CTS is not set, it means that the device on the other end is still busy and cannot accept the data yet. A simple example that demonstrates the usage of these two signals is when the system sends a large file to be printed. Usually, the printer accepts the data, stores it in an internal buffer, and then issues a print command. Sometimes there might be a problem (paper jam, no more paper, etc.) and in such cases the printer has to signal to the other end that it cannot accept any more data. This is done by not responding to the RTS and not raising the CTS. The other side understands that there is some problem that prevents the transmission and waits until the clear signal arrives.

- Data set ready (DSR) is a bit that signals that the device on the other end is ready (powered on, connected to the bus, and ready). If the telephone line disconnects, the signal will turn off since the device on the other end is not connected.

- Ground (G) is a signal line used for synchronizing the devices on the two ends. In many cases, this signal is connected to the PGND.

- Carrier detect (CD) is a control line that signals that the device has detected its counterpart on the other end. In an analogy to a fax machine, this bit is set when the machine on one end manages to connect to the fax machine on the other end.

This serves as an additional layer of communication. The telephone line provides the information that the communication was established; however, in the fax example, it may be that on the other end there is a human being and not a fax machine. Although the communication was established, it is not sufficient for transmitting the data. In a similar way, when the transmission takes place between computer systems, the CD will be set when the communication is established and the other end is capable of understanding and responding.

- Data terminal ready (DTR) is a control line that signals that the peripheral device is ready to initiate communication. This signal is similar to the DSR, but while the DSR is related to the communication device on the local side, the DTR is related to the remote side.

- Ring indicator (RI) is a control line that signals that the communication device has detected a call coming in (the other side is initiating a communication). In analogy to a standard telephone, this signal is what causes the telephone to start ringing. Only after we accept the call can the telephone signal to the other end that the call was established, and the person on the other end can start talking.

Contrary to the parallel buses described at the beginning of the chapter, in which in every cycle the bus transfers several bits, the serial bus sends one bit at a time. The data is transferred in groups of bits (seven or eight bits at a time based on the definition) on the TXS channel. Sending seven bits, for example, is achieved by sending the first bit on the first cycle, the second bit on the second cycle, and so on until the whole block has been sent. The convention is that when there is no transmission, the signal is set (logical "one").

Every group sent on the serial bus starts by sending a start bit and ends with a stop bit. The start bit is a logical "zero" that signals the following bits are the actual data. The stop bit, which is a logical "one," signals the end of block. In most cases, there are additional parity bits added to the transmission to protect its integrity, as will be explained later in the chapter. Figure 7.23 shows the serial communication, depicting the transmission of the character "a." Its binary value is 1100001 and the least significant bit is transmitted first. The transmission starts by sending the start bit, which signals that the additional bits transmitted represent the data. After the start bit, in the following cycles the data bits are

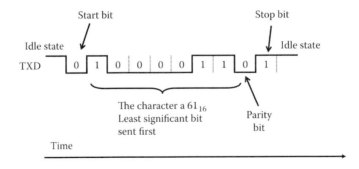

FIGURE 7.23   Serial communication.

transmitted. Since the transmission starts with the least significant bits, the first bit to be sent is a "one," which will be followed by four "zeroes" and then two additional "ones." It should be noted that there are various settings for the communication. One of these is the length of the byte. It can be a 7 bits byte or an 8 bits bytes. Alternatively the parity (to be explained later in this chapter) can be defines as even or odd parity. In this example, the transmission settings were set to seven bits bytes, so the character "a" is represented by seven bits. The next transmitted bit is a parity (explained later) and the last bit (the stop bit) signals the end of communication.

Although there is still some use for the RS-232C serial bus, it was replaced by USB, which became the de facto industry standard. It popularity stems from the fact that it is not intended just for communication between computer peripherals but also supports many other appliances, such as cameras, mobile phones, media players, and so on. Furthermore, USB is also used for supplying electric power to some of the lower power consumption devices. Due to its popularity, several versions were developed, mainly aimed at enhancing its speed.

Extending the Bus Concept

Most modern commercial systems are based on PC architectures, which means that the basic components are the ones that exist in PCs. Even with PCs, the buses sometimes create bottlenecks so a hierarchy of buses is used. In large parallel systems that include many PCs working on a common memory, sometimes even the bus hierarchy is not sufficient as can be seen in Figure 7.24.

Figure 7.24 depicts the architecture of the J90* supercomputer designed and manufactured by Cray.[†] The system included several (8, 16, or 32) processors, each one with its own cache memory. Each cache memory is connected to the appropriate processor using a private internal and fast bus. The system has a common global memory for sharing the application and data among the various processors. The communication between the global memory and the processors was done using a fast bus (1.6 GB/sec for each processor).

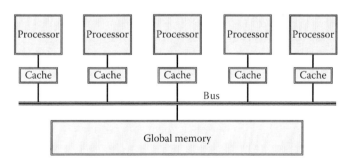

FIGURE 7.24　An example of a parallel system.

---

* The J90 was a supercomputer that was developed during the mid-1990s, and it did not require a special cooling system. This, one of the first parallel systems, supported 8, 16, or 32 processors. It had a common memory of 4 GB and an additional high-speed bus capable of transferring 4 GB/sec.

† Cray is an American supercomputer company that started in the early 1970s when Seymour Cray founded the company in Minnesota. For years, Cray had paved the way in designing and developing superfast computers and has vast experience with multiprocessor systems.

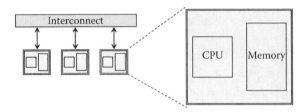

FIGURE 7.25 Cray T3E architecture.

Despite the high-speed transfer rate, it was obvious that for larger systems with a larger number of processors, the bus would become a bottleneck. For that reason, the next supercomputer designed by Cray (the T3E) implemented a different approach. The T3E included several versions and originally used the Alpha chip (see the section in Chapter 4 on "Processor Types"), which was very fast in performing floating-point calculations. The T3E was designed to support many processors, and the entry-level model had 1480 processors. It was also the first computer to reach the 1 Teraflops (10^{12} floating-point calculation per second). To achieve these speeds, that architecture had to be modified. Figure 7.25 describes part of the new architecture.

In order to support the high degree of parallelism and overcome the inherent limitations of buses, even the extremely fast ones, the system was based on standalone computing units (processing elements [PE]). Each such element is a system that can work independently and includes a processor and memory (it has its own cache memory as well, but this was not included in the figure for simplification reasons). In order to connect the PEs and the global memory, a new communication grid was developed. Contrary to the bus, which is based on one channel that connects all the devices, the grid is based on multiple channels in which each PE is connected to a small number of other PEs and to the memory using different channels. In order to simplify the implementation, the architecture used was based on the torus* geometrical shape. The main attribute of the topology is that each PE is connected to exactly four neighbors and no PE is located at the end. Figure 7.26 depicts an architecture for connecting many computing units by using multiple buses. In the diagram, there are 16 units that share eight different buses.

It should be noted that a bus architecture that is based on a grid in which each PE is connected to each other PE (as described on the right side of Figure 7.2) is faster. However, when the number of components to be connected by this type of grid is very large, the implementation of the grid becomes extremely complicated due to the number of connections required. Recall that the number of connections required for n elements is given by

$$\text{Number of connections} = n * \frac{(n-1)}{2}$$

So, for a 1480 components and a global memory, as designed for the entry level T3E, the number of channels required will be 1,094,460!

---

* A torus is a geometric shape and it is created by rotating a circle in three dimensions. The shape created resembles the inner tube of a tire.

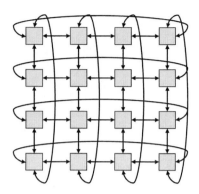

FIGURE 7.26   A torus-based bus.

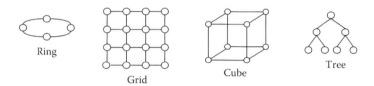

FIGURE 7.27   Additional topologies.

There are, of course, various other topologies applicable for designing a parallel system as demonstrated by Figure 7.27. At the bottom line, the decision should take into consideration the needs (required transfer rate, bus length, reliability, survivability, etc.) and costs.

The ring, grid, and cube topologies contain a degree of survivability that ensures continued work even in the event of a bus failure. In every circular topology, if part of the network goes down, it is still possible to get to all the elements. In such a case, the network (or the topology used for implementing the network) is said to contain built-in survivability. The tree topology on the right-hand side of Figure 7.27 does not contain survivability since if just one route goes down, one or more components will become inaccessible. The chances of a problem regarding a bus in a parallel system is very small since all components are in close proximity. Nevertheless, the same type of connection may apply to distributed systems, even systems that are remotely located. The fast development of the Internet in the last decade has somewhat reduced the importance of the distributed systems topology, since in most cases the connectivity will be based on the Internet. Nevertheless, for more critical systems where uptime is a considerable factor, network topologies are still relevant and important.

The cube, or any other topologies in which there are several routes to get from one component to another, provides a simple mechanism for determining the optimal path. This is done by allocating binary numbers to each node. In this way, the node's number is different by just one bit from the numbers of its neighbors (Figure 7.28).

Let us assume that

X defines the source node number (the format is $X_0X_1X_2X_3...X_n$)

Y defines the destination node number (the format is $Y_0Y_1Y_2Y_3...Y_n$)

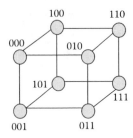

FIGURE 7.28   A cube topology node's numbers.

Then R defines the number of stations in the route.

R is given by the number of bits that are set in the expression

$$R = X \oplus Y$$

The symbol $\oplus$ represents the XOR.*

For example, if in Figure 7.28 we have to get from node number 2 (010_2) to node number 7 (111_2), we will have to go through two stations since

$$010 \oplus 111 = 101$$

The result contains two bits that are set, which means two stations. In a similar way, moving between two opposite vertexes, such as 0 and 7 or 5 and 2, requires three stations (the XOR result contains three set bits)

$$000 \oplus 111 = 111$$

or

$$101 \oplus 010 = 111$$

Bus Expansion beyond the System Boundaries

At the beginning of the chapter, the bus was defined as a means for connecting the various components of the system. As a matter of fact, the computers of the 1970s and 1980s used the bus mainly for connecting the internal components of the system. As such, the bus length was very limited, measuring several feet at the maximum. As the systems evolved, the buses had to be longer, for example, for connecting a printer that was located in a different room. Additional developments that included, for example, common arrays of storage devices required additional increases in the bus length to up to 30 feet (Figure 7.29).

The 1990s are considered the era of networking. Sun Microsystems even defined the network as the computer (see the section "The Network is the Computer" in Chapter 1).

---

* The logical operator $\oplus$ (XOR or exclusive OR) returns a true value if, and only if, the two operands are different (one is true and the other is false).

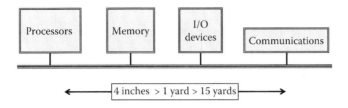

FIGURE 7.29   Bus length over the years (1970–1990).

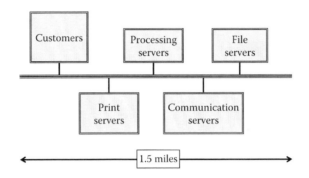

FIGURE 7.30   1990 bus (local area network).

Currently, with modern systems, the user works on a virtual system that may include a variety of servers, each one dedicated to a different computing function. The user who works on the system does not know and definitely does not care which system he or she is working on or where this system is located. All the user cares about is getting the required service. In this sense, the organizational network and the systems that are connected to it form a collaborative virtual system. This mode of operation started in the 1990s, during which the LANs were developed. Originally, the LANs were limited to less than a mile, but, using various repeaters and boosters, the length was extended up to approximately a mile and half (Figure 7.30).

During the early 2000, the Internet advanced at a very fast pace replacing many of the old computing concepts. The increased speed of data transmission and the variety of communication alternatives has changed the computing industry. Currently, many of the organizational system are spread over the globe since distance is no object anymore. Furthermore, the cloud-computing technologies are slowly transforming the local computing department by outsourcing larger chunks of the applications and their supporting infrastructure to other dedicated and experienced organizations. As far as the bus length is considered, it means that the new "buses" have become limitless (Figure 7.31).

Reliability Aspects

The fast development of the various buses, some of which are widely distributed, required special attention to reliability aspects. While in the past, the distance was short and the bus length was limited, it was maybe safe to assume that if the wires were not cut, the bus would continue to work and the data would be transferred reliably. Currently, the situation is different. Although the buses inside the computer are extremely reliable, reliability is

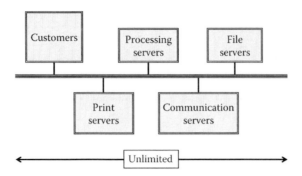

FIGURE 7.31   The 2000 bus (Internet).

not confined to the system itself and has to apply to all aspects. In many cases, the data is transmitted over wide-area networks that use different transmission media; some of these are based on wireless communications, which may disconnect due to the device location.

For increasing the transmission's reliability, several methods were developed over the years. It should be noted that although the methods are described as part of this chapter on buses, the methods are applicable to other devices as well, for example, disk drives. In the case of the disk, the controller has to make sure that the data received from the disk is actually the data that was written and that no bits were changed in the process.

Over the years, several methods for protection and increased reliability were developed. The most basic method is based on error correction code (ECC). Several methods implement ECC, and in all cases the idea is to augment the data transmitted with some additional bits that will allow the receiving end to check that the transmission was received properly. The bits to be added are calculated using a known algorithm. On the receiving end, the algorithm is used once again to calculate the ECC. If a match is found then no error was detected, which means that the data block received is identical to the data block sent. If, on the other hand, the calculation reveals some mismatch, the block can either be corrected (in some methods) or will have to be retransmitted.

The most basic and primitive method is based on a parity bit. The parity can be either odd or even. The parity type (odd or even) has to be known to both sides prior to the transmission. The method is based on counting the number of bits in the transmission that are set (one) and adding the necessary parity bit to the transmission block. Assuming the method is using even parity, then the number of bits set in the transmission block, including the parity bit itself, will be an even number. In all cases, the parity bit is responsible for making sure that the total number of bits that are being set, including the parity itself, obey the definition (it is either an odd number or an even number).

For example, let us assume that the communication is using even parity and the following 8-bit byte is to be sent:

D_0	D_1	D_2	D_3	D_4	D_5	D_6	D_7
0	1	1	1	0	1	1	0

The number of bits that are set is odd, and since the communication is based on even parity, then the parity bit should be set. This means that the total number of bits sent, including the parity bit itself, will be an even number. The block of bits transmitted will be

D_0	D_1	D_2	D_3	D_4	D_5	D_6	D_7	P
0	1	1	1	0	1	1	0	1

The bit on the right-hand side is the parity bit.

The receiving end is responsible for checking the block that was received. This is done by using the agreed-upon algorithm. In this specific case, the number of bits that are set will be counted, and if this number is an even number, the assumption is that the transmission was received with no errors.

On the other hand, assuming the block that was received contained

D_0	D_1	D_2	D_3	D_4	D_5	D_6	D_7	P
0	1	1	1	0	1	0	0	1

In this case, the receiving end counts the bits that have been set and realizes this is an odd number. This means that the block received is not the block sent and that something happened during the transmission. This basic method just gives an indication of the error but does not provide the means to correct it. In this specific case, the receiving end will have to ask the sender to send the block once again. It should be noted that the parity method is capable of detecting errors only if one bit was changed, or alternatively if an odd number of bits were changed. If two bits or any other even number of bits were changed, the method will still assume the block received is OK.

For example, we will once again use the block from the previous example. In this case, the method uses odd parity so the parity bit will be clear:

D_0	D_1	D_2	D_3	D_4	D_5	D_6	D_7	P
0	1	1	1	0	1	1	0	0

Unfortunately, the block received was

D_0	D_1	D_2	D_3	D_4	D_5	D_6	D_7	P
1	0	1	0	1	0	1	1	0

The receiving end checks the number of bits that are sent and realizes there is an odd number of bits, so it assumes the block was received properly. Unfortunately, there is very little resemblance between the two blocks. This is an artificial example, but it was chosen to demonstrate the shortcomings of the method.

A very simple and effective way to solve the problem raised by the previous example is based on the fact that, in most cases, the transmission block contains several bytes. This means that the parity can be applied horizontally and vertically. The previous method provided a horizontal check, and the vertical check will be implemented by adding an additional parity byte.

In this example, we will assume the parity type to be used is odd. Let us assume we have to send an 8-byte block defined thus:

D_0	D_1	D_2	D_3	D_4	D_5	D_6	D_7
0	0	1	1	1	1	0	0
0	1	0	1	1	1	0	1
1	1	0	0	1	1	0	0
1	1	0	1	0	1	1	1
1	1	0	1	1	1	1	1
1	1	1	1	0	1	1	1
1	1	0	1	1	1	0	0
1	0	0	0	0	0	0	0

In the first step, the parity bit for each of the bytes will be calculated. After all parity bits have been calculated and appended to the data bytes, the vertical parity byte is calculated. Once again, the type here will be odd parity, and the leftmost parity bit is calculated based on the leftmost bits of all the bytes in the block. In a similar way, all other bits in the parity byte will be calculated. Then the new parity byte will be added to the block and only then will the block be transmitted.

D_0	D_1	D_2	D_3	D_4	D_5	D_6	D_7	P
0	0	1	1	1	1	0	0	1
0	1	0	1	1	1	0	1	0
1	1	0	0	1	1	0	0	1
1	1	0	1	0	1	1	1	1
1	1	0	1	1	1	1	1	0
1	1	1	1	0	1	1	1	0
1	1	0	1	1	1	0	0	0
1	0	0	0	0	0	0	0	0
1	**1**	**1**	**1**	**0**	**0**	**0**	**1**	**0**

The new parity byte ensures that the number of bits set in each column is always an odd number.

This mechanism of vertical and horizontal checks can detect a bit that was changed and even correct it without the need to retransmit the block. Even when more than one bit was changed during the transmission, the method may succeed in correcting the situation (based on the location of the changed bits). On the other hand, the problem associated with this method is due to the need to wait for the whole block before that check can be done. When the checks are done by the hardware, it implies large buffers for holding the whole block. Currently, memory prices are very low, so the additional buffers do not provide a significant price factor. In the past, however, the situation was different, which drove the industry to search for additional cheaper solutions. An additional factor to be taken into consideration is the overhead associated with the method. Furthermore, the smaller the block, the larger the transmission overhead becomes. With the parity bit, the overhead is fixed. For each byte of 7 or 8 bits, an additional bit is added. This represents an overhead of 12.5% (for 8 bits) or a 1.3% (for 7 bits). Adding the parity byte may represent a very high overhead. If the blocks sent are of one byte, the parity byte adds 100% of overhead on top of the parity-bit overhead previously discussed. In many cases, to lower the overhead, the blocks that are transmitted are large. For example, for a 20-byte block, the parity byte will add an overhead of just 5%. However, in such cases, if an error occurs and the method does not succeed in correcting the problem, the whole block has to be retransmitted. Modern systems may have more sophisticated mechanisms in which the operating system uses a variable length block. In such cases, the block length is changed according to a set of conditions. This, however, relates to special software with the support of the operating system and is not part of this description.

It should be noted that in many cases, as already seen in this book, the solutions used today were developed to solve a problem that existed in the past but, due to rapid technological advancements, is not a real problem anymore. Nevertheless, we enjoy these solutions as they were developed or as a base to another better solution that was built on top of the previous one.

An additional method for checking the block that was received is based on checksum. In this case, there is no additional bit (like the parity bit). Instead, an additional byte is added. Let us assume that we have to transmit a 12-byte block. In addition, let us assume that the checksum is performed on chunks of three bytes each. The algorithm will add the first three bytes, ignoring any overflows and then transmit the three bytes followed by the byte that contains the checksum that was calculated. In this example, the process will repeat four times since there are 12 bytes to be transmitted. On the receiving end, the same checksum is calculated, and if the results match, the block was received properly.

For example, let us assume we have to transmit a 6-byte block:

1	2	3	4	5	6
0110 1100	1010 1100	0101 1011	0011 1100	1010 1111	1100 1101

Let us assume the method selected calculated the checksum for every three bytes. Then the first step calculates it for the first three bytes:

First data byte	0110 1100
Second data byte	1010 1100
Third data byte	0101 1011
Checksum	0111 0011

For calculating the checksum, a simple binary ADD is being used. It can be seen that by adding the three bytes, the correct sum is 0001 0111 0011; however, since the checksum is an additional byte, the overflow is ignored and only the rightmost eight bits are considered.

The bytes transmitted include the three data bytes appended by the checksum byte:

0110 1100	1010 1100	0101 1011	0111 0011

In a similar way, the checksum for the next (and in this case the last) group of three bytes will be calculated:

First data byte	0011 1100
Second data byte	1010 1111
Third data byte	1100 1101
Checksum	1011 1000

Once again a 4-byte block will be transmitted—the three data bytes and the checksum byte.

0011 1100	1010 1111	1100 1101	1011 1000

The overhead in this case is 33.3%, which means adding two bytes to the original six bytes. The method can be changed so that the checksum will be calculated for every five bytes, and then the overhead will be 20%, or choosing 10 bytes per checksum will lower the overhead to 10%.

It is possible to combine the methods, and in such cases, the parity bit will provide a horizontal check and the checksum will provide a vertical check.

Since the parity bit is calculated using a computerized algorithm, even when it is done explicitly by the hardware, it is possible to build a different mechanism. Instead of the ordinary method in which each parity bit "protects" the whole byte, it is possible to define which bits are protected by which parity bits. The main idea is that there are several parity bits. Each parity bit protects several predefined bits, and several bits are protected by the predefined parity bits. In such a case, if a bit was changed during the transmission, only the parity bits that protect it will be affected. This provides a mechanism for identifying the erroneous bit and correcting it, assuming only one bit was changed.

For example, let us assume the parity type is odd and the protection algorithm is as follows:

- Data bit 0 is protected by parity bits 0 and 1

- Data bit 1 is protected by parity bits 0, 1, and 2

- Data bit 2 is protected by parity bits 0 and 2

- Data bit 3 is protected by parity bits 1 and 2

This, of course, can be written in a different way that maintains the same meaning:

- Parity bit 0 protects data bits 0, 1, and 2
- Parity bit 1 protects data bits 0, 1, and 3
- Parity bit 2 protects data bits 1, 2, and 3

A more algorithmic notation will be

P_0 = odd parity (D_0, D_1, D_2)

P_1 = odd parity (D_0, D_1, D_3)

P_2 = odd parity (D_1, D_2, D_3)

Assuming the destination received a block that contained

D_3	D_2	D_1	D_0	P_2	P_1	P_0
0	0	0	1	0	1	0

The first step is to calculate the parity bits that should have been received. The assumption is that the data was received correctly, and this will be proved if the calculated parity bits match the received parity bits. For calculating the new values, we will use the algorithm formula previously defined but with the actual data values received:

P_0 = odd parity (1, 0, 0) = 0

P_1 = odd parity (1, 0, 0) = 0

P_2 = odd parity (0, 0, 0) = 1

This means that if the received block is the block that was transmitted, then the whole block, including the parity bits, should have contained

D_3	D_2	D_1	D_0	P_2	P_1	P_0
0	0	0	1	1	0	0

Unfortunately, the block received is different. It can be seen that there is a change in P_1 (parity bit 1) and P_2 (parity bit 2). It should be noted that although the difference relates to the parity bits, the bits that were changed are not necessarily the parity bits. The way to find the bit that was changed is to examine the parity bits.

To find the bit that could have caused the problem, we have to check the common denominator for the two parity bits. By checking the algorithm, it becomes clear that D_1 (data bit 1) and D_3 (data bit 3) are protected by the two bits. Theoretically, each one of these two data bits can cause the problem; however, since D_1 is protected by P_0, if D_1 was causing the problem, P_0 should have been wrong as well. Since it is not, it means that D_1 is fine and the problem was caused by a change to D_3.

In this specific case, the bit that was changed during the transmission was not only found but could also be easily changed back to its original value. This means that while the algorithm here requires a higher overhead, it does not require retransmission, assuming just one bit was flipped. If just one parity bit was flipped, then the data is fine and there is no need for correction or retransmission.

Hamming Codes

Hamming* codes are an ECC mechanism that, among other things, is used in memory reliability checks. The Hamming codes that serve as special parity bits are embedded in the binary message to be sent in predefined locations. These locations are all powers of two. The data bits start at location 1, leaving location 0 for another special purpose. All other locations in the message that are not powers of two are reserved for the data bits.

No.	1	2	3	4	5	6	7	8	9	10
Bin	0001	0010	0011	0100	0101	0110	0111	1000	1001	1010
D/P	P_1	P_2	D_3	P_4	D_5	D_6	D_7	P_8	D_9	D_{10}

The first line in the above table defines the address of the bit (in decimal). The second line defines the same address, but this time it is in binary notation. The third line shows if the bit is data or parity. As can be seen, all the locations that are powers of two are designated for parity bits.

The algorithm that was implemented by the Hamming codes was that the data bits are protected by the parity bits, whose address is contained in the data bits' addresses. In other words, the data bit in location 7 is protected by P_1, P_2, and P_4. Because 7 in binary notation is 111, this means that the bits that represent 1 (2^0), 2 (2^1), and 4 (2^2) are set in its address. As previously shown, the Hamming codes algorithm also defines a mechanism in which one parity bit protects several data bits. As can be seen from the table above,

- P_1 protects D_3, D_5, D_7, and D_9
- P_2 protects D_3, D_6, D_7, and D_{10}
- P_4 protects D_5, D_6, and D_7
- P_8 protects D_9 and D_{10}

The parity bit protects all data bits that contain the parity-bit address in their address.

For example, let us assume that we have to calculate the Hamming code for the binary value 1011. The first step will be to build the new number, which includes the parity bits

---

* Hamming codes are called after their inventor, Richard Hamming, who worked for Bell Labs in 1940.

(in the locations which are powers of two), without calculating the codes yet, just writing the data bits in their right locations. The leftmost bit will be placed in location number three; the next will be placed in location number five, and so on as described by the following table:

No.	1	2	3	4	5	6	7
Bin	0001	0010	0011	0100	0101	0110	0111
D/P	P_1	P_2	1	P_4	0	1	1

In the next step, we will calculate the Hamming codes.

- P_1 protects all data bits with an address (in binary) that has the bit 2^0 set. These are all the odd numbers. In this specific case, these are D_3, D_5, and D_7. The total number of bits that are set is two, so since we assume odd parity, $P_1 = 1$.

- P_2 protects all data bits with an address in which bit 2^1 is set. In this specific case, these are D_3, D_6, and D_7 so the parity bit will be zero.

- P_4 will be calculated in a similar way and it will be set to one.

Now the values can be stored in the table, which represents the value to be transmitted.

No.	1	2	3	4	5	6	7
Bin	0001	0010	0011	0100	0101	0110	0111
D/P	1	0	1	1	0	1	1

In addition to protecting the data that was transmitted, Hamming codes can be used for correcting the error in a case where only one bit was flipped.

In this example, we will assume the Hamming codes were calculated using even parity and a transmitted block was received and its content is as follows:

P_1	P_2	D_3	P_4	D_5	D_6	D_7	P_8	D_9	D_{10}	D_{11}	D_{12}
0	1	1	0	0	1	1	1	1	1	0	1

The first step is to calculate the Hamming codes of the data bits while ignoring the received parity bits. After calculating the codes, the message should have contained

P_1	P_2	D_3	P_4	D_5	D_6	D_7	P_8	D_9	D_{10}	D_{11}	D_{12}
1	0	1	1	0	1	1	1	1	1	0	1

Analyzing the two previous tables of what was received and what should have been received reveals that the blocks are different (bits P_1, P_2, and P_4). This implies that one or maybe more bits flipped during the transmission. Let us assume that just one bit failed (the case of more than one bit will be explained later in this chapter). The bit that failed is the one with an address containing the three parity bits, or in other words D_7 (bit number seven) was flipped. D_7 is the only one that is protected by these three parity bits. Once the information has been obtained, it is very simple to correct the problem and flip the bit back to its original state. A very simple check can be conducted by flipping D_7 and calculating the Hamming codes once again. In this case, the two blocks (the calculated one and the received one) should be identical.

The possibility of correcting a single-bit error is not unique to Hamming codes, and we have already seen that a simple parity can provide the same functionality. Furthermore, the assumption that only one bit was flipped is not sufficient, and there should be a mechanism to detect this situation or alternatively a situation in which two bits have been flipped. Even if the mechanism is unable to fix the problem, it still has to detect it. For that reason, the Hamming codes mechanism can be enhanced so that in addition to correcting a one-bit flip, it can detect (without correcting) a two-bit flip. This is called single-error correction, double-error detection (SECDED).

The detection of the single or double error is achieved by adding bit zero, which previously has been left out. This is referred to as P_0. The leftmost bit (P_0) protects the whole block, including the data and parity bits. If only one bit failed, the Hamming code will be wrong and the SECDED bit (P_0) will be wrong as well.

For clarification, we will use an example:

Let us assume a transmitted block received contained the following binary number:

$$0 \; 1101 \; 0110 \; 1101$$

We know it is a number protected by Hamming codes with odd parity and SECDED, which also uses odd parity. As in previous cases, we have to check if the number is correct. If it is not, and assuming just one bit flipped, the algorithm will correct it; and, if two bits have been flipped, it is impossible to correct but the algorithm should indicate it. In this case, retransmission is the only solution.

- We will place the bits in their locations:

P_0	P_1	P_2	D_3	P_4	D_5	D_6	D_7	P_8	D_9	D_{10}	D_{11}	D_{12}
0	1	1	0	1	0	1	1	0	1	1	0	1

- From the calculation, P_0 should have been one, but it is zero. This means that one of the bits flipped during the transmission.

- Then, we will check all the Hamming codes (the parity bits), and here we can see that P_2 and P_4 are wrong.

- The last step is drawing conclusions. If only one bit flipped, as found by the SECDED bit, and two Hamming codes are wrong, this means that one data bit was flipped.

The data bit is the one that these two parity bits are protecting, or in other words D_6 was flipped. Flipping it back corrects the problem.

- The original data, without the Hamming and SECDED codes, is 0001 1101.

If in the abovementioned example the received data was 0 0001 0011 1101, the results would have been different:

P_0	P_1	P_2	D_3	P_4	D_5	D_6	D_7	P_8	D_9	D_{10}	D_{11}	D_{12}
0	**0**	**0**	0	**1**	0	**0**	1	**1**	1	1	0	1

- As with the previous example, the SECDED bit is wrong, which means one bit was flipped.
- Calculating the values of the Hamming codes reveals that just one bit failed (P_4).
- This means that the parity bit failed and the data bits are fine, so no correction is needed.
- The correct data without the protecting bits (Hamming and SECDED) is 0001 1101.

We will continue and elaborate on the example a bit further and assume the transmission in this case contained 1 0000 0001 0101:

P_0	P_1	P_2	D_3	P_4	D_5	D_6	D_7	P_8	D_9	D_{10}	D_{11}	D_{12}
1	**0**	**0**	0	**0**	0	**0**	0	**1**	0	1	0	1

- In this case, the SECDED bit is correct, which means that either the whole transmission is correct or maybe two bits were flipped.
- When checking the Hamming codes, it is found that there is a problem with P_2, P_4, and P_8.
- This means that the transmission is erroneous, two bits were flipped, and it is impossible to correct (double error).

The method for assessing and calculating the Hamming codes, in which each parity bit is calculated separately, was intended to understand the method. In practice, all the codes are calculated using one XOR operation. The XOR is done on the binary values that represent the numbers of bits that are set in the transmission.

For example, let us assume that the net transmission (without the protection bits) is 101 0100 0101:

- The first step is to place the bits in their proper location, leaving the parity locations empty:

P_1	P_2	D_3	P_4	D_5	D_6	D_7	P_8	D_9	D_{10}	D_{11}	D_{12}	D_{13}	D_{14}	D_{15}
		1		0	1	0		1	0	0	0	1	0	1

- The next step is to perform an XOR between the numbers that represent the data bits that are set. In this example, these are D_3, D_6, D_9, D_{13}, and D_{15}, so the XOR operation will be between 3, 6, 9, 13, and 15:

$$0011 \oplus 0110 \oplus 1001 \oplus 1101 \oplus 1111 = 1110$$

- The first parity bit is zero (on the right side of the calculated value). The next parity bit is one, and so on.

- The next step is to place the parity bits in their proper locations: the first parity bit in location one, the second parity bit in location two, the third parity bit in location four, and so on until all the parity bits are in place. In this specific example, there are just four parity bits, but for longer transmissions, this number may be larger.

P_1	P_2	D_3	P_4	D_5	D_6	D_7	P_8	D_9	D_{10}	D_{11}	D_{12}	D_{13}	D_{14}	D_{15}
0	1	1	1	0	1	0	1	1	0	0	0	1	0	1

This single XOR operation produces the whole transmission (data and parity).

As with the previous example, we will enhance it a little bit. Let us assume that this block of information was transmitted but that D_{13} was flipped, so the received block contained

P_1	P_2	D_3	P_4	D_5	D_6	D_7	P_8	D_9	D_{10}	D_{11}	D_{12}	D_{13}	D_{14}	D_{15}
0	1	1	1	0	1	0	1	1	0	0	0	0	0	1

Once again, the checking process will include several steps:

- In the first step, the Hamming codes will be calculated. As in the previous example, we relate only to the numbers that represent the location of data bits that are set (the numbers in this case are 3, 6, 9, and 15).

- An XOR operation between these numbers will be performed:

$$0011 \oplus 0110 \oplus 1001 \oplus 1111 = 0011$$

- The calculated code (0011) is different from the code obtained in the transmission (1110). This means that there is a problem. Assuming just one bit failed (to simplify the example, the SECDED was not included).

- To find the number of the failed bit, all that is required is an additional XOR operation between the two Hamming codes (the calculated code and the code obtained from the transmission):

$$0011 \oplus 1110 = 1101$$

- The number obtained (13) represents the location of the failed bit.

The same method can be used to locate a parity bit that failed. In the previous example, we will assume that P_4 failed. This means that the original message was

P_1	P_2	D_3	P_4	D_5	D_6	D_7	P_8	D_9	D_{10}	D_{11}	D_{12}	D_{13}	D_{14}	D_{15}
0	1	1	1	0	1	0	1	1	0	0	0	1	0	1

However, due to the problems, the received message was

P_1	P_2	D_3	P_4	D_5	D_6	D_7	P_8	D_9	D_{10}	D_{11}	D_{12}	D_{13}	D_{14}	D_{15}
0	1	1	0	0	1	0	1	1	0	0	0	1	0	1

The calculation steps are

- Locating the addresses of data bits that are set in the transmission. In this case, the locations (addresses) are 3, 6, 9, 13, and 15.

- Performing an XOR between these numbers:

$$0011 \oplus 0110 \oplus 1001 \oplus 1101 \oplus 1111 = 1110$$

- The calculated code (1110) is different from the code in the transmission (1010), which means there is a problem. As in the previous example, we will assume just one bit failed.

- To find the number of the failed bit, an XOR between the two values (the calculated value and the value obtained from the transmission) will be executed:

$$1010 \oplus 1110 = 0100$$

- The number obtained is four, and this means that the bit in location four, which is a parity bit, has flipped. Even if the failed bit is parity, this shortened method finds it.

Key Takeaway

- *The bus logical structure*: The bus is logically divided into three main communication paths: one responsible for sending the commands, the second for data, and the third for control.

- *Bus management*: Can be from a central location (central arbitration) or distributed. The central arbitration is characterized by one central unit (arbitrator) that manages the bus transfers. Every device that wants to use the bus will first ask the arbitrator for permission and only after the permission is granted can the device use the bus for its purposes. Distributed arbitration is characterized by the fact that there is no central management for the bus activities. Instead of the central unit, the management is done collaboratively by all the devices by following the defined protocol.

- *Bus transactions*: The transaction can be a full transaction in which the devices hold the bus for the whole duration of the transaction. Alternatively, it can be a split transaction in which, each time there is a block to be transferred, the bus will be requested, used, and released.

- *Synchronous or asynchronous bus*: The bus, like any other communication media, can work synchronously, in which it is synchronized by an internal clock; or asynchronously, in which each operation will require a different amount of time or length of bus cycle.

- *The bus principle*: The first bus appeared in a PDP computer (manufactured by DEC). The idea behind implementing the bus concept was to lower the computer's price. Prior to the bus, each device was connected to all other devices on the system, creating a complicated and expensive mechanism of data transfer. The common bus that all devices connected to was cheaper, although slower.

- *The bus evolution*: The bus concept changed and evolved over the years. Originally, there was just one bus, but it became a bottleneck. Then there were several buses, and currently most computers utilize a bus hierarchy with numerous buses working at various speeds.

- *Reliability aspects*: Mechanisms are put in place to ensure the proper delivery of the data over the bus, such as parity bits and ECCs.

CHAPTER 8

Input and Output

INPUT AND OUTPUT

This chapter focuses and elaborates on various aspects of input and output (I/O). By using the general architecture figure, we can relate to the I/O devices in the system (Figure 8.1).

The peripheral devices, which are responsible for the I/O and for connecting the system to the outside world, are the main vehicle for obtaining the benefits from the system. The main purpose of a computer system is its output, and the peripheral devices are the means of displaying or communicating the system's results and sharing them with humans. There are some systems—for example, some embedded computers—that are not intended for communication with human beings; however, in these cases, the system still needs I/O devices with different functionalities. Despite the importance of enhancing performance, increasing the bus bandwidth and transfer rate, and so on, the I/O devices are equally important. Without these devices, there would be no way of communicating with the system in a beneficial way. These devices are responsible for entering the data into the system and obtaining the results in a clear and understandable fashion. In general, these peripheral devices can be divided into

- Input devices, such as keyboards, mice, microphones, scanners, cameras, and many more
- Output devices, such as printers, displays, speakers, and so on

There are some devices that have a dual role, such as mass storage, networks, and so on; these are both I/O devices. Due to the large variety of peripheral devices, there are significant differences in their capabilities and performance. A keyboard, for example, that is used by a human operator is a very slow device since it is limited by the operator's typing capabilities. Even the fastest operator will only be able to produce several keystrokes per second. This means that such a keyboard does not need to support more than 10 keystrokes per second. The keyboard controller can accommodate a very slow bus with a limited bandwidth and speed rate (see Figure 7.17). On the other end of the performance spectrum, the

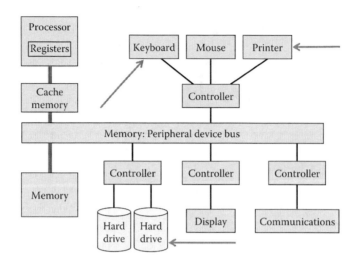

FIGURE 8.1   I/O devices.

network controller that supports superfast communication, or the display controller that needs to support a huge amount of data at a very high refresh rate, has to be extremely fast. Regardless of the specific functionalities of the different devices and controllers and their relative performance, the system has to be able to support all of them.

Usually, the peripheral devices are connected to the bus using a controller. Some devices, such as mass-storage devices, have an integrated controller, while other devices share an external controller. In both cases, the controller is responsible for translating the device's internal protocol to the protocol used by the bus to which it is connected.

Methods for Performing I/O

There are three main methods for performing I/O and these methods were developed over time:

- Programmed I/O, which implies that the running task or application is initiating the input or output command and is waiting for its completion. This type of I/O is usually used by various embedded systems. In such systems, the operating system may be very minimal so it does not support the interrupts mechanism. The application has to issue the I/O command and wait until the device completes it. Furthermore, in such systems, usually there is just one running process or application (monopro-gramming) so when it asks for some I/O, it waits, since there is no other use for the processor in the meantime. The application is checking the status of the device to see if the operation has finished. This type of I/O is sometimes referred to as "busy waiting" because the system is busy not because it is doing some productive work but just because it is waiting. Compared to modern general-purpose systems, such as personal computers (PCs) and even handheld and mobile devices, this may seem like a waste of the processor's resources, but for embedded systems it is different. Embedded systems are, in many cases, dedicated machines, which are responsible for performing just one task. One example is an alarm system. While it is in idle mode, it constantly checks the keyboard to see if the activation code has been entered. These checks are done using an endless loop, which ends only when the code is entered and the system is activated. Once activated, the alarm application checks each one of the sensors to see if it has something to report. Each sensor senses its environment, and, when addressed by the application, it replies with "everything OK" or, alternatively, if it felt a change such as a movement or an open door, it will report it. The main purpose of the system is to check these sensors and there is no other activity, so although it is in a busy-waiting state, there is no waste.

Figure 8.2 is a flowchart that elaborates on the programmed I/O mechanism. The processor (under the running application's control) executes an I/O instruction. The instruction is transferred to the peripheral device, which starts executing it; for example, it reads a character from the alarm system's keyboard or checks the status of a specific sensor. In the meantime, the application is waiting until the input is received. After the input character is entered, the device changes its status, signaling that the input is ready. The processor reads the device status and, when it sees that the input is ready, it will issue a read instruction. The status may signal that some error occurred and the application will have to handle it, or alternatively, the device may respond that it is still not ready and then the processor will continue its busy loop, waiting for the device. After the processor reads the input character, it will be stored in memory, and the application will check if additional characters are required. If this was the last character, and assuming the required input is the activation code, the application will have to check if this is the right code and act accordingly. If this was not the last character required for the code, the processor will repeat the whole process once again.

As previously noted, the "busy waiting" may seem a waste of time, and in another environment it might even be true, because in the meantime the processor could do

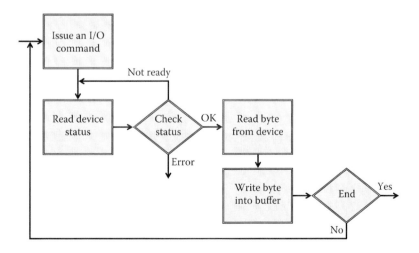

FIGURE 8.2   Programmed I/O flowchart.

some other productive work; in the case of an embedded system, however, the processor has nothing else to do, so it can wait. Another relevant example is a washing machine, in which the processor that controls all washing programs is embedded in the machine. Every program is divided into steps, and each step involves some instructions for the sensors or actuators in the machine. One such instruction may be to heat the water. The processor will be looping on reading the status of the heat sensor, and as long as the machine does not reach the required temperature, the loop as well as the heating will continue. Only when the required temperature is measured will the washing program continue to the next step. During the entire time, the processor was waiting for the right temperature to be reached, there was nothing else to do.

The busy-waiting method cannot be implemented in multiprogramming environments in which the processor has some other productive work to do while waiting, and in this case, the wait is just a waste of system resources.

- Interrupt-based I/O, which was developed mainly due to the inherent limitations of the programmed I/O. This method is intended for general-purpose systems that usually support multiprogramming, and in such cases it makes no sense to just waste processor cycles on waiting for an I/O instruction to complete. Unlike some embedded systems, where the processor has just one task, in multiprogramming environments, although the program that issues the I/O operation will have to wait, other programs and processes can use the processor during this time. The interrupt-based I/O requires, of course, the proper hardware and operating system that support interrupts.

Figure 8.3 provides a visual representation of the interrupt-based I/O. The processor executes the I/O instruction as it was written in the program. This I/O instruction is translated (during compilation) to a system call. The system call wakes the

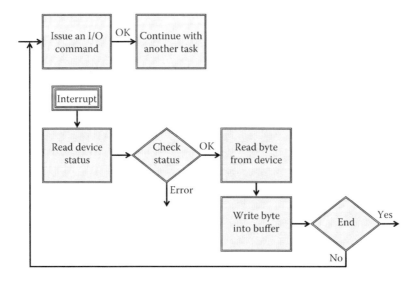

FIGURE 8.3   Interrupt-based I/O flowchart.

operating system, which sends the request to the device driver.* The device driver, in its turn, sends the request to the device (these steps, which are internal to the operating system, were not included in the flowchart). When the operating system finishes handling the request, the processor is assigned to a different program, and the current program (the one that issued the I/O request) is put on a waiting queue until the data it requested is available. When the device finishes its request and the data is available in its internal buffers, it issues an interrupt. The operating system that analyzed the interrupt calls the device driver, which reads the device status. This is required since it may be possible that although the device finished the request, it may also signal some problems it had in completing the request or in general. For example, a printer that received a block of data to be printed can signal it is ready for the next block, or it may also signal it has a problem, such as a paper jam or that there is no more paper. The device driver checks the status obtained from the device, and, if it is OK, it will issue a read instruction (assuming the original request was an input). In some cases, the instruction may read just one data item (byte or word), and in other cases, it may read the whole block. The data that was received from the device is written to memory following a check if the whole block was read, which implies that the program can resume running. If some data is still missing, the device driver will issue an additional request (another loop in the flowchart).

It should be noted that in a system that supports multiprogramming, there are several tasks running in parallel, and each one may request I/O; in addition, the operating system itself issues I/O operations. An example of the operating systems' I/O occurs in a virtual memory environment when handling pages that are missing. For that reason, during normal operation, there are many interrupts to be handled. There might be cases in which, during the time the operating system handles one interrupt, an additional one occurs. To prevent too many levels of nested interrupts, the convention is that after an interrupt, additional interrupts are locked out. It is the operating system's responsibility to unlock the interrupts when it is ready to accept new ones. Due to the importance of interrupts to system operation, the operating system will try to minimize the amount of time in which the interrupts are locked. It will be done for a short duration, which will enable the operating system to execute a critical segment of code or to update some system tables.

Figure 8.4 depicts one example of nested interrupts. The left rectangle represents a user program that is running. At some point, an interrupt occurs, and then the program is temporarily stopped, its entire environment is saved in the stack, and the operating system starts executing the code that is intended to handle this interrupt (the middle rectangle). In this case, the first instructions of this interrupt handler are being executed while the interrupts are locked, which means that additional interrupts will have to wait. After the interrupt has finished its critical code segment, it

---

* A device driver is a piece of the operating system responsible for managing the devices and acts as an interface between the device and the user programs.

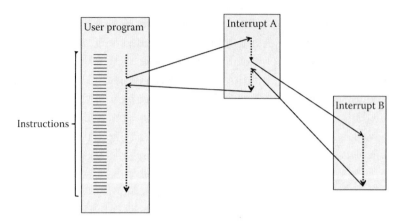

FIGURE 8.4 An interrupt during processing a previous interrupt.

will unlock the interrupts. At this stage, if a new interrupt was received (or it may have been received earlier and just waited until the interrupts will be open once again), the first interrupt handler will be interrupted. Once again, its environment will be saved in the stack and the second interrupt handler (right rectangle) will start executing. As with the previous case, initially the interrupts are blocked, but after some time this second interrupt handler will open additional interrupts. In this specific case, there are no additional interrupts, so the second interrupt handler will finish its mission. Only after it finishes will the control go back to the first interrupt handler, and its working environment will be loaded from the stack so it can continue running. When it finishes, the user program environment will be loaded from the stack, and it will continue running as if it had not been stopped.

If the first interrupt handler does not open the interrupts for the whole duration of its run, the second interrupt will be blocked until the first interrupt finishes (Figure 8.5).

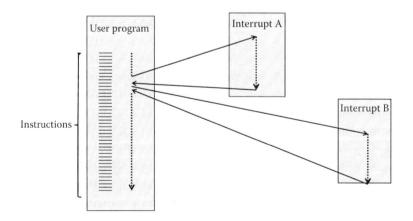

FIGURE 8.5 An interrupt after processing a previous interrupt.

- Direct memory access (DMA), which was developed to minimize the number of interrupts providing more productive time for the processor. The interrupt base I/O is more efficient compared with programmed I/O, but when there are many interrupts, the system overhead increases and its effectiveness drops. Although several systems have implemented sophisticated instructions for storing and loading the working environment, the overhead associated with interrupts is nevertheless significant, and lowering the number of interrupts increases the system efficiency.

The DMA method is slightly different (Figure 8.6). It starts exactly as in programmed I/O, where the application issues a system call with the request. The operating system checks it, and if it is OK, it is transferred to the device driver. The device driver translates it into a command to the device and reverts to waiting for an interrupt. The processor is assigned to a different application, which may be waiting for its turn. The application that issued the request is waiting for the block to arrive. Contrary to the programmed I/O method, in which the device issues an interrupt once it is ready, here the device is responsible for storing the data directly into memory without any intervention. It should be noted that not all devices (or device controllers) are capable of transferring the data directly. Usually, it will be applied to fast devices such as mass-storage devices. When all the requested data has been transferred to the designated memory location, the device will issue an interrupt to signal the end of the operation. Instead of an interrupt after each byte, word, or block as implemented by the programmed I/O method, the DMA method uses just one interrupt at the end of the operation.

This way, the processor is involved with the I/O operation just at the beginning and at the end. However, for allowing DMA transfers, some modifications are required in the device hardware or its controller, as well as changes to the operating system and device drivers.

To implement the DMA method, the controller has to be able to access memory (read and/or write). This means that the controller is using some of the memory

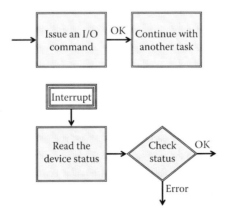

FIGURE 8.6 DMA I/O.

cycles for its purposes. For that reason, the DMA method is sometimes referred to as "cycle stealing." To maintain some order, the DMA controller can access the memory in specific instruction cycles: before it starts (prior to the instruction fetch [IF] step), after the instruction decode (ID) step, or at the end of the execution (EX) step. Interrupts on the other hand will occur only at the end of the instruction execution (end of the write back [WB] step; see Figure 8.7).

The efficiency of the DMA transfers is affected by the bus architecture that was implemented. A one-bus architecture, wherein the peripheral device is not directly connected to the controller, will experience very low efficiency. Furthermore, this implementation will slow down the processor as well.

The processor transfers the instruction to the controller using the bus. The controller itself has to send the command to the device, and since it is not directly connected, it has to use the bus once again (see Figure 8.8 for clarification).

This means that initiating each I/O operation requires two bus transfers. In this case, the same bus is also used for communication between the processor and the memory, so if it is busy for longer periods of time, it will slow the processor as well. When the data is ready, once again each transfer will use the bus twice: once to transfer the data from the device to the controller and the second time to transfer the data from the controller to the memory. The simple solution is to connect the device directly to its controller, which divides the number of bus transfers by two.

Figure 8.9 depicts a DMA controller that handles two devices. Sometimes, one controller can handle several (more than two) devices, and in such a case, it may have its own bus connecting its own devices (Figure 8.10). This private bus, which is used just for the devices, is handled by the controller and supports all communication

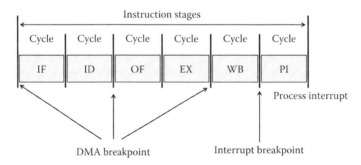

FIGURE 8.7   DMA interrupts.

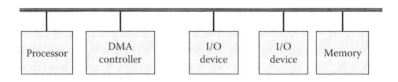

FIGURE 8.8   DMA on one-bus architecture.

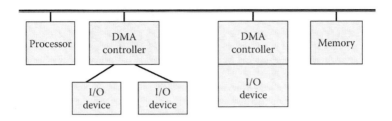

FIGURE 8.9   DMA—single bus and direct controller connection.

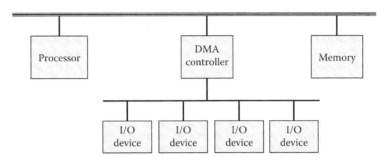

FIGURE 8.10   DMA using two buses.

between the devices and the controller. To handle the device, the controller has several internal buffers for the data read. This is necessary since the data is stored in these special buffers until it is ready to be transmitted to the memory.

There are a variety of DMA controllers with varying levels of sophistication. The simple way is to implement a controller that supports just one device. In this case, if there are several similar devices on the system, several controllers will have to be used. To lower the costs, more clever controllers were designed. Each one is capable of handling several devices (as shown in Figures 8.9 and 8.10). The first implementation was for a controller that supports several devices; however, only one device can be operational at a specific time. Such a controller can be equipped with one set of buffers, which will hold the data from the device that is currently active. This can be a good solution for connecting devices that rarely work in parallel.

The next step was cleverer: controllers that are capable of handling several devices working concurrently. Unlike the previous controller, which works like a selector in choosing the device that is working, the more clever controllers are capable of working as a concentrator. Such a controller will have several sets of buffers as well as several sets of registers to hold information about the devices, such as their hardware address and the address on the device where the data was to be written to or read from. All the connected devices can work in parallel, and no device interferes with the work of the other devices. Such controllers, when handling disk drives, for example, may include algorithms for assessing the pattern of reading and apply a read-ahead mechanism, which reads data before it was requested. If the application asks for that data, the controller will be able to provide it with minimal delay. It

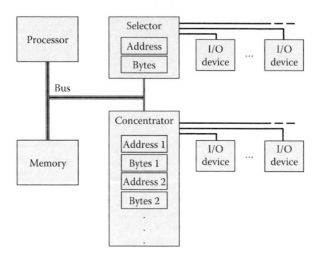

FIGURE 8.11   Selector and concentrator.

is implemented by assigning some of the available buffers for the read-ahead data (Figure 8.11).

Operating System Considerations

The division between operating system functions related to I/O and the hardware functions is sometimes artificial. Some hardware components are loaded by code that was designed to collaborate with a specific operating system. The device drivers are just one example. On the one hand, the device driver is designed to work with the specific device, and on the other hand, it is customized for a specific operating system. This section was added to enhance understanding related to the border between the operating system and the hardware architecture. The operating system has many aims and functions, but with regard to I/O, it has to provide two important capabilities:

- Efficiency, which is required mainly due to the limited speed of most of the peripheral devices. The operating system is responsible for ensuring high resource utilization, even if the devices are a limiting factor. As we have already seen, many developments were trying to solve past problems, and while currently these are no longer problems, we still enjoy these technological developments. The most important mechanism used for enhancing the efficiency and effectiveness of the system is multiprogramming, which enables the system to proceed with one process if another process is waiting for some event. This, of course, could not be achieved without additional development in the hardware, such as interrupts and DMA, which were developed for the same purpose.

- Generality, which is aimed at providing a common interface for accessing the large variety of different I/O devices. The general assumption implemented by the operating system is that the developer or the developed program does not have to know or care about the specific device it is using. The operating system provides a list of functions that define the characteristics of a peripheral device, and it will be the operating system's responsibility to translate these general functions into the specific device commands. This separation between the logical layer as implemented in the program and the physical layer that represents the devices is extremely important. The importance is even more significant in the open environment, where it is very simple to replace one device with a different one without any changes to the applications or the operating system. In general, working with a peripheral device is characterized by a short list of common functions such as lock, unlock, open, close, read, write, and so on, and the developer does not have to know exactly which device is being used.

I/O Buffering

I/O buffering is another mechanism that is used for enhancing the system's performance. It was partially implemented based on the pipeline mechanism that is used to enhance processor performance. Due to the large difference between the speed of processors and the speed of peripheral devices, the operating system implements several solutions to bridge these differences. In addition to the previously mentioned pipeline, buffering is also similar to the mechanism that loads the next block into the cache memory. When the operating system figures out the patterns of reading data from disk, it can issue a read instruction even before the program has asked for it. It should be noted that this is done by the operating system in parallel and in addition to a similar behavior exhibited by the disk controller. Furthermore, when the operating system works with internal buffers (in the operating system), it can read larger blocks than the blocks requested by the applications, and then the next time that the application reads additional data, it will be readily available. In such cases, the delay for the application will be minimal compared with the delay of ordinary reads, where the application has to wait for the block to be read from the disk.

When the operating system does not allocate buffers for the application and the only buffer is the one in the application itself, then the data read from the device is transferred directly to the buffer in the application. This mode of operation causes problems since it interferes with the operating system's optimization processes. For example, let us assume that an application is using an internal buffer (without a copy in the operating system), and it is waiting for data from a disk. In this case, if for some reason the scheduler wants to roll this application out (because it causes many page faults or for any other reason), it cannot do so. The device controller, assuming it is using DMA, has the real memory address, and it will copy the data to that location. In such a case, either the operating system will leave the application in memory, or it will roll it out while leaving several pages (the ones that contain the buffer). Finding these pages, of course, requires special and sometimes not trivial calculations.

In general, I/O can be performed in one of two ways:

- Blocked I/O, in which the I/O is done in blocks of data. This is the preferred method for faster devices.

- Continuous I/O, which transfers the characters one after the other. This is done for slower devices such as keyboards.

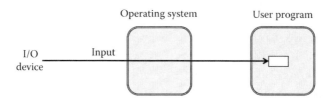

FIGURE 8.12   No operating system buffer.

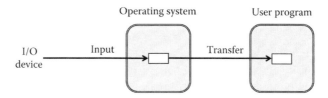

FIGURE 8.13   One additional buffer in the operating system.

Regarding buffers, there are several ways of implementing buffer mechanisms. The first, which was discussed previously, is to define a buffer only in the application without a copy in the operating system (Figure 8.12). In this case, where there is no buffer in the operating system, the data is transferred from the device directly into the application buffer. This approach uses minimal memory (just one buffer), but it is problematic in memory management aspects and interferes with improvements introduced in the operating system.

A slightly better solution is when, in addition to the buffer in the application, the operating system has another buffer (Figure 8.13). This approach solves the problems associated with the single buffer, since the data is transferred by the DMA controller to the operating system buffer. This means that the operating system has the flexibility to roll the application out, and its data will wait for it in the operating system buffer. On the other hand, this approach has a higher overhead due to the dual buffers and the need to copy the data between the two buffers. Each I/O operation includes an additional copy. In the case of output, the data is copied from the application buffer to the operating system buffer, and in the case of input, the data is copied from the operating system buffer to the application buffer.

For the application, in the case of output, copying the data from the application buffer to the operating system buffer is perceived as the end of the operation. As far as the application is concerned, once the data was transferred from the application to the operating system, the application assumes it was written to the destination device. In most cases, the data is still in the operating system, and the output operation has not yet started. For cases when it is important to verify that the data was written, for example, for security reasons, the operating system includes a special function (flush) that makes sure that the operating system buffer is written to the destination device before the application continues its execution.

A single operating system buffer is used when the application is using continuous I/O (Figure 8.14). In this case, the device issues an interrupt each time it has a character in its hardware buffer (e.g., the keyboard). The operating system, with the use of the device

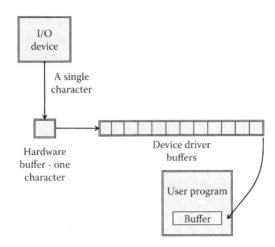

FIGURE 8.14   A single operating system buffer for continuous I/O.

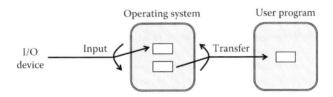

FIGURE 8.15   Double buffering.

driver, reads the character and stores it in the internal buffer. Later, when the application requests the next character, or even the whole line, the operating system will copy the content from its buffer to the application buffer. This mechanism allows the user to type in data even before the application has asked for it.

In continuous I/O, the hardware transfers the characters one at a time, and the operating system, by default, sends the whole line. Of course, the operating system provides the capability of reading each character, but this is not supported by all programming languages. The end of line is defined by the Enter key pressed by the user. This signals to the operating system that the input is finished, and the operating system can transfer the whole line to the application, assuming it is waiting for it.

Another improvement is the allocation of a double buffer in the operating system for each device (Figure 8.15). In the case of reading, the operating system can read the requested block into one buffer, and when it is filled up, it can read the next block into the second buffer. The mechanism of continuous reading can be implemented using a double buffering in the application as well. The idea of double buffering has been used and implemented by applications' developers in the past decades. However, when it is implemented by the operating system it is transparent to the application and provides the same functionality without the development efforts.

For description completeness, it should be noted that the double buffering mechanism that allows read ahead is implemented by several different components of the system. It is being used by the cache memory, which reads blocks larger than the actual requirements.

It is done by the virtual memory mechanism, which loads a page even if only one byte is required. It is used by the operating system that reads the data before the application has requested it and it is even used by the disk controllers that implement a read-ahead mechanism. In all these cases, the intention is to enhance the system's performance.

There are cases, especially with applications that require a high volume of I/O, in which two buffers are not enough. The simple solution is to increase the number of buffers. This means that a new layer of buffer management has to be provided. Alternatively, and in order to simplify the buffers' management, a circular buffer is implemented (Figure 8.16). Each item in the circle is a buffer by itself. In other words, the operating system defines an array of buffers. The management system is responsible for allocating and releasing the buffers and includes special locking mechanisms.

When there are just two buffers and one buffer is being processed, it is possible to read data into the second one. When there are several buffers, then some extreme situations have to be considered, for example, when the application is fast and it attempts to read from a buffer that does not yet contain data; or the opposite situation, when the application is slow and the data to be written is intended for a buffer that has not yet been processed. These types of synchronization between data producers and data consumers are very common and are handled successfully by the operating system.

The circular buffer mechanism is implemented for continuous I/O as well (as seen in Figure 8.17). In this case, the array of buffers is identical, but each buffer holds just one character. After every interrupt issued by the device, and assuming there were no errors,

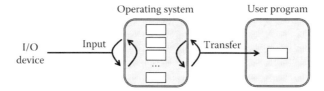

FIGURE 8.16   Circular buffers.

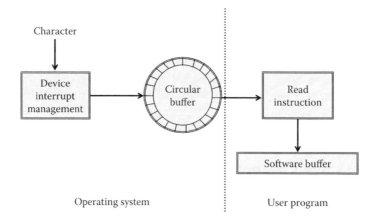

FIGURE 8.17   Circular buffer for continuous I/O.

one character is read from the device and transferred into the next empty location. The previously mentioned synchronization mechanisms are applicable here as well.

I/O and Performance

Despite the dramatic improvement in processors' performance, as predicted by Moore's law, the I/O speed increases only at a moderate rate. The disk drives are mechanical devices, and their speed is limited by the rotation speed (as will be explained in the next chapter) and the recording density. There are other newer devices, such as solid-state disks, that are faster; however, these are still expensive.

Let us assume that a program runs for 100 seconds (elapsed time or wall clock time). The time is divided into 90 seconds of processor time and 10 seconds of I/O time. For this example, we will assume that Moore's law continues to exist and that the processor time will be halved every 18 months while the I/O time remains unchanged (it should be noted that the I/O is improving but at a significantly slower pace, so for our example, we will assume it remains unchanged).

The following table outlines the times as well as the relative ratio between the processor time and the I/O time.

Years	Processor time	I/O time	Elapsed time	I/O as part of the time(%)
0	90	10	100	10
1.5	45	10	55	18
3	22.5	10	32.5	31
4.5	11.3	10	21.5	45
6	5.5	10	6.5	65

It can be seen that if the trends continue, the I/O times will become a significant bottleneck. While currently the I/O time is just 10% of the elapsed time, in 6 years it will become 65%. This means that special actions are required to address the issue.

Key Takeaway

- *Programmed I/O*: In which the running task or application has initiated the input or output command and is waiting for its completion, while constantly checking the status of the device.

- *Interrupt-based I/O*: In which the program or application initiates the I/O operation but does not wait. If it has other computations to perform, it may continue, or else it can relinquish the processor. When the device is ready with the I/O, it will signal the operating system by creating an interrupt.

- *Interrupt*: A signal that is created by the hardware or a running program with the intention of getting the operating system's attention. For example, if a device that was asked to read some data it stores is ready to deliver the data, it will issue an interrupt. The operating system will be involved and will handle the request further.

- *DMA (direct memory access)*: An I/O method in which the device transfers the data directly into memory (assuming it is an input command) and signals the operating system only at the end of the whole transfer.

- *I/O buffering*: Refers to the various possibilities for defining buffers to assist and enhance the I/O, starting with no buffers allocated in the operating system, one buffer, or many. When the operating system maintains several buffers, it can read larger blocks and even issue read-ahead commands to speed up the program's execution.

CHAPTER 9

Storage

MASS STORAGE

This chapter focuses and elaborates on various aspects of storage. By using the general architecture figure, we can relate to the storage devices (disks) in the system (Figure 9.1).

Storage Devices

Every computer system, like any living creature, includes the means to store and later retrieve data. As seen in Chapter 5, "Memory," which discusses the memory hierarchy (Figure 5.5), there are various levels of storage. In general, the memory—either the main memory or the various cache levels—is considered as the main level. However, these memories are volatile and temporary and maintain the data stored as long as it was not replaced or as long as the system is operational. This volatile memory includes the first levels in the hierarchy (registers, cache, and main memory). For that reason, additional devices for long-term storage are required. The following levels of hierarchy are for media storage that does not need to be connected to an electricity source to maintain the data stored. Furthermore, the data is saved even if the system is nonoperational.

The additional storage devices can be divided into several types, based on the access to the stored data and if they are online or not.

Access to the devices can be

- Serial access, which means that for reading a data item, all previous items have to be read or skipped. An example is various tape-based devices (similar to the tape cassettes that were used for storing audio information). This type of media was heavily used in the past, mainly for backup purposes, but in recent years, its usage has been limited. The major limitation of such devices is that the search time is influenced by the location of the searched item.

- Random (or direct) access, in which it is possible to get to the required item directly. Memory, for example, is a direct-access device. The access time for obtaining a data item using direct access is almost similar for all items, regardless of their location.

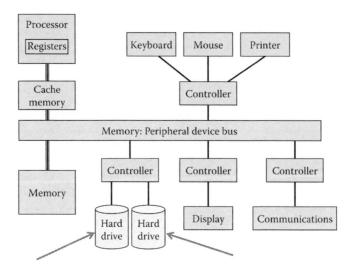

FIGURE 9.1   Disks as part of the architecture.

Another classification for storage devices is their online level:

- Fully online, which means that the device is always online and all its data is constantly available. Most magnetic disks installed in a computer system are fully online.

- Partially online, which usually involves a robotic system that holds a library of disks (e.g., optical disks); when a disk is required, it will issue the commands to stage it. This type of device provides limitless storage; however, the first access may require time, and sometimes even a significant amount of time (in cases where all the disk readers are occupied). As technology advances and online storage prices decrease, especially for the various cloud-based solutions that are being proposed, the usage and wide spread of partially online storage is decreasing.

- Off-line, which means the device is not connected to the system and its data is not available. The most trivial example may be the disk-on-key, which holds the data off-line, and when the need arises, the disk is connected to the system and its content becomes available. There are organizations that, for security reasons, use the same method but with removable hard drives. In both cases, these are off-line devices.

Disk Structure

Most magnetic disks share a very similar structure (Figure 9.2):

- The disk comprises one or more round platters on an axle, each one covered with a magnetic material.

- Each one of the sides of these platters is used. In the early disks, the outmost sides (the top of the upper platter and the bottom of the lower platter) were not used due to more physical problems associated with these two sides.

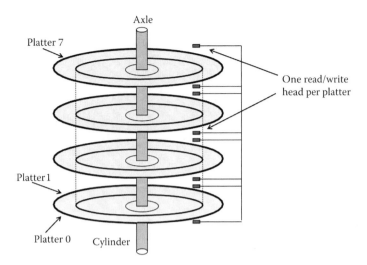

FIGURE 9.2   Disk structure.

- Each platter's side is divided into concentric circles called *tracks*. All the tracks that are on the same location on all the platters are called a *cylinder*.

- Each track is divided into smaller manageable chunks of data called *sectors*. The sector sizes vary between 512 bytes in the smaller disks to a common 4096 bytes in the larger disks. The sector is the minimal unit to read from or write to the disks. It contains additional headers and trailers, for example, an error correction code (ECC).

- The disk has special reading/writing heads (one per side of each platter) that are capable of reading and writing the data. The heads are mounted on a special arm that can move from one track to the other. Usually, all the heads are connected to a common assembly so that when one head moves, all the others move simultaneously to the same cylinder.

It should be noted that in the first disks, only part of the surface was used. The reason was that there is a difference between the lengths of the inner tracks and the outer tracks. The first disks used a common number of sectors per track, regardless of the track's location. This was done mainly to simplify the controller's task in calculating the sector's address. Usually, an address includes the disk number, the cylinder number, the reading or writing head number, and the sector number. When the number of sectors per track varies for different tracks, it will require a special table for the conversion. To decrease these differences, the tracks were recorded only on part of the surface.

As, on the one hand, the disk technology advanced and, on the other hand, the requirements for storage increased, it became clear that maintaining a fixed number of sectors per track was wasteful. While with a fixed number of sectors per track, the address calculation is simpler, only part of the surface is being used, and the longer tracks are underutilized. By providing a different approach, the amount of data stored on the disk can be increased

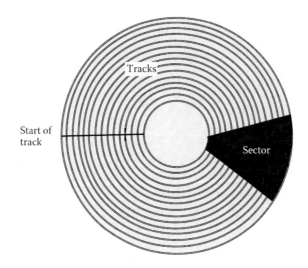

FIGURE 9.3   Tracks and sectors.

dramatically. The different approach was based on increasing the area used for tracks. The surface disk is depicted schematically in Figure 9.3.

The solution that was implemented is called *zone bit recording* (ZBR), and it defines different areas (zones) on the disk. Each zone includes several tracks. The tracks in the zone share a fixed number of sectors per track. The outer tracks, which are longer, have more sectors per track, while the inner tracks, which are shorter, have less sectors per track. Of course, locating the sectors becomes more complex; however, the algorithm is not too complicated, and it is performed by the controller. In modern disks, there might be tens of zones (Figure 9.4).

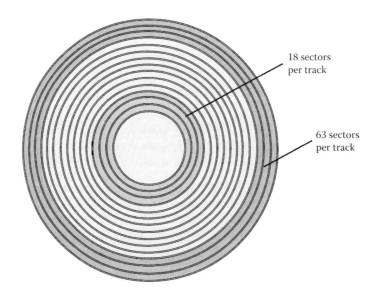

FIGURE 9.4   Zone bit recording.

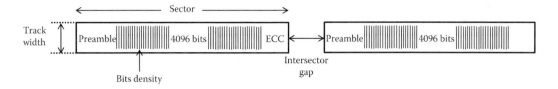

FIGURE 9.5   Sector structure.

The example shown in Figure 9.4 features an imaginary disk, the outer zone of which has 63 sectors per track. Its inner zone has 18 sectors per track, and all the zones in between have a varying number: $18 < n < 63$.

The sectors have a standard structure (Figure 9.5), which starts with a preamble that contains the synchronization information, such as the sector address. This preamble resembles the start bit in asynchronous communication transmissions. The preamble is created when the disk is formatted. During read and write operations, the controller calculates the sector's address and sends the reading and writing head to the required location. When the head is over the right sector, the controller issues an address read command just to make sure that the head is in the right location. If the address read is not the correct address, the controller issues a reposition command. This is done automatically by the hardware while the operating system and/or the application are not aware of the problem. If the address was damaged, the controller will continue trying to get the correct address, since it assumes that a mechanical problem caused the head to get to the wrong location. Just after the preamble, there will be 4096 bits (in case of a 512-byte sector). These bytes actually contain the data stored in this sector. Following the data, there will be an ECC to ensure the data integrity. After the ECC, there will be a small gap (intersector gap) followed by a new sector.

Usually, reading from or writing to the disk is done in blocks of data. Each block may contain one or more sectors. Even if the application issues a read for a smaller block, the controller will read at least a whole sector. For reading from or writing to the disk, the application has to provide the following parameters:

- Disk number

- Cylinder number

- Head number (or alternatively the surface number, since each head serves a specific surface)

- Sector number

- Number of bytes to read or write

As far as the operating system is concerned, the disk is one dimension of logical sectors. The sectors are mapped in a sequential order on a cylinder basis, starting from sector zero, which is the first sector on the first track (the outermost track, close to the platter's circumference). The mapping continues until the last sector of the track, and then it continues with the first sector on the first track but on the second surface. Then it continues to the first track on the third surface, and so on. Only after all the first tracks on all the surfaces have been accessed will the controller then continue with the first sector on the second track of the first surface. The idea behind this mechanism is to minimize the head movement for a sequential read or write.

One of the types of disks that has been very useful, but has disappeared due to its technological disadvantages, is the floppy disk (or diskette). Since the ordinary disk was referred to as the hard drive, the then "new" removable disk was called a floppy disk. Besides the name and some performance differences, the floppy disk's structure was identical to the hard drive's structure. The floppy disk had just one platter (two surfaces) and two reading and writing heads. Like ordinary disks, the floppy disk went through several generations that influenced its physical size and capacity.

The first floppy disk that used an 8 in. disk was developed by IBM with a very different intention. During the late 1960s, IBM developed a new family of computers (IBM 370) that was intended to replace the previous family (IBM 360). One of the major differences between the two designs was that the new family used microcoded instructions (see the section in Chapter 4 on "Instructions Execution"). Using microcode to define the instructions implies that the instruction can be changed while the system is on the customer's site. IBM needed a mechanism for delivering the new microcode (or firmware), and this was done using "new" technology, which was mainly a mobile and cheap device.

The most well-known floppy disk version was a 3.5 in. disk with a capacity of 1.44 MB. This diskette had 80 tracks with 18 sectors per track. The sector size was 512 bytes, which led to its capacity (2 sides * 80 tracks per side * 18 sector per track * 512 bytes per track = 1.44 MB). The floppy disk was extremely slow, and its rotational speed was six rounds per second. Despite its ability to provide a simple way to store and carry data, its disadvantages (reliability problems, limited capacity, and slow transfer rate) forced the industry to look for additional solutions, and diskettes practically disappeared.

Disk Speed

The disks' response time is determined by three main factors (Figure 9.6):

- Seek time, which is the time required for the head (or the arm assembly that holds the heads) to get to the required cylinder.

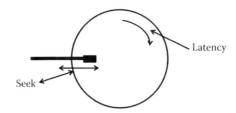

FIGURE 9.6   Disk speed.

- Latency, which is the time required for the disk to rotate until the requested sector is positioned under the head. On average, this is half the time required for one rotation. This time is directly affected by the disk's rotational speed.

- Reading or writing time, which is the time required for the head to read or write the data. Usually, this time is significantly lower compared with the other two times. While the first two times are dependent on mechanical operations, the reading or writing time depends on the electronic data transfer (the head is over the requested location, and all it has to do is read or write the data).

For example, assuming

S is the seek time

L is the latency time (half a rotation on average)

T is the transfer time

then, the overall time required for reading from or writing to the disk is determined by

$$Time = S + L + T$$

However, this formula is true only when there are no additional requests for the disk. In reality, the disk device driver as well as the controller have to respond to several requests, so the overall time may be longer and include the waiting time as well. There are several algorithms that the operating system may apply in trying to optimize the disks' access time (this will be explained later in this chapter), and these too may affect the waiting time.

In addition, although it can be understood from the above formula that the activities are performed serially, in modern controllers this is not the case. Modern disks usually partly overlap the two mechanical movements; however, the third activity can start only after the first two have been completed.

Some operating systems (such as Windows by Microsoft) do not ask the user to specify the size of the file that he or she intends to write. For every additional block appended to the file, the operating system looks for a free and available sector and assigns it to the file. As the file grows, there is an increasing probability that the newly assigned sector will not be physically close to the previous sector. The operating system handles this situation; however, it may have severe performance implications. If the file is written sequentially, there is only a minimal head movement. The head is located over a cylinder and writes the data without any mechanical movements. On the other hand, if the file is written in such a way that the sectors are spread all over the disk, the disk is accessed randomly and the heads have to be moved for every sector. While in modern disks the sequential read (or write) may take about one millisecond. If it is done randomly, it will require about 20 milliseconds, and sometimes even more. It of course depends on the disk and its attributes and the amount of fragmentation. These fragments, which represent sequential sectors that belong to the same file but are written in different locations on the disk, are a by-product of the way the system works (as was the case in managing the random access memory [RAM]). If the system does not impose an advance declaration of the file size, then over time, the fragmentations increase. The problem associated with the higher degree of fragmentation is that it increases the response time. The solution proposed by the system is running the defrag utility, which tries to copy the files into consecutive sectors.

Disk Capacity

Most of the currently available hard drives are Winchester disks. This means that the disk is hermetically closed, and neither the platters nor the heads or moving arm are visible from the outside. This is necessary in order to ensure that dust or any other particles will not enter the disk assembly. Any such external material poses a real danger to the disk's well-being, considering the high speed at which it rotates. The first of these types of disks was developed by IBM in 1973. The disk, which was sealed, was divided into two parts: a fixed part and a removable part. Each one was intended to store 30 MB. The disk was named after the famous Winchester 30-30 rifle.

The disk's capacity, as defined by its manufacturer, usually includes all the bits that exist on the disk. However, before it can be used, a disk has to be formatted, which, among other things, writes the sector addresses. For that reason, the actual usable capacity of the disk is always lower than the quoted capacity.

For example, consider a disk with the following characteristics:

- 8 (2^3) platters

- 2097152 (2^{21}) tracks per surface

- 128 (2^7) sectors per track (on average)

- 4096 (2^{12}) bytes per sector

The manufacturer will describe the disk as an 8.8 TB ($2^3 * 2^{21} * 2^7 * 2^{12} = 2^{43}$). In reality, about 10% of the bits will be used for overheard (intersector gapes, preamble, ECC), so in an optimal situation, the disk will contain less than 8 TB.

Developments in disk technologies can be divided into two parts. Since their introduction in the early 1970s and up to the 1990s, the main aim was to increase the capacity. This was achieved by increasing the recording density. During this time, the recording density increased by a factor of 40–50, while the capacity increased by a factor of 80–100. The result was that the early disks, which were physically large (the size of an average washing machine), increased in size, and in the 1990s, they were the size of a refrigerator. From the 1990s on, a greater emphasis was put on manufacturing smaller disks. As a result, there was a period by the late 1990s in which, instead of the capacity increasing, it was actually decreased, but the disk size was significantly smaller. The density recording, which was about 3 megabits per square inch, increased to several terabits per square inch.

Contrary to the rapid developments in disk technology related to the recording density, the disks' rotational speed, which directly influences the disk performance, has been constant for quite some time. There are fast disks with a rotational speed of 10,000 rpm; however, the fastest rotating disks, such as Cheetah by Seagate, have a rotational speed of 15,000 rpm. The Cheetah disk was introduced several years back, and the additional technological developments were mainly in the area of increasing its capacity, but its rotational speed remained unchanged. This limitation, combined with developments in the solid-state disk (SSD), has changed the focus, and currently for new developments, especially for appliances such as tablets and mobile phones, SSD is the common solution. These disks are slowly appearing in ordinary computer systems as well, although they are used only for tasks that need to be very fast, such as storing the applications' pages. This is because there is still a large cost difference per megabyte between SSD and ordinary disks.

Performance Enhancements

The hard drives, like any other peripheral devices, are connected to the computer's buses through a controller. In the early stages, controllers were mainly used to bridge between the bus protocol and the device protocol. As the disks' technology advanced, the controllers assumed a more important role. For example, with the implementation of zone bit recording (ZBR), it was the controller, through additional layers of logic, that managed the addresses calculations. Additional intelligence was added to achieve a higher degree of optimization and performance. This new logic is performed by the hardware (the controller) without any interference in the operating system or the application. The cooperation between the controllers and additional features in the operating system led to significant performance and reliability improvements. Some of the technics employed are

- Larger blocks: The controller can read larger quantities of data from the disk (compared with the amount requested by the application). The additional data is stored in buffers within the controller. The next time the system requests this data, the controller will retrieve it without the need to access the slow mechanical disk. This means that the controller has to manage the buffers, since it may happen that the controller reads the following data but the application does not need it. In this case, and after some predefined time has elapsed, the buffer will be freed so it can be reassigned. The modern controllers actually represent an embedded system with its own computer system. The software that is included with the controller is sometimes quite sophisticated due to the many special cases it has to manage. One example that is intended to increase the disk's reliability is related to bad sectors. In the past, if a bad sector was detected, it could have prevented the system from using the drive. The operating system was trying to mark some of the sectors as bad sectors so it would not try to write over them. Modern controllers have a specially designated area on the disk used as spare. Each time a bad spot, or a bad sector, is detected, the controller replaces it with another location in its spare area. When the operating system or the application tries to access that same location, the controller will substitute the original address with the new address. This is done on the fly without alerting the operating system or the application. The software embedded in the controller is not part of the operating system, and it is developed and supplied by the disk manufacturers.

- Pre-fetch (or read ahead): This has already been discussed. The controller can identify the application's patterns of behavior. When an application reads the sectors sequentially, the controller can read the next blocks even before they are requested. These read-ahead blocks are kept temporarily in the controller's buffers. This idea stems from the understanding that reading the following sector while the head is properly positioned requires very little time (no need for both seek and latency). This mechanism requires increasing the size of the controller's memory.

- Access algorithms: These are usually implemented by the operating system and are included in this chapter to provide an elaborated explanation and a more complete view of performance-enhancement methods.

- Disk array: This is a technology that increases the size of the single disk as well as its speed, reliability, and survivability.

Solid-State Disk (SSD)

Rapid developments in memory technologies (see the section in Chapter 5 on "Memory Technologies") was clearly observed by hard-drive manufacturers, who were facing increasing demand for enhanced disk performance. One of the first implementations was the disk-on-key, which uses flash memory.* The disk-on-key entered a market in demand and quickly replaced the removable media then available. As far as computers were concerned, there was a growing need to carry some information. Even with the introduction of laptops, users still needed a simple device to store information. Originally, this was done by using diskettes (see the section in this chapter on "Disk Structure"). Diskettes, however, were very limited and unreliable if carried out of a controlled environment. For a short period, diskettes were replaced by CDs, which are still being used for music, but when the disk-on-key arrived, it became the most used media for carrying files. The next stage, based on the successful user experience, was to use the technology for disk replacements. It should be noted that there were previous products that implemented this technology, even in the early 1990s; however, it was only in the last decade that the technology has entered mainstream computing. The significant advantages associated with SSD are related to the fact that it is actually a memory device with no rotating parts. As such, it can be extremely fast (no seek and latency) and relatively small with a low power consumption.

SSD, like modern disks, is not just storage but also a system that includes a processor, a bus, and memory (Figure 9.7). Compared with mechanical disks, SSD is extremely fast, especially for random reads.

As previously stated, the idea of replacing the rotating disks by memory as a means to improve performance is not new, and it has been implemented, for example by Control Data during the 1980s. The memory back then was physically large, so it could not be used as a mobile off-line device; however, memory was used as a system storage device mainly for rolling processes in and out as well as for copying large segments of memory.

---

* Flash memory is a nonvolatile memory that can be electrically written.

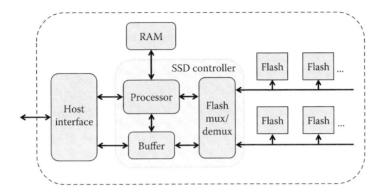

FIGURE 9.7   An example of SSD architecture.

The new technological developments regarding SSD and its small size pushed it and its usage at an increasing pace. The main usage of SSD is for server applications, in which the response time is extremely important. For example, the data stored on SSD will be the data that is causing the bottlenecks, such as parts of the database, swap files, and paging files.

The computing industry was locked in the rotating disks perception for over 60 years, and the introduction of such a new technology required some out-of-the-box thinking. In 2007, ASUS* introduced a notebook with a solid-state disk. Despite its very light weight, it was accepted with great caution (maybe because originally it ran Linux), although a couple of years later it included ordinary (rotating) disks and ran Windows as well. It took several years before the technology found its way into organizations. It should be remembered that in many organizations, there is a huge computing infrastructure that supports the organization. This infrastructure usually includes a large array of disks, and replacing these with new SDDs is extremely expensive, since SSDs are still significantly more expensive compared with mechanical disks. On the other hand, the technology opens up new possibilities for companies that were not active in the mechanical-disk industry, such as Intel, which currently offers solid-state disks.

Another significant factor favoring SSDs is their lesser power consumption and their higher resistance to hits and shocks; this makes them more applicable to laptops, notebooks, and so on. Despite their advantages and due to the large investments being made in current technology, the SSD will probably be used to extend the memory hierarchy by adding an additional level. It is important to note that SSD technology has some disadvantages. It is, and probably will be for quite some time, more expensive than ordinary mechanical disks. In addition, as with other flash-based products, there is a finite number of times the disk can be written. So, for a large number of such writes it may cause a problem. This happens because, like ordinary disks, SSD replaces bad sectors by sectors from its spare area. Unfortunately, there are some applications that use frequent writes, or a very busy system that uses SSD for paging and can reach this inherent limitation. For that reason, SSD, at least at its current state, cannot be used for the long-term storage of files that are being modified at a high frequency.

---

* ASUS is an international computers and services company with headquarters in Taiwan. In 2013, it was the fifth largest computers manufacturer.

Access Algorithms

In implementing various access algorithms, the operating system aims to increase the disk's performance. Usually, the dominant factor that limits performance in the mechanical disk operation is the arm (head) movement. So, if an algorithm for optimizing the movement can be applied, it will reduce the time spent moving the arm, which will increase the overall disk performance. This is the reason that various algorithms were developed.

In order to use a visual example for explaining the different algorithms, we will assume that

- The disk used in the example has 300 cylinders (0–299)

- The initial head position is cylinder 103

- The requests queue includes movement to cylinders 78, 21, 287, 211, 51, 79, 119, 3, 245, and 97

Some of the access algorithms used for enhancing performance include

- First come first served (FCFS), which handles the requests based on their arrival order. The first request will be served first, followed by the second request, and so forth. In this specific case, the head will first move to cylinder 78 and, after finishing this request, it will move to cylinder 21 and so on, as appears in Figure 9.8. The total number of cylinders the arm moves in order to fulfill the requests is 1098.

- Shortest time first (STF), in which the requests are handled based on their distance from the current head location. The first request to be handled is the closest one. In this specific example, the first request to be processed is the one that relates to cylinder 97 (the closest to the initial location—103). The next request is the one that accesses cylinder 79, and so on, as depicted in Figure 9.9. Before the next head

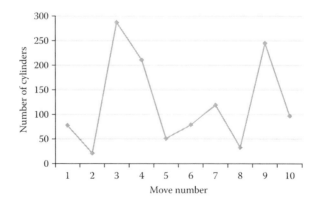

FIGURE 9.8   FCFS head movement.

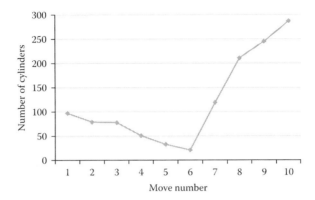

FIGURE 9.9   STF head movement.

movement, the operating system calculates the minimal movements and creates a prioritized list. In this specific case, since the head is at cylinder 103, the list will consist of

97, 79, 78, 51, 33, 21, 119, 211, 245 and 287.

For completing all the requests, the head will have to move 266 cylinders, which implies that this algorithm is more efficient than the previous FCFS algorithm. Unfortunately, implementing the algorithm as it is, without any additional precautions, may result in starvation, in which some requests may never be fulfilled. This happens if there are many pending requests all in close proximity, and the new requests are also for close-by cylinders, but there is, however, one request to a cylinder far away. Unfortunately, this request will wait forever, since always there will be a closer request that will be served earlier.

- Scan (or the elevator algorithm), in which the head starts at one end of the disk (usually at the first cylinder) and, while moving to the other end, handles all the requests it finds on the way. As part of the algorithm, the operating system sorts the requests and handles them according to the sorted order. When the head reaches the end of the disk, it starts its movement backward following the same mechanism, only this time the sorted numbers are handled from the largest downward. Assuming the head is in its movement toward the beginning of the disk, then the first request to be handled will be the one accessing cylinder 97, followed by 79, and so on until it reaches the beginning of the disk. Then it will change direction, going to the end of the disk and starting with the request that accesses cylinder 119, followed by 211, and so on, as described in Figure 9.10. To complete all the requests, the head has to move over 372 cylinders.

- C-Scan (or circular scan, Figure 9.11), which is very similar to SCAN with a minor change. The head starts at one end (usually at the beginning of the disk) and, while

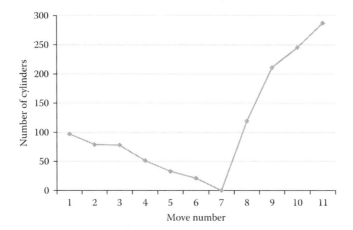

FIGURE 9.10   Scan head movement.

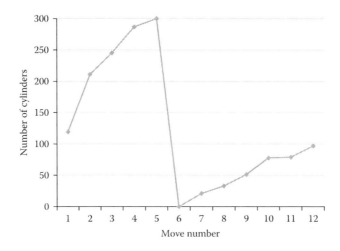

FIGURE 9.11   C-Scan head movement.

moving to the end of the disk, handles all the requests it finds. After it gets to the end of the disk, it starts once again from the beginning. In this specific case, since the head is at cylinder 103 moving forward, the first request to be served is for cylinder 119, followed by 211, 245, and 287. Then, the head will move to the end of disk, return to the beginning, and start going forward looking for requests in its way. The total number of cylinders it moves is 594 (including the 300 cylinders on its way back from the end of the disk to its beginning).

- C-Look (Figure 9.12) is an improvement to the previously described C-Scan. Unlike C-Scan, which moves from the beginning of the disk to its end (even if there are no additional requests near the end), in C-Look, the head moves forward until it finds the request with the larger cylinder number. The understanding is that there are no additional requests to cylinders that are located further away, so there is no need to

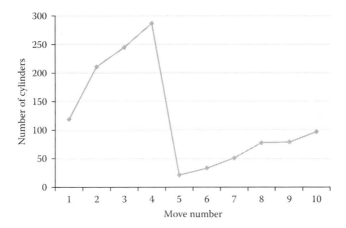

FIGURE 9.12   C-Look head movement.

move forward, and the head can go back to the beginning. However, when moving to the beginning of disk, since the controller knows which cylinders are requested, it does not have to move the head to the beginning of the disk but to the first requested cylinder. In this specific example, after the head reaches cylinder 287, it does not continue its move to the end of the disk but goes directly to cylinder 21. The total number of cylinders moved in this case is 526.

Disk Controller

The disk controller is responsible for some of the performance improvements described previously (see the section in this chapter on "Performance Enhancements"). One of these activities is managing the internal buffers as well as the whole memory structure, including caching the data and issuing the read-ahead commands for data to be pre-fetched. In many cases, the controller implements the read ahead by allocating multiple buffers and using double buffering or a circular buffers mechanism. In a sense, it is similar to the pipeline mechanism used by the processor for enhancing performance due to the parallel execution. While the application is processing one block of data, the next one is already available in the controller's buffers, and an additional one may be in the process of being loaded from disk.

For example, assuming

- P is the processing time of one block
- R is the amount of time required for reading one block
- n is the number of blocks to be processed (read or write)

Then the total time required for serial work using a single buffer is given by

$$\text{Time} = n * \left(P + R \right)$$

However, when working with two buffers or more (assuming the R > P), the total time is given by

$$Time = R + nP$$

This resembles the processor's pipeline, in which the actual reading of the next block is done while the central processing unit (CPU) processes the previous one. As with the processor's pipeline, in this case it is possible since two distinct components (buffers) are involved. These parallel activities can drastically reduce the application elapse time.

An additional benefit, already mentioned, of using a computerized controller is its ability to increase reliability. Although the disks are hermetically sealed, they rotate at a very high speed (up to 15,000 rotations per minute in the case of the Cheetah disks). For that reason, sometimes there might be defective spots, which cause bad sectors. These bad spots are due to a manufacturing problem or a problem that occurred during operation. Such a bad sector is usually an area on the disk that is not accessible. It may contain some data, and in such a case, the file containing the data that is on the bad sector will be unreadable (a corrupted file).

Usually, as part of their quality assurance process, disks are tested prior to leaving the manufacturing facility. One of these tests is to ensure that there are no bad sectors or that their number is less than a threshold defined by the manufacturer or the industry. Years back, there was a label attached to the disk with relevant information, including the number of bad sectors it had.

Currently, all disks include some additional spare sectors on each track. Each time a bad sector is discovered, it is automatically mapped to a different location. This new location is one of the additional spare sectors. This is done as part of the manufacturing and testing process, and it continues during normal operations. The controller maintains the mapping information on a separate (hidden) cylinder, which is used solely for that purpose and is not part of the calculated disk capacity. Using this mechanism, all disks leave the manufacturing facility with no bad sectors.

Most disks, and especially the modern ones, use direct memory access (DMA), which is performed by the controller. To better understand the technological developments in that area, it is important to note that originally the sectors were not written consecutively. The processor that used programmed input/output (I/O) was not fast enough to handle one sector while the disk rotates. This means that the processor read the first sector and it then had to write it into memory. By the time the processor was ready for the second sector, the disk had already rotated, and the processor had to wait for a whole new rotation. In order to fix the problem, the sectors were split to allow the extra time. This technique is called *interleaving* (as with memory interleaving), and it can be done using some variations (Figure 9.13).

Figure 9.13 demonstrates the interleaving method using three variations. The upper part represents the disk and the track recorded, while the lower side represents three examples. The first example, which demonstrates a three-to-one interleaving, uses a difference of three. Instead of the normal consecutive (one-to-one) recording, in this case the sectors are recorded so that, while the processor handles the first sector, the disk continues to rotate. When the

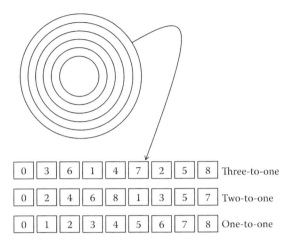

| 0 | 3 | 6 | 1 | 4 | 7 | 2 | 5 | 8 | Three-to-one |

| 0 | 2 | 4 | 6 | 8 | 1 | 3 | 5 | 7 | Two-to-one |

| 0 | 1 | 2 | 3 | 4 | 5 | 6 | 7 | 8 | One-to-one |

FIGURE 9.13   Sector interleaving.

processor is ready to access the next sector, two sectors have passed, and the next consecutive sector is ready for reading. In other words, the processor has more time for handling the read sector. The amount of time is defined by the time required for the disk to move two sectors.

In the two-to-one interleaving, the time difference is shorter. While the processor handles the read sector, the next sector rotates. When the processor is ready for its next sector, it is available for reading.

Modern systems that use other methods for I/O (DMA or interrupt-based I/O) are fast enough for reading and handling the sectors without any delay (one-to-one interleaving), especially due to the introduction of smart controllers and the use of DMA transfer, so interleaving is no longer needed.

Redundant Array of Inexpensive Disks

Redundant array of inexpensive disks (RAID) is a technology that was developed during the early 1990s. As with many other cases in the computing industry, the technology was developed to solve a problem that does not exist anymore; however, it laid the foundation for new and emerging technologies. RAID was driven by the costly disks of proprietary systems, which may have been fast at the time but were also extremely expensive. So, instead of paying large amounts of money for these proprietary disks, the idea was to use off-the-shelf disks and, by developing sophisticated controllers, to increase the speed, capacity, and reliability of these disks. During the 1980s, many companies offered large systems (mainframes and super computers). These companies emerged due to an increased demand for computing systems. In most cases, the bottlenecks that prevented optimal usage were the peripheral devices and especially disk drives. Despite heavy resources spent on increasing efficiency (in the processor, memory, and buses), the disk drives were a limiting factor. The companies spent large sums and much effort, including developing extreme solutions, in order to improve the situation. The large mainframes at that time were very expensive and provided the financial resources needed for research and development. The customers paid large sums for the disks, because, as previously explained, if the disks are not fast enough the system's performance is hampered.

One example of an exotic and very expensive disk was utilizing a fixed-head technology. Unlike current disks, which have one head per surface that moves to the required cylinder, the fixed-head disk had multiple heads per surface. As a matter of fact, the disk employed one head for each track, and it was also called *head per track*. Such a disk provides an elevated performance since it does not have to move to the cylinder (seek). There was no arm, since the disk did not have to move it. The only movement was the disk rotation.

Another example was the Hydra disk, so called because of its ability to read/write utilizing several heads in parallel. The heads were still connected to a common assembly and moved together, but once on the right cylinder, several heads could read/write in parallel. This led to a significantly higher transfer rate. This disk did not improve seek or latency times but only the transfer rate.

Most of the disks implemented by proprietary systems were not sealed, so dust and other microscopic particles could enter the disk, causing various crashes. Unlike the modern sealed (Winchester) disks, which have a mean time between failures (MTBF) of over one million hours, the proprietary disks of the 1990s had an average MTBF of 50,000 hours (or over 5 years of uninterruptable work). The capacity was also a limiting factor (tens to hundreds of megabytes), and if there was a need to store a very large file, an array of disks had to be defined. This array consisted of several concatenated physical disks, which, as far as the operating system was concerned, were one logical disk. Unfortunately, building such an array affected its reliability. If a single disk failed, it brought down the whole array. For example, if, for a large database, there was a need to define a logical disk that included 20 physical disks, the MTBF was significantly lowered ($50,000/20 = 2,500$). This means that such a system would fail on average every three months. The reliability figures would probably be worse, since the system probably has additional disks, which may fail as well.

The solution, which first appeared in a paper by Patterson, Gibson, and Katz, defined a mass-storage model that addressed three limitations that existed then:

- The problem of the capacity of the single drive was solved by concatenating several physical disks and creating a larger logical disk. This, of course, required some modifications to the operating system as well.

- Disk speed was improved by splitting the file on several disks and accessing the disks in parallel.

- Reliability and survivability was increased by implementing error corrections algorithms for finding and correcting information loss. In addition to the existing ECC, the model duplicated parts of the data on different disks to prevent loss of information.

The proposed model was defined using different levels (or submodels):

- RAID Level 0, sometimes called *striping*. This level does not provide additional survivability and concentrates on improving the read performance. The file is split into stripes, each one written to a different disk. When reading the data, the controller

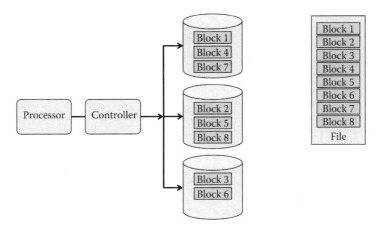

FIGURE 9.14   RAID Level 0.

issues several commands to several disks to read the data in parallel. This level is used when there is a need for a very fast response time in reading a file that seldom changes.

Figure 9.14 depicts a file that consists of eight blocks. These blocks were written on three disks, each block to a different disk. If the application needs to read three blocks at a time, then the controller will handle the reads concurrently, and after all the data has been read, it will be sent to the application as one combined block. If some problem occurs and one of the disks stops working, the file becomes inaccessible, since some of its parts are no longer available. RAID level 0 does not improve the MTBF but in fact worsens it. As has been seen, the MTBF in this case is calculated by the MTBF of the single disk divided by three. For that reason, if a system requires a high degree of reliability and survivability, RAID Level 0 is not the solution. On the other hand, as will be described later, combining this model with another model that is aimed at increasing reliability provides a solution that is both fast as well as reliable.

Using RAID Level 0 provides an additional benefit that is important for a multiprogramming and interactive environment. Unlike other disks whose activity depends on the programs that run in the system or the system setup, RAID Level 0 disks tend to be more balanced. For example, if a specific disk is defined as the disk that holds the system pages, then by definition the disk will be heavily used, especially if the system runs many processes in parallel. In general, due to the system setup, this disk will be used much more compared with a disk that is used just for storing files. For that reason, in such systems there will be a high degree of variance in the disks' activities, ranging from disks that are idle most of the time to disks that are very busy (like the paging disk). Figure 9.15 depicts the disks activity on a "standard" system, in which the disk accesses are not balanced. On interactive systems, the paging disk will be used more frequently,

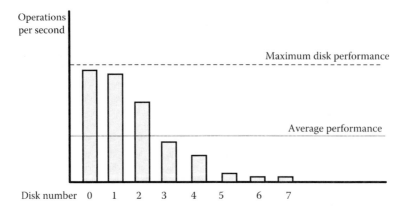

FIGURE 9.15   Disk activities on a "standard" system.

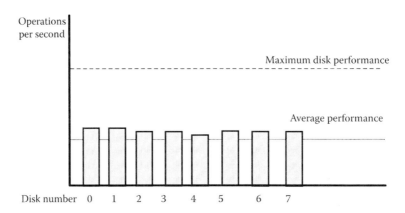

FIGURE 9.16   Disk activities on a RAID Level 0 system.

while on heavy batch–oriented systems, the disks that store the application data will be used more heavily.

Implementing RAID Level 0, where each file is split over several disks, produces a more balanced access, and the differences between the accesses of the different disks are minimal (Figure 9.16). This, of course, is true for both the system disks that store the applications' pages and the disks that hold the files.

Some operating systems, including Windows, support the definition of logical disks. This feature allows the definition of several logical disks on a single physical disk as well as several physical disks implemented as one logical disk.

It is important to note that, in addition to worse performance caused by unbalanced disks, which may have a negative influence on the whole system, there is nothing wrong with a disk that works more intensively, and it should not shorten its life.

- RAID Level 1, sometimes called *mirroring* or *shadowing*. This level provides a high degree of reliability since it duplicates the data on two different disks. If the MTBF of disks when the model was designed was 50,000 hours, then using RAID Level 1 increases the MTBF to $50,000^2$. If the current disks' MTBF is over one million hours, then applying RAID Level 1 increases the MTBF to practically an indefinite period of time $10^6 * 10^6 = 10^{12}$, or over one hundred million years. This improved survivability has its overhead since the number of disks has to be doubled. RAID Level 1 provides 100% redundancy, but in addition, it improves the response time. The controller (or the operating system) knows that there are two copies of the file, and it can access the two disks and choose the one that is the least busy. This, of course, is true for read operations; however, the write performance will be worse, since each write operation has to be performed twice. Figure 9.17 depicts RAID Level 1 and, as can be seen, a failure of one of the disks will not influence the system, which could continue working with the second disk.

- RAID Level 2 defines a theoretical model that has no practical or commercial implementations. The model defines a type of striping, but instead of defining striping on the block level, RAID Level 2 defines striping on a bit level. To implement the model, the system has to have a least 39 disks: 32 disks for data and seven disks for the ECC. Every word of 32 bits being written to a file is split into separate bits. Each bit is written to a different disk. Theoretically, this model provides very high reading and writing performance. During the time a single sector is written to or read from an ordinary disk, RAID Level 2 reads or writes 32 sectors. Of course, to achieve this level of performance, all heads on all disks should be synchronized.

- RAID Level 3 is an extension of RAID Level 2. It is a different type of striping, but instead of a bit striping, it is done on a byte level. Every byte in the block to be

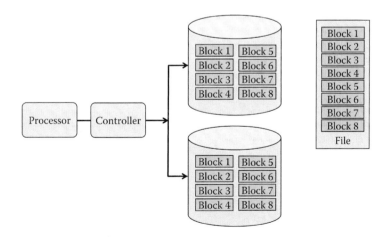

FIGURE 9.17   RAID Level 1.

written is sent to a different disk and, as a protection, the controller performs an XOR (Exclusive OR)* between two bytes. The XOR result, which occupies a byte, is written to a different disk (the parity disk). In case of the failure of one disk, it is simple to recreate the data that was on the disk by performing an additional XOR between the parity byte and the remaining byte. If the parity disk fails, it causes no problems since the data is maintained. RAID Level 3 provides enhanced performance for sequential reads due to the spread of the data over several disks; however, as in the previous case, all disks have to be synchronized. This model was used for streaming large volumes of data, such as movies, which could not be interrupted. The fact that the model allows easy recovery of lost data and that this recovery is done automatically by the controller provides the necessary continued streaming. On the other hand, writing is slower, since in many cases with heavy writing, the parity disk may become a bottleneck. Contrary to RAID Level 2, in this case, there is no need to purchase 32 disks for data. According to the available number of data disks, the controller will split the data. In addition, the integrity overhead is lower. There are an additional seven disks in the RAID Level 2 compared with one additional disk in RAID Level 3.

- RAID Level 4 (Figure 9.18) is an extension of RAID Level 3. Instead of a byte striping (as in Level 3), in this case the striping is on a block basis; that is, each block is written to a different disk, and the parity block (the result of the XOR) is written to the parity disk. All other attributes of RAID Level 3 are identical.

- RAID Level 5, as in previous cases, is an extension of RAID Level 4. Level 5 addresses limitations in Level 4 and corrects them. RAID Level 4 (as well as Level 3) has an inherent problem due to using just one parity disk. This only one parity disk may become a bottleneck, especially during writes, which always involved writing to two disks, one of them, will always be the parity disk. In case of failure, when one of the disks is not operational, the parity disk can also become a bottleneck, since to recover the lost data, the controller has to access both disks. The improvement introduced in RAID Level 5 was to split the parity blocks across all available disks instead of a dedicated disk. Therefore, when the parity block is written to a different disk each

---

* XOR (or Exclusive OR) returns true only if the bits are different. That is, one or the other bits is set, but not both, has a nice attribute that it can be used for reconstructing an original value.

Assuming:

$$A = 1011\ 1001$$

$$B = 0111\ 1101$$

Then:

$$C = A \oplus B = 1011\ 1001 \oplus 0111\ 1101 = 1100\ 0100$$

Using this value for an XOR with B will reconstruct A and using this value for an XOR with A will reconstruct B, as can be seen:

$$C \oplus B = 1100\ 0100 \oplus 0111\ 1101 = 1011\ 1001 = A$$

and

$$C \oplus A = 1100\ 0100 \oplus 1011\ 1001 = 0111\ 1101 = B$$

For that easy possibility to reconstruct lost data, XOR is being used as the parity mechanism.

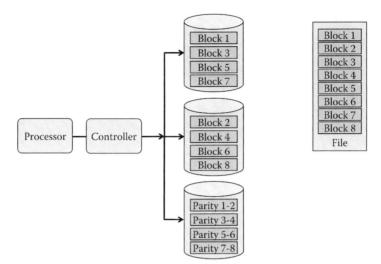

FIGURE 9.18   RAID Level 4.

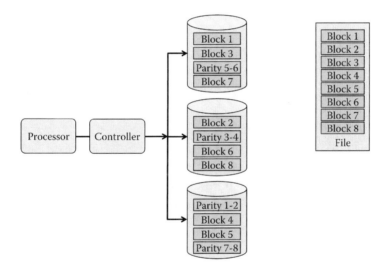

FIGURE 9.19   RAID Level 5.

time, it releases the possible bottleneck. Contrary to the improvement in the read performance, the write is still slower due to the need to write in parallel to two disks.

Figure 9.19 depicts the RAID Level 5 example. On the upper right side, there is a file and its list of blocks. During the write process, each block is written to a different block. For every two blocks, a parity block is calculated. The block is written to the next available disk in such a way that the two data blocks and the parity block are on three different disks.

- RAID Level 6 (sometimes referred to as RAID Level 10) is not a formal level defined by the RAID model and it was added de facto. Depicted in Figure 9.20, this level actually augments Levels 0 and 1 (and this is the reason it is sometimes called Level 10). The

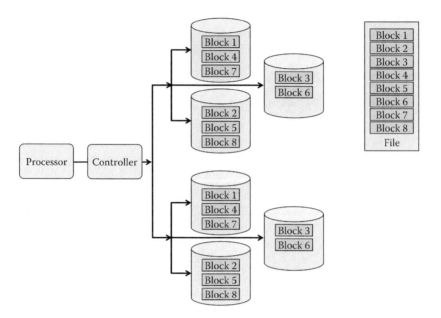

FIGURE 9.20   RAID Level 6.

level includes both mirroring and striping. It combines the performance enhancements achieved by Level 0 with the increased reliability of Level 1. Although it is fast and reliable, it also remains expensive due to the need to replicate the disks.

A very important attribute of a RAID system is its ability to reconstruct the data on the fly, but this capability was also extended to the whole disk. In a case that a disk has to be replaced, it is possible to disconnect it from the system and, due to the inherent recoverability capabilities, the system will continue working without it. This, of course, is not relevant for Level 0, which does not contain the recoverability possibilities. When a new disk is connected to the system, the controller will reconstruct the data that was written on the disk. This will be done in parallel to the work performed by the controller. It is also possible to add a hot backup, or a spare disk that is connected to the RAID system (Figure 9.21). If a problem is found in one of the other disks and it has to be removed, the hot backup disk will be put to work. The operating system as well as the running applications are not aware of the problem and will continue their execution as if nothing has happened.

To enable the hot backup capabilities, the system has to be designed accordingly (Figure 9.22). Generally speaking, the array management is done using three different layers:

- On the lower layer is the disk controller, which is responsible for managing the disk, including bad sectors, optimization, buffer usage, and so on.

- On the second layer is the RAID controller, which is responsible for all operations related to the array according to the specific level that was defined. It means managing

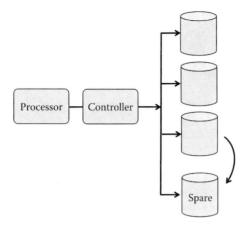

FIGURE 9.21   Hot backup.

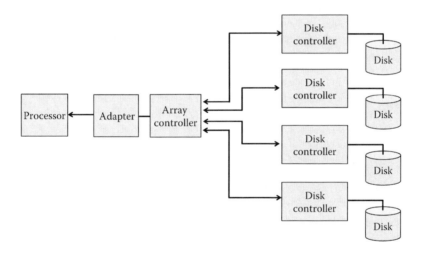

FIGURE 9.22   Controller responsibilities.

the array buffers (which are different from the disk control buffers), reliability issues, parity disk (one or more), hot backup, and so on.

- On the third and higher level is the system (or bus) adapter, which is responsible for protocol conversion, DMA management, and so on.

The amount of resources spent on ensuring the survivability of the organizational data is driven by the importance of the data for the organizations' well-being. Many modern computerized systems, especially in the Internet era, have to be operational 24/7. If the system fails, it may involve severe losses as well as a degraded reputation, which may lead to a loss of customers. Some systems in the twenty-first century cannot and should not stop providing service. For example, the cellular network, which involves a variety of computerized systems, should be always available.

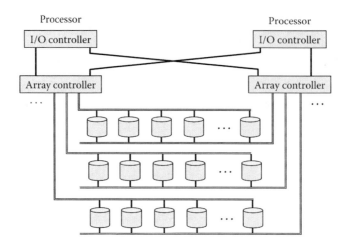

FIGURE 9.23   Full redundancy.

Using the RAID technology can provide some level of assurance, but sometimes there is a need to protect the computer itself (the processor, memory, controllers, etc.). In such cases, organizations use multiple systems that may be connected to a common array of disks. The dual or more systems replicate all hardware in order to minimize the chance of a hardware failure. Figure 9.23 depicts such a system, which has two computers, each one with its own set of controllers. The RAID system is managed by two controllers; each one has two connections so it is connected to the two systems using two different buses. All the disks are connected to two buses; each one belongs to a different RAID controller.

Storage Attached Network (SAN)

SAN is a local area network intended to handle large amounts of data and provide fast transfer rates to organizational data. In the past, mass-storage resources were connected to a single computer and, to access the data, it was necessary to go through that computer. Due to the increase in the number of servers that have to access this organizational data, it has to be available to all. Such a local area network usually uses a high-speed connection such as a fiber channel and supports a variety of configurations that can be modified and enhanced on the fly (like RAID). The advantages of using SAN are mainly that it provides the user community with simple, coherent access to common corporate information. This is due to the organizational need to improve its decision-making process by integrating all its information resources and preventing the creation of separate islands of information. A good decision-making process has to relate to all available information, and if for some reason these islands of isolated information are not taken into account, it hampers the process as well as the decision made.

SAN has additional advantages that relate to the operational aspect. It is much simpler to handle and manage mass-storage resources that are located in a central site, especially in the current heterogeneous and flexible working environments. Thus, a common and shared management leads to significant cost savings.

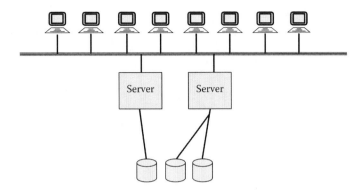

FIGURE 9.24 Mass-storage "ordinary system."

To provide these advantages, SAN systems have to be fast and use a variety of interfaces. Most systems use fiber-optics, which became almost a standard for connecting high-speed peripherals due to their speed and ability to stretch over long distances. To enhance the speed of the internal bus, the SCSI interface is usually used.

Figure 9.24 depicts an "ordinary" system in which the upper part relates to the users' various working devices (personal computers, handheld devices, mobile phones, etc.). All these devices are connected to a network, and through that network they connect to the organizational servers. Each server handles its data resources and the associated applications. When the application on the user's device needs some organizational information, it has to access one of these servers to obtain it. It should be noted that sometimes a disk or an array of disks is connected to more than one server, but usually this is done for reliability reasons and not for concurrent work. Over the years, several infrastructure tools, such as distributed databases, were developed to help the applications locate the information; however, for other files, the application has to do it.

Figure 9.25 depicts a storage attached network. The upper part of the figure is identical to the previous figure, but here the servers can access the data on the SAN disks. It should be noted that SAN provides the lower-level protocols, and the connecting server still has to

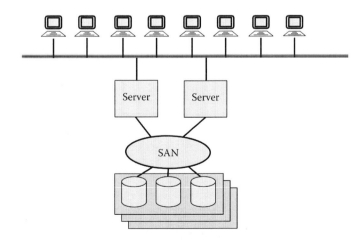

FIGURE 9.25 Mass storage on a SAN architecture.

manage the upper level. For that reason, the file-system management remains part of the servers, and the SAN provides the raw data management. Nevertheless, the SAN includes additional software components and not just hardware. Such a system will contain a communications infrastructure (a fast network), the storage devices, and a management layer that is responsible for resource management and access management as well as communication. This layer is responsible for fast and efficient data transfer as well as fault recovery.

Network Attached Storage (NAS)

NAS represents a different approach to solving the same problem. Using NAS, the storage resources are connected directly to the network, unlike SAN, in which the storage resources are part of the network. This approach has been around for a long time, and it was implemented by Novell, Inc.* as a method for sharing files. It also supported a network file system (NFS), which was a distributed file system developed by Sun Microsystems. Contrary to the SAN approach, which allows access only on a block basis, NAS relates to the whole files. The difference is better explained by Figure 9.26.

The figure depicts an ordinary system and the two SAN and NAS systems. The three components relevant for the explanation are the application, the file-system management component, and the disks themselves. Usually, the control flow starts with the application that needs some data, and then it accesses the operating system. The relevant component will be the file-system management, which is responsible for access rights, locating the file's address, and so on, and, assuming the access is valid, it will eventually get the information from the relevant disk and transfer it to the application. This order of events in all three architectures is identical. The only difference is the network's location in the process. In the ordinary system, in which the disks are directly connected, there is no network. In a SAN-based system, the network resides between the file-system management software and the disks themselves. This is the reason that SAN uses blocks as the communications components, since the network does not know about files and their locations; all it manages is raw blocks. In the NAS approach, on the other hand, the network is between the application and the file system. In this case, the NAS can provide access to the files since the file management software resides on the NAS system.

Key Takeaway

- *Storage devices*: There are many storage devices used by computers, which serve a variety of needs and purposes. Some may provide serial access (such as tapes) and others provide random access (such as a hard drive). Some of the devices may be fully online, providing constant access, and others may be partially online (such as robotic libraries that automatically stage the device, per request; this may take some time, however). There are of course devices that are off-line (such as disk-on-key, also called a *memory stick*).

---

* Novell is an American company that was very successful during the last decades of the twentieth century. Its major success was related to the understanding that standalone PCs have to be connected. Novell developed a network operating system, which later was called NetWare. As of 2011 Novell is part of The Attachmate Group.

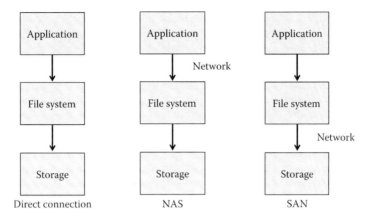

FIGURE 9.26   SAN–NAS comparison.

- *Disk's structure*: The mechanical disk (hard drive) usually contains one or more magnetic platters and a moving arm with reading/writing heads. The platter is divided into tracks and sectors.

- *Disk reading/writing speed*: This is determined by

  - The rotational speed

  - Seek time (the time required for the head to reach the required track)

  - Latency (the time required for the disk to rotate until the requested sector is under the reading/writing head)

- *SSD* (*solid-state disk*): A relatively new type of hard drive that has no moving parts and on which all data is stored electronically (as in memory or a disk-on-key).

- *Access algorithms*: These are various algorithms that are implemented by the operating system in order to optimize the disk access time. Some of these algorithms include

  - First come first served (FCFS)

  - Shortest time first (STF)

  - Scan

  - Circular scan (C-Scan)

  - C-Look

- *RAID* (*redundant array of inexpensive disks*): A technology that was intended to overcome some of the 1980s disks' limitations. The technology provides capabilities for creating virtual disks, which may include several physical disks, as well as for increasing reliability by providing various error-correction mechanisms.

- *SAN* (*storage attached network*): A local, usually high-speed network that is used for connecting a pool of storage resources so they will be available for many computing servers and workstations.

- *NAS* (*network attached storage*): A storage device that provides access for users that are connected to the network.

CHAPTER 10

Additional Architectures

ADDITIONAL ARCHITECTURES

This chapter focuses on additional developments related to computing architectures and the needs that led to these developments.

Despite rapid technological development and the increase in systems' performance, as defined by Moore's law, for example, current needs surpass the available solutions. For that reason, manufacturers as well as research and development organizations are constantly looking for new and innovative ideas to address these needs. Some of these developments were discussed in Chapter 4, "Central Processing Unit" as an example of instruction-level parallelism (ILP). Others relate to adding central processing units (CPUs, or cores), increasing the amount of memory, or to designing new memory hierarchies. In all these cases, the driving force was user needs for additional computer power.

Computer Classification

Before continuing to the definition of additional computer architectures, we have to define the current available ones. Unfortunately, there is no agreed-upon definition for classifying parallel systems. The Flynn* taxonomy, which was defined in 1966, can still be used as the basic ground rules. The taxonomy classifies a system by the stream that flows into it: data and instructions. Each one can be either a single stream or multiple streams. Thus, the taxonomy defines four possibilities:

- Single instruction, single data stream (SISD), which represents the old and ordinary computers based on the von Neumann architecture. Every instruction executed uses a single stream of data. There are, of course, instructions, such as the arithmetic ones that are executed using two operands, but these belong to the same stream (Figure 10.1).

- Single instruction, multiple data stream (SIMD), which represents a system with one control unit and several execution units (Figure 10.2). These models were implemented

---

* Michael J. Flynn is an American professor emeritus at Stanford University.

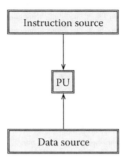

FIGURE 10.1   SISD-based architecture.

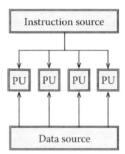

FIGURE 10.2   SIMD-based architecture.

in the past by a variety of manufacturers in an attempt to improve performance. In most cases, these used an array of connected processors working on the same instruction. When relating to the steps in instruction execution (see the "Processor" section in Chapter 3), then the control unit is responsible for the instruction fetch (IF) and the instruction decode (ID), and then it is transferred to all the available processing units. These processing units execute the same instruction; however, each processing unit executes it on a different input.

For example, assuming the instruction was

ADD R3, R4, R5

This means that the content of register number 4 will be added to the content of register number 5, and the sum will be placed in register number 3. All the processors will execute the same instruction; however, each one will be using its own registers.

One of the benefits of implementing this parallel method is the reduction in the amount of electronic circuits. In complex instruction set computer (CISC)-based systems, a large percentage of the electronic circuit was dedicated to the control unit. Using SIMD, in which only one control units handles all the arithmetic and logic units (ALUs, which are processing units) lowers this overhead.

One of the implementations of SIMD is vector computers, which were the main technology used during the last two decades of the twentieth century for building supercomputers. Currently, many of the modern CPUs implement some vector instructions, and this technology is most commonly used in video-game consoles and many of the high-end graphic controllers.

The vector computer was intended for fast calculations related to arrays (vectors) of data. These computers were aimed at the scientific community, in which many of the programs use mathematical transformations on large arrays and matrices of numbers. In computing terms, a vector is a one-dimensional array of the same type of data (integers, floating-point numbers, etc.). In the ordinary way, in order to access all the vector's elements, a loop will be required, which will address a different array item in each cycle. The vector computers had vector instructions that could do the calculations on the whole array. Of course, the compilers were adopted for using the new instructions. As far as programming is concerned, the array instructions in Excel 2010 (and beyond) resemble the old vector instructions. The most commonly used programming language for scientific applications at that time was formula translation (FORTRAN), which was developed by IBM and was intended for mathematical programming. For that reason, many of the instructions resemble mathematical notation. When the vector computers started to emerge, the FORTRAN compilers were modified to accommodate the new instructions.

For example, let us assume that A, B, and C are three vectors of equal length and we need to add every item in A to the appropriate item in B and place the sum in C. Or in other words, to perform

$$C[i] = A[i] + B[i] \text{ for every } i$$

The ordinary way is by using a loop over the items in A and B. However, when using the FORTRAN compiler that was modified for vectors, it required just one instruction:

$$C = A + B$$

Figure 10.3 depicts the schematic execution of the instruction in the vector computer.

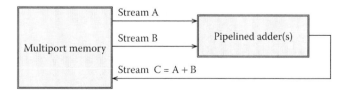

FIGURE 10.3   Addition in a vector computer.

The vector computers lost their leading role as the primary technology for high-speed computing systems, mainly due to their very high costs. The industry moved to parallel computing using many off-the-shelf systems. Nevertheless, the lessons learned helped improve the processor's pipeline, and some vector capabilities are still being implemented.

- Multiple instructions, single data stream (MISD), which is only a theoretical model (Figure 10.4). There were attempts to implement this model, especially in systems with a very high survivability, for example, in spacecraft. MISD means that several processors execute a similar program on similar data in order to make sure the results obtained are correct. In current high-reliability and high-survivability systems, this mode is not sufficient. In some of the implementations, for example, for in-flight computers, the system is based on different computers produced by different manufacturers. The computers run the same algorithm, but the programs were developed by different teams and use different programming languages.

- Multiple instructions, multiple data streams (MIMD) are the most widely used of the four types (Figure 10.5). These parallel systems are available in a variety of configurations, and some even utilize off-the-shelf components. The constant improvements in networking technologies followed by rapid developments in software development methodologies provide new ways of collaboration between remotely located systems and have contributed to further enhancing this model.

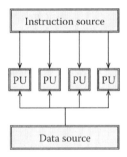

FIGURE 10.4   MISD-based architecture.

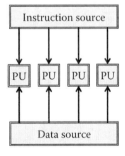

FIGURE 10.5   MIMD-based architecture.

Commercial implementations of systems with two or more processors have existed for several decades, and the von Neumann architecture was especially designed for multiple processors. However, in the early stages, the parallelism was at the system level. A parallel computer could run several applications in parallel, each application on a different processor. There was no simple and easy way of running an application on more than one processor.

The new developments in the MIMD technology are implemented in all the currently available computer systems, and PCs implement parallelism in the multiple cores that exist in most modern systems. Furthermore, new trends in software development that utilize thread programming allow a better utilization of the cores, even for the single application.

Most of the currently available computer systems are MIMD, which is characterized by a system that includes several processors, each one working on different applications. Utilizing threads, the system can run a single application so it uses more than one processor. As in many cases related to the computing industry, various configurations were developed over the years, for example, systems with a common shared memory that is accessible by all processors, or, alternatively, configurations in which each processor has its own memory. There are, of course, many variations on each type, including buses that are used for connecting the processors (see the section in Chapter 7 on "Extending the Bus Concept"), as depicted in Figures 10.6 and 10.7.

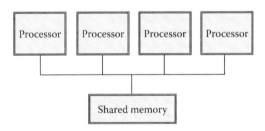

FIGURE 10.6   Shared memory architecture.

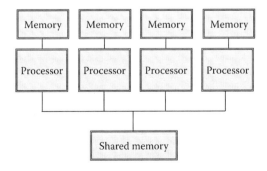

FIGURE 10.7   Another shared memory architecture.

In general, as was described in Chapter 7, "Bus," such an implementation of buses utilizes several logical buses. One control bus controls and coordinates the communication between the processors, so it will not disturb the higher priority transfers. The disadvantage of this implementation is that in such architectures, the bus can become a bottleneck, especially if the number of processors connected is increasing. In architectures with a very large number of processors (hundreds or thousands), this method is inefficient. Additional ideas were suggested in order to extend the model to a large number of processors, although the common method is to use a distributed memory (see the section in Chapter 7 on "Extending the Bus Concept"). In this implementation, each processor has its own memory, and there is no shared memory. Sharing is done by sending the data from one processor to the other. This, of course, increases the data transfers on the bus; to improve performance, the bus itself has to be modified (Figure 10.8). As can be seen, as long as the number of processors increases, the standard linear bus has to be extended and enhanced. During the course of development, some attention was paid to survivability as well. The simple linear bus provides a good solution if the number of connected devices is small. However, if there is a physical problem that splits the bus into two different sections, the system cannot work properly. The solution is to implement a circular bus, and in this case, a single physical problem will degrade the performance but will not stop the system.

The solutions described can be divided into two types. One is a complete solution that provides communication between any two devices, as with full connectivity; however, this involves a network of buses that, although it provides the best performance with minimal delays, is associated with extra costs, which, in many cases, cannot be justified. This is similar to the method used in the early days of computing for connecting peripheral devices (see the beginning of Chapter 7). Another type of connectivity, described in Figure 10.8, is an indirect communication. In all types

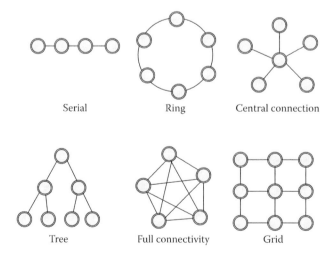

FIGURE 10.8   Connectivity types.

(linear, ring, central communication, grid, and tree), the data may need to transfer through several stations before it gets to its destination. The number of stations on the way and the associated delay depend on the specific type of implementation. For example, for a system that uses a hierarchy of processors, the tree communication may provide a good solution. The solutions described are usually relevant for large and expensive systems in which the configuration is tailored to specific needs. The modern approach is that the system should use off-the-shelf components and should be cheap; and it should not be a tailor-made solution that solves only a specific need that might later change. For simplifying the problems associated with these configurations as well as the number of stations through which the data has to pass, some mechanisms were designed for optimal data transfers.

Figure 10.9 elaborates on a similar one (Figure 7.28) in Chapter 7, "Bus." The numbers associated with adjacent nodes are different by one bit. This provides the means for a simple algorithm to calculate the difference, or the number of stations on the optimal route. The method can be extended to larger numbers of nodes as a hypercube (Figure 10.10), as was the case with the Cray computers, which used a torus-based hypercube (Figure 7.26).

The Cray computers used a hybrid memory in which there was a large shared memory, and each one of the processors had its own memory (Figure 10.11). This

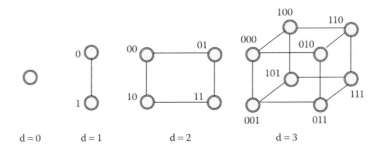

FIGURE 10.9　Nodes in the network.

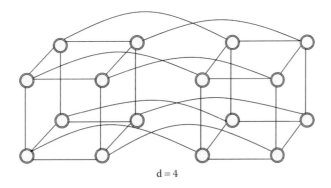

FIGURE 10.10　Hypercube.

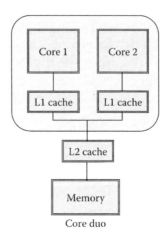

Core duo

FIGURE 10.11   PC memory configurations.

is very similar to the memory hierarchy used today, which divides the memory into several levels: registers, cache memory (usually implemented using several levels), main memory, and disks. This implementation is based and relies on the previous supercomputer architectures.

As in other cases, this approach that once was relevant just for large and very expensive systems paved the way for the architectures currently used in off-the-shelf systems. Even if it is not called a shared memory, each one of the processors accesses the memory and in addition, to enhance performance (Figure 10.7), each system has its own cache, which is very similar to the J90 system by Cray (see Figure 7.24).

The PCs that have been sold in recent years have adopted a very similar architecture, in which several cores share a common memory.

All have implemented some hierarchy in which at least two levels of cache memory are present. The configuration depicted in Figure 10.11 uses only one cache level on the processor chip and an additional external one, while the configuration depicted in Figure 10.12 has two levels of cache on the chip; the third level is connected via a bus. The third level and the memory are shared by all cores.

The difference in the implementation affects the performance that can be achieved and the cost associated with each one. The doubts of the 1990s about the best way to configure the system—to provide the required performance, on the one hand, and on the other to be cost-effective—are still relevant, even currently. While modern computers usually implement three levels of cache, the thinking about how many levels should be on the chip and how many levels should be considered shared memory is still relevant. For that reason, in addition to the configurations depicted in Figures 10.11 and 10.12, additional configurations are implemented by Intel or AMD (Intel's competitor) as described in Figures 10.13 and 10.14.

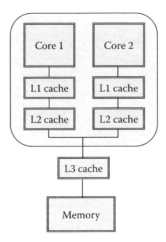

FIGURE 10.12   Two cache levels on chip.

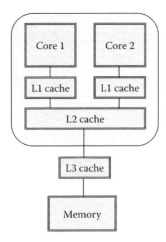

FIGURE 10.13   Common L2 cache.

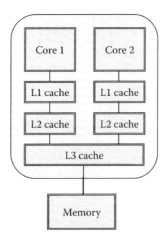

FIGURE 10.14   Common L3 cache on chip.

Grid Computing

As already stated, the increased demand for computing power led to a variety of solutions. Some of these solutions were discussed as part of the developments related to CPU technologies (ILP, additional cores and processors, memory hierarchy, etc.). Others took a different approach based on the assumption that the wide area networks are constantly improving and are no longer a bottleneck.

Grid computing is a method that connects computing resources that are available as part of the network in order to form a large virtual computer. This virtual computer can be assigned a task, which usually cannot be solved using the currently available resources. The idea was developed based on many of the services provided by modern society, such as banks, the post office, repair centers, and so on. All these operations have to deal with an unknown amount of work (customers), and the common way to handle the workload is by using several resources working in parallel and providing the service. Grid computing, which is basically a distributed environment, uses many systems as computing resources. The workload is broken into manageable chunks. Each chunk (a defined piece of work) is sent to a different system, and at the end all the results are merged into the result set (Figure 10.15).

A very famous example of the use of grid technology is the SETI@home* project. In addition to the scientific importance of the project in trying to locate extraterrestrial intelligence, the project proved the feasibility of such a virtual system. Since then, additional initiatives have been developed for using a similar idea and building a virtual system that uses idle cycles at users' computers around the world. Most people in modern society have a computer, and in some cases even more than one. In most cases, these systems' resources are underutilized. Even if someone uses his or her system extensively, the system is idle when the person is involved with other activities or is asleep. A solution that combines many of these systems into a virtual system produces capabilities that are significantly higher that any of the currently available solutions. Furthermore, this virtual system is very cheap (incurring no real costs besides the software development).

To implement the solution, the software components had to be developed. The server side had to be capable of handling a large number of systems as well as the layer that divides the data to be analyzed into different segments. Each segment is sent to a different PC, and then the results are combined. In this case, the system can be viewed as a cluster of distributed computers working in parallel. Such a system can be defined using organizational computers or computers at university laboratories and even computers that are spread out and connected by the Internet networks, as in the case of SETI.

---

* Search for Extraterrestrial Intelligence (SETI) is a project carried out by the University of California that looks for patterns that can be associated with extraterrestrial intelligence. The project consists of radio-telescope sensors that collect signals from outer space and a software package that analyzes the signals. When the project started, the computing resources required were several orders of magnitude of the largest available systems. The idea that was implemented was to use many personal computers that are spread over the world. The implementation took several years, and in 1999, the first version was ready. Users all over the world downloaded the software, which runs on their computer, but only when the computer is idle. The software connects to the main server and gets a file of signals to be processed. The number of active users who were involved in the project through the donation of their computers varied over the years, but the average performance has been estimated at several hundred terraflops.

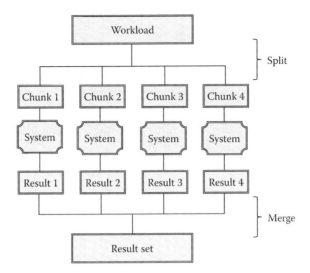

FIGURE 10.15 The grid concept.

Despite its potential, the technology was not successful beyond scientific applications due to some difficulties in its implementation. Dividing the application and distributing the parts to different systems, without the explicit involvement of a developer, is not a trivial matter. To use the variety of resources freely available, without manual intervention, a standard has to be developed, as is the case in many other service-oriented markets.

Service-Oriented Architecture

Service-oriented architecture is mainly a collection of services that run on different computers and provide services that are available for other applications. The services are applications that can connect with each other and transmit data and information. The idea behind this architecture is not new (e.g., see the section in Chapter 1 on "Terminal Services," which discusses client/server architecture). To define an architecture that provides services in an efficient way, the term *service* has to be defined. Service in a computing context is a specific and well-defined function that is not dependent on the situation or on other services.

Developments in the definition of a service-based system are no different than developments in other fields that are not related to computers. In fact, modern society is heavily based on services. If someone has to travel from one place to another, it is possible to drive by car. Sometimes, people prefer to use public transportation; this happens when the person does not own a car, or if public transportation provides a better, faster, or cheaper solution. If the destination is very far, sometimes there is no alternative, and the only solution will be public transportation; to go by airplane, for example. In this case, public transportation provides some kind of service. Even purchasing a product is a service provided by the store (physical or digital) for some fee. Prehistoric humans used only tools they created or food they grew or captured. However, one of the attributes of modern society is the variety of services we use in almost every area, from basic services such as water and electricity to knowledge workers who provide services based on their knowledge and experience, such as lawyers, physicians, accountants, and so on.

Many of these services were developed in order to satisfy a need. Usually, the person who seeks a service cannot provide it for himself or herself due to lack of the required expertise; or he or she seeks it because the service provides a more cost-effective solution. Another typical example is the increase in the consumption of ready-made food. In some cases, this is because the consumer does not know how to cook, or maybe the ready-made food tastes better. In addition, sometimes this is a free choice because the customer prefers to use the time required for cooking for other better, more enjoyable, or more profitable activities.

To develop a service-oriented market, several conditions have to exist:

- A standard interface has to be defined. If the service is purchasing goods, the interface is the store where the transaction can be performed. If the service is a doctor's consultation, the interface is defined by the meeting with the physician. In purchasing infrastructure services, the interface is much simpler. One can purchase electricity from the electricity supplier only after connecting to the electric grid using one of the agreed-upon electric plugs.

- The service has to be provided as a package deal. If, each time a person opened the faucet at home and used water, there was a need to contact the local municipality, ask for a quote, sign a contract, and so on, probably other more simple solutions would have emerged.

- The service should always be available (based on the type of service). For example, water, electricity, or communications (phone, Internet) are expected to provide a 24/7 service. Garbage collection or mail delivery can be performed periodically on an agreed-upon basis. Other services are provided based on specific norms. Some services are delivered during working hours; however, some other (e.g., emergency) services should always be ready and available.

- The service has to be easy to use. Purchasing electricity or water is very simple (turning on the switch or opening the faucet). To purchase other goods, one has to get to the store, talk to the service provider or a sales assistant, pay, and get the product. If it is a purchase over the Internet, it requires browsing the online store, selecting the product, and paying, and the product will be delivered in a couple of days according to the sales terms. In using a public transportation service, one has to wait for the bus, taxi, or train; and, when it gets to the station, one must board, pay (either by using money, a smart card, or the phone), and enjoy the ride. There are cases in which the customer pays for the service in advance; for example, for flights and most train rides as well as some cellular services (prepaid), and so on.

- In many cases, the service is not directly connected to the users' surroundings. It is possible that the service is enjoyed at the customer's premises but was created or manufactured somewhere else. For example, one may use electricity at home, but the electricity was produced at a power plant somewhere. Alternatively, we enjoy TV broadcasts at home or using our smartphone while on the move, but these broadcasts were created somewhere else.

- The service can include several other services as well. For example, on some toll roads, when a car stops due to a problem, sometimes the road service people provide help as a free additional service. Public health services in some countries are performed in clinics, which sometimes include laboratories and a pharmacy in addition to the examining room.

- In a service-based system, although the service provided is important, in many cases the way the service is provided is even more important. When one rents a car, it is obvious the car is operational. However, there are additional very relevant and important issues, such as the size of the car, the cost, the quality of the service, and so on. The question about how the service is provided depends on the service itself. If it is a competitive service, price may be an important factor. In other cases, the quality may be important or even the speed. For example, when sending a parcel to a different country, one can use the services of the post office. In most cases, these services will be cheaper compared with other alternatives. However, if the parcel is an important one, or contains documents that have to reach their destination on time, then the customer may choose to use an international delivery company that charges more but is responsible for delivering on time.

If we want to develop a computerized system that will deliver a service, several preliminary activities have to be established. First, the interface between the customer and the provider has to be clearly defined. This is identical to client/server architecture, in which a standard protocol is defined prior to the service delivery. The customer sends a request, which may be some declaration of intention or a definition of a need. In the next stage, the provider submits a proposal and, after the terms are finalized, the service provision can start. For example, let us assume that a person wants to register with a cellular communication company. The person addresses one or more suppliers and defines the need. The suppliers' representative suggests the most appropriate package; after the terms have been agreed upon and, as in most cases, the customer has provided a credit-card number for future billing, the service provision starts. The service in this sense is to use the cellular network by calling, receiving calls, and benefiting from all the other capabilities the network provides. The service is provided automatically.

There are cases in which, as part of the negotiations toward the service provision, an additional mechanism is required to find the relevant service providers. For example, say a customer is looking for a lawyer in a specific area or a doctor that specializes in a specific field. In such cases, the customer has to use some directory, such as the yellow pages, for example.

Similar service-oriented environments were developed for computer-based systems. These systems are not new, and parts of the technology appeared as network computers (see the section in Chapter 1 on "Computing Attributes") and terminal services (see the section in Chapter 1 on "Terminal Services"). What was needed was an additional layer for web services.

Web Services

The term *web services* refers to a computing infrastructure that integrates Internet-based applications. Such an infrastructure supports easy sharing of information—for example, between organizations and their suppliers and/or customers—without the need to specifically define the communication protocol. Unlike client/server technology, web services are intended for communication between applications and not for the end user, and for that reason they include only a general user interface (see the section in Chapter 1 on "Client/ Server"). While using standard components, web services are used to integrate applications that run on a variety of operating systems, use various different databases, and were written using a variety of programming languages. For these reasons, web services easily integrate third-party products as well.

Web services are currently being used by many applications, and a growing number of companies are offering application programming interfaces (APIs) for applications to seamlessly connect and use their services. The main idea, of course, leads to the development of new innovative solutions to attract more buying users, or even just to create more traffic. For example, Google provides an API to its map services so that an application that needs to integrate some geographic information systems (GIS) can use the API to draw the appropriate map and include the appropriate route. Another example is sites that provide price comparisons for a variety of products and services. Such applications usually use web-services APIs to connect to the many online stores and service providers, retrieve the relevant information (products, description, prices, etc.), and display the aggregated information. The innovation is not the data, which is publicly available, or the fact that it was obtained from the different sites, but it is the added services, such as the comparisons between the products or services, a better user experience, and so on.

Developments using web services, the large availability of solutions and tools, and worldwide connectivity provided all the necessary ingredients for marketing professionals to come up with the idea of software as a service. The underlying assumption is that all the requirements for a service (see the section in this chapter on "Service-Oriented Architecture") have been fulfilled. The new model is intended to provide significant organizational benefits in a competitive and constantly changing environment.

FIGURE 10.16 Software as a service.

The new computing architecture (service-oriented architecture [SOA]) is a natural development of the previous architecture, which utilizes technological developments (Figure 10.16).

Cloud Computing

*Cloud computing i*s a term that appeared in the last decade; in a relatively short period, it became an important issue that changed some basic computing principles, and it will change computing further. The main problem associated with the term cloud computing is that many use it but understand it in different way (just like the term *Internet*). Some customers and service providers define cloud computing as an extension to organizational computing facilities, providing additional virtual servers located anywhere. Others regard cloud computing as computing services provided for the organization by others (nonorganizational personnel) using systems located in the Internet cloud somewhere.

The most important issue, and the significant benefits introduced by cloud computing, come through the understanding of the computer center manager. Such a manager, who is sometimes referred to as the chief information officer (CIO) due to his or her role in managing the organizational information and providing the tools and services required by the organization's personnel, usually uses a very large budget. However, despite this extensive spending, there are cases in which a significant increase in computing resources is needed. Sometimes, this requirement is only temporary and for a very limited duration. Unfortunately, the CIO cannot cater to this need without spending additional funds on additional hardware resources, probably more licenses for software, and sometimes the additional training that is needed. In other words, the current computing model is very rigid and does not provide the flexibility required by the rapidly changing modern business environment. Cloud computing is intended to provide a more flexible environment, for example, by enhancing the provided capabilities, even temporarily followed by a pricing model of payment only for use. The economic benefits associated with cloud computing have attracted many new players into the market, and among the many companies that provide cloud infrastructure, there are many companies that are new in the computing industry. In a sense, this is a normal behavior of the market, as was seen already in the past. When a large technological shift occurs, several of the old organizations were slow to react and their offerings were replaced by other more competitive solutions. Most of the large computer companies of the 1970s have disappeared; or, like IBM, which then accounted for most of the market, have changed their offerings and services. The new wave of solutions in the 1980s, which included mini computers, created business opportunities for new computer companies. Unfortunately, in the 1990s, most of these systems were replaced by reduced instruction set computer (RISC)-based machines. Once again, the market was dominated by additional new companies. The next stage was the PC era, during which new companies emerged and replaced some of the older players. The latest development, cloud computing, is no different. Some of the existing infrastructure suppliers will have to adopt it, or their solution will no longer be used, paving the way for new companies and new offerings.

Cloud computing is a term that defines the provision of computing services through the Internet. This concept has three major attributes that are significantly different from current computing configurations:

- The service is provided on demand and is charged by usage. Contrary to the budgets spent by computer departments on hardware and software without a direct relation to real usage, cloud computing holds the potential for a better price/performance ratio.

- The service volume is fully flexible, and the client can define the amount of resources required for processing. This is an additional benefit, since current organizational computing departments cannot provide more resources than those physically available.

- The provider is responsible for managing the operations. The customer is not involved in any of the management issues, and all that is needed on the client's side is a workstation (usually a PC) and an Internet connection. As far as the CIO is concerned, these management responsibilities can be translated into large savings, since most of the site's personnel who are responsible for the systems' operations, including backups and restore activities, monitoring, and technical help desk, become partially redundant. These human resources, some very experienced, account for a large portion of the IT budget.

New developments related to virtualization (this will be elaborated on in the following section) and distributed processing, combined with faster networks, simplify the construction of the required infrastructure for the service. On the other hand, the global economic situation, which limits organizational ability and the willingness to spend large amounts on enhancing infrastructure, has fueled the move to the new technology. The cloud can be implemented as a private or public cloud. A private cloud is based on a private computer center and a virtual private network* that provides services to designated groups of customers. A public cloud, such as Amazon or Google, sells its service to everyone that is interested. The private cloud can use a public network to define a virtual private cloud.†

Regardless of the type of cloud (private or public), its main use is to provide easy and on-demand access to a flexible pool of resources and computing services. The cloud-computing model is based on other, non-computing-related services, such as electricity or telephone. All that is required is that the user turn on the electric switch or dial a number, and the service provision starts automatically. With cloud computing, the service provision is very similar. The user starts an application that may reside on a local server and uses services provided by other servers in the cloud. Or alternatively the user starts an application which is provided as a service and executed somewhere, which resembles using Google's search engine.

---

* A virtual private network is a logical extension to the private network. Instead of using a "real" private network that is extremely expensive, a site can choose to use the public network as part of its "private" network. The data sent uses the public network, but to prevent the use of unauthorized users, several technologies are used for security and management, such as point-to-point or tunneling; these provide a secure tunnel for data transfers between two points on the network.

† A virtual private cloud is a cloud, with all its pool of shared resources, which dedicates some part of those resources to a specific request. The dedicated part is isolated from the other resources, preventing public users from accessing the dedicated resources.

Cloud-computing services can be divided into three typical types of solutions, each one representing a different functionality:

- Infrastructure as a service (IaaS), which provides access to a virtual server. This service allocates a designated number of processors and storage areas required for a specific task. The system provides a set of basic tools for defining the proper configuration required as well as loading the programs and the files needed for the run. These tools are very similar to tools available at the local environment for running the application.

- Platform as a service (PaaS), which provides an additional functionality over IaaS. PaaS provides not only the infrastructure but also the required environment, for example, for development. This is a complete environment on which the customer can run all its operations, and it is provided as an alternative to the local computing infrastructure. For example, if an organization that uses a local server anticipates a significant increase in the number of entries to its organizational portal, there is very little it can do. On the other hand, if the organization is using cloud computing, all that will be required is to increase the usage of the pool resources during these peak times.

- Software as a service (SaaS) is a total solution in which the vendor is responsible for the whole solution, including hardware, software, communication, and especially the management. The customer gets access to a simple portal to define the attributes of the required services.

A very famous example of using cloud computing relates to the diaries kept by Hillary Clinton during the time she was first lady (1993–2001). There were many requests by journalists asking that the diaries be made public, quoting the Freedom of Information Act. On March 19, 2008, the documents became public. There were a total of 17,481 scanned pages. Peter Harkins, who worked for the *Washington Post*, realized the potential of the documents; however, he also understood that in their initial form, finding meaningful information would take too much time. Peter started looking for technological tools such as optical character recognition (OCR) to help transform the images into a searchable version. Preliminary tests revealed that it would take about 30 min to process a single page. The main aim in this case was to provide a solution that not only would be usable but also would be available as early as possible (or at least before any of the competitor journals). However, using a single processor for the task would require one year! Due to the importance of the documents, and as part of the race against time and against other journals, Peter decided to use cloud computing. He uploaded the files to the Amazon cloud and selected a virtual system with 200 processors working in parallel. Nine hours later, the images had been transformed into searchable files, and 26 hours later, a site with the documents, including search capabilities, was put in place. The bill for the transformation was $144, but regardless of the price, this experiment demonstrates some of the capabilities of cloud computing that had not been possible with earlier technologies.

The forces behind moving the organizational infrastructures to cloud computing are driven by upper management, who understand the economic implications. In many cases, IT departments object to the move, since it threatens their own existence. With or without the support of IT departments, the better solutions provided by cloud computing have already transformed many businesses, and many others will follow. The trend of using more services from external professional bodies that are experts in their fields will continue, and it will affect computing activities as well. For example, there is no need for an organization to have a legal department, unless their business really requires it. For that reason, many organizations have contacted specialized firms that provide the required service on demand. This trend, especially due to its additional benefits, will affect IT departments as well.

Figure 10.17 depicts a standard system with its resources usage over a typical working day. The dotted line defines the total resources available (or the maximum the system can provide). During normal operations, the demand for these resources varies, but it will never cross the dotted line, since the system will not be able to provide resources beyond those it has. On the other hand, there are times when these resources are waiting idle, since there is no demand for them.

Figure 10.18 refers to the resources available and used in a cloud computing–based system. It can be seen that the availability is very close to the real demand, and there is no waste (resources purchased but not being used). The difference between the required and available resources in both cases depends on many factors. For example, interactive systems that have to provide online services to customers tend to have larger spare margins to accommodate unforeseen loads. Nevertheless, the extra resources that are purchased and seldom used may have significant economic implications with no real benefits.

For dealing with the reduced budgets imposed on some organizations, the IT department may decide to configure the system so it will be over utilized. The resources available will not be sufficient for handing the peak activities, as shown in Figure 10.19.

This overutilization implies that there will be times when the system will not be able to cope with the workload, and some tasks will have to be delayed. If the main users who use the system are internal employees, this means that their productivity will decrease,

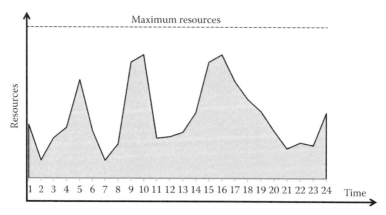

FIGURE 10.17   Resources usage (standard system).

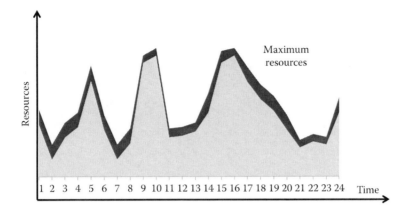

FIGURE 10.18   Resources usage (cloud computing).

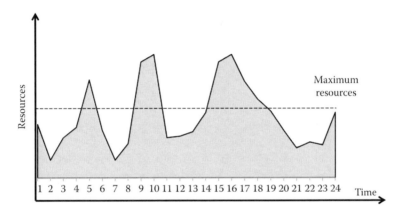

FIGURE 10.19   Underutilization.

which has its own costs. This, of course, contradicts the main idea behind using computers, which stems from the need to increase users' productivity. On the other hand, if the main users are external customers, then these service limitations may have severe disadvantages that may lead to negative consequences. In the open world of the Internet, where every product or service has many alternatives, bad service may persuade the customer or the potential customer to look elsewhere. All that is required is to click on the "back" button. Overutilization can cause loss of revenue (Figure 10.20). All the requested resources that are above the dotted line are requests that cannot be fulfilled, or else the required costs for granting them are too high. In such cases, the requests for resources above the maximum may translate into revenue loss. The net result will be that the benefits of overutilization may turn into a loss that is significantly larger than the savings.

Unfortunately, revenue loss does not represent the end of the problem. When the resources are not sufficient, the work is delayed and products are delivered late, which may affect the relationship with the customer. The loss of customer goodwill is not always easy to measure.

If the problem continues, it is not just the customers' goodwill that is at issue; some of these customers may decide to look for alternate solutions. This trend will continue as

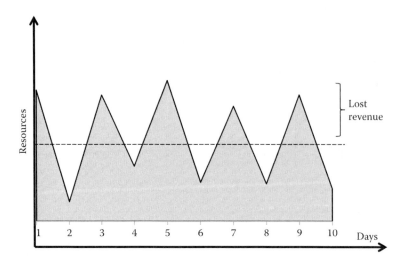

FIGURE 10.20   Loss of revenue.

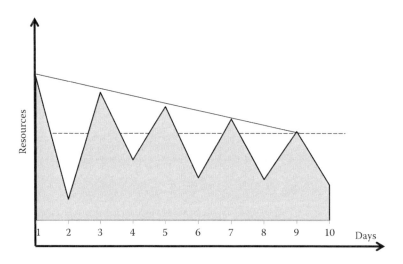

FIGURE 10.21   Customer loss.

long as the system is overutilized. If the number of customers or orders drops, the number of transactions will drop as well, until the system stops being overutilized. For example, consider an online store that sells various products to its customers. If the site is very slow, or does not respond at all, the average customer will not wait too long and will look for a different store. This will continue until the number of customers decreases to a point where the system will be able to handle all requests, and it is no longer overutilized (Figure 10.21). For better accuracy, however, it should be noted that the purchasing decision is usually not based only on the site's speed but on other considerations as well.

Virtualization

Virtualization is a term that defines a higher level of abstraction. The term *abstraction* is used in the computing industry at several levels. At the level of the various peripherals (input–output [I/O] devices), the operating system provides abstraction by using the required virtual layer, which hides the specific device and its attributes from the application or the developer. The modular approach, in which the application is responsible for its level (accessing files) and the operating system is responsible for its level (managing the physical devices), ensures that the application will continue running even if the specific device is replaced. Another level of abstraction is achieved by the device driver, which bridges the standard I/O interface and the actual device (see the section in Chapter 8 on "Methods for Performing I/O"). Even the virtual memory mechanism is an additional level of abstraction. Virtualization is a higher level of abstraction that intends to hide the whole specific system and its physical attributes from the application or the developer.

Most computers (desktops, laptops) are based on ×86 architecture, which was developed by Intel in the early 1980s. In recent years, the 64-bit systems that are based on the Intel 64 architecture have gained popularity. Originally, the ×86 architecture was intended for an operating system that runs just one program (see the section in Chapter 1 on "Personal Computers"). It was only later that the hardware was modified to allow several processes to be executed in parallel. There were additional changes introduced to the operating system as well (such as the appearance of Windows). Despite all of the improvements intended to enhance systems' performance, some of the resources remained idle (this led to the development of infrastructures for using idle resources, such as SETI@home; see the section in this chapter on "Grid Computing").

Virtualization takes this abstraction one level further, and it provides the means to run several virtual systems on one physical computer. Each such virtual system shares the resources with the other operating systems. Every virtual machine can run a variety of operating systems as well as several processes in parallel. It should be noted that for quite some time, there were tools that supported the running of two operating systems on the same physical computer. However, these tools required that the operating system be defined at boot time and would not be changed until the next boot, and, when the computer ran, it used just one of the operating systems. Virtualization is different, since it allows the running of several operating systems in parallel while sharing the resources.

Figure 10.22 depicts an "ordinary" computer that runs one operating system and just one program/application. Most of computers are intended to execute several applications in

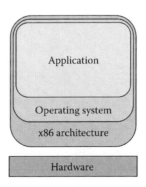

FIGURE 10.22   A physical system.

parallel, especially due to developments introduced into the operating system (as described in Chapter 1, "Introduction and Historic Perspective"). However, in many computing centers, and due to the division of applications to different servers, a different trend is taking place. Since most computer centers provide a large range of services, some of which are interactive, the response time becomes an important factor of the service quality. Among the various services, one can see print services, fax services, storage services, e-mail, Internet access, database services, data mining services, and many more. In an attempt to provide better response times, especially due to the decreasing costs of PCs (which, in many cases, are used as the server running the service), the applications are divided, and each one runs on a different machine. Consequently, large organizations have installed large server farms. The management of such farms, as well as the resources shared among them, becomes a very complex issue. An additional factor to be considered is the amount of electric power consumed by the center, which includes that used by the systems as well as the required air conditioning.

In a virtualization project that was performed in the research laboratories at Los Alamos, one million dollars per year were saved. The computer center had 300 servers, each one with one or two CPUs. After virtualization, the number of servers went down to 13. Each server was an AMD computer with four CPUs, and each CPU had two cores. In addition, each server was equipped with 32 GB of memory. The servers ran 210 virtual systems with an average utilization of 50%. Over 100 servers were decommissioned as well as three computing centers that were no longer needed. The return on investment was very fast, and just 9 months after the virtualization project started, the organization broke even.

Figure 10.23 depicts a physical system that, by using virtualization, became three logical (virtual) systems.

To provide a similar base for comparing the two (Figures 10.22 and 10.23), each virtual system in Figure 10.23 runs only one application. All three virtual systems are executed

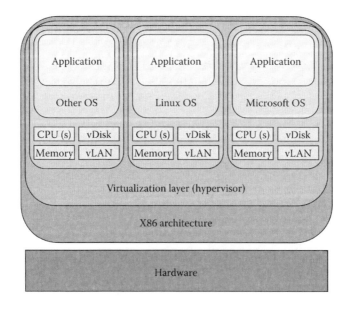

FIGURE 10.23   Virtualization.

on the same physical machine, but each one has its own virtual resources. These resources include the processor, memory, and I/O devices. It should be noted that although the systems share the resources, there is a complete separation, and one system does not know there is another system on the same physical machine.

The virtualization is implemented using a new software layer (hypervisor), which resides just above the hardware. The hypervisor is responsible for providing each operating system that runs above it with the feeling that it is running directly on the hardware. There are, of course, many variations of the hypervisor that were developed by different companies, and each one tries to improve its functionality. This layer mimics the hardware and should be 100% compatible so the operating systems can run above it without any changes. The operating system is identical to the one running on a standalone physical machine.

There are many benefits associated with virtualizations, starting with the possibility of decreasing the number of servers in the organizations (as was the case with the Los Alamos laboratories). This decrease has an immediate impact on the cost associated with the operations as well as the costs that will be required for future upgrades. In the modern era, which is characterized by the green revolution, decreasing the number of servers lowers the electric bill and supports the move to a greener environment. Additional sophisticated capabilities of migrating virtual systems from one physical system to the other improves efficiency, availability, reliability, and error recoverability.

The fact that the virtual system is actually software provides additional capabilities, as software is more flexible than hardware systems. The virtual system is saved in a container, which makes it easy to move it to a different physical system. Such a move is done transparently, and the connected users are not aware of the fact that their applications or services are being run on a different physical system.

The computer usage is provided at a high abstraction, which, for the user, is not directly linked to a specific physical system. It is similar to receiving communication services from a phone company, without knowing (or caring) which types of switches or other connectivity equipment are involved in the process. This knowledge is important at the infrastructure level and for maintaining a high level of reliability and survivability. In case of malfunction, the application, including its operating system, can be migrated to a different physical machine. These transfers can be initiated to obtain a more balanced workload, which may lead to a better response time. The most important development based on virtualization is cloud computing. Since virtualization provides the means to define a virtual system that is based on as many as needed physical systems and in addition it provides automatic migration of applications between these virtual systems, it is used as the cloud computing infrastructure.

As with many other developments in our modern society, the driving force is economic. Although various attempts to develop virtualization using proprietary systems were made decades ago (e.g., by IBM), the real push forward was made by implementing the idea in the PC environment. There are no real accurate or reliable statistics regarding the servers' resources usage percentage; however, the assumption is that the percentage is very low. For that reason, a virtualization mechanism that provides the capability of running additional environments on the same physical system provides significant economic benefits.

However, in the modern world, which is constantly changing, virtualization provides an additional important benefit—the flexibility to launch new services and the immediate possibility of doing so. In a world without virtualization, launching a new service requires purchase and installation (or at least to utilize existing) hardware, software installation, and integration; only then can it start providing the service. In a virtualization world, the activation is immediate. This fast response time to various market changes has improved organizations' ability to react and seize various opportunities.

Virtualization is one of the main technologies that provide large organizations, such as Amazon or Google, with the ability to support their user communities while providing a fast response time. Such organizations experience unpredictable workloads and still have to maintain a reasonable level of response time. The amount of computers employed by these companies is so large that they are capable of providing cloud computing services for external uses as well. Like many other cyclic trends in the computing industry, cloud-computing technology resembles the service bureaus that were common in the early days of computing. Such a service bureau provided computing services for organizations that could not afford to buy a computer. The service bureau was usually run by the computers' manufacturers, who shared some of their computing resources. Similarly, some of the large current cloud computer service providers are organizations who use large farms for their own purposes and, in parallel, sell their services.

Key Takeaway

- *Computer classification*: Based on Flynn's taxonomy, there are several computer classifications:

  - Single instruction, single data (SISD)

  - Single instruction, multiple data (SIMD)

  - Multiple instruction, single data (MISD)

  - Multiple instruction, multiple data (MIMD)

- *Grid computing*: A method that connects computing resources that are available as part of the network in order to form a large virtual computer.

- *Service-oriented architecture (SOA)*: Refers to a collection of services that run on different computers, which are available for other computers. The services are applications that can connect with each other and transmit data and information.

- *Web services*: Refers to a computing infrastructure that integrates Internet-based applications. Such an infrastructure supports easy sharing of information without the need to specifically define the communication protocol.

- *Cloud computing*: A technology that appeared in the last decade and, in a relatively short period of time, became an important issue that changed some basic computing principles. Cloud computing is designed to provide three main services:

  - Infrastructure as a service (IaaS), which provides access to a virtual server

  - Platform as a service (PaaS), which provides an additional functionality over IaaS, such as the required environment

  - Software as a service (SaaS), a total solution in which the vendor is responsible for the whole solution, including hardware, software, communication, and especially the management.

- *Virtualization*: A term that defines a higher level of abstraction. Virtualization provides the means to run several virtual systems on one physical computer. Each such virtual system shares the resources with the other operating systems. Every virtual machine can run a variety of operating systems as well as several processes in parallel.

CHAPTER 11

Software Architectures

SOFTWARE ARCHITECTURES

This chapter focuses on software architectures, which are used by solution designers to define and plan effective and high-quality software-based solutions using a variety of platforms, both hardware and software. The chapter will elaborate on architecture development over time and the principles behind this development. However, the architectures defined and explained represent an outline for the solution and not a detailed blueprint.

The fast and frequent developments related to hardware that have been described in the previous chapters of this book have just one purpose: to provide a better platform for developers so that more advanced solutions can be tailored, either in response to users' requests or by defining brand-new technologies for enhancing activities, processes, and society as a whole.

Software Architecture

The software architecture of an application or computer-based system is a diagram that depicts the main system's components and their mutual interactions. As computer systems evolved and became more complex, a systematic approach to software development had to be used. This led to a long trail of developments related to software engineering, some of which will be addressed in this chapter.

Software architecture, unlike hardware architecture, can be regarded as a blueprint for the system to be developed. As such, it also provides a checklist of activities to be performed as part of the development. Such an architecture can detail some of the deliverables to be produced during the development, deliverables that are required for the proper functioning of the system. As such, a system's architecture can be viewed as a structured organization of components required for the proper operation of the system. In addition to the components, the architecture depicts their interconnections and sometimes even puts constraints on their integration. While originally, software architecture was intended mainly to define the software components, such architectures are currently used for addressing additional nonfunctional* requirements such as security, performance, scalability, and so on. These and other nonfunctional requirements are sometimes even more critical than the functional requirements and, as such, have to be considered in the early stages of the design.

The software architecture depends on the requirements elicitation, which takes place[†] during the system's analysis phase, and it is intended to provide a solid infrastructure for the software to be developed. Furthermore, with the advancements in software development methodologies, similar advancements have been required in software architecture designs to accommodate new capabilities. While in the past, the architecture was designed mainly to support a smooth operation (functional as well as nonfunctional requirements), new designs address the development process as well, with a greater emphasis on changeability and maintainability.

The importance of the system's architecture is derived from the benefits it provides. As the systems become more complex, the architecture provides a simpler mechanism of communication between the various parties involved. It enables a discussion without the need to dive into technical terms and issues, which sometimes are not too clear to users. It is produced during the conceptual phase so it can be free from specific solutions and provides just an overview of the solution. In addition, each architecture type has some inherent benefits and limitations, which can be addressed fairly early in the process. For example, a system that requires a high degree of security may be better implemented using a single architecture.

In addressing software architectural trends, we may relate to several important stages that followed the hardware technological developments: the prearchitectural era, client/server, component-based architecture, layered architecture, tier architecture, object-oriented architecture, and service-oriented architecture. Despite the many names, there is some degree of overlap between these architectures.

Prearchitectural Era

The first computers, developed during the first half of the twentieth century, were aimed mainly at scientific computing, and software development was in its infancy. The main concern was to get the program to run and to produce the required results. There was no real thinking about architecture, as the hardware was limited and did not provide too many features for different designs (see the sections in Chapter 1 on "The First Computers," "Attributes of the First Computers," and "1970s Computers: The First Mainframes").

The first attempt to think about architectural impacts and to implement a preliminary design was when the memory required for solution was larger than the physical installed memory. A mechanism for dividing the software into independent pieces (or overlays) was implemented in order to overcome the physical limitations (see the section in Chapter 5 on "Virtual Memory"). Future hardware developments, related mainly to the memory management unit and the implementation of segments and pages, provided a better solution,

---

* In software engineering, nonfunctional requirements describe how the system will work, including any constraints it has to be aware of. Functional requirements, on the other hand, describe what the system should do.

† In software engineering, requirements elicitation is the step in which the analyst gets a comprehensive understanding of the system to be developed as well as the project's needs.

and the overlays, in many cases, became redundant. Furthermore, a vital component in modern architectures is the network that provides the communications between various components. Therefore, before moving to multiplatform architectures, proper networking mechanisms needed to be in place, and this only occurred during the 1980s. In addition, the technological quantum leap in the development of the personal computer and the role it played in modern computing environments was an additional main contributor to architectures' capabilities and flexibility, and this trend also only occurred during the 1980s.

Client/Server Architecture

A major step in the development of software architectures was fueled by several requirements and technological progressions. The very high costs associated with mainframes in the 1970s and 1980s, on the one hand, and, on the other, the appearance of the personal computer, paved the way for new and exciting architectures (see the sections in Chapter 1 on "Historic Perspective," "Personal Computers," "Computer Networks," "1970s Computers: The First Mainframes," and "Terminal Services").

Although in the first implementations, personal computers (PCs) replaced proprietary terminals, their additional capabilities were quickly realized, and the trend of switching some of the workload to the PC started. This, of course, provided economic benefits and better response times. Contrary to the mainframe that supported many concurrent users, the PC, which initially was relatively slow and supported just one task (see the section in Chapter 1 on "1980s Computers: The Last Mainframes" and "The Network is the Computer").

The first usage of the PC was in a standalone mode. Some tasks were performed locally on the PC, similar to running a local copy of Word or Excel. This implementation has nothing to do with software architecture. However, if local files are required by other users, or the local user has to access a common file that resides on a different PC or on the organizational server, a networked architecture is required. The client/server architecture is a type of distributed system that is implemented on separate systems. The client, which is usually a PC; and a server, which might be any computer, are connected by a network. The client/server architecture itself went through several stages trying to respond to various market requirements. Originally, the client was responsible only for the user interface (UI) or the presentation layer. In the next step, in addition to the UI, an additional layer (or layers) was performed locally on the PC. As a matter of fact, the first implementation of networked computers was for sharing files and expensive, one-of-a-kind peripheral devices (see the section "File Server" in Chapter 1). The next step was the development of a "real" client/server architecture in which the work was divided between the server and the client (see the section "Client Server" in Chapter 1). The application was split into several layers (presentation, logic, and storage), and each implementation could define where each layer would be executed. In most cases, the presentation layer is executed on the local PC, and the data (or storage) layer is on the remote server. Of course, there might be other implementations as well, for example, where the business logic resides on the server, on the PC, or even on both. This type of client/server provides faster speed, since the response time is, in many cases, the local PC's responsibility. On the other hand, reliability and data security are maintained by the remote server with its trained IT staff.

Over the years, there were several attempts to implement various client/server architectures. The rapid development of the PC and the added functionality and capabilities led to the concept of a thick client that could run most of the layers defined. On the one hand, this approach provided each user with a personal system at his or her disposal; however, this approach had other implications related to security and reliability. Leaving the data, which in many cases has organizational value, on the user's PC without adequate backup or safety means may pose a security threat in which data may be lost, stolen, or hampered by viruses or other malware. These inherent disadvantages led to a different approach that utilized thin clients provided the local PC only with the presentation layer, and all other layers were implemented on the server side. This approach is safer and eliminates (or minimizes) the threat of viruses. In addition, and based on technological developments related to fast communication media, many of the thin client implementations do not have local disk storage (or alternatively have minimal storage). In these network terminals (or network devices), the applications are downloaded from the network. This architecture is very efficient and helpful in cases in which the application needs to be updated, which, in the thin client's case, is achieved automatically. Each time the client is turned on, it will load the most recent application.

It should be noted that the client/server architecture is not confined to just one client or one server, and the configuration may be based on numerous clients and servers as a function of the functionality required. A simple example of one or several servers that support many clients may include a database server, mail server, print server, and so on. In modern computing environments, this type of architecture is sometimes referred to as application servers, which may be part of a service-oriented architecture (defined later in this chapter). In such a case, the application servers actually provide various services for the client applications.

Although client/server systems still exist, the contribution of this architecture type is that it paved the way for other derivative architectures that are better suited to modern computing environments.

One such implementation that expands the traditional client/server architecture is the client-queue-client architecture, sometimes referred to as a passive queue. In this architecture, the server acts as a data queue for the clients. A common implementation is for clients to communicate with each other using a server-based queue. In other words, the clients exchange data among themselves by storing it on the server in a special store (or queue). A simple example may be the communication carried out between web crawlers* when indexing web pages.

---

* A web crawler, also known as a web spider or web bot, is a program that automatically browses web pages. This is used by all search engines for indexing data on the web and maintaining an up-to-date view. Crawler technology can be used for additional purposes, such as locating broken links or mining specific information (e-mail addresses may be an example). Due to the magnitude of the task, usually a search engine will use numerous crawlers. These crawlers have to communicate with each other, and this can be done using a client-queue-client architecture.

Peer-to-Peer (P2P) Architecture

Another important development that stems from client/server architectures is the peer-to-peer (P2P) communication or architecture. The original design behind the Internet (or the World Wide Web) was to provide a mechanism of communication between all its nodes. Each user can edit and contribute by creating and sharing content. The sharing was done using a linking mechanism. One of the earliest implementations was for Usenet. This was a platform for distributed discussions developed originally during the 1980s. The main idea was to develop the capability that allows the user to read and post messages related to various categories. It may be considered as one of the early predecessors of Internet forums. Usenet used Unix-to-Unix copy (UUCP), a protocol and related programs that provided file transfer between remote computers as well as remote execution. However, P2P architectures became very popular and well known by specific applications that were developed and utilized the architecture—file-sharing applications such as Napster and Kazaa.

Napster came to life with the idea of sharing music (mainly MP3* files). It was a revolutionary idea since all music at that time was distributed via albums. Napster provided a solution that appealed to many users. According to various estimates, at its peak, there were about 60 million users in the Napster community. The first step in implementing such a solution was to use a common repository (like the original mp3.com) that users could use for uploading their files. Other users could connect to the site, search for their preferred type of music, and, when they had found it, download it to their PCs. This is an example of a client-queue-client architecture, and it has some inherent limitations. The data has to be copied from the clients to the server, and if there are many songs, the server needs large storage. It should be noted that with the rapid developments in storage capabilities, currently storage is very cheap and is no longer a limiting factor. However, when Napster started at the end of the twentieth century, the situation was different. In trying to overcome these limitations, the next step that was implemented by Napster eliminated the redundancy of copying the files to the server. Instead, the files remained on the users' computers, and the Napster server provided indexing services. Each Napster user had to download a small application that communicated with the Napster server. The application provided the users with the possibility of sharing some of their music folders. Sharing in this sense meant that the Napster server maintained a link to the folder, and the MP3 files that were on the folder became available for anybody looking for these songs. The Napster implementation was a true P2P architecture in which communication (file uploads and downloads) was maintained between peers. The Napster server did not host the files but simply served as a large index (Figure 11.1).

---

* MP3 (MPEG-2 Audio Layer 3) is an algorithm for decoding and compressing data, especially audio files. Although it is a lossy data compression, it became the de facto standard, since it manages to compress digital audio files to 10%–20% of their original size with a limited impact on the human ear. This is done by reducing the accuracy of the sound on the spectrum that is beyond the hearing capabilities of most humans. The format, which was designed by the Moving Pictures Experts Group (MPEG) opened up new possibilities related to music and especially streaming music (and video) over communication lines. It also helped develop architectures for the distribution of music, Napster and Kazza being some examples.

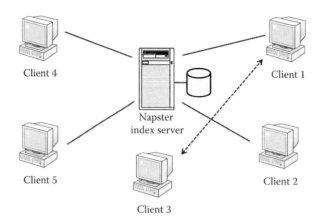

FIGURE 11.1   Napster P2P.

The process of uploading and downloading songs using Napster included several steps:

- The Napster client connects to the server.

- It uploads a list of files (songs) while providing access to the folders containing the files.

- The server maintains the list of keywords, including the PCs' IP addresses.

- The downloading client searches the Napster index for the required files.

- The addresses of the PCs containing the required files are returned.

- The downloading client pings the addresses received, looking for the best candidates.

- Download starts without the Napster server being involved (the dotted arrow on Figure 11.1).

An inherent limitation of the Napster approach, and of P2P in general, is related to the download reliability. If, for example, a song was found only on one peer (one user computer), it starts downloading using this one source. If the user turns off the computer or disables the Napster client, the download will stop. There is no way of knowing if the download will resume or when.

The main limitation associated with the Napster approach was that, although the file transfer was decentralized, maintaining the index information and locating content was highly centralized. It provided a single point of failure and a possible bottleneck. However, apparently the main issue with the architecture is that it allowed the music industry to sue Napster for their involvement in large-scale copyrights infringement. Although the Napster server did not store the songs, it helped in illegal downloading as defined by the U.S. Ninth Circuit Court, which ordered Napster to prevent the trading of copyrighted music on its servers.

In trying to overcome these limitations, and especially Napster's legal problems, Gnutella, Kazaa, and others that use P2P file sharing in a similar way to Napster, introduced a simple change. Unlike the centralized approach implemented by Napster, Gnutella uses a decentralized system in which the peers communicate with each other without a centralized server. As with other cases of P2P, there is no hierarchy. The node sends the query to its neighbors. If the neighbor has the requested object, it sends a message back to the querying peer. If the neighbor does not have the object, it forwards the query to its neighbors. Implementing this architecture implies that each peer has similar responsibilities, and no one maintains an index or directory information. On the other hand, the architecture produces heavy traffic. To limit this flooding effect, the default parameters set by Gnutella limit the number of queries created by each node. If the requested peer does not have the requested file, it will query only seven of its neighbors. If the neighbors do not have the file, they will query up to seven of their neighbors. Furthermore, the maximum hop count was set to 10, meaning that the query forwarding in cases when the file was not found will be repeated at most 10 times. This flood prevention mechanism causes an additional problem. There may be cases when the requested file is in the network, but since it is not in the 10-hop radius, it will not be found.

In trying to overcome some of the Gnutella limitations, Kazaa introduced several changes. It implemented node hierarchy, queue management, and parallel download. As part of the parallel download, each user could configure the maximum number of simultaneous uploads and downloads on his or her computer. This was done mainly to increase speed. Kazaa could download the song from various users' computers concurrently. This was achieved by splitting the song files into chunks and loading different chunks from different systems. Popular songs that were found on many users' computers were downloaded very fast (limited only by the network's bandwidth), while rare songs may have required longer downloading times. In addition, each peer was either a supernode or an ordinary node. Usually, supernodes were the ones with higher bandwidth. Each such supernode acted as a mini Napster hub, managing the content indexes and the IP addresses of its ordinary nodes. This was achieved by using a FastTrack* protocol in which some of the nodes acted as proxies for other ordinary nodes. The process of finding and downloading contents followed several steps:

- A new peer is looking for an operational supernode. An initial list is provided as part of the client software that was installed.

- When an operational supernode is found, the peer connects and obtains an accurate and up-to-date list of supernodes.

- The peer pings some of the supernodes and connects to one.

---

* FastTrack protocol, sometimes referred to as a second-generation P2P, uses two types of nodes: Supernodes and ordinary nodes. The supernodes serve as a proxy server that relays information from the ordinary nodes. When responding to a request, a supernode may connect with other super nodes it knows. Each of these supernodes may further connect other supernodes. This multilevel relay may extend to up to seven levels of propagation.

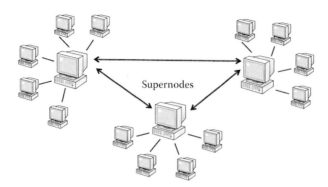

FIGURE 11.2   Kazaa hierarchical nodes.

- If the supernode stops responding, for example, due to turn-off by the user, the peer will look for another supernode in the list.

- The peer sends the query to the supernode.

- If the supernode finds matches within its dependent nodes, the IP addresses will be returned and the transfer will start.

- Otherwise (i.e., if the dependent nodes do not have the file), the supernode will forward the request to other supernodes.

- If the file is found, the IP addresses will be sent to the requesting node, which will start the transfer.

- Otherwise the query will be forwarded further.

Figure 11.2 depicts the hierarchical nature of the nodes in a Kazaa architecture, showing how each node is connected to a supernode and each supernode communicates with other supernodes.

The P2P architectures, which over the years produced a variety of systems—SET@home (see the section in Chapter 10 on "Grid Computing") being one example—continue to evolve into other markets, and one famous example of using this architecture is Skype. The implementation used by Skype is based on a central server that manages the login process. In addition to the authentication, the server has to ensure the user names are unique across all of Skype's names. The Skype architecture, which was developed by Kazaa, uses a similar approach involving two types of nodes (a supernode and an ordinary node). Due to its different aim, which was to establish a voice-over-Internet Protocol (VoIP)* telephone network, the architecture implements additional codecs† for maintaining the call quality, but these are not part of the general architecture.

---

* VoIP is a methodology and underlying support technologies that provide the means to make telephone calls using a broadband network and utilizing the Internet Protocol (IP).

† Codec (coder-decoder) is a computer program that is designed to decode and encode a digital stream of data. In the early days of communication, the modem was a hardware device that was responsible for coding and decoding the analog data. Currently, most codecs are software based, with specific formats such as audio compression, video compression, and so on.

Client/server architecture may be a good solution in situations where the main application is executed on a server and has to support many clients. It should be noted that client/server architecture is applicable for clients that use web browsers to connect to the servers and not just organizational PCs. One of the main benefits of this type of architecture that it maintains and secures the centralized organizational storage through the information technology (IT)-managed operations. On the other hand, client/server architecture, which is designed using two types of entities (clients and servers), is sometimes limited in imposing an artificial bond between the various application layers. A simple example may be an architecture in which the business logic and the data storage are both on the server, although, from an architectural point of view, it may be better to separate them. In trying to overcome these limitations, client/server architecture has changed into other more flexible architectures such as a tier architecture that may contain several levels and not just two as in the case of client/server.

Layered Architecture

The main concept behind layered architecture is to split the application into separate modules, each one representing a different functionality, and then to group similar modules into layers. The layers are placed in a hierarchy with a means of communication between them. Each such layer has a distinct role and responsibility and a predefined access protocol (or interface). The layered architecture is flexible and provides a high degree of maintainability. It is possible to replace a layer with a different piece of code with a similar functionality without affecting all other layers.

Contrary to client/server architecture, in which there are at least two different separate systems, the layered approach can be implemented using just one physical system, or alternatively it can be implemented using separate physical systems.

The hierarchical nature of layered architecture implies that each layer depends on the layer beneath it and enhances its functionality.

One of the best-known examples of a layered architecture is the open systems interconnection (OSI) model, which is a conceptual model for representing standard communication functions. It is a conceptual model since it defines the functionality without the underlying implementation.

The layers defined by the OSI include

- Physical: Responsible for transmission and reception of raw data over the physical link.

- Data link: Responsible for the reliable transmission of data between two points (nodes) connected by the physical layer underneath.

- Network: Structuring the data into packets (datagrams) and managing the transmission through the network by utilizing multinode addressing, routing, and flow control.

- Transport: Reliable transmission of data segments between various points on the network. The transmission includes acknowledgements, data segmentations, and multiplexing.

- Session: Management of a communication session that is based on repeated exchange of information between two nodes.

- Presentation: Managing the translation of data between network nodes, such as a client and a server or service provider. These translations may include character encoding, encryption, and decryption as well as data compression and decompression.

- Application: The layer close to the application or the end user. This layer identifies the communication partners and synchronizes the communication and the resources available.

Figure 11.3 depicts the layered architecture of the OSI model.

Layered architecture can be implemented as a closed architecture, which implies that each layer can communicate only with the adjacent lower layer (if it exists), and this is the case with the OSI implementation. On the other hand, open architecture implies that each layer can send messages to any lower level and not just the one adjacent.

Closed layered architecture reduces the impact of changes since it minimizes dependencies. Open-layered architecture, on the other hand, provides simpler code, since an upper layer can directly connect any lower level without the intermediate level, which requires additional code for transferring the message through all the middle layers. However, open-layered architecture increases the dependencies between the layers and, as a result, increases the complexity of the code and the system.

Figure 11.4 depicts a layered architecture. The left side is an example of a closed architecture, and, as can be seen, each layer addresses only the layer underneath. The right side, on the other hand, represents an open architecture, in which each layer can access any other layer, not just the one underneath.

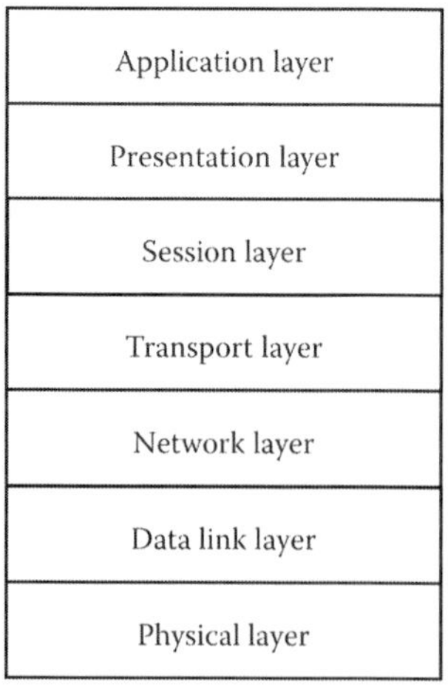

| Application layer |
| Presentation layer |
| Session layer |
| Transport layer |
| Network layer |
| Data link layer |
| Physical layer |

FIGURE 11.3 The OSI model.

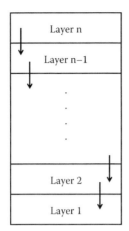 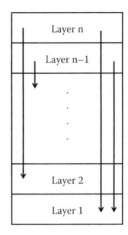

FIGURE 11.4   Opened and closed layered architecture.

The layered architecture, either closed or open, has some considerable benefits:

- Abstraction, which means the architecture can be defined in an abstract way that hides the physical implementation. The level of abstraction can be defined as a function of the purpose of the design. If the architecture is used for communication with the users, it may be at a higher level of abstraction. On the other hand, if it used to communicate to more technical personnel, it may be more detailed.

- "Divide and conquer," which implies that the layered approach provides a higher degree of isolation between the layers, increasing modularity and maintainability. Changes, both technological and functional, can be introduced into the layers without affecting other layers or the total functionality of the system. These changes, of course, cannot change the interfaces used to communicate with the changed layer.

- Better manageability through the separation of control. Each layer has a predefined functionality, which can be tested separately. This, in turn, increases the system's maintainability and manageability.

This architecture is useful in cases in which some of the layers required for implementing the solution are readily available. Another case in which layered architecture would be beneficial is that of a large and complex application, which requires parallel work by many development teams. Using a modular development approach and splitting the application into separate layers, each one with its distinct functionality, may decrease the time to market and reduce development risks. It should be noted, however, that software engineering methodologies have developed other approaches for addressing the complexity of large projects and reducing development risks.

Tier Architecture

Tier architecture is very similar to layered architecture since it combines similar functionality into common segments. However, in tier architecture, each tier may be implemented using a different physical machine. Like layers, tiers are implemented using a hierarchical structure, and each tier is separated from all other tiers except the one above (if it exists) and the one underneath (if it exists).

The architecture is based on dividing the application into functional components, each one with a predefined role and interface. Each such component can be deployed on a different system, which increases the overall scalability, flexibility, and maintainability. In this sense, tier architecture can be viewed as an enhancement of client/server architecture. The presentation layer will be deployed on the client system, while the business logic may be deployed on a different server. Figure 11.5 depicts a simple architecture for a common information system. Three layers (tiers) are implemented. One is responsible for the presentation, the second for the business logic, and the third for the data. This architecture can be implemented as a client/server, and in such a case, the presentation will be part of the client's system, the data usually will be part of the server, and the business logics can be on either side or even on both sides.

If necessary, this logic server may be protected behind a firewall to prevent unauthorized access. The storage, or database layer, may be deployed on a different storage server. As such, a client/server architecture that contains only one client and one server may be defined as a two-tier architecture. A three-tier architecture usually will have some middleware components between the client and the server. There might be additional tiers deployed on different servers in case of a large online system that may be required to process many concurrent requests, for example, a large online transaction processing (OLTP) system. These multitier (or n-tier) architectures provide a higher degree of scalability due to the possibility of distributing the load to multiple nodes. On the other hand, this, of course, increases the traffic over the network. Figure 11.6 depicts a more complex system that was deployed using four tiers. The presentation and the business-logic layers remain

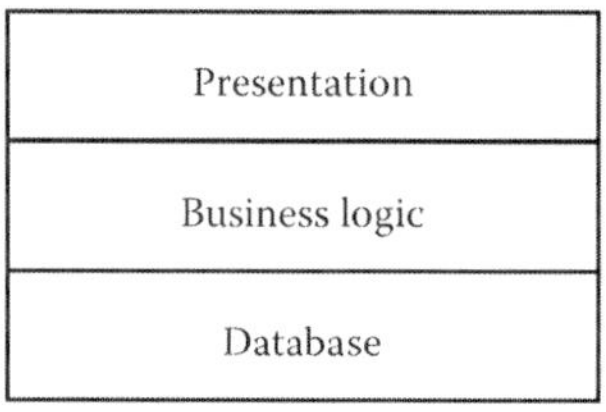

| Presentation |
| Business logic |
| Database |

FIGURE 11.5   A three-layer architecture.

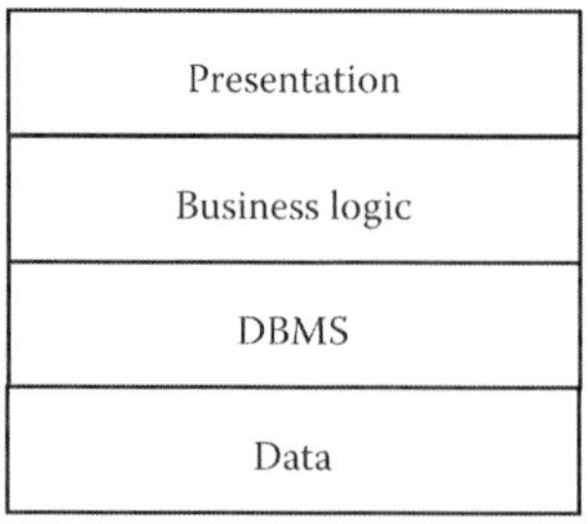

| Presentation |
| Business logic |
| DBMS |
| Data |

FIGURE 11.6   A four-tier architecture.

unchanged; however, since the data storage is distributed over several systems, an additional database management system (DBMS) layer is required. For security or maintainability reasons this later may be implemented as an additional tier on a different system.

The flexibility built into layer- and tier-based architectures is not limited to horizontal partitioning (as seen in Figure 11.6), which allows the addition of more layers or tiers. The architecture provides vertical partitioning as well. As part of vertical partitioning, each layer (or tier) can be partitioned based on its functionality. For example, let us assume that the architecture outlined in Figure 11.6 has to support two distinct devices. As such, the presentation layer can be divided vertically into two presentation subsystems, as shown in Figure 11.7.

In this specific case, the requirements are for an application that can be executed using a standard PC and a mobile phone. Although all mobile devices support a browser, which can run the application, the different characteristics sometimes require a different presentation layer. The application, in this case, is designed to use two different presentation subsystems.

There are, of course, situations in which not only does the presentation have to be vertically split but the additional layer as well. For example, if the application displays advertisements, then on the PC screen, some ads can be displayed on the left and right sides. On the mobile device, due to its limited display, the ads should be managed differently. In such a case, the business-logic layer will have to be divided as well (Figure 11.8).

Of course, vertical partitioning can be extended to additional layers as well. For example, a system that uses more than one storing mechanism, or utilizes more than one database, may require more than one DBMS layer.

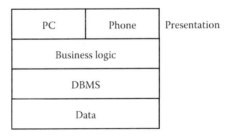

FIGURE 11.7   Vertical partitioning.

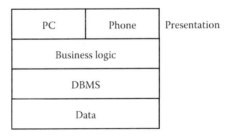

FIGURE 11.8   Two-layer vertical partitioning.

The main benefits of using tier architecture are

- Increased availability due to the modular design and the possibility of replicating servers as the load increases, or in case of a server malfunction

- Increased scalability, since each tier can be deployed on one or more servers, and each such server can be scaled based on the anticipated load

- Increased flexibility, which is gained by the modular design and the fact that each tier can be managed and scaled independently, with no required changes to the other architectural components

- Simpler maintainability, which is achieved due to the separation of the tiers and the fact that each one can be maintained independently without interfering with other components

Compared with layered architecture, tier-based architecture provides additional benefits and, mainly, flexibility. If the processing done in one layer is intensive and may interfere with the processing required in other layers, then tier architecture is a much better option because of its utilization of a different computer. Furthermore, in some cases, the different layers are executed on the same machine, even if there is very little interaction between them. With the rapid developments in communications technologies as well as distributed processing, tier architecture may provide a significantly better solution.

Object-Oriented Architecture

The object-oriented paradigm was developed originally as a new programming approach in the 1960s with the introduction of Simula, a language developed by a group of Norwegian researchers to simulate real systems. Additional developments were performed by researchers at Xerox with the introduction of Smalltak, which was a real object–oriented programming language. Only during the 1980s, with work by Grady Booch, did it develop from mainly a programming language into an object-oriented design method. In the 1990s, additional capabilities were introduced, such as object modeling techniques (OMT) by James Rumbaugh and object-oriented software engineering by Ivar Jacobson.

The main idea behind object-oriented analysis (OOA) is that software, like the real world that surrounds us, should be modeled using many objects that interact with each other. The main difference between OOA and other types of analysis is that in OOA, the requirements, model, and implementation are based on objects. Contrary to the procedural approach, in which software is based on two separate entities—procedures, representing the logic; and data—in the object-oriented approach, objects are integrated units that contain both the object's data and logic.

In previous and other forms of systems' analysis, requirements are gathered to form the required functionality of the system. In OOA, the requirements are needed in order to

- Identify the participating objects

- Build the object model diagram that defines the objects and their interactions

- Elaborate on the objects' attributes and characteristics or the information they maintain

- Define the behavioral aspects of the objects or the operation they can perform

As part of the tools developed for supporting OOA, the unified modeling language (UML) was defined. UML is a set of specifications and diagrams used for modeling the architecture, structure, and behavior of the system as well as the business processes it supports. As part of the OOA, the common models used are use cases[*] and object models[†].

The next stage in the software development life cycle is the design. The object-oriented design is about implementing the conceptual model defined as part of the analysis. The analysis stage and the conceptual model defined are technology independent. Only during the design are the specific technologies (e.g., databases, development frameworks, middleware) defined, which requires revisiting the object model and defining the class data and methods. As part of the object-oriented design component[‡] and deployment[§] diagrams may be used.

After finishing the design stage, then starts the programming, which is mainly about developing the classes that include both data (class attributes) and behavior (class methods). An important side effect of the OOA is its advantages related to modularity and reusability. Although modularity and reusability were available in previous development methodologies, the object-oriented paradigm is straightforward and can easily be implemented using the class and object building blocks. This, of course, has architectural implications.

Since object-oriented architectures are implemented by integrating different reusable objects, each one of which is self-sufficient and contains the attributes and methods it requires, the design of such a system involves actually defining these building blocks. Each such object has its own responsibility, and it communicates with other objects using a predefined interface of exchanging messages between the objects. The interface is implemented by calling a specific method, which resembles a procedure call in the ordinary and procedural programming. The object-oriented development paradigm has some inherited

---

[*] Use-case diagrams are used to capture the high-level requirements of the system. They represent the functionality required by each of the participating actors. In this sense, actors are human beings or other internal or external systems that interact with the system to be developed. In addition, use-case diagrams are used to define the events the system handles as well as their flows. Used as part of the analysis, use-case diagrams define the input, output, and the required functionality but not the way to implement it.

[†] An object diagram is derived from the class diagram. In object oriented architectures, classes are blueprints or templates for creating objects, and objects are specific instances of the class representing real-world entities. For example, a bank account is a class with all it attributes and behaviors. This class can be used to create many different bank accounts, each one being an object that represents a different instance of the bank-account class. The purpose of the class diagram and the derived object diagram is to model the static view of the system to be developed.

[‡] Component diagrams are used to model the physical aspects of the system. These aspects may include libraries to be used, the executable code, files, and so on. These diagrams' contribution is in defining the relationships between the components and the way they are organized.

[§] Deployment diagrams are used for representing the physical components' topology. As such, the deployment diagrams will consist of nodes representing the system and their relationships. In this sense, nodes are hardware components used for storing software components. Although UML was designed mainly for describing the software attributes of the system, component and deployment diagrams consider some hardware aspects as well.

benefits for software engineering; however, most of these benefits are relevant for defining object-oriented architectures. Some of these benefits are

- Encapsulation, which means the object hides the implementation from the outside world. A client object that requires some service from the object is exposed only to the interface or the way of interacting with the object providing the service. This contributes to the modular design, since it is relatively simple to replace an existing object by a different one, provided the interface remains unchanged.

- Composition, which refers to the fact that objects can be constructed by integrating other objects while providing a combined functionality. Nevertheless, the internal structure is unknown to the client objects. As with encapsulation, composition increases the modularity and flexibility of changes.

- Inheritance, which refers to the object's ability to inherit from a parent object and use the functionality that was already defined by the base or parent object. From a software-engineering perspective, this represents an important feature that allows rapid development of derived classes and objects. This ability has its merit in lowering the costs associated with maintaining the system and introducing changes.

- Polymorphism, which, while it is based on inheritance, provides the means not only to inherit the behavior from the parent object but also to modify it. By overriding some of the inherited behavior, an object can benefit from the two worlds. On the one hand, it can inherit the required functionality, and, on the other hand, it can replace the undesired behavior with a different one.

The object-oriented development paradigm reflects on all previous architectures, since each one of the previously described architectures can be implemented using an OOA. Figure 11.9 depicts and object-oriented system and the communications between the subsystems defined. Subsystems, or packages of components, are depicted as folders (a rectangle with a small rectangle on its top left side). The left side of the figure defines a general overview of a client/server architecture. The client sends messages to the server (in the

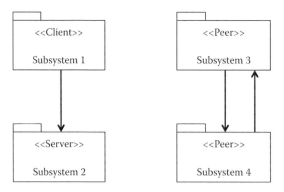

FIGURE 11.9   Object-oriented communication.

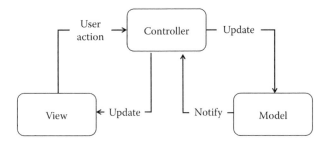

FIGURE 11.10   MVC architecture.

direction of the arrow), but the server does not initiate communication with the client. On the right side, there are two peers that communicate by sending messages in both directions. As previously defined, a P2P architecture maintains communication between all peers, and each one can act as both a server and a client.

Furthermore, for implementing best-practice solutions, there is a list of design patterns[*] that define known and proven solutions for various architectural problems. One of the earliest models for defining the architecture was the model-view-controller (MVC), which resembles the layers used in an information system architecture. The model represents the knowledge maintained by the system so it corresponds to the data. The view is the visual representation, so it may use part of the fields represented by the model based on the required query. The controller is the layer that links the view and the model, or, in the client/server and layered architectures, it is the logic. As with other cases, the MVC architecture was intended to increase modularity and separate the system into different modules, each one responsible for a specific task.

Figure 11.10 depicts the MVC model. The view layer is responsible for communication with the outer world (users or other systems). Following the user actions, a message will be sent to the controller. Based on the type of action, the controller may choose to update the data in the model, or, alternatively, query the model and obtain the required results. These results will be sent back to the view layer for presenting to the user. As with previous cases, the architecture supports several views and controllers.

With the development of UML, the terms *model*, *view*, and *controller* changed to *entity*, *control*, and *boundary* (ECB). The ECB pattern is a variation of the previous MVC pattern. UML has some special icons for representing the stereotypes of the classes, which helps in better understanding the architecture and its components. Using UML notation provides a "drill down" capability that allows the architecture to be defined in more detail, as shown in Figures 11.11 and 11.12.

Figure 11.11 depicts a system with UML icons. On the left is the user that interacts with the boundary objects. These objects interact with the control objects, and,

---

[*] Design patterns represent a list of conditions found in object-oriented systems. Many of these conditions were solved already and there is no need to reinvent the wheel. So the main reason for defining the design patterns was to learn from the experience of others, especially when there are proven and working solutions. A design pattern is a solution to a problem that appears in various ways. A pattern may have several variants or solutions that take into account various planning considerations.

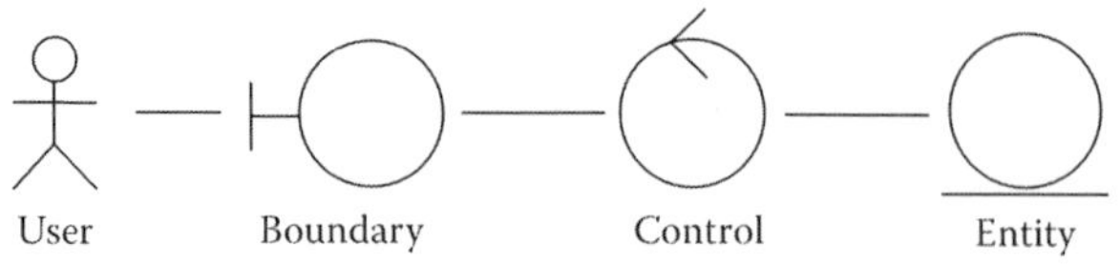

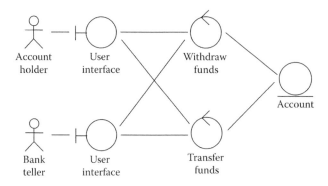

FIGURE 11.11   Entity control boundary overview.

FIGURE 11.12   Detailed ECB diagram.

depending on the required action, the control will have to interact with the entity objects. The same diagram can be used for depicting a more elaborated architecture as shown in Figure 11.12.

This figure describes the previous architecture but with added functionality. For clarity reasons, only part of the architecture is described. This is a banking application that is intended for a variety of users; however, only two are described. The system provides a large range of functionalities, but the diagram relates only to two of these (withdraw funds and transfer funds). While each one of the two types of users has a different user interface, both can perform the same transactions. This is illustrated by the lines connecting each of the two user interface objects to the common control objects. The control responsibilities include verifying the transaction, for example, if the account has sufficient funds; and then performing it. In both cases, the control object will have to interact with the account object, once for checking the balance and, if the action was taken, again to update the balance. In the case of transferring funds, there might be an additional access to the entity objects for updating the other account (if it is managed in the same bank).

The main benefits of using object-oriented architecture are when the system to be developed (or modeled) is based on real-world entities. These entities have a status and behavior, which can easily be translated to objects. Each such object has attributes (defining its status) and methods that represent its activities. In addition, the application to be developed can benefit from other available classes and objects that provide additional capabilities (methods) that can be integrated as part of the solution.

It should be noted, however, that the object-oriented methodology can and is used not only for common information systems but also for many other systems, applications, and web-based components.

Service-Oriented Architecture

Service-oriented architecture (SOA), which can be seen as a normal advancement of the object oriented concept, defines the system's functionality as an integration of services. A new system is implemented by defining a simple layer that interacts with many service provides. Each such service provider is a software component with a predefined responsibility and an interface. As part of SOA, each service has a standard interface that can be published, so it will be automatically discovered and used. As with OOA, the interface is implemented using a message sent between the client and the service provider. Each such service can be executed on a different system, since, with modern developments in data communications, distance and geographic locations are no longer important. Services can be combined to provide a higher level of components that provide lists of services residing on various different hardware platforms.

The most important benefits associated with SOA are that

- The services are only loosely coupled, which implies that each one is self-sufficient and independent and as such can be replaced or updated as needed without any effects on the system as a whole.

- The services are autonomous, which means that each one can be developed and maintained independently and can run on different heterogeneous platforms.

- The services are distributed, so there is no limitation regarding their location. For example, using Google's API* for map drawing provides the service, but the client application does not know where it was computed. Furthermore, with the high degree of distribution, it is possible that each time the service is called, it is executed on a different machine and in a different location.

SOA provides a higher degree of modularity, transparency, and flexibility. A system or an application is not limited to a specific platform, and it can augment services executed on a variety of computing environments. SOA is applicable in cases where there is a large amount of services that can be easily utilized. Many modern architectures that utilize software as a service (SaaS) or various cloud-computing services are SOA based.

For a service-oriented architecture to be highly effective, it should employ a mechanism or a layer for service discovery. Originally, such distributed architectures that employed a variety of services used broker-based architecture. The broker is a component responsible for the communication between the various decoupled and distributed components. It is responsible for the mechanism that forwards the messages (requests) and returns the results.

In its basic configuration, a broker architecture will utilize three components: clients, servers, and a broker. The clients mainly implement the user interface (similar to the presentation layer in a client/server architecture). In addition, the client sends requests to the servers utilizing the broker. The servers implement the services they provide, register the

---

* An application programming interface (API) is a set of tools that serves as an interface to another software component.

services through the broker, and respond to incoming requests by executing the service and sending back the results. The broker has to register and maintain a list of available services, provide a common interface for the clients to interact with, transfer the messages (request) to the appropriate server, and handle various exceptional situations.

Using this method of communication, in which each client sends its requests to the broker instead of communicating directly with the server, and the broker forwards the messages to the appropriate servers, reliability and flexibility are increased. The client does not have to know where the server is located or which server it is. The broker, through its discovery and registration mechanism, will automatically take care of these technical issues (Figure 11.13).

The architecture depicted in Figure 11.13 is sufficient for a simple homogeneous configuration. The single broker represents an elevated risk, since, if it malfunctions, the whole system stops working. Furthermore, when a larger system has to be designed, a single broker may become a bottleneck that limits the systems throughput. For that reason, larger broker systems will usually have additional three components: proxies for the client and server sides, and bridges to connect the numerous brokers allocated for the system.

These additional components are required for additional transparency and flexibility. The client-side proxies are implemented as a layer between the clients and the broker. The main purpose of a proxy is to hide the implementation details in such a way that a remote object will appear to the client as if it resides on the same computer. The client/side proxies are responsible for the translations required between the client objects and the broker objects. As previously noted, each one of the clients, as well as the brokers, may be written using a different programming language and on a different platform. Such a heterogeneous environment may require these translations.

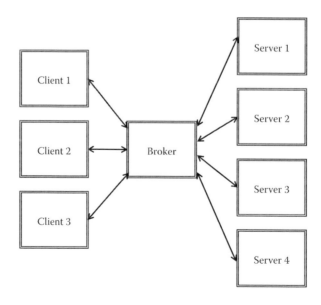

FIGURE 11.13   Simple broker architecture.

On the other end, the server-side proxies perform similar actions. The proxies receive the request messages, convert them to the proper format, and call the required services on the server. It should be noted, however, that the translations were included here for the sake of explanation, and most web servers have implemented these translations as part of their offerings. The last component added is bridges, which are used for connecting several brokers. Figure 11.14 depicts a larger broker system, but for clarification reasons, it contains only two brokers and a limited number of servers and clients.

The development stages that the P2P architecture followed are relevant and applicable for the broker architecture as well. The configuration defined by Figure 11.14, even if it implements numerous brokers, may introduce a bottleneck, since all messages from the clients to the servers, as well as the responses from the servers to the clients, have to go through the broker. For that reason, another type of broker architecture was defined: the direct-communication architecture. In direct-communication broker architecture, the broker is responsible just for the initial setup. Once the initial communication between the client and the server is established (the handshake), all future message are transferred between the client proxies and the server proxies without any broker involvement. Related to Figure 11.14, in a direct-communication broker architecture, an additional messages (or data) communication link will be implemented between the proxies, as shown in Figure 11.15.

The importance of distributed architectures to the development of better and more adapted computing solutions was clear, and not only to specific organizations or designers. Distributed architectures in this sense represent all possible client/server configurations. The clients and the servers could be on the same machine, on different machines but on the same network, or on different machines on different networks. Figure 11.16 depicts the general concepts behind a distributed system. On the rectangle on the left, which represents a client application, a specific object needs to communicate with an object that resides on the server (the dotted arrows). The middleware layer, which defines the distributed architecture and provides the glue for its components, is responsible for providing the means of communication. By using the middleware, the calling object on the client's side

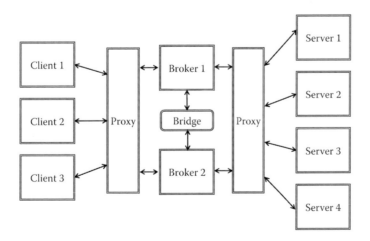

FIGURE 11.14   Larger broker architecture.

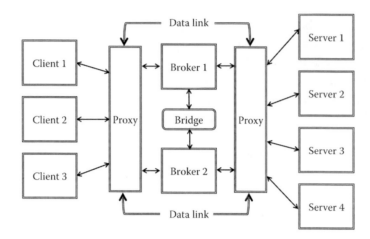

FIGURE 11.15   Direct communication broker architecture.

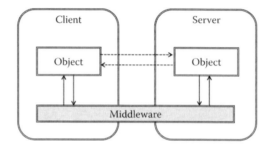

FIGURE 11.16   Distributed system generic architecture.

interacts with the server object as if it was running on the same machine. All the necessary operations such as service discovery, massage transfer, parameter conversion, exception handling, and so on are performed automatically by the middleware.

CORBA: Common Object Request Broker Architecture

The benefits obtained from a distributed computing environment are due to the possibility of sharing resources, even scarce ones; it provides better load balancing and supports the running of applications on a variety of hardware platforms. Considering these benefits, larger organizations and standards bodies looked for a more standard, open way to define and implement a heterogeneous, distributed computing environment. The Open Management Group (OMG)* developed the common object request broker architecture (CORBA), which was intended for defining and specifying an object-based distributed system. The main idea was to define the architecture and interfaces required for designing a system that allows communication between various software modules. These modules can

---

* The Open Management Group is an international, open-membership, not-for-profit technology standards consortium. OMG was founded in 1989 and is driven by vendors, end users, academic institutions and government agencies.

reside on heterogeneous systems, in different locations developed by different vendors. The CORBA specifications were adopted as standards by ISO.*

As with previous implementations, CORBA defines an object request broker (ORB). In a distributed system with clients and servers running on different computing platforms, it is the ORB that ensures seamless communication. Each client, which may be an object, can request services from the servers (which are also implemented as objects). The client does not have to know where the server is located or what interface it uses. To bridge the possible different interfaces and ensure that the client request is understood by the server and the server replies are understood by the client, the ORB defines a special interprotocol: the general inter-ORB protocol (GIOP) and the Internet inter-ORB protocol (IIOP) for Internet-based systems. The difference is that IIOP maps the GIOP requests and replies to the Internet's transmission control protocol (TCP) layer on each computer. The TCP is the transport layer of the OSI model (see Figure 11.3).

Due to the Internet's dominance and the fact that it has become the main communication media for computing environments, the IIOP is a critical module in the implementation of CORBA. IIOP provides the capabilities for programs written in one programming language to communicate over the Internet with other programs, without knowing or caring about their detailed implementation. All that is needed is the service and its name.

In implementing the inter-ORB protocol, CORBA is using one of the object-oriented principles: encapsulation (see the section in this chapter on "Object-Oriented Architecture"). Encapsulation, in the object-oriented context, implies that the internal structure of the object and the mechanism it uses to implement its methods are hidden. The client using the object receives the service just by using the interface. For that reason, CORBA uses an interface description language (IDL), which describes the interface in a language-independent way. This way, all objects' interfaces are defined so that all clients and servers can communicate regardless of their hardware platform, operating system, programming language, and so on. As such, the interface definition has to clearly specify the function to be performed as well as the input and output parameters, including their types. An important issue with a distributed system that includes service discovery and wide-area networks† is that unpredicted errors may occur. As such, an extensive and powerful exception handling is provided.

Since the IDL is language independent, each vendor developed a compiler that generated the appropriate required source code for the specific programming language. The generated code provides stub and skeleton interfaces for the object. A client stub is responsible for the conversion (sometimes called marshaling) of parameters used in the clients' call for a service and the deconversion (sometimes called demarshaling) of the results passed from the server after execution. A server skeleton is a stub on the server side that is responsible

---

* The International Organization for Standardization (ISO) is an independent, nongovernmental membership organization and the world's largest developer of voluntary international standards.
† In communication, a wide-area network (WAN) refers to a computer network that spans over a large geographic distance.

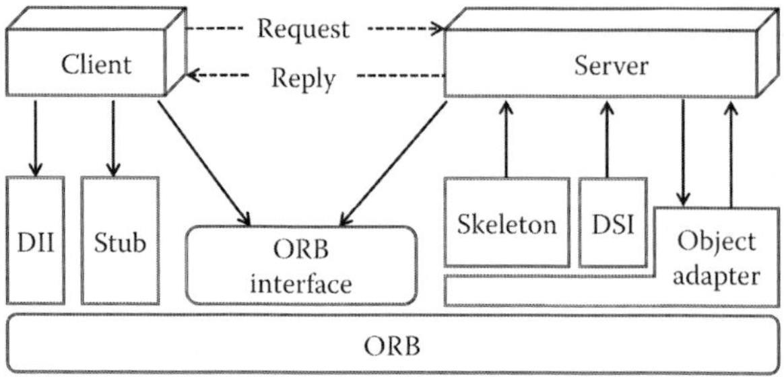

FIGURE 11.17   CORBA architecture.

for the deconversion of the parameters sent by the client as well as the conversion of the results obtained from the server.

Figure 11.17 depicts the generic CORBA architecture. The upper part illustrates the client, one of whose objects requests a service that resides on the server. Since it is a distributed system, the client's object cannot access the server, and it needs the CORBA middleware. As already mentioned, the ORB provides the communication infrastructure that is required for transferring the requests, as well as their parameters, to the designated servers. The ORB will make the connection to the server, marshal the parameters, and return the results back to the client. The IDL-compiled code provides the stub defined in the figure. The dynamic invocation interface (DII) allows the client to issue requests to objects that are not statically linked using the client stubs. This mechanism is used for requesting services from objects discovered during run time. The main advantage in using DII is that the request on the client side looks identical in both cases (statically linked and dynamically linked). The ORB interface is a list (repository) of all the object's interfaces that were registered by the ORB. Interfaces are added to the ORB interface by the IDL stub, or dynamically through object invocation.

On the server side, the CORBA architecture consists of the implementation of the service objects (described as the server box), skeletons, an object adapter, and the ORB interface.

The server objects are the ones responsible for doing the work and sending the results back to the clients. The interface for these working objects is defined by the IDL skeleton. As with the stubs, these skeletons are generated from the source code, which is the result of the vendors' compilers. The skeleton can be regarded as an interfacing bridge between the ORB and the actual objects' implementations. As with the client, the server can choose between static and dynamic invocation of the objects. It can rely on static skeletons (generated from the object's IDL definitions) or its objects can use a dynamic skeleton interface (DSI). The object adapters are an additional layer between the objects implemented and the ORB. Their main role is to help in activating the requested objects and delivering the requests to the objects. For modularity reasons, usually an object adapter will be defined to support just one type of object implementation. For example, one object adapter may be used for C++ objects, while another will be used for Java objects, and so on.

By splitting some of the functionality to the object adapters, the ORB can be smaller, especially in cases where it supports a functionality that is seldom used. On the other hand, due to its constant use, it usually resides in memory. Therefore, if the system is using a large memory, a larger ORB can be designed, which will improve the overall system's performance.

Component Object Model (COM) and Distributed COM (DCOM)

In parallel to the OMG definition of CORBA, Microsoft has designed and developed its own component object model (COM) technology. A component, in this sense, is a set of software elements that can be grouped into a reusable entity. The entity provides some services through known interfaces with a hidden implementation (encapsulation). COM is a platform-independent, distributed, object-oriented system for creating binary components that can communicate. The COM technology was intended to help to develop reusable software components and link these components in order to form an application. For increasing flexibility, the COM components can be developed using a variety of programming languages. The developed components can interact with other components in the same process (Figure 11.18), or components of a different process executed on the same computer (Figure 11.19), and even components that execute on different computers, as shown in Figure 11.20.

Figure 11.18 depicts a simple configuration in which both the client and the server run within the same process. The small circle denotes the interface connection point.

Contrary to the situation depicted in Figure 11.18, in which the objects communicate using the same process, Figure 11.19 depicts a communication between objects that are part of different processes. In this case, the COM infrastructure has to be used on both sides of the communication link.

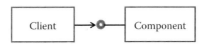

FIGURE 11.18   COM using same process.

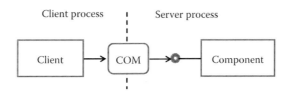

FIGURE 11.19   COM using same computer.

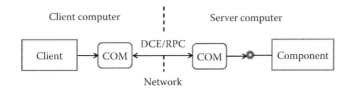

FIGURE 11.20   COM using different computers.

Figure 11.20 depicts a more complex integration. Client objects that run on one computer have to communicate with server objects that execute on a different computer. In this case, the COM infrastructure runs on each of the computers. The communication between the two COM layers is based on a distributed computing environment/remote procedure call (DCE/RPC).*

The RPC is initiated by the client, which sends a request message to a server. The request causes the execution of a procedure on the remote server, and the results are sent back to the client. There are several implementations of RPC, but in general, the sequence of event may include the following steps:

1. The client initiates the RPC by calling a local stub. This is done just like calling any other local procedure. The call includes the parameters needed for the remote procedure.

2. The client stub packs the parameters into a message and makes a system call to send the message to the server. The parameter packing is called *marshaling* (as was the case with CORBA).

3. The operating system on the client side sends the message to the server as requested.

4. On the server side, the operating system receives the message and forwards it to the server stub.

5. The server stub unpacks the message into its components—the parameters for the remote procedure. This unpacking is called *unmarshaling* (as was the case with CORBA).

6. The server stub then calls the server procedure and provides the required parameters.

7. The server procedure executes and produces the results, which are sent back to the client using the same steps but in the reverse direction.

8. Normally, from the time the client sent the request until it gets the result, it is blocked, unless it sends an asynchronous request, which enables it to continue working while the request is being processed.

Distributed COM (DCOM) is an application-level protocol for object-oriented integration, and it is intended for developing applications for distributed computing environments. Each client connects to the server using an interface, which is a contact point that consists of a group of related encapsulated functions. The interface definition specifies the functions to be executed, their parameters, and the return values and their types. DCOM

---

* The distributed computing environment (DCE) is a software system developed in the early 1990s by a consortium of companies. The DCE is a framework for developing client/server applications. The framework includes various tools such as a remote procedure call (RPC), a naming directory, authentication services, and so on.

   An remote procedure call (RPC) is an interposes communication mechanism that allows a program to call and execute a procedure that resides on a different computer, without explicitly programming the details for that call. Although in this sense RPC is part of DCE, over the years many other implementations of RPC were developed.

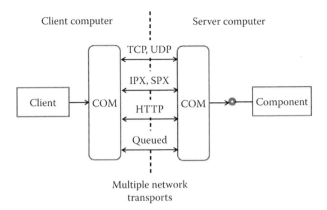

FIGURE 11.21   DCOM using multiple network transports.

can be viewed as an extension to COM, and it provides components interaction across heterogeneous networks and a larger variety of tools, services applications, languages, and components developed by other vendors as well.

Figure 11.21 depicts the DCOM architecture; the additional capabilities related to COM are mainly the ability to integrate several networks (including the Internet) and to support other vendors' proprietary but COM-compliant components.

In addition, Microsoft provides COM+, which is an extension to COM that implements a set of operating-system services for the running components. For example, COM+ supports run-time event notification. This means that components may ask to be notified when events occur; for example, when a sale is completed, an inventory update component will be issued so that the inventory can be updated. In addition, COM+ supports the logging of transactions that can be used for security analysis and queuing requests waiting for a service.

Java RMI and Java Beans

Java, which was originally introduced by Sun Microsystems (currently part of the Oracle Corporation), is a programming language that was developed for large-scale interoperability (see the section "The Network is the Computer" in Chapter 1). Applications developed using Java depend on the Java virtual machine (JVM) for proper execution. JVM is an abstract computer or environment capable of "understanding" the Java code. The main idea behind the development of Java was to create a platform-independent application suitable for the networked computing environment. To achieve the goal of network mobility, Java makes extensive use of the object-oriented paradigm.

The Java architecture is based on four integrated technologies/components:

- The Java programming language
- The Java class file format (bytecode)
- The Java application programming interface (Java API)
- The Java virtual machine

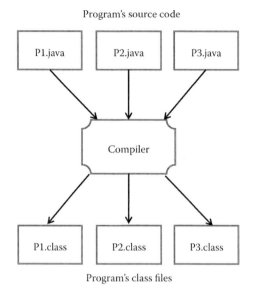

FIGURE 11.22   Java compile-time environment.

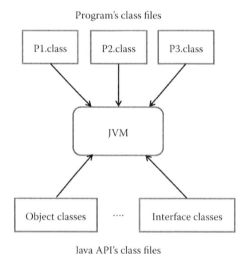

FIGURE 11.23   Java run-time environment.

The process depicted in Figure 11.22 starts by developing the software using the Java programming language. The code is then compiled into Java class files. The class files are special files that can be executed on the JVM. While running (Figure 11.23), the class file can access the various system resources by using methods available as part of the Java API. This is done by invoking methods in class files that implement the Java API.

Figure 11.22 depicts the compile time environment, which includes three Java source files (P1, P2, and P3) which are compiled and produce three Java class files. These class files are moved to the run-time environment and are executed (Figure 11.23).

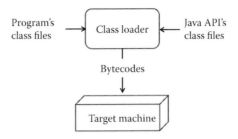

FIGURE 11.24   JVM functionality.

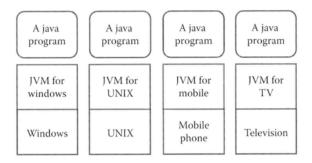

FIGURE 11.25   The Java flexible environment.

The idea incorporated in the Java architecture is that, using the JVM concept, programs can be executed not only on traditional platforms (e.g., Windows and UNIX) but on a large variety of appliances as well. The JVM is responsible for loading the class files and executing their bytecodes while augmenting the required Java API. This is done by utilizing a special class loader that interprets the class files and executes the bytecodes on the target machine, as depicted in Figure 11.24.

Combining these elements (the Java programing language, the Java API, and the JVM) forms the Java platform, which enables the execution of a Java program on any computerized platform, assuming it provides a JVM-compatible environment (Figure 11.25).

Considering the flexibility inherited in the Java concept, it was only natural that Sun introduced its own distributed architecture. Initially, Java supported sockets for object communications. Sockets, however, require that both the client and the server be engaged in application-level communication, which means that each object is responsible for encoding and decoding the messages. Due to the additional work needed, the next step was to implement an RPC mechanism (similar to CORBA and COM). The main benefit of RPC over sockets is that it provides a procedural interface; in other words, the procedure can call a distributed and remote service. However, originally RPC was designed for structured programming languages, so it was intended for calling a remote procedure. Java, on the other hand, is an object-oriented language, so it requires a different approach. In an object-oriented approach, sometimes it is necessary to reference a remote object and invoke its methods. For that reason, Sun implemented the remote method invocation (RMI), which is intended explicitly for objects and supports many of their characteristics, such as inheritance, polymorphism, and dynamic invocation.

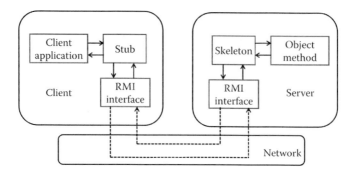

FIGURE 11.26   RMI architecture.

Figure 11.26 depicts a general RMI architecture. On the left side, the rectangle represents the client. The application needs a service that is implemented on the server (the right rectangle). The application calls the client stub, which marshals the call's parameters. The message is then sent to the RMI interface, which sends it over the network to the RMI interface on the server side. The next step is to send the message to the server skeleton, which demarshals the parameters; and to call the specific method in the object implementation. After the method has completed the process, the results are sent back to the calling client using the same steps, but in the reserve direction.

However, an RMI that communicates between methods of Java classes is just a communication protocol. As such, it can be viewed as a natural advancement of the remote procedure call (RPC). In parallel to the development proposed by Sun, Microsoft has developed its own protocols and tools. One of the first solutions, originated over 20 years ago, was based on dynamic data exchange (DDE). It provided a mechanism for sharing data between applications, for example, an Excel graph embedded into a Word document. DDE had some severe limitations. To change the graph, the Excel application had to be invoked, and the links did not work when the files were moved. The solution proposed by Microsoft was object linking and embedding (OLE), which, in addition to the DDE linking, provided embedding, which allowed users to embed a copy of the original data. Instead of linking the graph to Excel, embedding its copy in the Word document. This solution led to a definition of compound documents, which are documents that contain objects maintained by different programs. The unbreakable link between the component and the application that handles it required an additional tool to simplify the creation, display, and modification of the components. This led to the development of COM, which is basically a set of protocols that allow the components to communicate with their original programs. As with many layered development projects, COM includes OLE as part of its implemented standards. By developing the OLE custom extension component (OCX), the COM added new capabilities for developing customized applications. OCX is a small piece of code with its own user interface, and it allows the integration of other components into a new program. The next step implemented by Microsoft was the ActiveX, which is a group of methods for sharing information and functionality among programs. One popular technology is the ActiveX controls, which are objects used to attach a program to a web page. Originally, ActiveX controls were intended for Windows only; however, after their source code was made public, additional vendors provided support for ActiveX on their non-Windows-based platforms. The built-in interactivity between the various components and programs, and the fact that developers could easily create new ActiveX controls, provided a high degree of flexibility and increased development speed. For that reason, ActiveX, which was originally used by only Internet Explorer, was later implemented by Mozilla and Firefox as well. Such an ActiveX control was downloaded by the browser and executed with full access control, which raised some serious security issues.

During the time that Microsoft was developing various tools and technologies to support distributed environments, Sun implemented a different solution—the Java bean. A Java bean is a reusable software component that can be easily manipulated. The main idea is to create components that include Java classes. These components are self-contained and reusable. Furthermore, the components can be composed into larger components, applets,* applications, and servlets† using a visual building application.

The Java beans or components are a step forward from the ordinary object-oriented (OO) paradigm. The idea behind OO is to develop standalone and self-sufficient classes that can be integrated into an application. The classes and their instantiations, the objects, are the raw materials for the application. As the applications grew and became more complex, implementing tiers and layers, the need for building blocks changed as well. Currently, a software architecture does not care about detailed raw materials but about components. This is especially true since the component can be implemented in various ways, some of which are hidden from the developer. On the other hand, the developer is concerned about the interface and whether the component is capable of providing the required service.

Beans are classes that were developed according to specific conventions regarding their properties and interface definitions. Beans can be manipulated using a visual builder tool to form larger beans or an application. For that reason, the beans have to publish their attributes and behaviors using special method signature patterns. The visual builder tool recognizes these patterns when integrating the beans.

For communicating between objects, Java uses messages sent from one method to another. Beans originally were designed to be graphical components such as buttons, lists, and so on, and for that reason, the communication model was changed. Beans use an event-based model in which classes listen to the events in which they are interested. This is the same mechanism implemented by AWT‡ and Swing.§ Schematically, the event model has three main components:

---

* An applet is a Java program that runs in the browser (similar to an ActiveX control). The applet is embedded in the HTML code and it is downloaded automatically to the user's machine. As all other Java programs, it needs a JVM to run. To avoid various malicious access attempts, the applet has strict security rules enforced by the browser. If the applet needs additional classes, these will be loaded as well.

† A servlet is a Java program that runs on an application server and connects incoming requests with the database or the application.

‡ The abstract window toolkit (AWT) is the original platform-dependent windowing graphics and user interface toolkit implemented by Java. It is part of the Java Foundation Classes, which is the standard API for Java's graphical user interface (GUI).

§ Swing is a GUI tool kit for Java and it was developed to provide more sophisticated and robust GUI components than AWT. The Swing components are not platform specific, but use Java to create a platform-independent code. Like AWT, Swing too is part of the Java's Foundation Classes.

- The event object, which encapsulates the information relevant to the specific instance of the given event. The event object will contain a reference to the event source, so it can be notified when the event has been processed.

- The event source, which is the object that originally triggered (sometimes called fired) the event.

- The event listener, which is an object that has been listening and waiting for the event. Once it has happened, the event listener will be notified. There might be situations in which there are many event listeners. The listener concept is a common principle used by many web-based applications and database servers. When a request comes in on an appropriate port, the web server understands it has work to do.

Figure 11.27 depicts the Java beans communication mechanism. It starts by registration of the available event listeners. Then, when the need arises, the event source fires the event, including the event object, for the event listener to process. The results or notification will be sent back to the event source.

Despite the very different approaches to distributed components architecture, there are some clear commonalities between the Java beans and ActiveX methods. However, these layered architectures are not limited to just two layers, as in the case of client (source) and server (listener). There are cases in which the listener class may become complex and difficult to maintain. For example, when the listener reacts to several different events, or when it reacts to events that were sent by different sources, the number of sources is especially large. A relatively simple solution to this situation is to introduce another layer between the event source and the event listener. This new layer is an object, called the *event adapter*. Its main purpose is to adapt the source to the requirements of the listener. The adapter knows the listener's method, so it can forward each event object to the proper method. It is possible to implement the adapter classes as part of the listener component. However, if increased maintainability is required, it is better to define separate components for the adapters. Furthermore, the event adapter can provide some queuing mechanisms that improve flexibility, resource utilization, and response times.

Figure 11.28 depicts the adapter-based communication. The event listener creates an instance of the adapter. The adapter starts by discovering the listeners' classes and their methods. The adapter registers itself as the listeners (the service providers). When the need

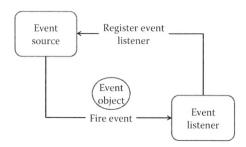

FIGURE 11.27   Java beans communication.

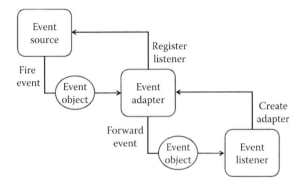

FIGURE 11.28 Adapter-based communication.

arises, the source will forward the event object to the adapter, which, in turn, will invoke the listener's appropriate method.

Java 2 Enterprise Edition

J2EE, or Java 2 Enterprise Edition, is the solution developed by Sun (currently part of Oracle) for distributed applications. J2EE is a suite of software specifications for the design, development, and deployment of distributed, multitier, component-based, and loosely coupled applications. Through its history, Sun has been looking for innovative solutions to the industry's problems. It was one of the first companies to understand the importance of networks to organizational computing (see the section "The Network is the Computer" in Chapter 1) and was one of the founders of network computers (see the section "Network Computers" in Chapter 1). Oracle Corporation, on the other hand, as one of the leading database management systems, has developed experienced client/server architectures for increased flexibility and response time and better ROI (see the section in Chapter 1 on "Terminal Services"). Furthermore, for increasing architectural functionality, such as cross-platform support; increasing the developer base; and gaining a larger industry visibility and support, currently the technical specifications of the Java technology are developed by the Java Community Process* program.

J2EE, which is built on top of the Java technology, followed several industry trends in trying to provide a solution to users' needs. Currently, J2EE concentrates on enterprise needs, which can be summarized by developing better and faster decision-support systems, while reducing the costs of these systems. It is the responsibility of IT departments to provide powerful and high-quality services at an affordable cost. Each enterprise may define its emphasis; however, in general, these powerful and high-quality services imply high availability, utility, flexibility, and security.

The aim behind the definition and development of the J2EE architecture is to provide an enabling technology that defines standards for developing applications. The common architecture will provide common infrastructure functionalities such as security, scalability, and session management. To achieve these aims, J2EE uses a multitier architecture; this

---

* Java Community Process (JCP) is an open program that provides a mechanism for everyone to participate in defining future Java specification requests (JSRs), either by reviewing future directions or suggesting new ones.

partitions the application into several parts, which in turn simplifies both development and future maintenance. Furthermore, using several tiers increases flexibility, scalability, and reliability. The standard-based modular approach provides a relatively simple mechanism for components replacement, which prevents the known vendor lock-in situations.

A brief history of industry development (the problems and the solutions provided) will aid a better understanding of the J2EE architecture. The original computer architectures, back in the mainframe era, can be described as a two-tier architecture in which the client was a thin client (or dumb terminal) and all business logic as well as the data was kept on the server (see the section in Chapter 1 on "Historic Perspective" and Figure 11.29).

The main disadvantages associated with the two-tier architectures related to the server side. The server usually was a large and expensive computer with very limited scaling. Adding functionality to the business-logic application was also expensive due to the lack of appropriate development tools.

In addressing some of these disadvantages, a three-tier architecture emerged. In a three-tier architecture, it is possible to dedicate each tier to a different function; the client will be responsible for the presentation or the user interface, the middle layer will be responsible for the business logic, and the third layer will be responsible for the data (see Figure 11.5). This approach is similar to the layered approach; however, there might be other ways to divide the functionality among the tiers. The client may run some parts of the business logic in addition to the user interface, or the server may perform other business-logic parts as well. Nevertheless, as J2EE is based on Java, an object-oriented language, it adopted the standard three-tier architecture derived from the MVC model (see Figure 11.10) and implemented the three-tier architecture as depicted in Figure 11.30.

The three-tier architecture addressed some of the two-tier architecture's disadvantages. The individual application server is easier to control and manage, and it provides a higher degree of scalability. The application server can be divided horizontally by adding additional application servers. Furthermore, the different application server introduced new market opportunities for a variety of software tools aimed at rapid application development (RAD). On the one hand, these development tools and environments connect to the client, and on the other hand, they link to the organizational database. The three-tier

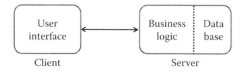

FIGURE 11.29 Two-tier architecture.

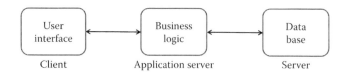

FIGURE 11.30 Three-tier architecture.

client/server architecture peaked during the 1990s with many RAD tools intended for the development of standalone applications. It took some additional years to understand the value of the organization's digital resources for better decision making and increased competitiveness. In parallel with the development of the concept of the "total cost of ownership," the disadvantages of the standalone three-tier architecture emerged. Although the application development time decreased with the use of the various RAD tools, the installation and maintenance costs associated with geographically dispersed systems skyrocketed. In trying to integrate several three-tier client/server architectures, additional business-logic tiers were added. However, by adding additional tiers and layers, the system became more complex due to the connectivity required between some of these newly added business-logic layers. On the other hand, additional end-user devices started to emerge, so additional support layers were required, which further increased complexity, as depicted in Figure 11.31.

The left side of the figure represents the various possible user devices. The business-logic layers represent not only the "pure" business logic but also the additional functionality required for handling users' devices. For that reason, there are many communication paths between the various business-logic components. In addition to the added complexity, these architectures did not fit properly in the web environment, so a different approach was required.

The developed solution was based on analyzing the components' behavior. A component, like any other system, can be viewed as a process of three stages: input, processing, and output. A message sent from one object is actually the input of the next object. This input is processed and produces an output message that is sent back to the source object; or forwarded to another object, where it serves as an input once again. In many cases, the input and output have to deal with standard functions required by the users' devices. Therefore, the J2EE architecture uses microcomponents that are divided vertically into the three or more distinct functions of input, processing, and output. Figure 11.32 is a schematic view of the architecture.

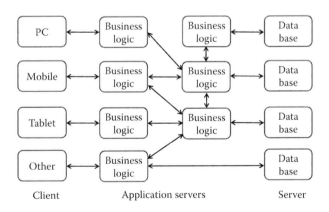

FIGURE 11.31   Additional tiers.

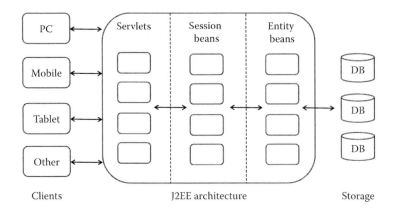

FIGURE 11.32　A schematic view of the architecture.

Aspect-Oriented Architecture

Aspect-oriented programing (or architecture) was developed following two major trends:

- The increased complexity of software-based systems and the understanding that one architecture, flexible and sophisticated as it may be, cannot fit all possible needs. New technological trends require additional functionality not directly related only to business logic but also to other operational aspects.

- Standardization processes, which allow the development of new layers of functionality that can easily be integrated into existing architectures such as J2EE. These processes opened up a new market for off-the-shelf components to augment standard and existing architectures.

In general, software architecture was developed to provide an abstract model of the system to be developed. Originally, the most important characteristics of the system were derived from its functional requirements. At a later stage, the nonfunctional characteristics became important as well. There are even cases in which the nonfunctional requirements, if not met, may prevent the system from being used. For example, such systems may include very slow interactive systems, which annoy their users; or unreliable systems, which crash often or do not secure their data; and so on. Many software engineering methods and methodologies were developed to deal with the complexity derived from functional as well as nonfunctional requirements. Software engineering, which is mainly about the process of producing and delivering the software, influenced the architecture as well. Since its beginning, software engineering emphasized dividing the system into smaller, more manageable pieces. The previous sections have described various methods of development as well as the complimentary architecture for supporting this trend. As a matter of fact, this "divide and conquer" approach is used by most engineering disciplines. A car, for example, is built of many parts and components, and in a case of failure, just one part has to be fixed or replaced. Software engineering uses the same approach. Large and complex systems are broken into modules. The modules are further split into submodules, and so forth. This simplifies the development process, allows for parallel development, and has the potential to produce a better product. An additional concept borrowed from the engineering disciplines was the modular approach. Defining the functionality of a component and its interface provides much-needed flexibility. Each such component can easily be replaced by another component that provides the same functionality and maintains the agreed-upon interface. In the early programming languages, only part of the system was modular. In various programming languages, these modular pieces of code were called subroutine, function, procedure, and so on. Examples of such modular functions are all the mathematical functions supported by all programming languages. The current variety of existing functions reduces the time required for development and increases the systems' reliability by using tested and working components. A further step forward in the modular approach to development was the introduction of object-oriented architecture. While in previous approaches, only some parts of the system were modular, the object-oriented approach introduced a new level of modularization in which the whole system is modular. This, of course, made it simpler to implement the various architectures previously described.

Aspect-oriented software development represents a new level of modular design. Most previous architectural designs aimed to provide a better method for defining the functional components required for the system. However, in many cases, there are common or crosscutting concerns that have to be addressed, and aspect-oriented architecture design addresses this issue. An example of such crosscutting concerns may be as part of the requirement elicitation. There are various functional requirements, however; all of them probably share the need for security or fast recovery. In this sense, security and fast recovery are crosscutting requirements. Aspect-oriented software development provides an abstraction mechanism for issues relevant for multiple components. Aspect-oriented architecture is a way to model the nonfunctional requirements of the system as well as other quality and behavioral aspects. Examples of such aspects may include logging services, security issues, and error handling. By defining these crosscutting components, a higher degree of modularity is achieved (Figure 11.33).

Figure 11.33 depicts the two situations. On the left is the nonaspect architecture. There are two classes, and the concerns are depicted as the small rectangles representing code as

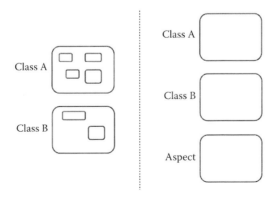

FIGURE 11.33   Aspect and non-aspect classes.

part of the functional logic. On the right side, the concern code is contained in an additional aspect class that provides the required functions to the two original classes.

Usually, crosscutting concerns are caused by two problems: code that is separated across multiple modules (called *tangling*), and code that is intermixed with other pieces of code (called *scattering*). As part of aspect-oriented programming, developers do not have to be concerned with the various aspects of the system. Once these aspects are developed, they can be used many times across the system.

As previously explained, object-oriented programming represents a significant improvement compared with the previous procedural programming. However, as the systems became more complex, some inherent limitations of the object-oriented approach became noticeable. For reducing complexity, object-oriented programming emphasizes simple objects. On the other hand, a large system may require the execution of many different objects to perform a specific task. Usually these interrelated objects will be combined into a component, which, by definition, creates some degree of interdependency between the objects and the components, especially in an SOA environment. This, in turn, sacrifices the notion that objects are independent. Enhancing or maintaining such a system may pose additional problems due to the fixed, and sometimes hard-coded, nature of communication between the objects and the components in which they reside.

To reduce complexity and development risks, design patterns were developed. These design patterns provide some well-defined methods of addressing given problems. However, although there are many design patterns, they still do not cover all possible requirements and situations. Furthermore, even if the design patterns are correctly implemented, they may be tailored to a specific problem and lose their modular and reusable characteristics. However, the main limitation associated with design patterns is that they are mainly concerned with functional requirement implementation. For that reason, aspect-oriented architectures are used to encapsulate nonfunctional concerns, which usually crosscut various different components. Aspect-oriented programming is the mechanism for defining these concerns. For defining the concerns, some special programming languages were developed; however, current object-oriented compilers cannot process these new languages.* In order to overcome this issue and still integrate the aspect code in the existing classes, the aspect weaver was developed. Aspect weaving is the process that merges the aspects into the code. The aspect weaver is a programming tool that understands the aspects and builds the appropriate code. It actually runs before the compilation and inserts new instructions into an object so it adheres to the defined concerns (as defined by the aspect). The new classes, sometimes called *woven classes*, consist of the integration of the original class with the additional aspect code. This is an automatic process, described in Figure 11.34.

The aspect weaver uses the two classes on the left and automatically inserts the behavioral additions to handle the aspect code. These behavioral additions, or the aspect code,

---

* A common and widely used example is AspectJ, which is an aspect-oriented programming extension for Java. AspectJ uses the standard Java syntax and adds some special constructs called aspects. These constructs provide the mechanism for defining the operations to be performed (methods) and the specific locations where the methods will be invoked.

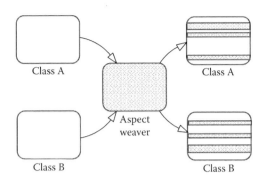

FIGURE 11.34   Aspect weaver.

are described by the pattern rectangles within the classes. As part of the aspect definition, there are two main issues to be considered: (1) the aspect code (or behavioral addition), and (2) the joint point, which defines the specific code location where the aspect has to be applied. Joint point may represent a specific method or even a variable assignment.

There are two ways to implement aspect weaving: (1) static and (2) dynamic. Static weaving means inserting the aspect code at the joint point. A simple example may be logging functionality. If the requirement is to maintain a log file for each modification of a database table, then the aspect code for logging the activity will be augmented into the original class. Static weaving is very efficient in terms of resource utilization, since it can be viewed as an additional method call. On the other hand, static weaving is very difficult to maintain, since it is not simple to identify the aspect code in the woven class. A significant limitation of static weaving is when there is a need to modify the aspect code at run time. Although in most cases, especially in the past, the aspect code was static in nature, and run-time modification flexibility was seldom needed, nevertheless, in complex and newly emerging systems, it may be required. An example of a dynamic changing aspect is when dealing with a high-volume transaction system that implements a load-balancing aspect. The load-balancing aspect is dynamic, and it has to provide the capability of distributing all or part of the load to different systems. For that reason, the dynamic aspect weaver is needed. The dynamic weaver maintains static aspects but, in addition, some dynamic ones. The static weaving is done prior to the compilation, and the dynamic weaving is done at run time. The dynamic weaving is based on aspect classes that are capable of adding, modifying, and removing some of the aspects based on the running environment. The dynamic weaving provides the required flexibility, and it is easier to maintain; however, it requires more computing resources due to the additional level of abstraction.

Additional Architectures

The computer hardware industry has changed significantly due to the various standardization processes that started during the 1980s. As part of these processes, standard interfaces, protocols, and communication links were defined and developed. From the hardware perspective, the PC revolution drastically changed the market and its leading players. From a market dominated mainly by large corporations that provided wall-to-wall solutions, the new standards opened up new opportunities for many innovative smaller players with specific solutions. These trends had a significant economic impact on the market by providing new and sophisticated solutions at a very competitive price. Furthermore, it also fueled competition, which in turn advanced technology further and at an increasing pace. This mix-and-match trend allows users to build their own PC from components manufactured by a variety of vendors. The only limitation, of course, is that in such systems, it is not always easy to locate and correct a problem when it happens. For that reason, some of the vendors apply an old–new mechanism of locking in the customer. The brand PCs, for example, are systems that were designed, integrated, and tested by the manufacturers, which provide support in cases of problems. This approach is also used by some of mobile phone manufacturers, which do not provide the means to connect to other peripherals. This trend resembles the approach taken by the manufacturers of the old mainframes.

Standardization processes are not confined to hardware or only to the hardware industry. These processes are not new to the software industry, and many have already been discussed. For example, in the design and development of the various software architectures, such as client/server, layered architectures, SOA, and so on, standard protocols had to be defined. The various operating systems were among the first to implement such standard protocols. Supporting the hardware plug and play requires a mechanism of communication between the system and the device driver, which, in many cases, was developed by the manufacturer. All the services provided by the operating system are actually a definition of a set of APIs that govern the integration between the operating system and the various applications that use it.

However, as systems become more and more complex, additional architectures for supporting increased functionality were developed. Some of these architectures have already been described in this chapter. Each such architecture has its strengths and limitations. The Internet revolution has changed the basic thinking regarding systems infrastructure. Most modern systems are communication based and utilize readily available components and protocols. The device separation, applied as part of client/server architecture and later as one component of tier architecture, is simple yet fundamental. Currently, one can access sites on the Internet using any device (PC, mobile phone, tablet, etc.) without caring or knowing about the protocols the message is using or the properties of the server that replied. The object-oriented paradigm, which originated from the need to provide better development processes and more successful projects, emerged as the dominant architectural building block. The software development industry followed a layered path, in which each new development is based on previously produced and adopted knowledge. All these developments were possible due to many standardization processes and protocols. One common example used as a standard for Internet page definition is HTML.* By using HTML both on the server and on the client (by the browser), a common definition of the content and how it should be displayed is achieved. The server adds the HTML tags to the document, and then it is sent to the browser. The browser strips the tags but uses

---

* Hyper Text Markup Language (HTML) is a language that is used to define web pages. It is based on a set of markup tags. Each such tag represents a document content and/or attribute.

them in order to determine how to display the document. The HTML is just one example of the standardization processes applied in the software industry. The first browsers supported only text and were limited to just one font and one size. HTML, with the appropriate browser support, extended the functionality to colors, fonts, and pictures. However, with new technological advancements, additional market-driven requirements for sound, animations, and video had to be addressed and implemented. Various operating systems and browsers handle the support for these new media types differently. Furthermore, there are many types and formats, and some of them require helper utilities (browser plug-in). To better address these new media types, HTML5 was introduced. The specific capabilities of HTML5,* and its ability to create interactive graphics without the need for additional plug-ins, are not the main issue. HTML5 is indicative of the software development process. There were previous revisions of HTML, but HTML5 is a standard defined by the W3C† with the aim of providing a common infrastructure for development.

As previously stated, HTML is just one example of the stepwise approach to software development and architecture building. The newly developed applications and systems sometimes have a wide range of considerations to address. While in the past, the most important issues were the functional capabilities of the system, the nonfunctional requirements followed closely. Currently, there are additional, sometimes critical issues. Some of these issues stem from the nonfunctional requirements, and others relate to the development process itself. In a networked world, where a system is based on components executed on remote servers, issues such as security, reliability, and disaster recovery become of paramount importance. On the other hand, to decrease software development risks and increase development credibility, most development projects prefer using available components instead of developing new ones. This is one of the cornerstones of modular development—the object-oriented paradigm—and it led to the development of SOA. SOA (see the section in this chapter on "Service-Oriented Architecture") is a collection of services that communicate with each other. SOA is an advancement of the previous DCOM and CORBA specifications (see the sections in this chapter on "CORBA: Common Object Request Broker Architecture" and "COM and DCOM"). It once again demonstrates the phased (layered) development of systems architectures, wherein each architecture is based on the previous architecture while augmenting it.

Another important trend that affected systems architecture is cloud computing. As in previous cases, the main benefits associated with cloud computing are mainly economic;

---

* HTML5 is a new revision of the previous version so it supports previous functionality (and some deletions that became redundant). However, it also supports a set of new technologies for easier development and the creation of more professional and sophisticated pages. Some of the main new features include
  1. New tags for defining content
  2. New ways to connect to the server
  3. New graphics effects for presenting data
  4. New multimedia capabilities applicable for ordinary (nonprofessional) users
  5. Storing data on the client side for off-line operation
  6. Better performance and speed optimization by better utilizing the hardware resources.
† W3C: The World Wide Web Consortium is an international community that works to develop and promote web standards. Its famous mission statement is "Web for all and web on everything."

however, the issues caused by cloud computing have to be considered and fixed before it can be implemented. As with SOA, the issues to be considered are security, recoverability, response time, and so on. Cloud computing involves additional considerations, such as quality of service and the dynamic allocation of resources. Some of these issues, especially the ones that relate to cloud computing, are handled by the suppliers. For example, each such supplier provides a set of APIs for the automatic allocation and release of computing resources. However, as far as SOA is concerned, other issues have to be considered. SOA, as previously defined (see the sections in this chapter on "Service-Oriented Architecture" and "Web Services"), outlines an ideal situation in which an application (or a system) is divided into logical computing units, or components. These components, which represent control as well as business logic, are provided as services. To apply SOA, new standard layers of abstractions were required to define the type of services offered and the way to invoke them per request. The components that provide the services are the core functionality behind the SOA. Successful implementation of these components should include

- Component description: Like specifying requirements for a system to be developed. The main purpose is to define the business-related functions. This description deals with "what" the component should do and not "how" it should do it. In other words, the description is technology independent.

- Service definition: This is a list of components that, when combined, provide some predefined functionality. As with the components description, at this stage the definition is technology independent.

- Interface definition and description: The mechanism for calling and establishing communication between the components. It may resemble an object-oriented interface class.*

- Service registration and discovery: This is a mechanism for service registration in a common public services directory. Applications (consumers) that require the services use the service discovery mechanism to locate and access the required services.

- Application or consumer interface: This is the mechanism used by the application to interface with the available services. It is an interface that has to be implemented at run time, which enables the communication. Usually, an additional abstract layer responsible for describing a specific method, such as web services or EJB, will be implemented for such an interface.

Since the early days of computing, most systems architects and developers have been looking for a possible way to integrate various existing components, add the "glue" (logic), and produce a working solution. The object-oriented paradigm provided some part of the

---

* Interface class: In object-oriented programming, an interface class is an abstract class that defines a generic interface. Like any other class, the interface class contains methods and variables; however, the interface class may choose to implement the methods or leave them unimplemented.

solution, and SOA added much-needed capabilities. Aspect-oriented programming was introduced to address other, crosscutting capabilities. However, as information and computing systems grew larger, additional new architectural concerns evolved. In the twenty-first century, most companies, small and large, depend on their computing systems. Many of the services provided by modern society are information based, such as e-commerce, e-content provision, social networks, and so on. By using the Internet, combined with fast communication links, customers for modern society's services are all around the world. The underlining assumption, of course, is that the systems providing these services will be available 24/7. Some, or even many, of the architectures previously discussed are capable of providing such availability. However, this means that, in cases of maintenance or the deployment of new features, the system will have to be brought down, which translates into losing money and sometimes even losing customers. To better deal with such operational constrains, architectures that support continuous deployment were required.

The previously described architectures lack some significant capabilities required for continuous deployment. In a layered architecture, it is possible to deploy the whole layer; however, it becomes problematic if there is a need to deploy a new version several times a day. In a tier application, such deployment will require one or several tiers to be deployed as a function of the changes introduced. In this sense, SOA provides a good infrastructure; however, for continuous deployment, the services should be kept at a minimal level. This microservices architecture can be considered as an additional level developed on top of the SOA.

The microservices architecture consists of many small services that run as different processes. Each of these services is independent and usually deployable by an automatic deployment procedure. Large applications may consist of tens of thousands of such services; each one can be deployed independently. Development and testing is on a single service, which increases both reliability and scalability. Reliability is enhanced since it is significantly easier to develop and test several independent small components compared to a large application. Scalability is increased since several teams can work in parallel on different services. In addition, by deploying several copies of the services, the availability of the overall system is increased. On the other hand, microservices architectures have some inherited limitations. It is very complicated to identify run-time errors due to the on-demand, long trail of services calling. As such, while microservices support continuous deployment, the overall operation complexity increases as well. While operating a single service may be simple, when tens of thousands of services are involved, the complexity that arises due to the volume becomes an issue.

The various architectures, the increased demand for features (functional, nonfunctional, and operational), and the development of standardization have led to a new type of component—middleware. The importance of a common middleware that addresses various aspects of the system has already been discussed as part of aspect-oriented programming. Nevertheless, middleware is not limited just to aspects. In its very simple form, middleware is a software layer for connecting various components and applications. As such, some of the architectures described earlier utilize middleware, for example, RPC, which allows calling a remote procedure; or ORB, which provides the ability to send objects and initiate services in an object-oriented system. Nevertheless, the standardization in recent years has allowed for the development of new middleware layers with extended functionality. Furthermore, to increase even more the interoperability among solutions and vendors, several initiatives and alliances were formed. One example is OSGI—the Open Service Gateway Initiative, which promotes software componentization and interoperability of applications and services across various devices. The main idea is to define a set of specifications that will help in developing dynamic, shared, virtual, and automated service-oriented applications. In addition to various initiatives, there is also a wide variety of solutions provided by various vendors. For example, IBM's WebSphere is defined as "Software for SOA environments that enables dynamic, interconnected business processes, and delivers highly effective application infrastructure for all business situations."[1] Another example is JBoss by RedHat, which is defined as "a family of lightweight, cloud-friendly, enterprise-grade products that help enterprises innovate faster, in a smarter way"[2]; there are, of course, additional vendors as well.

A closing remark: A very large variety of potential architectures have been developed to address existing and emerging needs. The days of a single solution that fits all problems have long gone. In designing a software architecture, there are many issues and aspects to be considered and then a large variety of solutions to choose from.

Key Takeaway

- *Software architecture*: A diagram that depicts the main system's components and their interaction. Software architecture can be regarded as a blueprint for the development and integration activities to be performed during the development process.

- *Prearchitecture era*: Refers to the early stages of computer usage, when the most important issue was to have the program run and produce the required results.

- *Client/server architecture*: Refers to an architecture that is based on two main components, the client and the server. Although both the client and the server can reside on the same computer, usually these will be two distinct systems. There are many possibilities for implementing a client/server architecture, starting from both running on the same computer, through two systems that are connected by a local area network, and up to a configuration that implements the communication over a wide-area network like the Internet.

- *Peer-to-peer architecture*: Refers to an architecture in which each peer on the network can connect to any other peer and exchange information. Over the years, various types of such architectures were designed, starting with a central server for management and indexing, up to a totally distributed architecture without any central management.

- *Layered architecture*: Refers to a concept in which the application is divided into several logical layers. In most cases, the layers are organized in a hierarchical order, and each layer can access only the layer underneath it.

- *Open and closed layered architecture*: Refers to two types of implementation of the layered architecture. In the closed layered architecture, each layer can access only the layer underneath, while in the open layered architecture, each layer can access any other existing layer.

- *Tier architecture*: Refers to an architecture that is similar to the layered architecture. The difference is that in a tier architecture, each layer can be implemented using a different computer. The client/server architecture can be implemented using a three-tier architecture (presentation, business logic, and storage) or a four-tier architecture, and then the database management system will be assigned a different layer (between the business logic and the data).

- *Object-oriented architecture*: Refers to architectures that emerged from the developments in the object-oriented field. Most modern developments are based on the object-oriented approach due to the benefits associated with this paradigm (encapsulation, inheritance, and polymorphism). As such, appropriate architectures that will take into account these benefits had to be developed.

- *MVC architecture*: Refers to a model in which the application resembles the three-tier architecture. The application is built using three distinct parts: the model that represents the knowledge maintained by the system; the view, which is the visual representation; and the controller, which represents the glue between the two—the business logic.

- *SOA (service-oriented architecture)*: Refers to a collection of services that run on different computers, which are available to other computers. The services are applications that can connect with each other and transmit data and information.

- *Broker architecture*: Refers to an implementation of SOA in a distributed environment. The broker is a component responsible for communication between the various decoupled and distributed components. It is responsible for the mechanism that forwards the messages (requests) and returns the results.

  In its basic configuration, a broker architecture will utilize three components: clients, servers, and a broker. The clients mainly implement the user interface (similar to the presentation layer in a client/server architecture). In addition, the client sends requests to the servers utilizing the broker. The servers implement the services they provide, register the services through the broker, and respond to incoming requests by executing the service and sending back the results. The broker has to register and maintain a list of available services, provide a common interface for the clients to interact with, transfer the messages (request) to the appropriate server, and handle various exception situations.

- *CORBA (common object request broker architecture)*: A standard implementation of a broker architecture. It was developed mutually by various interested organizations and was adopted as a standard by OMG and ISO.

- *COM and DCOM*: The Microsoft architecture for distributed systems. COM is a platform-independent, distributed, object-oriented system for creating binary components that can communicate.

- *Java RMI and Java Beans*: Remote method invocation (RMI) is a Java mechanism that provides reference to a remote object and invokes its methods. RMI, which was developed explicitly for objects, supports many of their characteristics, such as inheritance, polymorphism, and dynamic invocation. Java beans are classes that were developed according to specific conventions regarding their properties and interface definitions. Beans can be manipulated using a visual builder tool to form larger beans or an application. For that reason, the beans have to publish their attributes and behaviors using special method signature patterns. The visual builder tool recognizes these patterns when integrating the beans.

- *J2EE*: Java 2 Enterprise Edition is the solution developed by Sun (currently part of Oracle) for distributed applications. J2EE is a suite of software specifications for the design, development, and deployment of distributed, multitier, component-based, and loosely coupled applications.

- *Aspect-oriented architecture*: Aspect-oriented architecture is a way to model the non-functional requirements of the system as well as other quality and behavioral aspects.

- *Aspect weaver*: The aspect weaver is a programming tool that understands the aspects and builds the appropriate code. It actually runs before the compilation and inserts new instructions into a class so it adheres to the defined concerns (as defined by the aspect). The new classes, sometimes called *woven classes*, consist of the integration of the original class with the additional aspect code.

REFERENCES

1. IBM. (n.d.). WebSphere software. Retrieved from http://www.ibm.com/software/websphere.
2. Red Hat. (n.d.). Technology. Retrieved from http://www.jboss.org/technology/.

Bibliography

A report on the ENIAC (Electronic Numerical Integrator and Computer), Contract No. W-670-ORD-4926 between Ordnance Department, United States Army Washington, DC and University of Pennsylvania, Moore School of Electrical Engineering, Philadelphia, PA, June 1, 1946.

Aleksy, M., Korthaus, A., and Schader, M. (2005). *Implementing Distributed Systems with Java and CORBA*. Berlin: Springer Science & Business Media.

Al-Husainy, M. A. (2007). Best-job-first CPU scheduling algorithm. *Information Technology Journal*, 6(2): 288–293. Retrieved from http://docsdrive.com/pdfs/ansinet/itj/2007/288-293.pdf.

Alonso, G., Casati, F., Kuno, H., and Machiraju, V. (2004). *Web Services* (pp. 123–149). Berlin: Springer.

Alter, S. (2008). Service system fundamentals: Work systems, value chains, and life cycle. *IBM Systems Journal*, 47(1): 71–85.

Amdahl, G. M. (1967). Validity of the single processor approach to achieving large scale computing capabilities. In *Proceedings of the April 18–20, 1967, Spring Joint Computer Conference* (pp. 483–485), New York, ACM, April.

Anderson, J. R. (2000). *Learning and Memory*. Washington, DC: American Psychological Association.

Ang, J., Arsanjani, A., Chua, S., Comte, P., Krogdahl, P., Luo, M., and Newling, T. (2004). *Patterns: Service-Oriented Architecture and Web Services*. IBM Corporation, International Technical Support Organization. Retrieved from https://www.researchgate.net/profile/Ali_Arsanjani/publication/200167132_Patterns_Service-Oriented_Architecture_and_Web_Services/links/5488c92e0cf289302e30b950.pdf.

Arizona State University, (2008). Cloud computing: The evolution of software-as-a-science. W.P. Carey School of Business, http://research.wpcarey.asu.edu/.

Arlow, J. and Neustadt, I. (2005). *UML 2 and the Unified Process: Practical Object-Oriented Analysis and Design*. London, England: Pearson Education.

Ashmore, D. C. (2014). *The Java EE Architect's Handbook*. Bolingbrook, IL: DVT Press.

Barker, R. and Massiglia, P. (2002). *Storage Area Network Essentials: A Complete Guide to Understanding and Implementing SANs* (Vol. 7). New York: Wiley.

Barney, B. (2012). What is parallel computing? Introduction to parallel computing. Retrieved May 9, 2015, from https://mavdisk.mnsu.edu/alleng/courses/EE%20613/Reading/DrDobbs_1.pdf.

Barry, D. K. (2012). *Web Services, Service-Oriented Architectures, and Cloud Computing: The Savvy Manager's Guide*. Burlington, VT: Morgan Kaufmann.

Behzad, S., Fotohi, R., and Effatparvar, M. (2013). Queue based job scheduling algorithm for cloud computing. *International Research Journal of Applied and Basic Sciences*, 4(11): 3785–3790.

Berger, A. S. (2005). *Hardware and Computer Organization—The Software Perspective*. Amsterdam: Elsevier.

Berlekamp, E., Peile, R., and Pope, S. (1987). The application of error control to communications. *IEEE Communications Magazine*, 25(4): 44–57.

Bernus, P., Mertins, K., and Schmidt, G. J. (Eds). (2013). *Handbook on Architectures of Information Systems*. Berlin: Springer Science & Business Media.

Berson, A. (1992). *Client-Server Architecture (No. IEEE-802)*. New York: McGraw-Hill.

Bertsekas, D. and Gallager, R. (1992). *Data Networks*. Englewood Cliffs, NJ: Prentice Hall.

Bhandarkar, D. (1997). RISC versus CISC: A tale of two chips. *SIGARCH Computer Architecture News*, 25(1): 1–12. Retrieved from http://www.cs.inf.ethz.ch/37-235/mat/ACM-tale-of-2-chips.pdf.

Blake, R. P. (1977). Exploring a stack architecture. *Computer*, 5: 30–39.

Bleuler, E. and Haxby, R. O. (2011). *Electronic Methods*. Orlando, FL: Academic Press.

Brader, M. (Ed.) (1994). A chronology of digital computing machines (to 1952). Retrieved from http://www.davros.org/misc/chronology.html.

Brichau, J. and D'Hondt, T. (2006). Aspect-oriented software development (AOSD): An introduction. Retrieved May 9, 2015, from http://www.info.ucl.ac.be/~jbrichau/courses/introduction ToAOSD.pdf.

Brown, M., Fukui, K., and Trivedi, N. (2005). Introduction to grid computing. IBM, International Technical Support Organization. Retrieved May 9, 2015, from http://www.redbooks.ibm.com/redbooks/pdfs/sg246778.pdf.

Burke, B. and Monson-Haefel, R. (2006). *Enterprise JavaBeans 3.0*. Sebastopol, CA: O'Reilly Media.

Buyya, R., Yeo, C. S., Venugopal, S., Broberg, J., and Brandic, I. (2009). *Cloud Computing and Emerging IT Platforms: Vision, Hype, and Reality for Delivering Computing as the 5th Utility, Future Generation Computer Systems*. Amsterdam: Elsevier Science.

Campbell, S. and Jeronimo, M. (2006). *Applied Virtualization Technology*, pp. 69–73, Hillsboro, OR: Intel Press.

Campbell-Kelly, M., Aspray, W., Ensmenger, N., and Yost, J. R. (2013). *Computer*. Boulder, CO: Westview Press.

Carruccio, E. (2006). *Mathematics and Logic in History and in Contemporary Thought*. Piscataway, MD: Aldine Transaction.

Carvalho, C. (2002). The gap between processor and memory speeds. In *Proceedings of the IEEE International Conference on Control and Automation*. Retrieved May 9, 2015, from http://gec.di.uminho.pt/discip/minf/ac0102/1000gap_proc-mem_speed.pdf.

Cerami, E. (2002). *Web Services Essentials*. Sebastopol, CA: O'Reilly Media.

Chappell, D. (2008). *A Short Introduction to Cloud Platforms*. Washington, DC: Microsoft Corporation.

Chawathe, Y., Ratnasamy, S., Breslau, L., Lanham, N., and Shenker, S. (2003). Making gnutella-like p2p systems scalable. In *Proceedings of the 2003 Conference on Applications, Technologies, Architectures, and Protocols for Computer Communications* (pp. 407–418). New York: ACM.

Chiueh, S. N. T. C. and Brook, S. (2005). A survey on virtualization technologies. *RPE Report*, 1–42. Retrieved May 9, 2015, from http://www.computing.dcu.ie/~ray/teaching/CA485/notes/survey_virtualization_technologies.pdf.

Chu, S. L., Li, G. S., and Liu, R. Q. (2012). DynaPack: A dynamic scheduling hardware mechanism for a VLIW processor. *Applied Mathematics & Information Sciences*, 6–3S(3): 983–991. Retrieved from http://t.www.naturalspublishing.com/files/published/1mshk1mf1638x5.pdf.

Citron, D. and Feitelson, D. (2002). Revisiting instruction level reuse. In *Proceedings of the Workshop on Duplicating, Deconstructing, and Debunking (WDDD)*. Retrieved May 9, 2015, from http://www.cs.huji.ac.il/~feit/papers/MemoRevisit02WDDD.pdf.

Clark, T. (2003). *Designing Storage Area Networks: A Practical Reference for Implementing Storage Area Networks*. New York: Addison-Wesley Longman.

Cox, M. (2000). The development of computer-assisted reporting. In a paper presented to the newspaper division, Association for Education in Journalism and Mass Communication, Southeast Colloquium, March, University of North Carolina, Chapel Hill, NC (pp. 17–18).

Cragon, H. G. (1980). The elements of single-chip microcomputer architecture. *Computer*, 10: 27–41.

Crump, T. (1992). *The Japanese Numbers Game: The Use and Understanding of Numbers in Modern Japan*. London: Routledge.

Daintith, J. (2004). EDVAC. *A Dictionary of Computing*. Retrieved from http://www.encyclopedia.com/doc/1O11-EDVAC.html.

De Gelas, J. (2008). Hardware virtualization: The nuts and bolts. AnandTech. Retrieved March 17, 2008, from https://impact.asu.edu/cse591sp11/HardwareVirtualizationAnandTech.pdf.

Dixit, K. M. (1993). Overview of the SPEC benchmarks: IBM Corporation, International Technical Support Organization. Retrieved from http://research-srv.microsoft.com/en-us/um/people/gray/BenchmarkHandbook/chapter9.pdf.

Dodge, R. C., Menascé, D. A., and Barbará, D. (2001). Testing e-commerce site scalability with TPC-W. In *Proceedings of 2001 Computer Measurement Group Conference*. Orlando, FL, December.

Dubey, A. and Wagle, D. (2007). Delivering software as a service. *The McKinsey Quarterly*, 6 (pp. 1–7). Retrieved from http://www.executivesondemand.net/managementsourcing/images/stories/artigos_pdf/sistemas_informativos/Delivering_software_as_a_service.pdf.

Duckett, J. (2011). *HTML and CSS: Design and Build Websites*. New York: Wiley.

Eberts, M. and Gisler, M. (2006). *Careers for Computer Buffs & Other Technological Types*. New York: McGraw-Hill.

Elerath, J. G. and Pecht, M. (2009). A highly accurate method for assessing reliability of redundant arrays of inexpensive disks (RAID). *Computers, IEEE Transactions on*, 58(3): 289–299.

El-Sayed, M. and Jaffe, J. (2002). A view of telecommunications network evolution. *IEEE Communications Magazine*, 40(12): 74–81, December.

PBS LearningMedia (1998). ENIAC is built 1945. (n.d.). Retrieved from http://www.pbs.org/wgbh/aso/databank/entries/dt45en.html.

Erl, T. (2008). *SOA Principles of Service Design*. Upper Saddle River, NJ: Prentice Hall.

Fernandes, A. L. (2004). Current architectures for parallel processing. Portugal: ICCA. Retrieved from http://gec.di.uminho.pt/discip/minf/ac0304/ICCA04/Proc/T3-ParArch.pdf.

Flynn, M. J. (1972). Some computer organizations and their effectiveness. *IEEE Transactions on Computers*, C-21(9): 948–960.

Fowler, M. (2004). *UML Distilled: A Brief Guide to the Standard Object Modeling Language*. New York: Addison-Wesley Professional.

Freeman, R. (2005). *Fundamentals of Telecommunications*. New York: Wiley.

Fritts, J. and Wolf, W. (2000). Evaluation of static and dynamic scheduling for media processors. In *2nd Workshop on Media Processors and DSPs in conjunction with 33rd Annual International Symposium on Microarchitecture*. Retrieved May 9, 2015, from http://mathcs.slu.edu/~fritts/papers/fritts_mpdsp00_1.pdf.

Gardner, M. (1986). *Knotted Doughnuts and Other Mathematical Entertainments* (pp. 85–93). New York: W. H. Freeman.

Gibson, G. A. (1999). Performance and reliability in redundant arrays of inexpensive disks. In *1989 Computer Measurement Group Annual Conference Proceedings* (pp. 1–17), December 1989.

Gibson, G. A. and Van Meter, R. (2000). Network attached storage architecture. *Communications of the ACM*, 43(11): 37–45.

Glanz, J. Google details, and defends, its use of electricity. *New York Times*, September 8, 2007. http://www.nytimes.com/2011/09/09/technology/google-details-and-defends-its-use-of-electricity.html?_r=1&.

Goldstein, A., Weyl, E., and Lazaris, L. (2011). *HTML5 & CSS3 for the Real World*. 1st Ed. SitePoint, Victoria, Australia.

Good, N. S. and Krekelberg, A. (2003). Usability and privacy: A study of Kazaa P2P file-sharing. In *Proceedings of the SIGCHI Conference on Human Factors in Computing Systems* (pp. 137–144). New York, ACM, April.

Grega, A. (2012). A brief history of the mainframe world. *IBM Destination Z: Destination Z Community*, 1. MSP TechMedia, Minneapolis MN. Retrieved from http://destinationz.org/Academia/Articles/A-Brief-History-of-the-Mainframe-World.aspx.

Grego, P. (2009). *Astronomical Cybersketching* (p. 12). Berlin: Springer.

Gupta, M. (2002). *Storage Area Network Fundamentals*. Indianapolis, IN: Cisco Press.

Halacy, D. S. (1970). *Charles Babbage, Father of the Computer*. New York: Crowell-Collier Press.

Henderson, H. (2009). *Encyclopedia of Computer Science and Technology* (Revised Edition). (p. 13.) New York: Infobase.

Hennessy, J. L. and Patterson, D. A. (2005). *Computer Architecture: A Quantitative Approach*. (4th edn), Burlington, VT: Morgan Kaufmann.

Henning, J. L. (2000). SPEC CPU2000: Measuring CPU performance in the new millennium. *Computer*, 33(7): 28–35.

Hess, K. and Newman, A. (2009). *Practical Virtualization Solutions: Virtualization from the Trenches*. Englewood Cliffs, NJ: Prentice Hall.

Hiremane, R. (2005). From Moore's law to Intel innovation: Prediction to reality. *Technology@Intel Magazine*, April.

Horne, C. (2007) Understanding full virtualization, paravirtualization and hardware assist. White paper, VMware Inc.

Howells, M. (2000). High tech in the 90s: The 1890 Census. *Ancestry Magazine*, March/April.

Hunt, J. (2012). *Java for Practitioners: An Introduction and Reference to Java and Object Orientation*. Berlin: Springer Science & Business Media.

Hunt, J. and Loftus, C. (2012). *Guide to J2EE: Enterprise Java*. Berlin: Springer Science & Business Media.Internet World Stats. Internet users in the world by regions: November 2015. Miniwatts Marketing Group, 2015. Retrieved from http://www.internetworldstats.com/stats.htm.

IBM. (n. d.). WebSphere software. Retrieved from http://www.ibm.com/software/websphere.

Intel. Microprocessor quick reference guide. 2008. Retrieved from http://www.intel.com/press-room/kits/quickreffam.htm#XeonIII.

Ishii, Y. (2007). Fused two-level branch prediction with ahead calculation. *Journal of Instruction-Level Parallelism*, 9: 1–19. Retrieved May 9, 2015, from http://www.jilp.org/vol9/v9paper4.pdf.

Ivar, J. and Ng, P. W. (2004). *Aspect-Oriented Software Development with Use Cases*. New York: Addison-Wesley.

Jain, R., Werth, J., and Browne, J. C. (Eds). (2012). *Input/Output in Parallel and Distributed Computer Systems* (Vol. 362). Berlin, Germany: Springer Science & Business Media.

Johnson, R. and Hoeller, J. (2004). *Expert One-on-One J2EE Development without EJB*. New York: Wiley.

Josuttis, N. M. (2007). *SOA in Practice: The Art of Distributed System Design*. Sebastopol, CA: O'Reilly Media.

Juola, P. (2005). *Principles of Computer Organization and Assembly Language*. Upper Saddle River, NJ: Prentice-Hall.

Kahan, W. (1996). IEEE standard 754 for binary floating-point arithmetic. *Lecture Notes on the Status of IEEE*, University of California, Berkeley, CA, pages: 1–30. Retrieved from http://i-n-d-e-p-t-h.googlecode.com/files/IEEE754.pdf

Kanizsa, G. (1955). Margini quasi-percettivi in campi con stimolazione omogenea. *Rivista di Psicologia*, 49(1): 7–30.

Kanizsa, G. (1976). Subjective contours. *Scientific American*, 234(4): 48–52.

Khan, D. M. and Mohamudally, N. (2011). From mainframe to cloud computing: A study of programming paradigms with the evolution of client-server architecture. *Journal of Computing*, 3(12): 21–27.

Khattar, R. K., Murphy, M. S., Tarella, G. J., and Nystrom, K. E. (1999). *Introduction to Storage Area Network, SAN*. Kenya: IBM Corporation, International Technical Support Organization.

Koivisto, D. (2005). *What Amdahl's Law Can Tell Us About Multicores and Multiprocessing*. Technical Report 238112, EETimes Network, Santa Clara, CA.

Kumar, R. and Singh, P. K. (2013). Instruction level parallelism: The role of architecture and compiler. *Proceeding of ICETSTM, 21, 22*. Retrieved May 9, 2015, from https://www.researchgate.net/profile/Rajendra_Kumar24/publication/260424013_INSTRUCTION_LEVEL_PARALLELISM__THE_ROLE_OF_ARCHITECTURE_AND_COMPILER/links/00b7d53130980ce2ab000000.pdf.

Kurose, J. E. and Ross, K. W. (2012). *Computer Networking: A Top-Down Approach*. (6th edn), New York: Addison Wesley.

Lai, S. (2001). Future trends of nonvolatile memory technology. Retrieved May 9, 2015, from http://www.eecs.umich.edu/courses/eecs598/handouts/week5_Muller_NVM_IEDM2004.pdf.

Larman, C. (2005). *Applying UML and Patterns: An Introduction to Object-Oriented Analysis and Design and Iterative Development*. London: Pearson Education.

Laskey, K. B. and Laskey, K. (2009). Service oriented architecture. *Wiley Interdisciplinary Reviews: Computational Statistics*, 1(1): 101–105.

Li, K. (2003). Error correction code. Retrieved May 9, 2015, from http://midas.herts.ac.uk/reports/plato/Reports2003/027/2003-27.pdf.

Liang, J., Kumar, R., and Ross, K. W. (2004). *Understanding Kazaa*. New York: Polytechnic University.

Lilja, D. J. (2000). *Measuring Computer Performance: A Practitioner's Guide*. Cambridge, MA: University Press.

Lindholm, T., Yellin, F., Bracha, G., and Buckley, A. (2014). *The Java Virtual Machine Specification*. London: Pearson Education.

Lister, A. (2013). *Fundamentals of Operating Systems*. Berlin: Springer Science & Business Media.

Löwy, J. (2001). *COM and NET Component Services*. Sebastopol, CA: O'Reilly Media.

Ma, D. (2007). The business model of "software-as-a-service". *InServices Computing, 2007. SCC 2007. IEEE International Conference on* (pp. 701–702). Salt Lake City, UT: IEEE.

Mahoney, M. S. and Haigh, T. (2011). *Histories of Computing*. Boston, MA: Harvard University Press.

Marshall, D. (2007). *Understanding Full Virtualization, Paravirtualization, and Hardware Assist*. vmware.

Martin, R. and Hoover, J. (2008). Guide to cloud computing. *Information Week*, June 21, 2008, www.informationweek.com.

Matick, R. E., Heller, T. J., and Ignatowski, M. (2001). Analytical analysis of finite cache penalty and cycles per instruction of a multiprocessor memory hierarchy using miss rates and queuing theory. *IBM Journal of Research And Development*, 45(6): 819–842.

McCartney, S. (2001). *ENIAC: The Triumphs and Tragedies of the World's First Computer*. New York: Berkley Publishing Group.

McHoes, A. and Flynn, I. M. (2013). *Understanding Operating Systems*. Boston, MA: Cengage Learning.

Mell, P. and T. Grance. 2009. The NIST definition of cloud computing. National Institute of Standards and Technology, Information Technology Laboratory, Version 15, 10-7-09. Retrieved May 9, 2015, from http://www.csrc.nist.gov/groups/SNS/cloud-comjputing/index.html.

Metropolis, N. (ed.). (2014). *History of Computing in the Twentieth Century*. Amsterdam: Elsevier.

Michael, G. (n. d.). The Univac 1 computer. Retrieved from http://www.computer-history.info/Page4.dir/pages/Univac.dir/index.html.

Micheloni, R., Marelli, A., and Ravasio, R. (2008). Error correction codes. In *Error Correction Codes for Non-Volatile Memories* (pp. 35–59). Berlin: Springer.

Microsoft. The OSI model's seven layers defined and functions explained. Microsoft Support. Retrieved May 9, 2015, from https://support.microsoft.com/en-us/kb/103884.

Miller, L. C. (2012). *Server Virtualization for Dummies*. Oracle Special Edn, New York: Wiley. Retrieved May 9, 2015, from http://www.oracle.com/oms/hardware/extremeperformance/assets/ept -eb-dummies-server-1641465.pdf.

Moore, G. E. Moore, G.E. Cramming more components onto integrated circuits. *Electronics*, 38, 114, 1965. (Reprinted in *Proc. IEEE*, 86, 82–85, 1998.)

Newcomer, E. and Lomow, G. (2005). *Understanding SOA with Web Services*. New York: Addison-Wesley.

Orfali, R. and Harkey, D. (2007). *Client/Server Programming with Java and Corba* (with CD). New York: Wiley.

Ormrod, J. E. and Davis, K. M. (2004). *Human Learning*. New York: Merrill.

Pappas, T. (1989). *The Joy of Mathematics* (pp. 64–65). San Carlos, CA: Wide World.

Parameswaran, M., Susarla, A., and Whinston, A. B. (2001). P2P networking: An information-sharing alternative. *Computer*, 34(7): 31–38.

Patterson, D. A. and Hennessy, J. L. (2008). *Computer Organization & Design: The Hardware/Software Interface*. (4th edn), Burlington, VT: Morgan Kaufmann.

Patterson, D. A., Gibson, G., and Katz, R. H. (1988). *A Case for Redundant Arrays of Inexpensive Disks (RAID)* (Vol. 17, pp. 109–116). New York: ACM.

Peter, A. (1995). *IBM PC Assembly Language and Programming*. (3rd edn), Upper Saddle River, NJ: Prentice-Hall.

Phansalkar, A., Joshi, A., Eeckhout, L., and John, L. (2004). Four generations of SPEC CPU benchmarks: What has changed and what has not. Technical Report TR-041026-01-1. Austin, TX: University of Texas.

Pugh, E. W. (2002). Origins of software bundling. *IEEE Annals of the History of Computing*, 24(1): 57–58.

Randell, B. (Ed.). (2013). *The Origins of Digital Computers: Selected Papers*. Berlin: Springer.

Red Hat. (n. d.). Technology. Retrieved from http://www.jboss.org/technology/.

Redin, J. (2001). *A Brief History of Mechanical Calculators*. Retrieved May 9, 2015, from http://www.xnumber.com/xnumber/mechanical1.htm. Part II. http://www.xnumber.com/xnumber/mechanical2.htm. Part III. http://www.xnumber.com/xnumber/mechanical1.htm.

Reese, G. (2009). *Cloud Application Architectures: Building Applications and Infrastructure in the Cloud*. Sebastopol, CA: O'Reilly Media.

Risvik, K. M., Aasheim, Y., and Lidal, M. (2003). Multi-tier architecture for web search engines. In *Web Congress, 2003. Proceedings. First Latin American* (pp. 132–143), IEEE, November.

Roff, J. T. (2001). *ADO ActiveX Data Objects*. Sebastopol, CA: O'Reilly Media.

Roger, R. F. (2002). *Computer Sciences* (p. 175). Indianapolis, IN: Macmillan.

Rosen, M., Lublinsky, B., Smith, K. T., and Balcer, M. J. (2012). *Applied SOA: Service-Oriented Architecture and Design Strategies*. New York: Wiley.

Saroiu, S., Gummadi, K. P., and Gribble, S. D. (2003). Measuring and analyzing the characteristics of Napster and Gnutella hosts. *Multimedia Systems*, 9(2): 170–184.

Schildt, H. and Coward, D. (2011). *Java: The Complete Reference*. New York: McGraw-Hill.

Seznec, A. and Fraboulet, A. (2003). Effective ahead pipelining of the instruction address generation. In *Proceedings of the 30th Annual International Symposium on Computer Architecture* (pp. 241–252), San Diego, CA, IEEE, June.

Shanley, T. (2010). *×86 Instruction Set Architecture*. New York: MindShare.

Siegel, J. (2000). *CORBA 3 Fundamentals and Programming* (Vol. 2). New York: Wiley.

Sikora, M. (2008). *EJB 3 Developer Guide*. Birmingham, England: Packt.

Silberschatz, A., Galvin, P., and Gagne, G. (2013). *Operating System Concepts*. (9th edn.), New York: Wiley.

Silberschatz, A., Galvin, P. B., Gagne, G., and Silberschatz, A. (1998). *Operating System Concepts* (Vol. 4). New York: Addison-Wesley.

Silc, J., Robic, B., and Ungerer, T. (2012). *Processor Architecture: From Dataflow to Superscalar and Beyond*. Berlin: Springer Science & Business Media.

Sklar, B. (2001). *Digital Communications: Fundamentals and Applications*. Englewood Cliffs, NJ: Prentice Hall.

Smotherman, M. (2001). Understanding EPIC architectures and implementations. South Carolina: Department of Computer Science, Clemson University. Retrieved May 9, 2015, from https://www.cs.auckland.ac.nz/courses/compsci703s1c/resources/Smothermanacmse_epic.pdf.

Stallings, W. (1987). *Handbook of Computer-Communications Standards; Vol. 1: The Open Systems Interconnection (OSI) Model and OSI-Related Standards*. Indianapolis, IN: Macmillan.

Stallings, W. (2000). *Local and Metropolitan Area Networks*. (6th edn.), Upper Saddle River, NJ: Prentice Hall.

Stallings, W. (2013). *Computer Organization and Architecture, Designing for Performance*. (9th edn.), London: Pearson Education.

Stephen, S. (2011). *Object-Oriented and Classical Software Engineering*. New York: McGraw-Hill Education.

Swedin, E. G. and Ferro, D. L. (2007). *Computers: The Life Story of a Technology* (p. 26). Baltimore, MD: JHU Press.

Tanenbaum, A. S. (1979). *Structured Computer Organization*. Englewood Cliffs, NJ: Prentice-Hall.

Tanenbaum, A. S. (2003). *Computer Networks*. Upper Saddle River, NJ: Prentice-Hall.

Tanenbaum, A. S. (2006). *Structured Computer Organization*. London: Pearson Education.

Tanenbaum, A. S. (2010). *Computer Networks*. (5th edn.), Englewood Cliffs, NJ: Prentice-Hall.

Tanenbaum, A. S. and Bos, H. (2014). *Modern Operating Systems*. (4th edn.), Englewood Cliffs, NJ: Prentice-Hall.

Tatnall, A. (2012). *History of Computers: Hardware and Software Development. Encyclopedia of Life Support Systems*. Ramsey, Isle of Man: UNESCO-Eolss.

Thornton, J. (1970). Design of a computer: The control data 6600. Glenview, IL: Scott, Foresman. Retrieved May 9, 2015, from http://ygdes.com/CDC/DesignOfAComputer_CDC6600.pdf.

Tritsch, B. (2004). *Microsoft Windows Server 2003 Terminal Services*. Washington, DC: Microsoft Press.van der Meulen, R. and Pettey, C. Gartner Says More than 1 Billion PCs In Use Worldwide and Headed to 2 Billion Units by 2014. Gartner Newsroom, June 23, 2008. Retrieved from http://www.gartner.com/newsroom/id/703807.

van der Meulen, R. and Rivera, J. Gartner says global devices shipments to grow 2.8 percent in 2015. Gartner Newsroom, March 19, 2015. Retrieved from http://www.gartner.com/newsroom/id/3010017.

Van der Spiegel, J., Tau, J. F. Ala'ilima, T. F., and L. Ang, P. (2000). The ENIAC: History, operation and reconstruction in VLSI. In R. Rojas and U. Hashagen (eds), *The First Computers: History and Architectures* (pp.121–178), Cambridge, MA: MIT Press.

Vecchiola, C., Chu, X., and Buyya, K. (2009). Aneka: A software platform for NET-based cloud computing. In W. Gentzsch, L. Grandinetti, and G. Joubert (Eds), *High Speed and Large Scale Scientific Computing* (pp. 267–295), Amsterdam: IOS Press.

Veerasamy, B. D. (2010). Concurrent approach to Flynn's MPMD classification through Java. *International Journal of Computer Science and Network Security*, 10(2): 164.

Velte, T., Velte, A., and Elsenpeter, R. (2009). *Cloud Computing, A Practical Approach*. New York: McGraw-Hill.

Von Neumann, J. (1988). *John von Neumann*. New York: American Mathematical Society.

W3 Counter. May 2007 market share. Awio Web Services, 2015. Retrieved from http://www.w3counter.com/globalstats.php?year=2007&month=5.

W3 Counter. September 2014 market share. Awio Web Services, 2015. Retrieved from http://www.w3counter.com/globalstats.php?year=2014&month=9.

Weng, N. and Wolf, T. (2004). Pipelining vs. multiprocessors—Choosing the right network processor system topology. In *Proceedings of Advanced Networking and Communications Hardware Workshop (ANCHOR 2004) in conjunction with The 31st Annual International Symposium on Computer Architecture*, ISCA, IEEE, Munich, Germany.

Wexelblat, R. L. (ed.). (2014). *History of Programming Languages*. Orlando, FL: Academic Press.

Winkler, I. and Cowan, N. (2005). From sensory to long-term memory evidence from auditory memory reactivation studies. *Experimental Psychology,* 52 (1): 3–20.

Wolf, C. and Halter, E. M. (2005). *Virtualization: From the Desktop to the Enterprise*. New York: Apress.

Woods, D. and T. Mattern. (2006). *Enterprise SOA: Designing IT for Business Innovation*. Sebastopol, CA: O'Reilly Media.

Woody, T. Google is on the way to quietly becoming an electric utility. *Quartz,* Sept 18, 2013. Retrieved from http://qz.com/125407/google-is-on-the-way-to-quietly-becoming-an-electric-utility/.

Glossary

access algorithms: various algorithms that are implemented by the operating system in order to optimize the disk access time. Some of these algorithms include (1) first come first served (FCFS), (2) shortest time first (STF), (3) scan, (4) circular scan (C-Scan), and (5) scan but only up to the last request (C-Look), which represents an improvement over C-Scan which scans to the end of the disk.

accumulator: a register used by the processor during computations. The first computers had just one register, called accumulator; later, when the number of the registers increased, their name changed as well.

accumulator-based architecture: an architecture that uses one register, called *accumulator*; it resembles the common calculator. For adding two numbers, for example, one number is stored in the accumulator and the second number is part of the ADD instruction. The result will be stored in the accumulator.

address translation: the process that translates the virtual addresses used by the running programs into the real location (physical) in memory. The memory management unit (MMU) is responsible for the address translation. After the translation, the physical address is checked against the cache. If it was found, it is a hit; otherwise, it is a miss.

addressing modes: refers to the way instructions can access variables that are stored in memory. CISC computers implement many such modes, which may include immediate (the address is in the instruction); pointer (the address is in a register); displacement (a fixed number specified in the instruction is added to a pointer or an immediate address; memory indirect, in which the memory address is a pointer to the real address; and many others.

ADSL (asymmetric digital subscriber line): a fast data communication technology that enables high transfer rates.

algorithm: a systematic procedure intended for achieving a specific goal or performing some purposeful computation.

ALU (arithmetic and logic unit): the electronic circuit within the processor that executes the instructions. Usually, it will receive the opcode (the instruction to be performed) and one or two operands and will produce an output result.

Amdahl's law: defined by Gene Amdahl, it states that that the performance enhancements to be gained by some component are limited by the percentage of time the component is being used.

API (application programming interface): refers to a set of definitions and tools designed for accessing and application. The API is the protocol that governs the interaction with the application.

application programming interface: see API

aspect-oriented architecture: a way to model the nonfunctional requirements of the system as well as other quality and behavioral aspects.

aspect weaver: a programming tool that understands the aspects and builds the appropriate code. It actually runs before the compilation and inserts new instructions into a class so it adheres to the defined concerns (as defined by the aspect). The new classes, sometimes called *woven classes*, consist of the integration of the original class with the additional aspect code.

assembler: a special compiler that translates the assembly language instructions into object code.

assembly language: sometimes called *assembler*, a low programming language in which usually the object code mnemonics (instructions) were replaced by more human-readable and understandable names.

asymmetric digital subscriber line: see ADSL

BCD: A method for representing numbers wherein each number is written as a corresponding 4-bit binary pattern. The number 4096, for example, would be written in BCD as 0100 0000 1001 0110.

benchmark programs: refers to a large set of existing as well as artificial programs that were used for assessing the processors performance.

big and little endian: refers to the direction the bits are transferred to and from memory. Big endian starts with the most significant bit first, while little endian starts with the least significant bit first. Neither direction has any effect on the running program/application.

binary: a numbering system in which all digits are either 0 or 1. The number 15, for example, is written as 1111. The binary system is just an additional system; however, it is important in the computing context. Since computers use two values (on, off) the binary system uses two digits (called *bits*—binary digit).

bit (or binary digit): the minimal unit of digital data. It stores a single binary value (0 or 1).

branch prediction: a hardware mechanism that tries to predict the behavior of conditional instructions based on their previous execution.

broker architecture: an implementation of SOA in a distributed environment. The broker is a component responsible for the communication between the various decoupled and distributed components. It is responsible for the mechanism that forwards the messages (requests) and returns the results. In its basic configuration, a broker architecture will utilize three components: clients, servers, and a broker. The clients mainly implement the user interface (similar to the presentation layer in a client/server architecture). In addition, the client sends requests to the servers utilizing the broker. The servers implement the services they provide, register the services through the broker, and respond to incoming requests by executing the service and sending back the results. The broker has to register and maintain a list of available services, provide a common interface for the clients to interact with, transfer the messages (requests) to the appropriate server, and handle various exception situations.

bus: in computing, the communication system responsible for the data transfer between the various devices within the computer. There is a large variety of buses with various widths and speeds. The bus concept changed and evolved over the years. Originally, there was just one bus, but it became a bottleneck. Then there were several buses, and currently most computers utilize a bus hierarchy, with numerous busses working at various speeds.

bus logical structure: The bus is logically divided into three main communication paths: one responsible for sending the commands, the second for data, and the third for control.

bus management: can be from a central location (central arbitration), or distributed. The central arbitration is characterized by one central unit (arbitrator) that manages the bus transfers. Every device that wants to use the bus will first ask the arbitrator for permission, and only after the permission is granted can the device use the bus for its purposes. Distributed arbitration is characterized by the fact that there is no central management for the bus activities. Instead of the central unit, the management is done collaboratively by all the devices by following the defined protocol.

bus principle: The first bus appeared in a PDP computer (manufactured by DEC). The idea behind implementing the bus concept was to lower the computer's price. Prior to the bus, each device was connected to all other devices on the system, creating a complicated and expensive mechanism of data transfer. The common bus that all devices connected to was cheaper, although slower.

bus transactions: The transaction can be a full transaction in which the devices hold the bus for the whole duration of the transaction. Alternatively, it can be a split transaction in which each time there is a block to be transferred, the bus will be requested, used, and released.

bus width: the number of bit (or bytes) that are transferred by the bus in one cycle. Visually, it may resemble a road in which the width corresponds to the number of lanes and the number of cars that can go through at the same time.

byte: a unit of digital information. Usually, it refers to 8 bits of data.

cache hit: the situation in which the required datum is found in the cache.

cache memory: a special type of memory, used mainly by the CPU and intended for reducing the access time to main memory. The cache memory is faster and smaller and contains copies of the frequent used data located in main memory.

cache miss: the situation in which the datum is not in cache and has to be brought from the lower memory level.

central processing unit: see CPU

CISC (complex instruction set computer): uses many addressing modes and many instructions with varying lengths and execution times. The variety of instructions was made possible by using microinstructions. The main problem associated with CISC technology is that the CU is extremely complex, which slows down the development of new processors.

classification of computers: categorizing computers by their size or functionality (minicomputers, microcomputers, mainframes, servers, supercomputers).

client/server architecture: refers to an architecture that is based on two main components, the client and the server. Although both the client and the server can reside on the same computer, usually these will be two distinct systems. There are many possibilities for implementing a client/server architecture, starting from both running on the same computer, through two systems that are connected by a local area network, and up to a configuration that implements the communication over a wide area network (WAN) like the Internet.

cloud computing: a computing model that is based on using a network for accessing computing resources. One of the important capabilities of cloud computing is its elasticity, which provides a dynamic configurable infrastructure. Cloud computing business models stress the use of public resources with a pay-per-use mechanism instead of the existing computing infrastructure.

COM (component object model) and DCOM (distributed component object model): the Microsoft architecture for distributed systems. COM is a platform-independent, distributed, object-oriented system for creating binary components that can communicate.

common object request broker architecture: see CORBA

complex instruction set computer: see CISC

compiler: a computer program that reads the source code (instruction written in a specific programming language) and translates it to a different language or into object code (the binary code understood by the hardware).

component object model: see COM

computer systems: every computer system, regardless of its classification or type, has a common architecture that consists of a processor, memory, buses (or communication channels) and I/O devices.

computers' generation: an old term that was used for classifying computers by the hardware technology that was used for their design. The modern terms relate to the specific role the computer plays in the organization and not the hardware technology it uses, which, for the ordinary user, is irrelevant.

context switching: the process that changes the process that is being executed by the processor. Before the processor can switch to a different process, all the registers' content has to be saved, as well as other running variables. Then the registers and the running environment of the new process have to be loaded (including reloading the registers with their original content).

control unit: see CU

CORBA (common object request broker architecture): a standard implementation of a broker architecture. It was developed mutually by various interested organizations and was adopted as a standard by OMG and ISO.

core: In computing, core refers to an independent processing unit. A multicore processor is one CPU, which consists of several processing units, each one capable of executing a different process.

CPI (cycles per instruction): measures how many cycles are required for executing one instruction. Since different instructions may require different number of cycles, CPI is usually an average number or is provided per a specific instruction. CPI is one of the performance indicators. While two or three decades ago, executing an instruction required several cycles, modern systems can execute (on average) several instructions per cycle.

CPI-based metric: a performance metric intended to estimate the execution time based on CPI. For using a CPI-based metric, we will have to estimate the mix of instructions used in a specific program. Each instruction has its CPI, and the total execution time will be given in cycles.

CPU (central processing unit): the hardware component within the computer that executes the instructions. The CPU speed is one of the most important factors that define the computers performance. In the past, the speed was increased by reducing the CPU's cycle time. In the last decade, speed has been gained by incorporating additional cores.

CPU time (or processor time): the amount of time the processor worked on the program.

CU (control unit): the electronic circuit within the processor responsible for all the processor's "housekeeping." While the ALU executes the instruction, the CU is responsible for bringing it from memory, fetching the operands, and storing the result back in its location (memory or register) as specified by the instruction.

cycles per instruction: see CPI

database management system: see DBMS

DBMS (database management system): the software that creates, retrieves, updates, and manages the data.

decimal numbering system: the standard system used by humans. It includes 10 symbols (digits), so its base is 10. The value of the number is obtained by multiplying each digit's value by a power of 10 designated by the location and summing up all values.

difference engine: a mechanical calculator design by Charles Babbage. It was intended to tabulate and solve polynomial functions.

direct memory access: see DMA

disk reading/writing speed: determined by (1) the rotational speed, (2) seek time (the time required for the head to reach the required track), and (3) latency (the time required for the disk to rotate until the requested sector is under the reading/writing head).

disk's structure: The mechanical disk (hard drive) usually contains one or more magnetic platters and a moving arm with reading/writing heads. The platter is divided into tracks and sectors.

DMA (direct memory access): an I/O method in which the device transfers the data directly into memory (assuming it is an input command) and signals the operating system only at the end of the whole transfer.

dynamic scheduling: refers to a hardware mechanism that changes the order of the instructions executed in order to minimize hazards.

ECC (error correction code): a method used for ensuring the integrity of digital data stored or transferred. There are various methods, and in most cases, it is achieved by adding data to the original content. The extra data provides the receiver with the possibility of validating the content and, in some cases, even correcting the error introduced.

EIS (enterprise information systems): a term that defines an information system that improves overall organizational efficiency and effectiveness. Usually, this is achieved by integrating many or all computing resources and data.

elapsed time: sometimes called wall clock time; the amount of time that was required to run the program. This time includes the processor time as well as any other time needed, such as that taken to read the information from the hard drive, access memory, and so on.

ENIAC (Electronic Numerical Integrator and Computer): the first electronic general-purpose computer with reprogrammed capabilities. The ENIAC was designed by John Mauchly and J. Presper Eckert of the University of Pennsylvania.

enterprise information systems: see EIS

error correction code: see ECC

extensible markup language: see XML

file server: a concept for overcoming some of the PC's limitations. The server is connected to the network and provides access to its files. The concept was later enhanced to support many other types of servers such as print servers, e-mail servers, compute intensive servers, and so on.

forwarding: see loop buffer

GB (gigabytes): or a billion (10^9) bytes; a size unit used to define memory size in the current generation computers and disks.

Harvard architecture: an architecture that uses two separate memories, one for instructions and the other for data. This architecture can produce more predictable response times, so it is used by signal processing and real-time systems.

hexadecimal system: the system that uses 16 digits (the ordinary 0–9 and A, B, C, D, E, F). It is important since 16 is a power of 2, so hexadecimal numbers can be used to represent binary numbers so they be more readable. This is especially true for large numbers.

HTML (hypertext markup language): a standard language for defining and building websites. The browser reads the HTML files and displays the content embedded in the files according to the HTML definitions.

hypertext markup language: see HTML

IAS machine: a computer built by the Institute for Advanced Study (IAS) at Princeton University based on the von Neumann design.

IEEE 754 Standard: a standard for representing real binary numbers. The standard resembles scientific notation with some minor modifications. The binary number is divided into three parts: (1) the number's sign, (2) a biased exponent, (3) the mantissa. The 32-bit floating-point format consists of one sign bit, 8 exponent bits, and 23 mantissa bits. When using 64-bits, the floating-point format consists of one sign bit, 11 exponent bits, and 52 mantissa bits.

ILP (instruction-level parallelism): a pipeline mechanism that splits the single instruction into its microinstructions and executes these in parallel.

ILP hazards: a list of possible hazards that may stop or delay the pipeline, such as an unbalanced pipeline, read after write (RAW), write after read (WAR), and write after write (WAW).

information technology: see IT

instruction execution: involves several steps: (1) fetching the instruction, which involves calculating the address in memory and bringing the appropriate bytes containing the instruction and its operands; (2) decoding the instruction for evaluating if it is a valid one and, if it is valid, figuring out how many operands it has; (3) copying the operands from their locations (memory and or general-purpose registers) into the internal ALU registers; (4) issuing the instruction to be executed by signaling the ALU that all input data is available; (5) copying the result from the ALU internal register to the defined destination (memory or register). Each of these steps can be further divided into additional substeps.

instruction level parallelism: see ILP

instruction pointer: see IP

Internet of things: see IoT

Internet service provider: see ISP

interrupt: a signal that is created by the hardware or a running program with the intention of getting the operating system's attention. For example, if a device that was asked to read some data is ready to deliver the data, it will issue an interrupt. The operating system will be involved, which will handle the request further.

interrupt-based I/O: in which the program or application initiates the I/O operation but does not wait. If it has other computations to perform, it may continue, or else it can relinquish the processor. When the device is ready with the I/O, it will signal the operating system by creating an interrupt.

I/O buffering: refers to the various possibilities for defining buffers to assist and enhance the I/O. This ranges from no buffers allocated in the operating system, to one buffer, or many. When the operating system maintains several buffers, it can read larger blocks and even issue read-ahead commands to speed up the program's execution.

IoT (Internet of things or network of things): refers to an environment in which a large variety of entities have unique identifiers and are able to communicate over a network. This is an elaborated form of communication. Originally, communication started with human-to-human; it then moved on to human-to-computer, and the last stage is machine-to-machine communication. Usually IoT requires an integration of hierarchical networks, such as personal networks, local area networks (LAN) and wide area networks (WAN).

IP (instruction pointer): an internal register used by the hardware, which holds the address of the next instruction to be executed. During sequential execution, the register will point to the next instruction. In cases of branches, it may point to a different address rather than the next one based on the evaluation of the executing instruction.

iron law of processor performance: says that the time required to run a program is a product of the number of instructions to be executed, the cycles required per instruction, and the cycle time.

ISP (Internet service provider): an organization that provide access to the Internet. In many cases, the ISP provides additional services such as hosting websites, e-mail services, enhanced security, and so on.

IT (information technology): a general term that refers to the organizational computing infrastructure; in other words, it is the usage of computers and communication to create, process, store, retrieve, and secure the organization's digital resources.

J2EE (Java 2 Enterprise Edition): a Java-based, platform-independent environment for the design, development, and deployment of web-based applications.

Java: a programming language developed by Sun microsystem (currently part of Oracle Corporation). Java is part of a universal architecture capable of running common code on a variety of platforms by using JVM (Java virtual machine).

Java remote method invocation (RMI) and Java Beans: RMI is the Java mechanism that provides reference to a remote object and invokes its methods. RMI was developed explicitly for objects and supports many of their characteristics, such as inheritance, polymorphism, and dynamic invocation. Java beans are classes that were developed according to specific conventions regarding their properties and interface definitions. Beans can be manipulated using a visual builder tool to form larger beans or an application. For that reason, the beans have to publish their attributes and behaviors using special method signature patterns. The visual builder tool recognizes these patterns when integrating the beans.

Java virtual machine: see JVM

JVM (Java virtual machine): an abstract (virtual) machine that can run the Java instructions. The JVM is a software layer that understands and runs Java binary codes (Bytecode).

KB (kilobytes): or a thousand bytes; a size unit used to define memory size in very old computers or in modern limited appliances.

LAN (local area network): a computer network that connects computers and other related devices in a relatively small area, such as a campus.

layered architecture: a concept in which the application is divided into several logical layers. In most cases, the layers are organized in a hierarchical order, and each layer can access only the layer underneath it.

local area network: see LAN

loop buffer (or forwarding): another hardware mechanism that is intended to reduce delays. In some cases, the next instruction needs an operand that is the output of the previous instruction, and the mechanism copies the content of the internal output register into the internal input register.

mainframe: a high-performance computer that was used as the main organization's computational engine. The mainframe was very large and expensive and was gradually and partially replaced by other cheaper and more efficient solutions.

MALLOC: an operating system function intended for dynamic allocation of memory to the running process. Usually, there are two types of variables: static variables, which reside in the program and exist as long as the program is running; and automatic variables, which can be stored in the process stack every time the program calls a new function (or method). There are cases in which these two types of variables are not flexible enough, and then the software developer can use a third type to be stored in a newly acquired piece of memory. The program uses the MALLOC function to get these additional memory cells, and when they are no longer required, the memory will be returned to the operating system.

Mark I—The Harvard Mark I: also called the IBM Automatic Sequence Controlled Calculator (ASCC); a general-purpose electromechanical computer. It was designed by Howard Aiken and built by IBM, and was later used during World War II.

MB (megabytes): or a million bytes; a size unit used to define memory size in older computers or in modern limited appliances.

MVC architecture: a model in which the application resembles the three-tier architecture. The application is built using three distinct parts: the model that represents the knowledge maintained by the system; the view, which is the visual representation; and the controller, which represents the glue between the two or the business logic.

memory hierarchy: a term that defines the actual memory organization used by modern computers. Usually, there are several levels of memory, and data may be moved between them automatically without any involvement of the developer or the application that is being executed.

memory organization: The memory may be organized using various methods; however, in all cases, the developer's view is of a one-dimensional array of cells.

memory performance: important to the overall system's performance, this is enhanced using several techniques: technology that improves the memory speed, increased memory hierarchy levels, interleaving, and a wider bus.

memory–register-based architecture: an architecture in which there are several registers; however, the instructions use just one register, and other operands, if they exist, are in memory.

microinstructions: sometimes called micro code; a set of instruction's building blocks. Each instruction executed by the processor has some predefined components, such as fetching the instruction, decoding it, and so on. These building blocks are called microinstructions.

miss penalty: refers to the actions to be performed when a miss occurs and the time penalty it costs.

Moore's law: an observation made by Gordon E. Moore (the cofounder of Intel). In 1965, he projected that the number of components in an integrated circuit will double every year. Later he changed it to doubling every two years.

NAS (network attached storage): a storage device that provides access for users that are connected to the network.

negative binary numbers: Contrary to the "-" (the minus sign) used in decimal notation, the sign in the binary notation is actually part of the number. There are three ways of representing signed numbers: (1) Sign and magnitude, in which the first bit is the sign bit (one denotes a negative number) and the other bits are the value (or the magnitude of the number). This representation resembles the normal decimal notation of a sign followed by a number. (2) One's complement, in which the positive number is migrated to a negative one by flipping each bit. (3) Two's complement, in which the binary number is obtained by the one's complement plus adding a binary one. Most systems use the two's complement notation.

.net: (pronounced dot net) a framework developed by Microsoft. It includes a large set of tools (classes) that provide programming language interoperability and access to a variety of runtime services.

network attached storage: see NAS

NC (network computer): a type of computer with a limited memory, storage, and processing power. The idea of the NC started in the late 1990s, and it matured a decade later. These computers, which are connected to the network, get all the required services from servers on the network. Usually NCs are cheaper, provide a better price/performance, and are more secure. In a sense, NCs are the predecessors of the many Internet-based appliances currently available.

no operation: see NOP

NOP (no operation): an instruction that does nothing. It is sometimes used by the compiler for various timing issues that are related to the hardware architecture.

number's range: refers to the understanding that binary numbers that are part of a byte (8 bits) are limited in range. When using the first two negative representations (sign and magnitude and one's complement) there are two possible values for zero. Two's complement has one zero, but the two sides of the number (positive and negative) are of different lengths (there is one additional negative value).

network computers: see NC

numerical system: an order method for representing numbers using "digits" (or some agreed-upon symbols). For being used in calculations, such a system should include a limited number of digits and support infinite numbers.

object-oriented architectures: architectures that emerged from developments in the field of object oriented. Most modern developments are based on object oriented due to the benefits associated with the object-oriented paradigm (encapsulation, inheritance, and polymorphism). As such, appropriate architectures that would take these benefits into account had to be developed.

opcode (operation code): defines the instruction to be executed, such as add, divide, move, if, and so on.

open- and close-layered architecture: two types of implementing the layered architecture. In the close-layered architecture, each layer can access only the layer underneath, while in an open-layered architecture, each layer can access any other existing layer.

open source: an initiative to produce open-source software. Contrary to many of the "usual" software packages that are sold, open-source software can be freely used and modified by anybody. Open-source software is developed by many people who volunteer their time and knowledge.

operation code: see opcode

other numbering systems: It is possible to define additional numerical systems using any base. The digits participating in such a system for base n are 0, 1, 2,...,n-1.

page: an atomic unit that is loaded and stored in memory consecutively. The program is split into pages and the memory is also divided into same length segments. The fixed-size implementation makes it very simple to handle and manage.

page table: a table in memory that is used by the hardware to translate the logical address into a physical one. In addition, entries in the table hold security and access bits.

paging: a term that refers to the situation in which a page is requested but it is not in memory. The hardware detects the problem and signals the operating system by issuing an interrupt. The operating system will put the process on hold until the request page is loaded from disk. Only then will the program continue running.

paragraph: in the ×86 architecture, a sequence of 16 bytes. A paragraph always starts on the boundary of a paragraph, that is 0, 16, 32, 64..., which means that paragraph addresses always will have four zero bits on their right side.

partitions: executing areas within the memory that hold programs to be executed. Originally, the number of partitions was fixed (determined at boot time), while later, the operating system could change their number and size.

PB (petabytes): or 10^{15} bytes; a size unit used to define the current generation of large multiple-disk storage systems known as "disk farms."

peer-to-peer architecture: an architecture in which each peer on the network can connect to any other peer and exchange information. Over the years, various types of architectures were designed, starting with a central server for management and indexing, up to a totally distributed architecture without any central management.

prearchitecture era: the early stages of computer usage, when the most important issue was to have the program run and produce the required results.

processor's internal clock: a clock inside the processor that synchronizes all instruction executions.

processor's paths: relates to the data communication links that exist inside the processor. The paths are responsible for transferring the data between the processor's various internal components, for example, transferring the content of the input register into the ALU where the ADD instruction is performed.

programmed I/O: in which the running task or application initiates the input or output command and waits for its completion while constantly checking the status of the device.

punched card: a small piece of paper 7 3/8 in by 3 1/4 in (187 mm × 83 mm), originally used by Herman Hollerith. Each card contained 80 columns, each one representing one character. The characters were encoded on the card using punched holes.

RAID (redundant array of inexpensive disks): a technology that was intended to overcome some of the limitations of 1980s disks. The technology provides capabilities for creating virtual disks that may include several physical disks as well as increasing their reliability by providing various error-correction mechanisms.

RAM (random access memory): a device that holds the application's instructions and data during execution. It is called *random access* since any piece of information can be fetched directly (as opposed to sequentially), so the access time is similar regardless of its physical location.

random access memory: see RAM

reduced instruction set computer: see RISC

redundant array of inexpensive disks: see RAID

register: in computing, a small piece of memory inside the processor that temporarily holds some operands or data required for computation.

register–register architecture: an architecture with several registers, in which the instructions are performed on operands that reside in registers.

reliability aspects: the mechanisms put in place to assure the proper delivery of the data over the bus, such as parity bits and error correction codes (ECCs).

resource conflict: a situation in which two instructions are trying to execute the same microinstruction on the same cycle. Due to resource limitations, only one instruction will continue executing, while the other will have to wait for one cycle.

response time: the time that passes between the request being entered and the response being displayed on the screen.

RISC (reduced instruction set computer): a technology that refers to computers that were designed using a limited number of instructions and a few addressing modes. However, they use registers extensively to avoid excessive memory access.

SAN (storage attached network): a local, usually high-speed network that is used for connecting a pool of storage resources so they will be available for many computing servers and workstations.

scheduler: the part of the operating system that is responsible for scheduling the processes and deciding which one will be executed next.

scheduling algorithms: algorithms used by the operating system for scheduling tasks for execution. Some of the most famous scheduling algorithms are: (1) first come first served (FCFS), in which the processor works on the tasks as they were introduced. Each task gets the full amount of processor time it needs and only after it finishes does the processor move to the next task. (2) Shortest job first (SJF), in which the task has to declare the amount of time it requires, and then if a short task enters the system (shorter than the time remaining to the current executing task), the system will switch to the new task. (3) Priority, in which the operating system assigns a priority to each task to be executed, or alternatively the task can define its priority. The order of execution is defined by that priority. (4) Round robin, in which the processor executes all available tasks in a circular manner. Each task waits for its turn and then gets a predefined amount of time. If it did not finish, it waits for its next turn.

scoreboarding: a hardware mechanism that analyzes the registers used by the instruction for deciding if it can start execution or whether it has to be delayed since its operands (one or two) are still not ready.

SDK (software development kit): a set of tools for easy application development. The SDK is provided for specific system, packages, hardware, and so on.

segment size register: an internal register available only for the operating system, which holds the size of the segment. It is used in order to ensure that when accessing a segment the displacement is not larger than the segment size, which will give the program the possibility of accessing areas that belong to some other process.

server concept: As part of the division of work between the local computer and computers on the network, many services are provided by dedicated computers. Some relevant examples may be the file server, print server, database server, and so on.

service oriented architecture: see SOA

single, dual, and multiple-port memory: Usually when the system consists of one processor, the memory will use one port (an entry point for data communications). When there are two processors, they will have to compete for the single port, and for that reason the memory may have a dual port. When there are more processors, the memory may use multiple ports.

SOA (service-oriented architecture): a collection of services that run on different computers that are available for other computers. The services are applications that can connect with each other and transmit data and information.

software architecture: a diagram that depicts the main system's components and their interaction. Software architecture can be regarded as a blueprint for the development and integration activities to be performed during the development process.

software development kit: see SDK

solid state disk: see SSD

SSD (solid state disk): a relatively new type of hard drive that has no moving parts, and in which all data is stored electronically (as in memory or a disk on key).

stack: a data type that acts as a container. It implements the last-in, first-out (LIFO) mechanism, which means that data elements are inserted and extracted only from the top of the stack. A stack can be demonstrated as a stack of books in which one can only add a book on top of the stack and extract a book that is on top of the stack. In this sense, the top of stack is the location where the next book will be placed or the location from where the next book will be extracted.

stack-based architecture: a computer system that uses instructions without operands. The operands are stored in the stack. It is designed based on the Polish notation; for adding two numbers, for example, the numbers have to be pushed into the stack and only then is the ADD instruction issued. The results will be on top of the stack.

storage devices: There are many storage devices used by computers, which serve a variety of needs and purposes. Some may provide serial access (such as tapes) and others provide random access (like a hard drive). Some of the devices may be fully online, providing constant access, and others may be partially online (such as robotic libraries, which automatically stage the device per request, although this may take some time). There are of course devices that are off line (such a disk on key, also called a *memory stick*).

storage attached network: see SAN

stored program model: a computer that stores the program to be executed, in contrast to the first computers, which had to be programmed manually.

swap: a term that refers to swapping the whole program from memory to the disk. It may be done to improve the system's performance, for example, when there are many programs competing for a relatively small pool of pages.

synchronous or asynchronous bus: The bus, like any other communication media, can work synchronously, in which it is synchronized by an internal clock; or asynchronously, in which each operation will require a different amount of time or bus cycles.

system performance: refers to a set of measurements, benchmarks, and tools that were developed over the years for assessing systems' performance, such as (1) millions of instructions per second (MIPS), which measures the number of instruction the processor executes per second; (2) millions of floating point operations per second (MFLOPS), which measures the number of floating-point instructions the processor executes per second; (3) megabytes per second (MB/Sec), which measures data transfer capabilities, such as the input and output devices or internal paths (buses); and (4) transactions per second (TPS), which measures the system's ability to handle transactions.

table look a side buffer: see TLB

TB (terabytes): or 10^{12} bytes; a size unit used to define the current generation disk storage.

TCO (total cost of ownership): an estimate of the total cost associated with a computer-based solution over a predefined period of time.

terminal services: also known as remote desktop services (RDS); a Microsoft package that supports the thin-client implementation. For that reason, a remote desktop protocol (RDP) was developed, and the client receives all required services over the network from the server.

"The network is the computer": a term coined in the 1980s that represents some of the current computing environments. For example, web-based computing is a model in which the user works using a browser, and the requests are processed by some system spread over the network.

thick client: a powerful computer used for the presentation layer as well as some or all of the business logic.

thin client: an implementation of network terminals, a system with minimal resources that depends on the network for loading its software and storing the results.

thread: in computing, a part of a running program managed independently by the operating system. Multithreading, or dividing the application into multiple threads, simplifies development and testing. In addition, it is highly suitable for modern computer environments that consist of multicore CPUs.

three-tier architecture: involves three computers: the local client, the remote server, and an additional tier between the client and the server for a specific service, such as transaction management, application server, and so on.

tier architecture: an architecture that is similar to layered architecture. The difference is that in a tier architecture, each layer can be implemented using a different computer. The client/server architecture can be implemented using a three-tier architecture (presentation, business logic, and storage) or a four-tier architecture, and then the database management system will be assigned a different layer (between the business logic and the data).

time-sharing system: a computer system that is intended for running several users/tasks in parallel. Most current modern computers and even some appliances, such as smartphones, support time sharing.

time slice (or time slot): a term used by the operating system to define the amount of time a process will use the processor before it is put back to wait. Multiprocessing systems usually share the resources between the running processes, and the time slice defines the amount of time the processes use at one shot.

TLB (table look a side buffer): a special high-speed buffer used for caching the page table in order to speed up the address translation process.

total cost of ownership: see TCO

transistor: a device used to amplify and switch electronic signals. It is made of semiconductor materials.

two-tier architecture: involves two computers, the local client and the remote server. This is the simplest form of client/server.

unbalanced pipeline: a pipeline in which the various stages require different times. This hampers the ILP mechanism and may have a severe impact on performance. One slow stage not only increases the time of a single instruction takes to be executed but may also increase the time future instructions take to be executed.

vector processors: special-purpose processors that implement vector instructions. Unlike ordinary processors, in which a single instruction works on a single set of operands, the vector instructions work on multiple data. One instruction can add two vectors of numbers, creating a new vector of results. Vector computers provided a very fast computation engine, although at a very high cost. These systems were operational from the 1970s to the 1990s and were gradually replace by arrays of off-the-shelf microprocessors, which provided superior price performance. Although vector processing is not widely used, some vector capabilities exist in modern implementations, and both Intel and AMD use vector capabilities, for example, in the graphics processing unit (GPU).

virtual memory: a concept used by most modern computers. The virtual (or logical) addresses used by the program are mapped into physical locations. This is done automatically by the hardware every time a memory location is accessed. The program is automatically divided into pages, and the physical memory is divided into frames. The pages and frames are of the same size. If a page is not in memory, it is the operating system's responsibility to load it.

virtualization: In regard to computers, virtualization is the process of defining a virtual entity. For decades, computers have used virtual memory, which provides significantly better memory utilization. Currently, virtualization refers to a more abstract layer, in which a single machine appears as several different systems, each one with its own operating system.

von Neumann architecture: a model architecture designed by John von Neumann. It consists of three main components: (1) the memory used for data and instructions; (2) the processor, which is divided into the arithmetic and logic unit (ALU) and control unit (CU); and (3) input and output (I/O) devices.

WAN (wide area network): a computer network that connects computers and other related devices over a large geographical area, such as intercontinental communication.

web-based application: an application that may reside on a remote server and is accessed by the user through a standard browser.

wide area network: see WAN

Windows: a generic name for a family of operating systems developed and sold by Microsoft Corporation. Some Windows versions include Windows 95, Windows 98, Windows 2000, Windows XP, Windows 7, Windows 8, and Windows 10.

×86 architecture: a family of chips manufactured by Intel, beginning with the Intel 4004 and extending through the 8008, 8088, 80086, 80286, 80386, 80486, and the various Pentiums. These chips formed the basis of the IBM-PC and its successors until they were replaced by 64-bit architectures.

XML (extensible markup language): a markup language that uses a text-based format and a set of rules for decoding and encoding the data so it is bot-machine readable as well as human readable. XML may be considered an extension to HTML.

Index